Wildlife in American Art

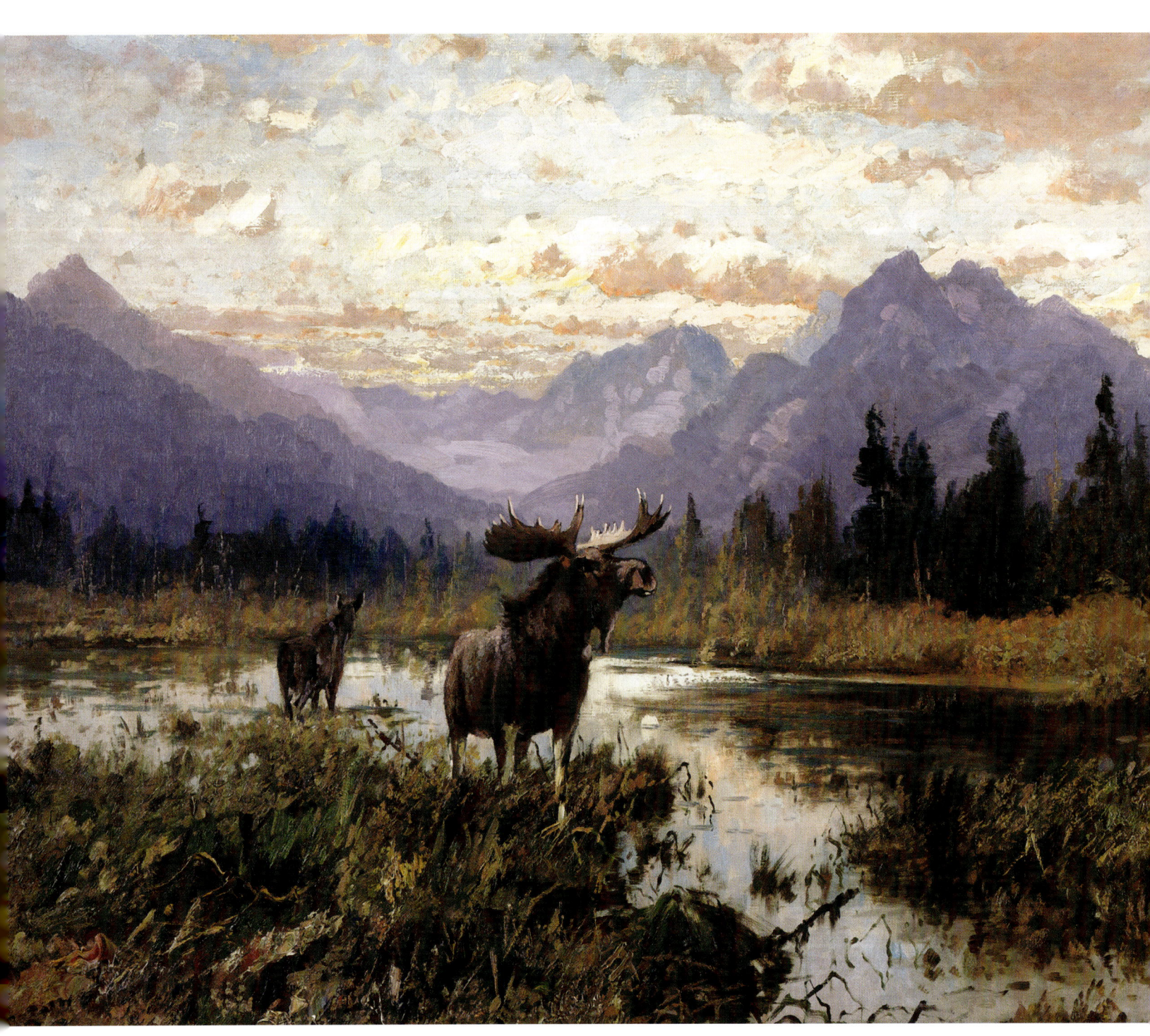

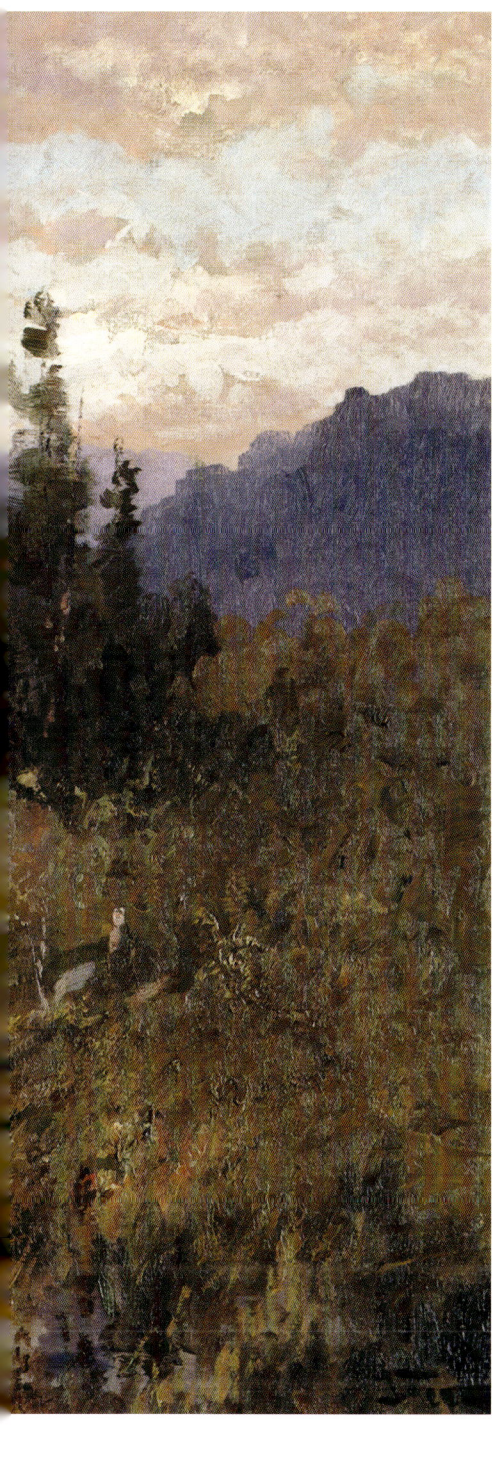

Wildlife in American Art

Masterworks from the National Museum of Wildlife Art

Adam Duncan Harris

Foreword by William G. Kerr

Preface by James C. McNutt

UNIVERSITY OF OKLAHOMA PRESS ✳ NORMAN

IN COOPERATION WITH

THE NATIONAL MUSEUM OF WILDLIFE ART OF THE UNITED STATES

JACKSON, WYOMING

ALSO BY ADAM DUNCAN HARRIS

Bob Kuhn: Painting the Wild (Jackson, Wyo., 2002)

"In Wild Style," in *Earthlings: The Paintings of Tom Palmore,* by Susan Hallsten McGarry (Oklahoma City, 2008)

"Lars Jonsson: The Beauty of Nature," in *Where Heaven and Earth Touch: The Art of the Birdpainter Lars Jonsson,* edited by Peter A. Reimers and Mamoun Fansa (Oldenburg, Germany, 2008)

Wildlife Art for a New Century II (Jackson, Wyo., 2005)

Wild Work: Animal Drawings by Alexander Calder (Jackson, Wyo., 2004)

Yosemite 1938: On the Trail with Ansel Adams and Georgia O'Keeffe (Jackson, Wyo., 2003)

Library of Congress Cataloging-in-Publication Data

National Museum of Wildlife Art.

  Wildlife in American art : masterworks from the National Museum of Wildlife Art / Adam Duncan Harris ; foreword by William G. Kerr ; preface by James C. McNutt. — 1st ed.

     p. cm.

  Includes bibliographical references and index.

  ISBN 978-0-8061-4015-5 (hardcover : alk. paper) 1. Wildlife art—United States—Catalogs. 2. Art, American—Catalogs. 3. Art—Wyoming—Jackson—Catalogs. 4. National Museum of Wildlife Art—Catalogs. I. Harris, Adam Duncan. II. Title. III. Title: Selections from the National Museum of Wildlife Art.

  N7660.N318 2009

  704.9'432097307478755—dc22

                                                          2009001394

Dedicated to the National Museum of Wildlife Art board of trustees, staff, and volunteers whose daily efforts help build, support, care for, and interpret this wonderful collection.

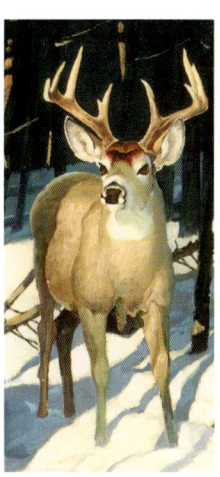

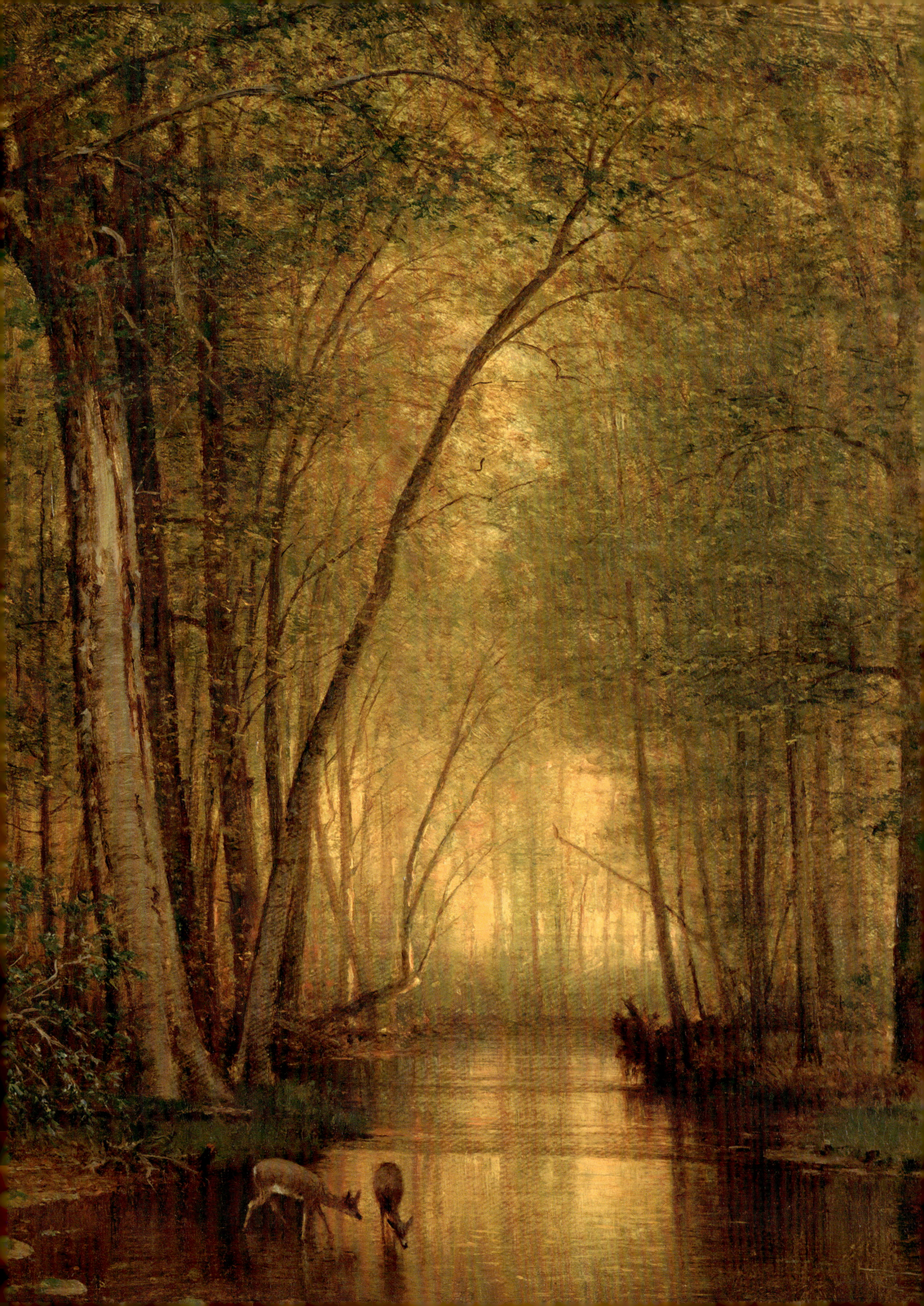

Contents

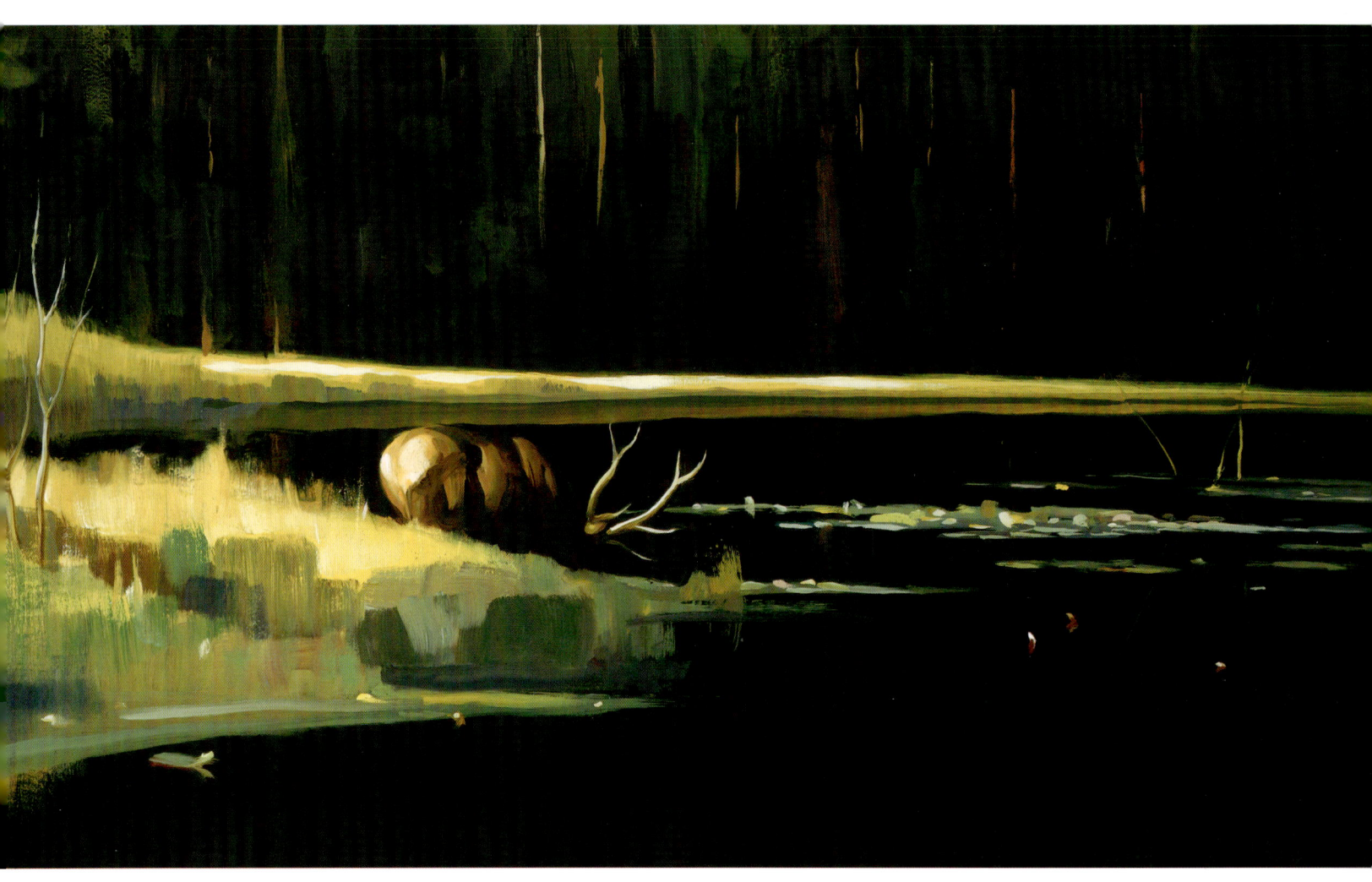

Foreword

The National Museum of Wildlife Art was spawned by a like-minded group of friends who envisioned a community-based institution that could grow through a singular, compelling focus to assume a national presence. Blessed by an extraordinary location, residing intimately with much of its subject matter, the museum has established a reach beyond the grasp of those founders. On its twentieth anniversary, in 2007, the NMWA saw its original vision being fulfilled and began to chart the journey to a global horizon. The museum's collections, professional stature, and accreditation provide a foundation to attain such a goal.

This lovely volume sets a high benchmark for the wildlife genre as mastered by American painters, sculptors, and printmakers. The museum's members and visitors can be confident that NMWA's board of trustees, professional staff, and dedicated volunteers will continue raising their standard for excellence as the national home for animal art moves through the twenty-first century.

May it long serve those who come to its place in search of the wild, the natural, the forgotten, and the serene.

William G. Kerr
Chairman Emeritus
National Museum of Wildlife Art

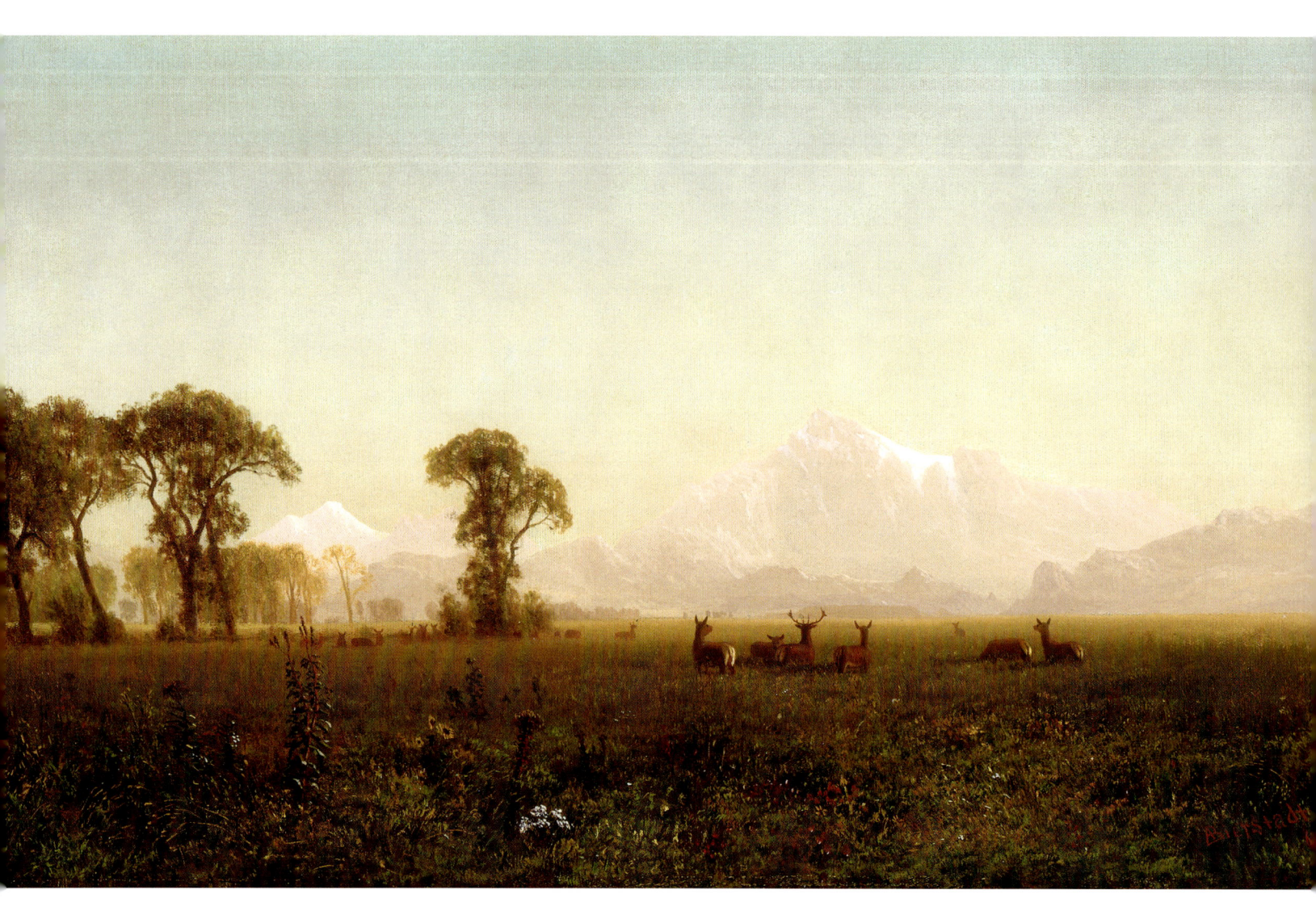

Foreword

The National Museum of Wildlife Art was spawned by a like-minded group of friends who envisioned a community-based institution that could grow through a singular, compelling focus to assume a national presence. Blessed by an extraordinary location, residing intimately with much of its subject matter, the museum has established a reach beyond the grasp of those founders. On its twentieth anniversary, in 2007, the NMWA saw its original vision being fulfilled and began to chart the journey to a global horizon. The museum's collections, professional stature, and accreditation provide a foundation to attain such a goal.

This lovely volume sets a high benchmark for the wildlife genre as mastered by American painters, sculptors, and printmakers. The museum's members and visitors can be confident that NMWA's board of trustees, professional staff, and dedicated volunteers will continue raising their standard for excellence as the national home for animal art moves through the twenty-first century.

May it long serve those who come to its place in search of the wild, the natural, the forgotten, and the serene.

William G. Kerr
Chairman Emeritus
National Museum of Wildlife Art

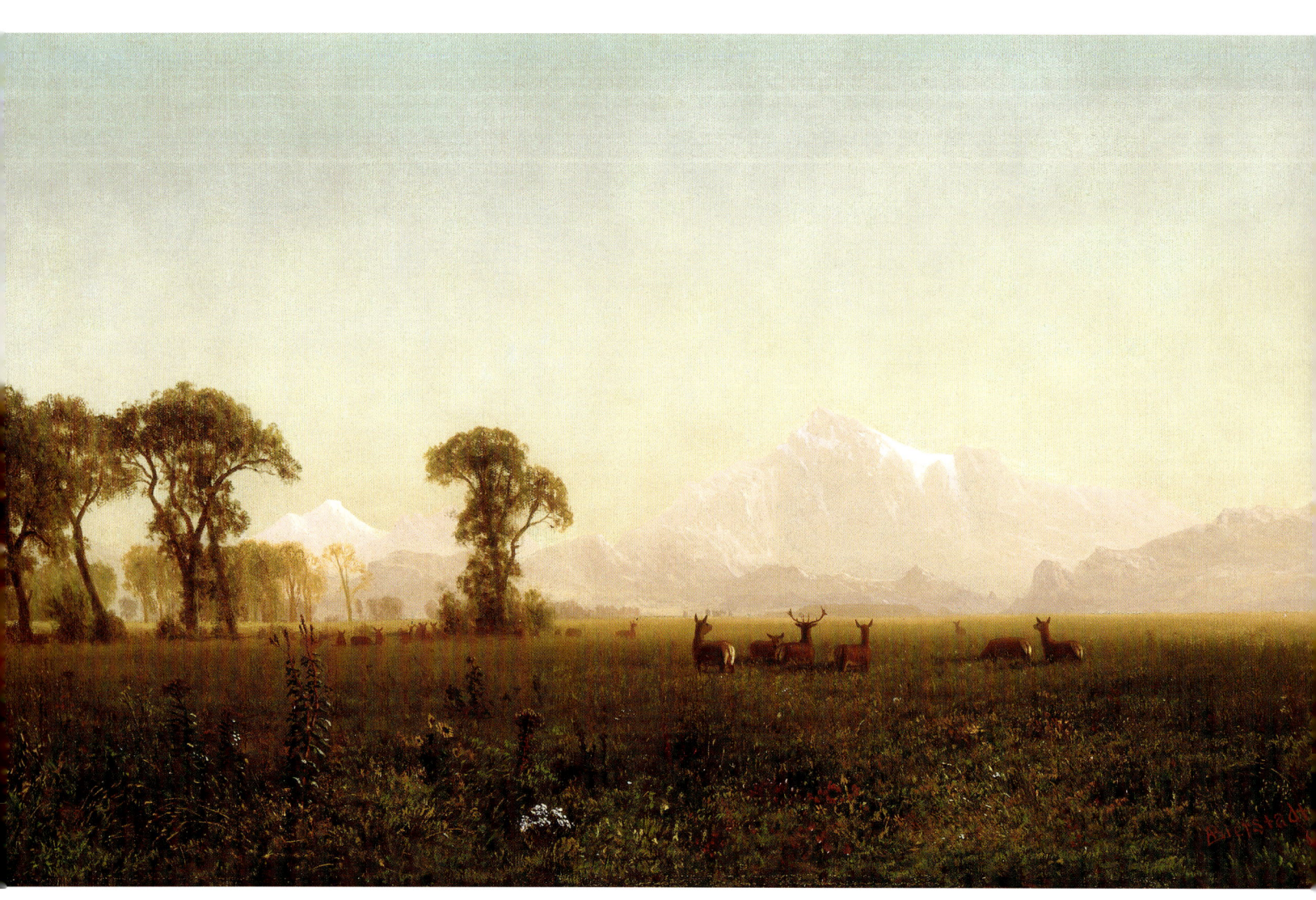

Preface

After more than twenty years of devoted collecting and programming, some might believe that the work at the National Museum of Wildlife Art has reached a culmination. Who would have thought in 1987 that this institution would have amassed, in such a short time span, a collection exceeding five thousand catalogued items, including paintings, sculptures, works on paper, and archival material? Adam Harris's account shows how art depicting wildlife emerges and relates to trends in the cultural life of the nation, and it gives no reason to expect that the museum's collection represents an end point. The test will be, of course, whether the museum has gathered a body of work that will consistently speak to the future. The congressional designation of the "National Museum of Wildlife Art of the United States," signed into law May 8, 2008, confers a special measure of intent on that process.

The path that connects Thomas Jefferson, Meriwether Lewis and William Clark, Ralph Waldo Emerson, John Wesley Powell, John Muir, Theodore Roosevelt, Olaus Murie, Rachel Carson, and E. O. Wilson to anonymous Native American carvers, Edward Hicks, Mark Catesby, John James Audubon, Edward Kemeys, Albert Bierstadt, Carl Rungius, Louis Agassiz Fuertes, Georgia O'Keeffe, Andy Warhol, and Robert Kuhn runs through an American landscape variously considered as wilderness, sublime creation, endless resource, and threatened habitat. Among the people who have lived and struggled in that landscape—often with one another—artistic representations of the land and the creatures that inhabit it have sometimes exacerbated and sometimes helped to heal the divisions created by politics, race, economics, religion, environment, national identity, and other imperatives. On the healing side, at least, the value of wildlife in art may be to point people's concerns away from themselves and toward other creatures, a first step in recognizing their mutual dependency. In this, the construction of the idea of wildlife art and its documentation in the museum acquire a significant function beyond the mere gathering of favored images. Wildlife art insists that a shared understanding of the world does exist and that we can achieve the necessary synthesis of ideas and arts to follow the path without getting lost.

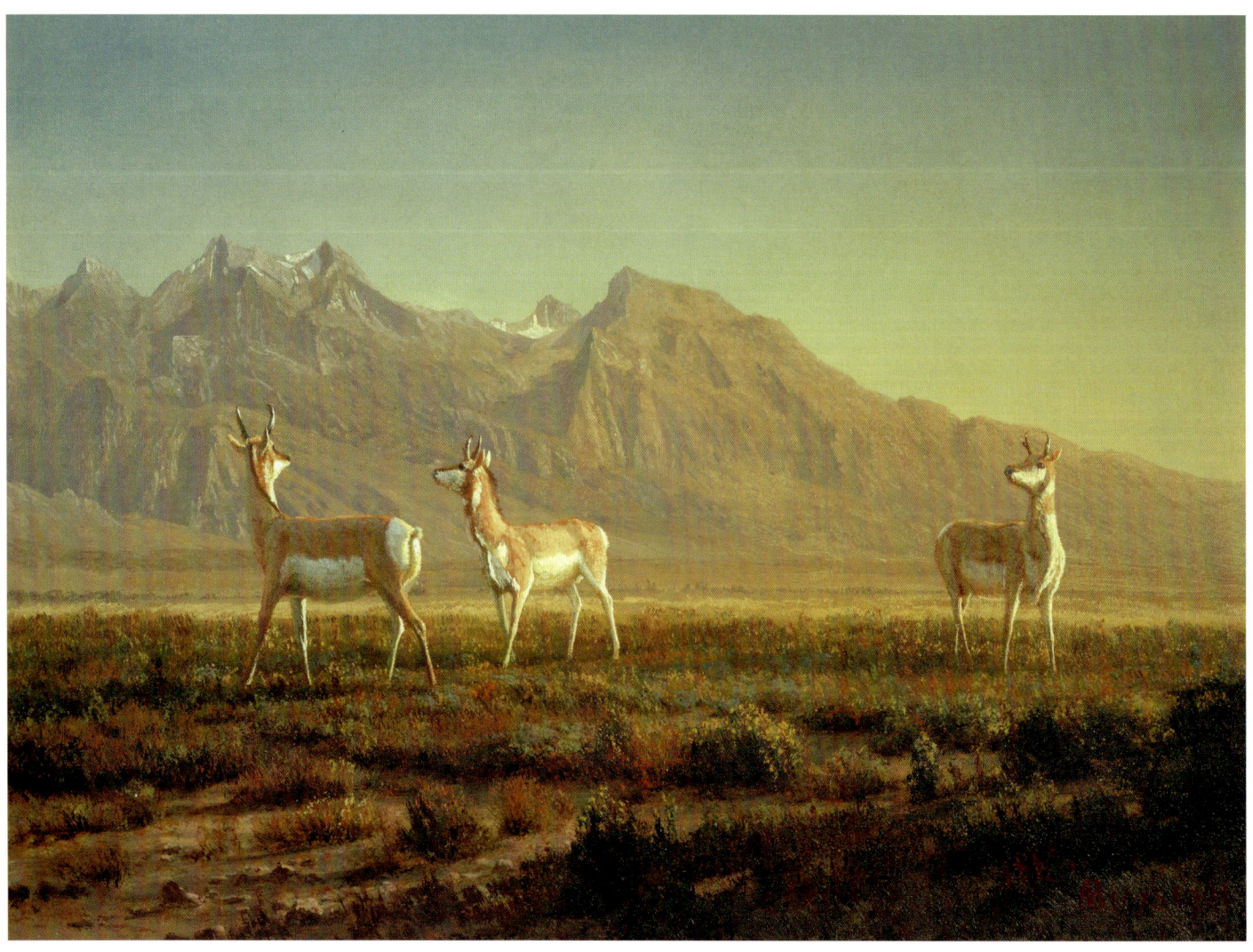

FIGURE P.1.
ALBERT BIERSTADT
Prong-Horned Antelope, c. 1865.
Oil on canvas; 16⅞ × 22½ inches.
Gift of the Stonehollow Collection.
W2008.018.

    This volume renews the task of making the connections between ideas and art and places the National Museum of Wildlife Art in a special position to draw together community, nation, and environment for the future. It is the most comprehensive publication to issue from the museum to date, and we expect that it will be far from the last.

James C. McNutt, Ph.D.
President and CEO
National Museum of Wildlife Art

Author's Note and Acknowledgments

Wildlife in American Art combines elements of a traditional collection catalogue with a scholarly treatment of pertinent topics. This hybrid approach seemed appropriate for the museum's first major publication, which aims to introduce readers to the museum's permanent collection and to salient topics related to wildlife and its place in American art. The selected artwork represents the breadth of the museum's holdings. Sometimes minor works were chosen over major ones to extend the time line, visual scope, and range of material. This book only begins to probe the depths of the museum's collection and of the importance of wildlife in the visual culture and history of the United States. The National Museum of Wildlife Art has assembled the premiere collection of American art related to wildlife (along with an unparalleled collection of European antecedents). By presenting a wide range of material, the museum and this catalogue aim to broaden perceptions of wildlife in art and open the door to further, in-depth study.

An essay at the beginning of each chapter introduces major topics in the history of wildlife art. Following the essays are entries on individual artists and artwork in the museum's collection. The entries are arranged chronologically by the time when the artist was having the greatest impact on the field. When many artists were active simultaneously, they are arranged chronologically by the year in which they were born. The book can be read straight through, but it can also be used as a reference to look up brief biographical material on artists and artwork in the collection.

This book would not have been possible without the formative vision of the founding trustees of the National Museum of Wildlife Art. Establishing a center for the study and appreciation of wildlife art in one of the most scenically beautiful places in the world was a stroke of genius from which the millions of visitors who come to visit this majestic corner of Wyoming benefit. The museum would not have been possible without the inestimable eye of Bill and Joffa Kerr and the ongoing dedication of the Robert S. and Grayce B. Kerr Foundation. The Kerrs' initial donation of approximately 250 works of art has grown into the most comprehensive public collection of fine art devoted to wildlife in existence. The current board of trustees carries on the vision of the founding members as the museum looks forward to the future. A great debt of gratitude goes to all of these individuals, whose ongoing work supports the museum's mission, programs, and collection.

Every department at the National Museum of Wildlife Art has contributed to the success of this project. In particular, I would like to thank Chief Preparator Ron Gessler and Registrar Fay Bisbee for their careful attention to the artwork. Before this book began in earnest, summer interns and curatorial assistants spent a portion of their tenure at the museum researching and writing individual artist biographies. As the book progressed, interns and assistants helped with additional research, editing, and proofreading. Much of the diligent work completed by these individuals is represented herein. Thanks go to Roy A. Hunt Curatorial Interns Anne Sterrett, Jan Schultheiss, Jessica Fertig, Cassie Wilkins, Kelly Kleinfelter, and Kristy Masten; Lillian Thomason Gemar Interns Hadley Jerman, Rachel Miller, and Matthew Smith; and Assistant Curators Michelle Lynch and Emily Hinckley. The amazing images of the works in the collection come thanks to the camera work of skilled photographer Garth Dowling.

Additional thanks go to James C. McNutt, William G. Kerr, Brian Dippie, and Sheila Hoffman for their insightful comments on various drafts of this manuscript; their careful critiques greatly improved the final product. On a personal note, I would like to thank Kristine and Grainger for providing the nurturing home life that supported the writing of this book.

Last, I would like to thank Lynn and Foster Friess, whose offer to underwrite the production of this book while it was still in its formative stages spurred the expansion of what was then a three-page proposal into the over-three-hundred-page manuscript it eventually became. My hope is that this volume will stand as a worthy representation of the museum's American art collection for many years to come and will inspire a deeper understanding of the importance of wildlife in the formation of a national identity.

Adam Duncan Harris, Ph.D.
Curator of Art
National Museum of Wildlife Art

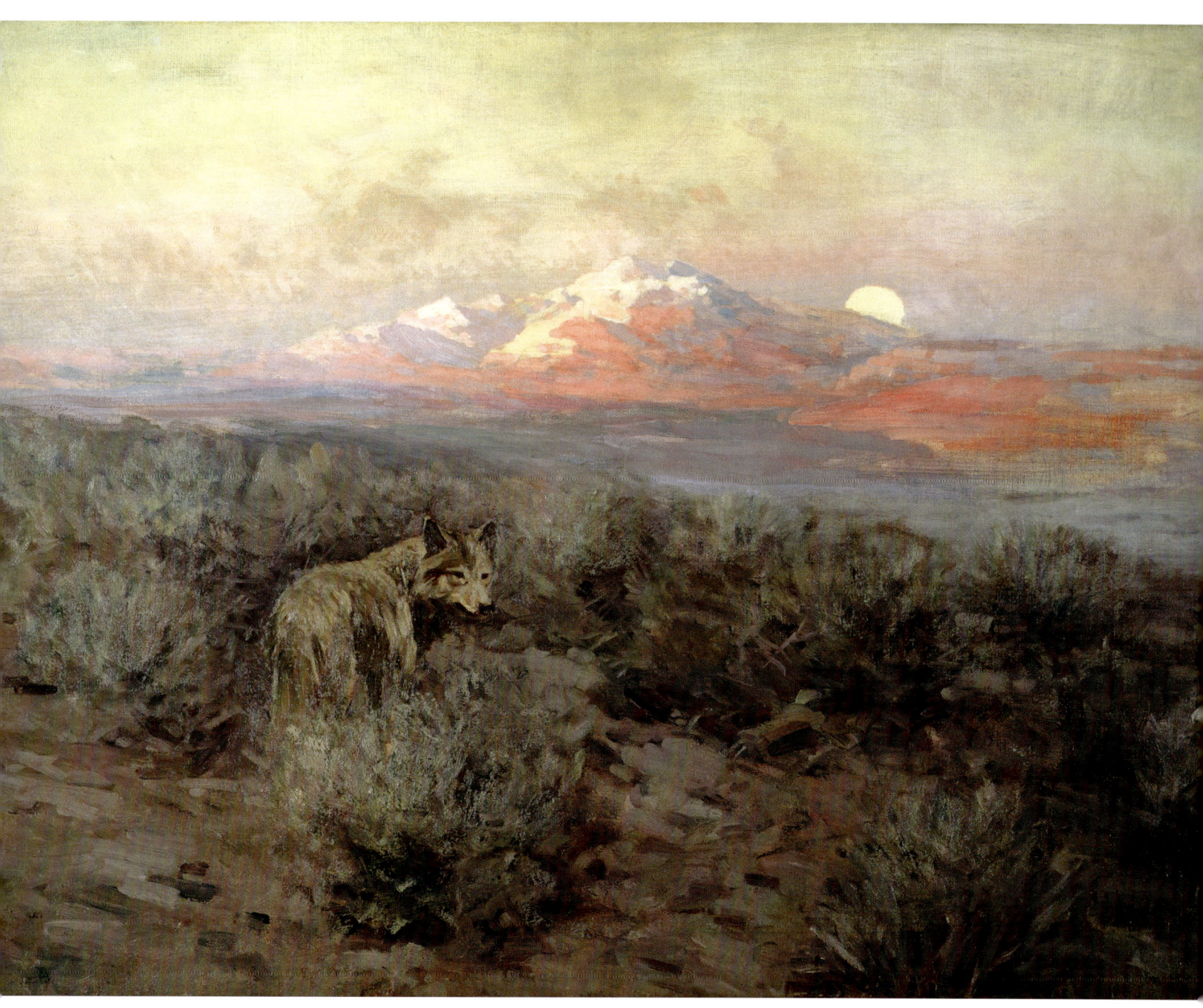

Wildlife in American Art

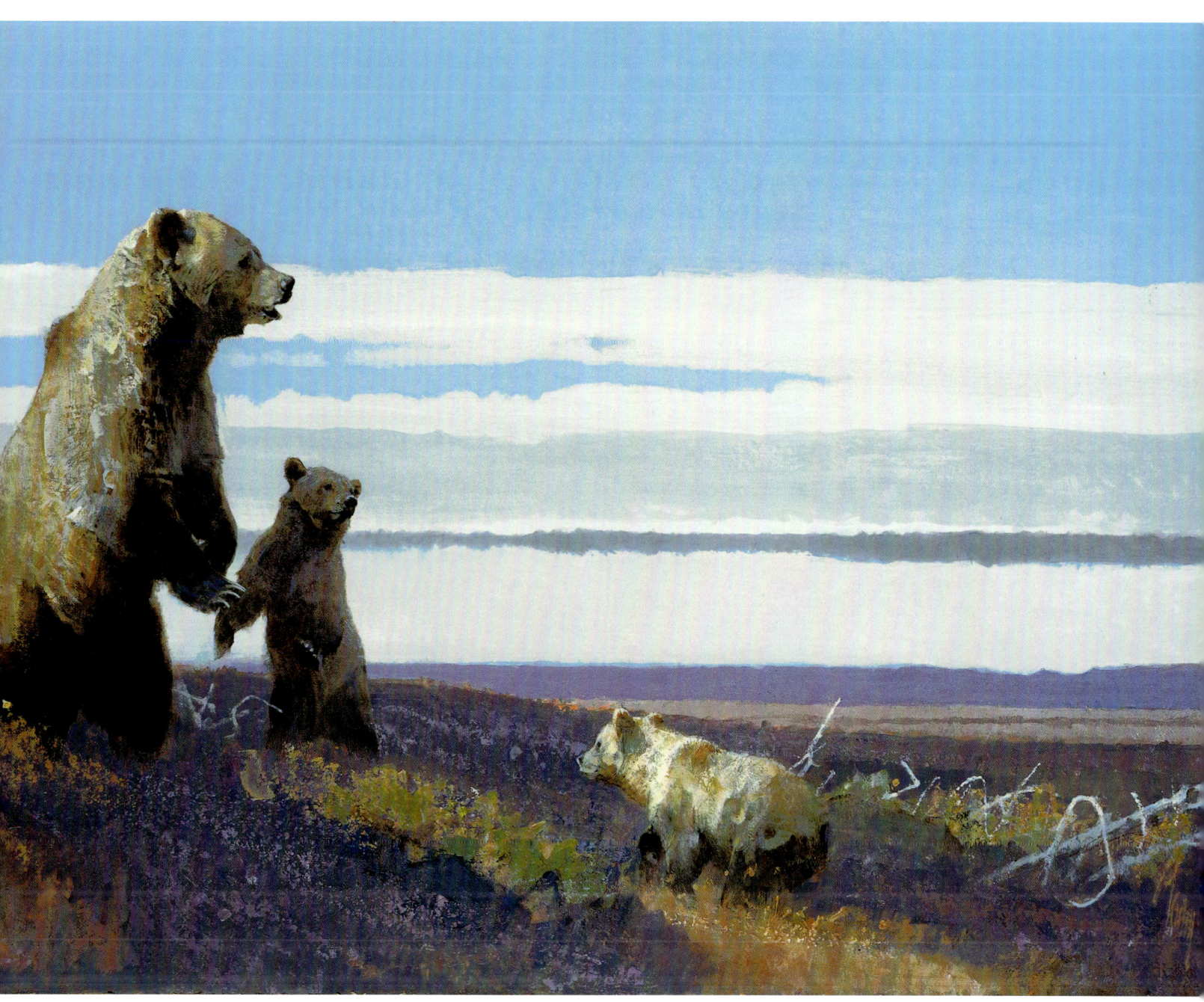

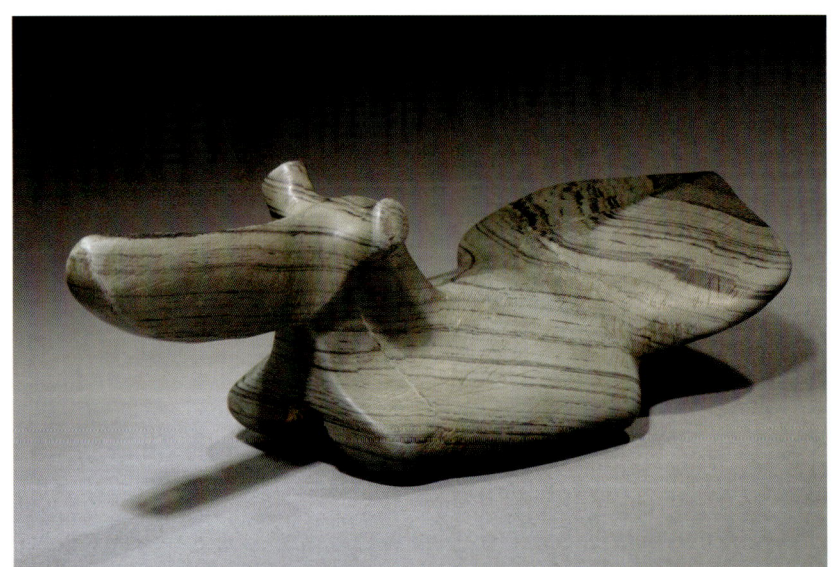

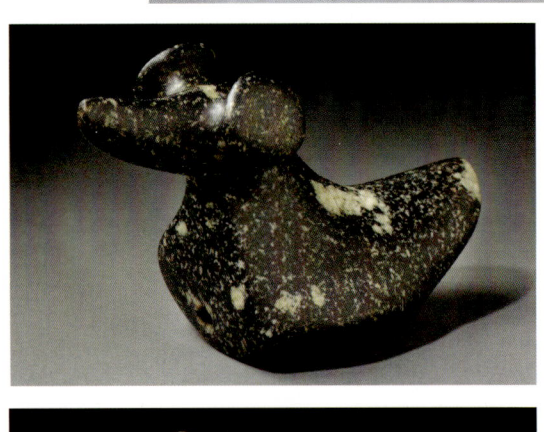

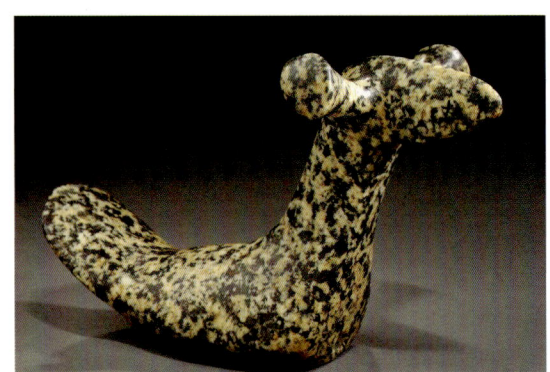

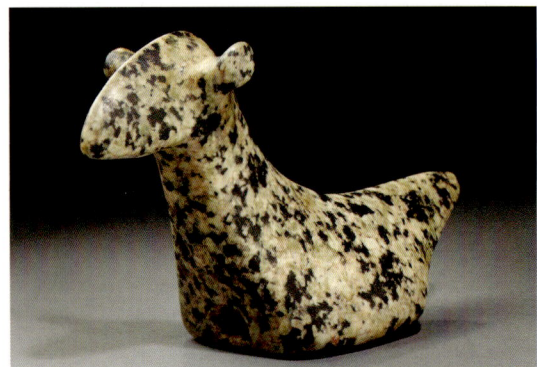

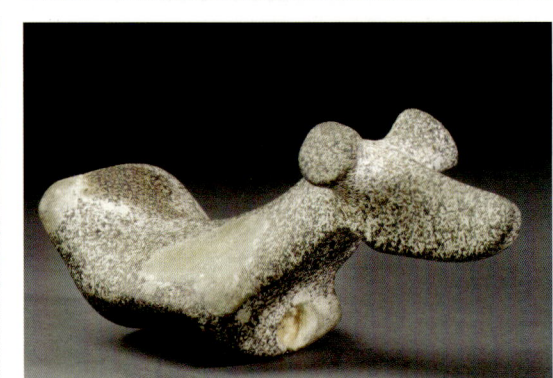

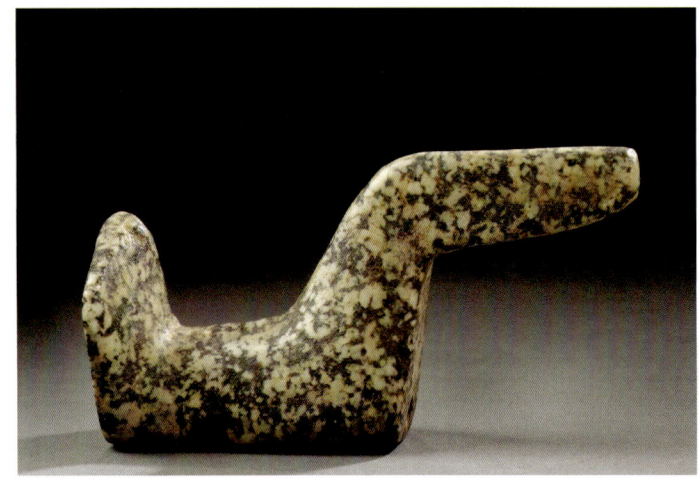

Introduction

Wildlife, Art, and Wilderness in the Formation of a National Identity

The earliest men of which we have any record, thousands of centuries ago, expressed their sense of beauty by leaving pictures drawn on their cave dwellings. These pictures are for the most part of animals—of deer, mastodons and wild horses.

Alexander Calder, *Animal Sketching*, 7

In approximately 2500 B.C., American Indian tribes in what is now southern Michigan and northern Indiana carved small bird sculptures out of native rock. Today, these objects are called birdstones, but their purpose remains a mystery. They have been interpreted as totemic figures, as personal decoration, or as weights for the spear-throwing device known as an atlatl, but no conclusive evidence supports one particular interpretation. Utilitarian value aside, these simply carved objects are among the most compelling in the museum's collection. The smooth, rounded sculptures present the shape of a bird without excess ornamentation (figure I.1). The outstanding features on some are the "pop-eyes" that extend from the heads. The birdstones are also the oldest objects in the museum's collection; the fact that the museum holds examples of wildlife in art separated in time by more than four thousand years speaks directly to the enduring power of animal imagery in the scope of human creation. In the future, as collections grow, the museum may be able to show how American Indian artists used animal imagery over the centuries, but for now, the primary focus of the collection remains on painters and sculptors of European descent.

In 1987, the National Museum of Wildlife Art began its existence in a small, commercial space on the town square in Jackson, Wyoming. A donation of approximately 250 paintings and sculptures depicting North American wildlife from Bill and Joffa Kerr provided the artistic foundation upon which the museum was built. The roster of deceased artists in the collection included Carl Rungius, Charles Russell, and Edward Kemeys, with contemporary artists such as Robert Kuhn, Robert Bateman, Ken Carlson, Ken Bunn, and Sherry Salari-Sander rounding out the collection. First known as the Wildlife of the American West Art Museum, the institution directed its energies toward a specific locale—the West.

As the collection grew, the museum retained its focus on wildlife but broadened the geographical area under consideration. Many artists who specialized in wildlife painted in diverse regions of this country and abroad; limiting the scope to the West soon became too restrictive. However, telling the complete story of how wildlife has been depicted by humans over the course of history was deemed too far-reaching. As the collection developed, it focused on depictions of wildlife across North America and Africa, the two regions of major wildlife populations in the world and, consequently, the two major inspirations for art featuring wildlife.[1]

In addition, the museum began to look toward Europe for antecedents and influences that impacted American artists depicting wildlife. Developing their own areas of specialization during the same era as Carl Rungius were German painters Wilhelm Kuhnert (1865–1926) and Richard Friese (1854–1918), as well as Swedish artist Bruno Liljefors (1860–1939) (see figures 5.4, 5.5, and 5.6, respectively). The sculpture of French animalier artist Antoine-Louis Barye (1796–1875) and his followers was widely studied by Americans abroad (see figure 3.1). In England, the work of Arthur Wardle (1865–1949) and Edwin Landseer (1802–1873) provided models upon which much twentieth-century wildlife imagery was built (see figures I.2 and 2.2, respectively). Supplementing the collection with European art has allowed the museum to present a broader history of how wildlife has been depicted across time and artistic movements.

The larger institutional parameters allow the museum to display a more complete history of wildlife in art, particularly as it has developed in America. The majority of the current collection spans from the middle of the nineteenth century to the late twentieth century and focuses on artists of European descent who painted the wildlife of North America as a way of substantiating and reiterating a national identity based on self-reliance, opportunity, bountiful resources, and a vast, unexplored wilderness. In 1994, the museum moved into a brand new facility three miles north of Jackson on a butte overlooking the National Elk Refuge. With a change in place came a change in name: the National Museum of Wildlife Art, reflecting the new, wider horizon in collecting, programming, and mission.

Since its inception, the museum's mission and collecting activities have been centered on wildlife art. Questions about the connection to two closely related areas arise on a regular basis: "How does this artwork differ from natural history?" and "Why doesn't the museum collect sporting art?" On the topic of natural history, Carl Rungius eloquently expressed his sentiments in a *New York Times* interview from 1913:

> I can't help feeling that the public regards an animal picture as an illustration, an explanation, something that is to make them understand natural history better, or preserve for them a "vanishing type." . . . Of course, the reason for this is that the animals of the wilderness—the

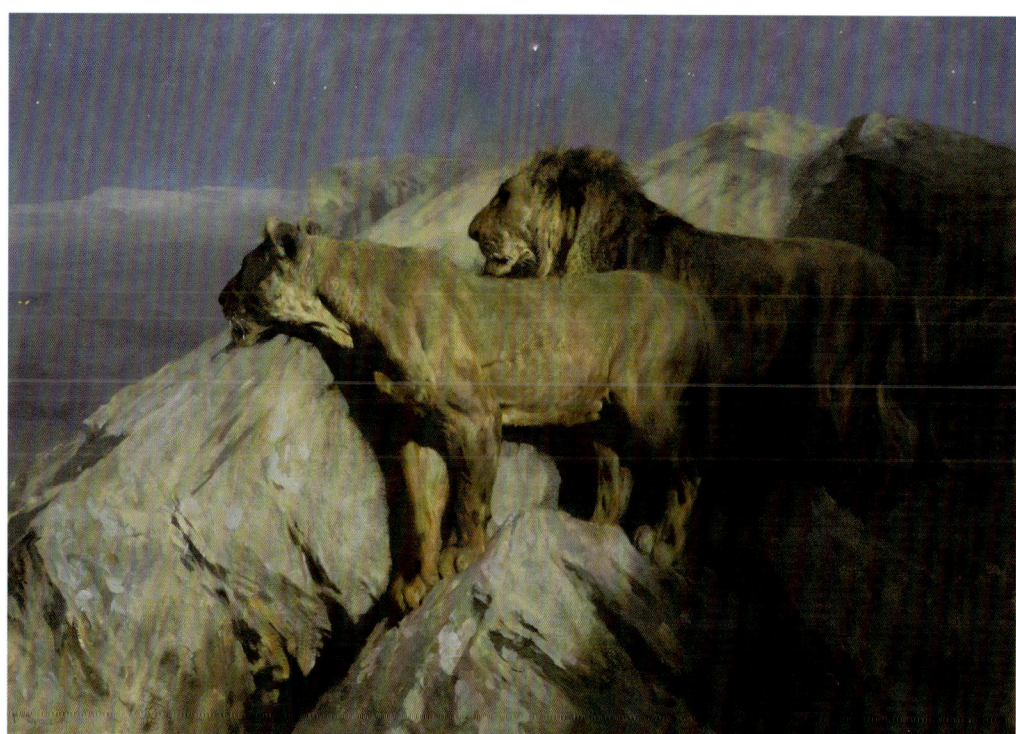

FIGURE I.2.
ARTHUR WARDLE
Silent Watchers, 1928.
Oil on canvas; 34 × 50 inches.
JKM Collection.
JL2003.064.

real "wild animals of America"—are utterly strange to the man and woman of the East to-day, and that in consequence a picture of them simply seems to tell a story; it isn't close enough, it doesn't strike a personal note enough, to be recognized or regarded as what it is— simply art.[2]

Rungius's cogent analysis of the situation, coming relatively early in his long career, pinpoints one of the central issues facing wildlife art: wildlife art that accurately depicts an animal in its natural setting engaging in natural behaviors *can* be used to teach natural history, and for the uninitiated, that realm of knowledge may be the first that springs to mind. Moreover, collectors drawn to the field often judged the merits of a picture or a sculpture based on its accuracy, which drove artists in the twentieth century to strive for even greater levels of authenticity, sometimes to the detriment of artistry. In addition, many of the artists who created masterful bodies of artwork also contributed to natural history displays at various points during their career. Chapter 4 in this volume deals directly with the sculpture produced by a group of artist-taxidermists working at the American Museum of Natural History in New York. In addition, the New York Zoological Society (now the Bronx Zoo) sustained Rungius during lean times with commissions for paintings of the animals of North America meant to educate their eager public.

The connections between wildlife art and natural history are undeniably deep, going back to the earliest artist-naturalists who traversed the western plains recording the fauna of previously unexplored country. However, the interesting thing about art, any art, is that it can be interpreted, analyzed, and appreciated on a variety of levels. Pictures at the National Portrait Gallery in Washington, D.C., might be employed to study anatomy but can also be used to examine the perspectives of the artists who painted them, the material culture of the eras in which they were created, or the cultural values of an evolving nation. Limiting interpretation to a single point of reference is shortsighted and robs the object of its full potential as a cultural artifact. Wildlife art can be most fully appreciated when it is considered from various points of reference, including art history, natural history, American history, and world history. One of the museum's goals is to open the field of interpretation, encouraging viewers to consider wildlife art on its own multifaceted merits.

The museum has not placed a great priority on collecting in the related area of sporting art even though the subject is interconnected with wildlife art; both speak directly to founding elements of a national identity, especially the vision of American nature as bounteous and the principle of personal freedom—notably, the freedom to hunt. Moreover, sporting and wildlife art have often shared patrons and dealers, and the same artists often created both types of work.[3] Arthur Fitzwilliam Tait was proficient at both, for example, and appeared not to favor one over the other. Rungius painted a few hunting scenes early in his career but abandoned them outright to concentrate on wildlife.[4] Many of the best wildlife artists were also hunters and were not averse to the sporting scene. Rungius famously said that in the beginning of his career he hunted six days a week and painted one, but he soon found that painting six and hunting one was more to his liking.[5] In addition, some of the artwork can be classified as sporting art just as easily as wildlife art. Thomas Hewes Hinckley's *Woodland Prince* (see figure 2.5) depicts a proud stag atop a podium-like rock outcropping; it can easily be interpreted as a trophy painting and would not look out of place hanging adjacent to a mounted head in a sportsman's library.

A simple, yet critical, distinction marks the difference between wildlife art and sporting art: sporting art presumes some interaction between human hunters (or their canine agents) and animal prey, while wildlife art does not. The lack of the hunter figure in wildlife art opens the door to a wider range of interpretation and makes wildlife art accessible to a broader range of people. Many look at an idyllic scene such as Arthur Fitzwilliam Tait's painting featured in this catalogue (see figure 2.6)—with rabbits in the foreground, deer in the middle ground, and ducks in flight over a calm Adirondack lake in the background—and see a peaceful depiction of nature untrammeled. However, reading the title of the painting, *Good Hunting Ground,* causes interpretation to shift; viewers see the scene through a hunter's eyes, rather than bringing their own perspective to the picture. The same would happen, on a more immediate basis, had Tait included a hunter in the picture.

With concern for the environment and endangered species on the rise, sporting art can appear one-sided in its point of view, while wildlife art, even if created with a sporting mindset, leaves room for interpretation across a wider range of positions, whether preservationist, conservationist, environmentalist, pro-hunting, or anti-hunting. Hinckley's *Woodland Prince* (see figure 2.5) thus can be read as a fine trophy painting or as an epitome of all that is magnificent about the wilderness (or it can be read simultaneously as both). With a mission to explore humanity's relationship with nature, the museum does have a segment of the collection that focuses on humans interacting with animals. What sporting art the museum has is contained in this group: for example, Alfred Jacob Miller's *Death of the Elk* (see figure 1.10) and Alexander Pope's *Hanging Grouse* (see figure 2.12). This area of the collection also contains nonsporting pieces such as *Bohemian Bear Tamer* by Paul Wayland Bartlett (see figure 3.9) and *The Peaceable Kingdom* by Edward Hicks (figure I.3).

As the museum has grown, the scope of the collection has broadened to include depictions of wildlife from a wider spectrum of art. The acquisition of Hicks's *Peaceable Kingdom* energized supporters to bolster the museum's already significant holdings by seeking more examples of canonical American artists. After the Hicks artwork, the museum was fortunate to acquire a skull painting by Georgia O'Keeffe, *Antelope* (see figure 6.7), as well as a portfolio of Andy Warhol's *Endangered Species* prints (see figures 6.10–6.19). These new additions help show the pervasive use of wildlife imagery across artistic time periods and styles. From birdstones to pop art, wildlife has played an essential role in the scope of American art history.

Edward Hicks (1780–1849) is one of the best-known early American artists to incorporate wildlife into his oeuvre. Borrowing from European traditions, Hicks used animals in his art as allegory, illustrating a passage from the Bible. In his remarkable *Peaceable Kingdom* series, Hicks drew inspiration from Isaiah 11:6: "The wolf also shall dwell with the lamb, and the leopard shall lie down with the kid, and the calf and the young lion and the fatling together, and a little child shall lead them." A commercial sign painter who later became a Quaker minister, Hicks created *Peaceable Kingdom* paintings as a way to balance his desire to paint with his religious beliefs, which did not endorse decorative art. By depicting a biblical passage promoting peace and harmony, Hicks was able to negotiate the difficult terrain between artistic freedom and religious strictures. He completed sixty-two known versions of *The Peaceable Kingdom* during his life as he continued to wrestle with these issues.

At first glance, the National Museum of Wildlife Art's *Peaceable Kingdom* appears to be a fairly literal translation of Isaiah 11:6. In the center of the canvas, a young child leads three pairings of animals that would not normally coexist in harmony: a lion with a cow, a wolf with a lamb, and a leopard with a goat, all

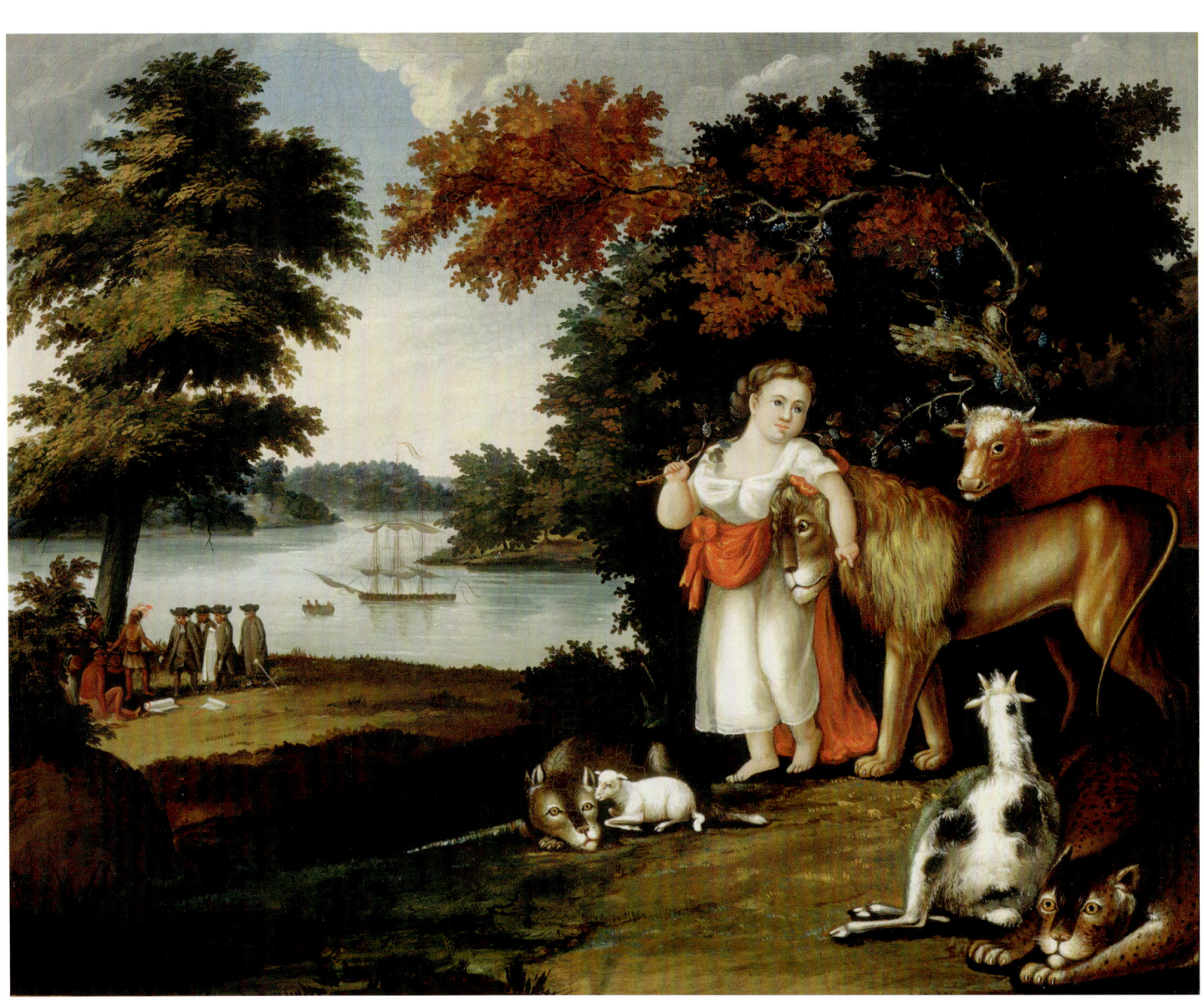

examples of predators coupled with prey. A closer look, however, shows that the painting is more complex. The young child holds a bunch of grapes, a reference to the redemptive blood of Christ.[6] Hicks divided the canvas in two, with a dark line of shadow and vegetation separating the foreground and background of the picture. In front of the line, Hicks painted an allegory of peace on earth (the child leading the animals); behind the line, he painted an actual representation of peace on earth (William Penn signing a treaty with the Lenni-Lennape Indians).[7] While the line separates the spiritual and temporal areas of the image, the harmonious message applies to both sides, indicating peace in heaven and on earth, an ideal Hicks did not experience in his personal or religious life.

The *Peaceable Kingdom* paintings were directly related to a rift between rival Quaker factions. Urban Quakers began to amass wealth and display it in a fashion unbecoming to traditional Quaker beliefs. Rural Quakers, less financially successful, resented their rich counterparts and more firmly adhered to pious teachings that placed value on simplicity and humility, not on materialistic gain.[8] Hicks sided with the rural Quakers but desired peace between the two groups. As he grew older, Hicks depicted the animals in a less naturalistic, more stylized fashion; they began to appear older, more grizzled, and less content, reflecting his continuing anxiety over the split in the church. This canvas presents one of the more harmonious visions in the series, a harmony reflected even in the vegetation: the long branch at the top of the canvas reaches across the picture, linking the allegory in the foreground with the historical event in the background.

Hicks's work provides a prime example of how animals have been used to tell greater stories and illustrate larger themes in American life. American artists during Hicks's time and after became increasingly interested in North American wildlife, especially as they began to accompany expeditions venturing west to explore the vast American wilderness. Titian Ramsay Peale, George Catlin, Karl Bodmer, and Alfred Jacob Miller created striking images of elk, bison, deer, wolves, and other native species. Instead of illustrating biblical passages, these artists described the native fauna of a largely unexplored continent and, in the process, helped a young nation create a sense of self based on a land rich with opportunity and full of natural resources.

Although specific biblical passages were not always the inspiration behind early depictions of American wildlife, seeing the land as a gift from God underlies much of the thinking about the importance of the wilderness to America. In *Wilderness and the American Mind,* historian Roderick Nash wrote, "In the early nineteenth century American nationalists began to understand that it was in the *wildness* of its nature that their country was unmatched. While other nations might have an occasional wild peak or patch of heath, there was no equivalent of a wild continent. And if, as many suspected, wilderness was the medium through which God spoke most clearly, then America had a distinct moral advantage over Europe, where centuries of civilization had deposited a layer of artificiality over His works."[9] Nash also noted that, in a gross contradiction, the conquest of the wilderness was what gave Americans a clear sense of self-worth.

Associated with pride in the wilderness was pride in the wildlife. After the French natural historian George Louis Leclerc, comte de Buffon, cast aspersions on the size and quality of American animals, Thomas Jefferson wrote *Notes on the State of Virginia* (1784), which praised the health and vigor of American wildlife, going so far as to postulate that wild mammoths might still roam the unexplored regions of the nation.[10] Minister Samuel Williams said of the debate, "Instead of finding nature but weak and feeble in America, her animals appear to be marked with an energy and a magnitude superior to what is found in Europe."[11]

In his 1803 letter of instruction to Meriwether Lewis, Thomas Jefferson asked Lewis to note with care the course of the Missouri River and to pay particular attention to the native peoples. He also asked Lewis to record "the animals of the country generally, & especially those not known in the U.S. the remains or accounts of any which may be deemed rare or extinct."[12] The fact that Lewis and Clark were charged with recording as much information as possible about the continent's wildlife population shows that Jefferson, at least, saw value in learning about the nation's native animals. The fauna-related notes and sketches with which the party returned paved the way for later expeditions that included artists whose main purpose was to record the animals. This growing body of information led American scientists to begin categorizing the natural history of the wild continent.

It is difficult to understand the importance of wildlife in American art without knowing how the definition of wilderness has developed over the course of the nation's history. Concepts of the American wilderness have changed as succeeding generations of immigrants have occupied the land and have used it in different ways. For the pilgrims, the wilderness was initially terrifying; they struggled to survive in the New World and had no safe haven from which to appreciate the territory surrounding them. Once stable settlements developed and colonists could think about nature and the American landscape in relative safety, the wilderness became a place of bounteous natural resources to be exploited. Seeing the wilderness as a resource instead of a threat coincided with the Enlightenment era in America at the end of the 1600s. The Enlightenment placed importance on rational thought and science as the way to a more civilized society. Learning about nature by recording and describing different species of animals and plants was seen as a worthwhile exercise in and of itself, but this knowledge was also used to advance the cause of civilization. Categorizing the wild was a way to tame it; understanding nature led to mastery over it, and what was once unknown and frightening became comprehensible. During the 1700s, cities began to grow and Americans began to transition from a pastoral to an urban existence; these developments led to the Industrial Revolution of the 1800s, with Enlightenment-influenced thinking guiding development.[13]

Thoreau scholar Bradley Dean in "Natural History, Romanticism, and Thoreau" noted, "Although pastoral landscapes tend not to alienate humans, industrialized landscapes generally do, and when humans feel physically safe but psychically alienated, they seek palliatives to ameliorate their sense of alienation."[14] City dwellers seek refuge and recreation in the wilderness or by surrounding themselves with reminders of the wilderness, which had (and continue to have) a similarly regenerative effect. By the end of the 1700s, as the nation continued to grow more urban in character, the Romantic period began; this era posed the wilderness as a therapeutic place, a place of personal and spiritual renewal. The Romantic wilderness was also a place that needed protection from the incursions of industry, a place separate from cities and landscapes already impacted by farming or logging. The notion of the wilderness as a separate space also conceptualized it as unaffected by ongoing human habitation, ignoring the long-time presence of American Indians but celebrating the presence of wildlife. Much of the artwork in the museum's collection reflects this Romantic vision of the wilderness.

The therapeutic quality of the Romantic wilderness functions not only for people who experience a specific wilderness firsthand but also for people who simply know that it exists; wilderness is valuable even to people who will never see it in person but may have reminders of it in their homes. Beginning with landscape painter Thomas Cole in the early 1800s, artwork depicting the wild provided a form of relief from the urban condition. In "The Fate of Wilderness in American Landscape Art," American art historian Angela Miller wrote, "The audiences of Cole's Catskill paintings . . . were deeply implicated in the market revolution that was rapidly transforming the metropolitan hinterlands, through their activities as entrepreneurs and businesspeople. Landscape art offered a therapeutic retreat from the forces of market development in which they themselves were involved, forces that were endangering the very wilderness to which they turned for refuge."[15] This situation—exploiting the land on the one hand and treasuring it (or representations of it) on the other—goes back to the contradiction Nash noted, in which Americans saw the land as a gift from God but then found self-worth by conquering it.

By the late 1800s, Romantic appreciation for the wilderness had begun to help create national nature preserves. George Catlin famously called for just such an action in 1841, when he wrote of the need for a *"magnificent park,* where the world could see for ages to come, the native Indian in his classic attire, galloping his wild horse, with sinewy bow, and shield and lance, amid the fleeting herds of elks and buffaloes."[16] The fates of wilderness, wildlife, and American Indian populations would never converge into Catlin's idyllic scenario, however. American Indian reservations and wilderness preservation areas developed as separate spaces (the former prior to the Civil War, the latter just as the war was ending). In 1864,

Abraham Lincoln signed a bill declaring Yosemite to be the property of the State of California, protected as a preserve for future generations against commercial development. In 1872, Yellowstone became the first official national park, set aside for the enjoyment of the American people.

Yosemite and Yellowstone were developed as places of relative safety, where nature could be contemplated, enjoyed, and appreciated without threat (this was not the pilgrim's wilderness). A healthy wildlife population became an essential component of these parks; a healthy American Indian population did not. Miller noted that "the creation of wilderness preserves after the [Civil War] once again failed to accommodate the Native Americans who had long occupied these lands."[17] During the late 1800s and early 1900s, tracts of the most beautiful parcels of the American landscape were being set aside as national nature preserves, while American Indian populations continued to suffer the effects of restrictive appropriation acts passed by the U.S. Congress. These acts limited their freedoms and gave them less and less desirable land on which to live. Wild animals, not American Indians, became a core focus of the national parks and other wilderness areas.[18]

The definition of wilderness promulgated in the national preserves as they developed during the late 1800s and early 1900s acknowledged, encouraged, and celebrated a living population of wildlife. After becoming the nation's first national park, Yellowstone became a preserve for one of the last remaining populations of wild bison in the United States. Art depicting the preserves also reflected this view, as can be seen in Worthington Whittredge's *Deer in Yellowstone National Park,* painted in 1893, just twenty-one years after the founding of the park (figure I.4). Whittredge highlights the namesake yellow stone and the wildlife population and even includes a wisp of steam rising from a geothermal feature hidden in the crags above the lush landscape. Natural beauty coupled with healthy wildlife became the principal attractions of the national parks and also became the principal subjects of wildlife art.[19]

This emphasis on animals in national nature preserves developed in part because of the link between wilderness preservation and wildlife conservation movements. Wild animals had powerful allies arguing on their behalf. In *American Sportsmen and the Origins of Conservation,* John F. Reiger provides a long list of influential people whose appreciation for hunting or fishing shaped a desire to preserve wildlife and wilderness areas. The list includes John Quincy Adams, Chester A. Arthur, John James Audubon, George Catlin, James Fenimore Cooper, William T. Hornaday, George Bird Grinnell, Washington Irving, Thomas Moran, Theodore Roosevelt, and Henry David Thoreau, among others. Reiger argues that in different ways and in different fields, these noted individuals contributed to the environmental movement of their day, which was interested in "'nature appreciation,' wildlife, parks, and forests."[20] Long-time owner and

FIGURE I.4.
WORTHINGTON WHITTREDGE
Deer in Yellowstone National Park, 1893.
Oil on canvas; 24 × 17 inches.
Promised Gift of Lynn and Foster Friess.
(Lost in 2009; see note 19.)

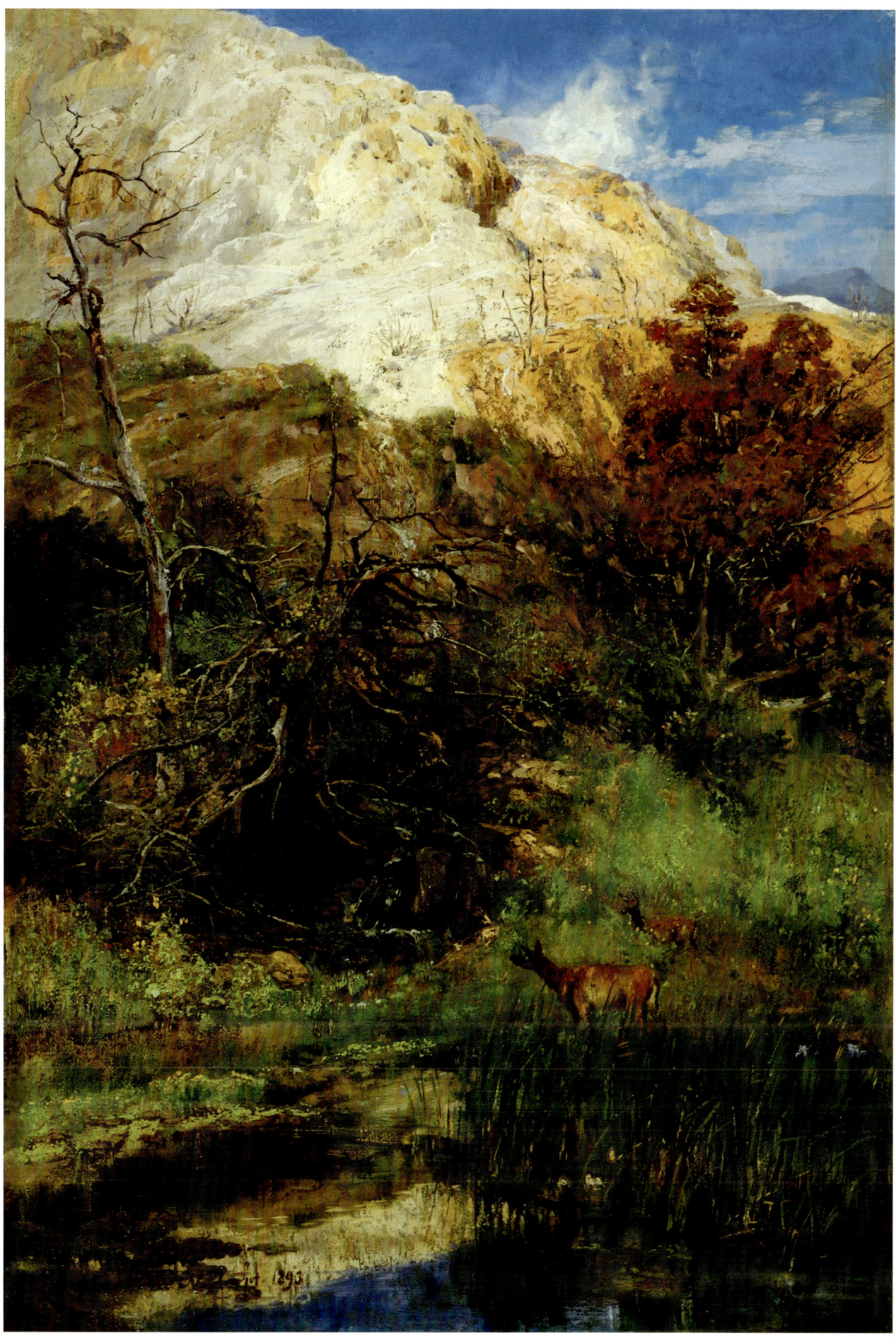

editor of the sporting periodical *Forest and Stream,* George Bird Grinnell used the influence he had among his readers to fight for wildlife preservation in Yellowstone (in the park's early years, the protection of wildlife was not assured). An avid sportsman, he clearly understood that without protection, the remaining herds of megafauna such as bison and elk would soon be eradicated, leaving no game to hunt.

In "Their Last Refuge," a *Forest and Stream* editorial from December 14, 1882, Grinnell wrote,

> We have seen it [the West] when it was, except in isolated spots, an uninhabited wilderness; have seen the Indian and the game retreat before the white . . . tide of immigration. . . . There is one spot left, a single rock about which this tide will break, and past which it will sweep, leaving it undefiled by the unsightly traces of civilization. Here in this Yellowstone Park the large game of the West may be preserved from extermination; here . . . it may be seen by generations yet unborn. It is for the Nation to say whether these splendid species shall be so preserved, in this, their last refuge.[21]

The construction of the passage above shows how easily American Indians disappeared from the definition of what the wilderness would be. At the beginning, Grinnell discusses "the Indian and the game" retreating before the "white tide," but at the end, he promotes Yellowstone as a refuge for the wildlife without again mentioning the American Indians—in effect, erasing them from the equation. These defining moments in conceptualizing the wilderness directly affected how it was portrayed and consumed by artists and art collectors. Wildlife pictured in wilderness settings reinforced the Romantic notion of wilderness as a pristine place, existing as it did for millennia, untouched by human hands.

Artists following in the footsteps of Lewis and Clark reiterated the changing conceptions of the wilderness in the imagery they created. Early artist-naturalists, including George Catlin, Karl Bodmer, and John James Audubon set out to document the inhabitants of a new continent. This scientific, Enlightenment-oriented goal had an underlying Romantic sensibility; if these ways of life and species of animals were not recorded, they might be lost forever. Alfred Jacob Miller, Charles Wimar, and William Jacob Hays had more purely Romantic ideals in mind, celebrating the wilderness and wildlife in their own right. Later, mournful renderings by William Cary and Arthur Verner of lost buffalo calves and dead bison displayed the effects of commercial greed on the inhabitants of the wilderness and reaffirmed a desire to save what was left.

With the development of the national nature preserves, paintings by the likes of Carl Rungius and those who followed him posed proud ungulates in untrammeled landscapes that mirrored the wildlife conservation and wilderness preservation definition of what constituted the wild. For audiences at the beginning of the 1900s, wildlife subjects in art recalled the prevailing, Romantic definition of the American wilderness, as succinctly stated by Miller: "Anglo-American Romanticism looked to nature as a source of personal renewal and as a pointed alternative to the disenchantments of modernity."[22] In addition, harkening back to Jefferson and Lewis and Clark, the underlying iconography of these wildlife works shows North America as a continent full of amazing animals, a key component in an overarching sense of national identity. Today, wildlife subject matter in art retains that Romantic, regenerative aspect but has been filtered through a century of modern art movements, which tended to promulgate artistic visions that were more personal. That wildlife remains a prolific subject speaks to its ongoing prominence in the American imagination. Images of wildlife not only were central to the formation of a national identity but also continue to be a powerful indicator of how we think about ourselves in relation to the world in which we live.

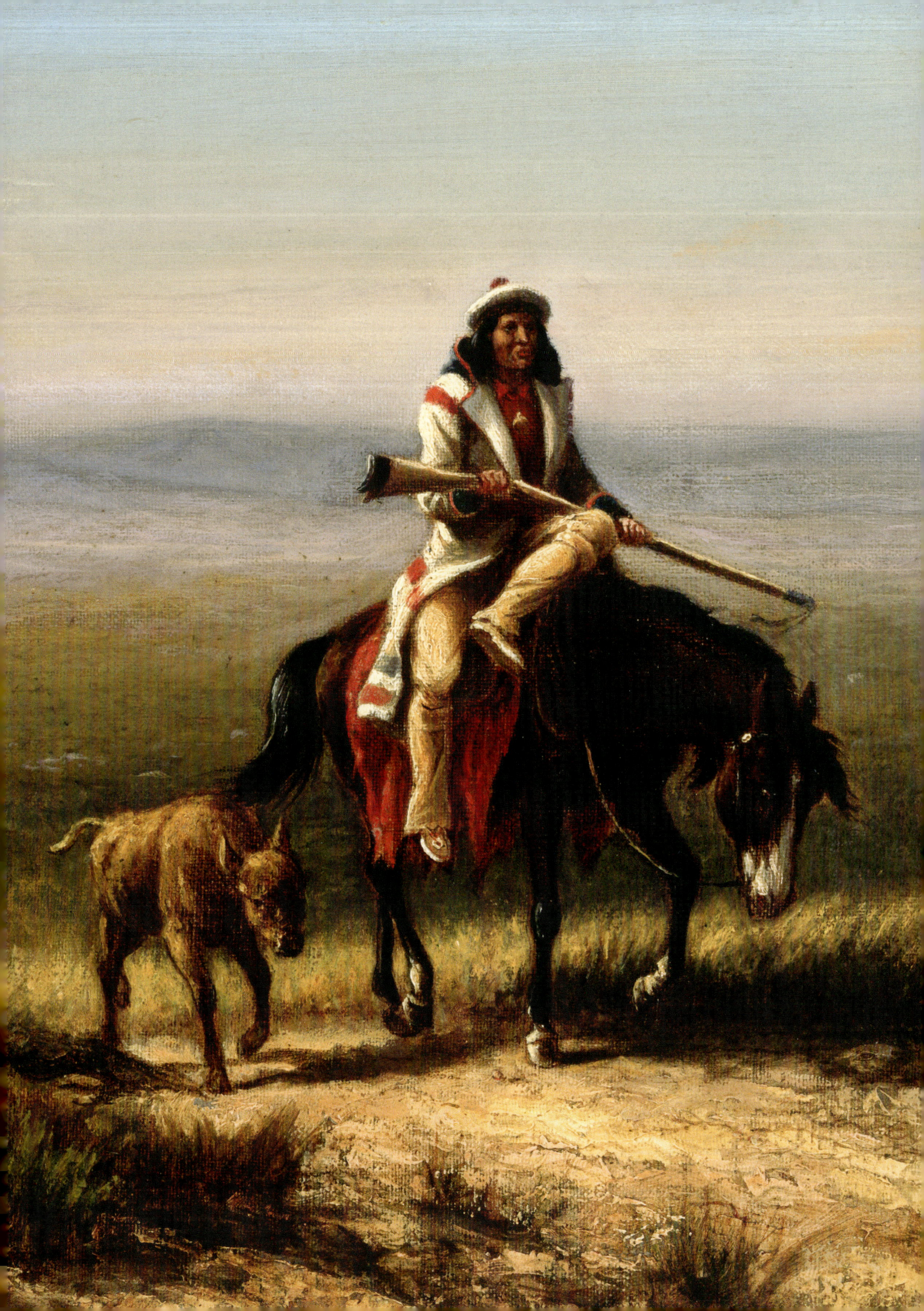

Chapter 1

Exploring New Ground: *Early Images of American Wildlife*

Images of American wildlife proliferated across the Atlantic before they found a large audience at home. The New World was a place full of engaging animals of great interest to many Europeans (both intellectually and financially). The bison became popular in print, in part because it was related to but noticeably different from the European wisent, in part because it might be domesticated (and therefore generate income), and in part because it was easier to approach and sketch than other, more timid animals. Deer, elk, bears, and pronghorns would be studied in time, but they proved a much greater challenge.

During the sixteenth and seventeenth centuries, much of the imagery depicting American fauna provided a distinctly distorted view of the New World. The version of the bison by North American explorer Father Louis Hennepin (Belgium, 1626–1705), for example, has the characteristic hump and shaggy hair, but it resembles a domestic ox much more than a wild buffalo (figure 1.1).[1] Even stranger than the bison is the monkey/opossum creature that dangles from the branch above. Sometimes, original sketches brought back from America or created in Europe were inaccurate to begin with, as artists drew animals based on memories, verbal accounts, or Old World species. When engravers translated sketches into prints, the images were often further altered. Subsequent artists then copied and modified the already muddled visions, resulting in fantastical creations that bore little resemblance to the animals they purported to depict. The firsthand experiences of artists such as John White and Jacques Le Moyne (both of whom ventured to America in the 1500s) suffered at the hands of engravers who altered their work. White's originals are available today and show a meticulous and confident handling of animals, but the majority of his images did not become widely known until 1865.[2] Not until 1731, when Mark Catesby began publishing his own work, did images that were more accurate become available to the general public.[3]

According to wildlife art historian David J. Wagner, Catesby's *Natural History of Carolina, Florida and the Bahama Islands* was the most popular reference book on American natural history for nearly one hundred years after his death in 1749 (see figure 1.2).[4] During that century, America grew into a nation in

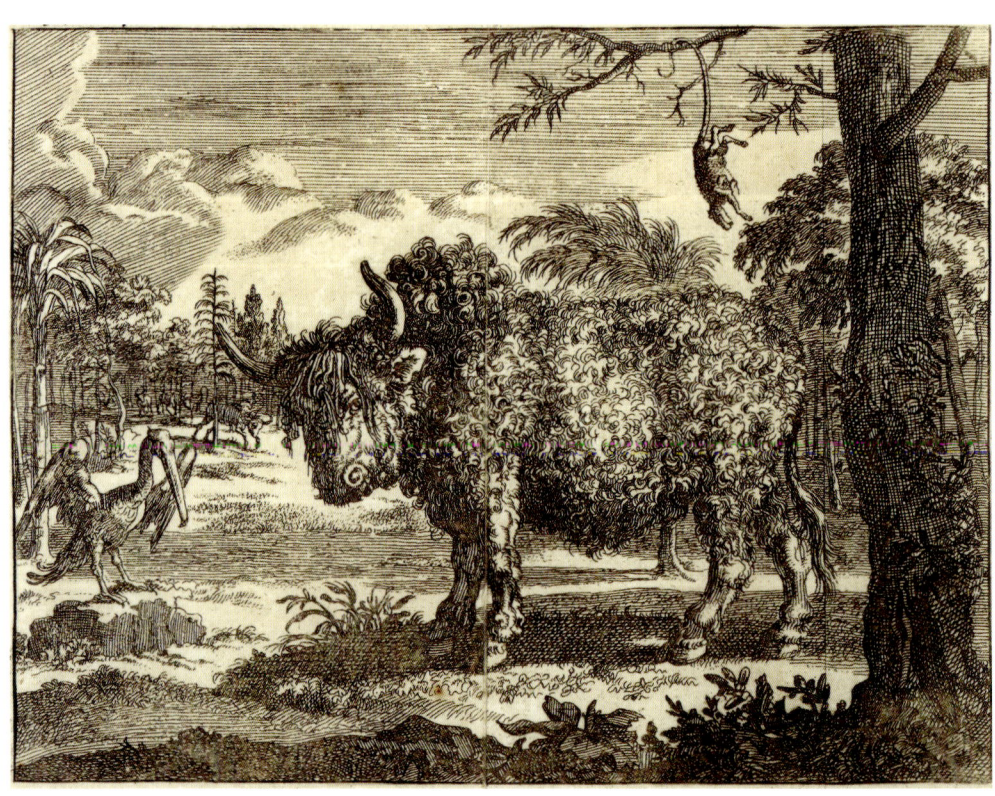

its own right, and images of native wildlife became of great interest in the United States while they also remained popular in Europe. After Catesby, the next major figure to impact the field was John James Audubon, whose work found success first in Europe and then in the United States.

Audubon, a singular force in American wildlife art, began seriously studying and drawing birds in the first years of the 1800s. For the next two and a half decades, he traveled widely, particularly along the Ohio and Mississippi rivers, adding images to his portfolio. In 1826, he embarked for England with 240 sketches, hoping to find a publisher for his work. His efforts culminated in *Birds of America* (1828–38), a four-volume set of double-elephant-sized prints that was the most complete record of North American birdlife ever published (eventually numbering over four hundred images). Praised for its artistry and accuracy, *Birds of America* remains one of the greatest achievements in American art. Audubon's success in selling subscriptions to the set (first in Europe and then in America) allowed him to embark on a second venture, *The Viviparous Quadrupeds of North America* (1845–48), a project that took him deep into the West, following in the footsteps of Lewis and Clark.[5]

In 1804, Lewis and Clark made their unprecedented journey up the Missouri River from Saint Louis to the Pacific Ocean, breaking trail for other expeditions to follow. After Lewis and Clark, Americans and Europeans alike explored the West; some had scientific goals in mind, while others had adventure as their primary motivation. Though no artist accompanied Lewis and Clark in an official capacity, Clark sketched landscapes, animals, and vegetation to complement his scientific notes. Later expeditions saw the merit of having an artist along, as visual documentation added veracity and interest to written text. When Major Stephen H. Long assembled his crew for an expedition into the Rocky Mountains in 1819, he included Titian Ramsay Peale to sketch animals and vegetation and Samuel Seymour to depict topography. Peale returned to the East Coast with 122 finished illustrations plus hundreds of field sketches depicting some never-before-seen species. An 1822 engraving of Seymour's *View of the Rocky Mountains on the Platte Fifty Miles from Their Base* was the first published view of the Rockies. His picture did not just depict a range of mountains, however; Seymour populated the middle ground with a herd of bison to illustrate just one of the many species encountered by the group on the journey. The Peale image from the expedition that was most often reproduced was a picture of an American Indian shooting a bison with an arrow. The bison also figured prominently in the work of George Catlin, who traveled up the Missouri in 1832, and Karl Bodmer, who made the trip in 1833. The subsequent publication of these artists' works again brought images of North American wildlife to eastern and European audiences hungry for pictures of the West.[6]

As the nineteenth century progressed, artists such as Alfred Jacob Miller, Charles Wimar, and William Jacob Hays journeyed west and brought back remarkable sketches of the animals they saw along the way.[7] Farther north, Canadians were engaged in a similar practice; Paul Kane, the "Catlin of Canada," painted the people and wildlife of his country in the middle of the nineteenth century. Kane's follower Frederick Arthur Verner documented dwindling bison populations as the twentieth century drew closer. By the 1880s, the majority of bison had been decimated from the plains, and the frontier era was coming to a close. Later artists depicted this change with paintings that mourned the wholesale slaughter of the American bison.

Coinciding with the lament over the loss of the bison was a related sentiment directed toward American Indians. After westward-moving Europeans had subjugated the native tribes in their path and eliminated the millions of bison on whom many of the Indians relied for food, shelter, and clothing, there was a sense of regret over what had been lost. This loss was tempered by settlers' success in colonizing the West, but there remained a mournful feeling that America had lost a part of what had made it exceptional, and that greedy easterners had despoiled a once-pristine continent. Thus arose the Romantic notion of the wilderness, which looked back to an idealized, unspoiled era but also projected the remaining wilderness as an entity in need of protection so that it could be enjoyed by future generations.

Linking the land, bison, and American Indian populations, Catlin wrote, "Nature has no where presented more beautiful and lovely scenes, than those of the vast prairies of the West; and of *man* and *beast,* no nobler specimens than those who inhabit them—the *Indian* and the *buffalo*—joint and original tenants of the soil, and fugitives together from the approach of civilized man; they have fled to the great plains of the West, and there, under an equal doom, they have taken up their *last abode,* where their race will expire, and their bones will bleach together."[8] The bison and the American Indian came to represent the West, in all of its complexity, as both a celebrated space and a locus for sadness and guilt. Seventy years after Catlin published his thoughts, the association endured: James Earle Fraser's 1913 Indian head–buffalo nickel epitomized the sentiment. The nickel features an American Indian man's profile on one side and a silhouette of a bison on the other: two iconic images of the American West, one the flip side of the other. The Fraser nickel is an elegy to the people and wildlife that once roamed the plains: where there were bison, there were American Indians, and vice versa.[9]

The fate of wildlife compared with that of American Indians has much to do with who was advocating for them at the time of their greatest peril, during the last half of the 1800s and the early 1900s. With powerful figures in the U.S. government, such as Theodore Roosevelt, using their influence to save the bison, the species escaped extinction. At the same time, American Indians (who had been relegated to reservations) struggled to retain any sense of their traditional ways of life.[10] The iconography of the American bison grew ever more powerful during this period as it came to symbolize the loss of the frontier and the squander of once-abundant natural resources. Images of the vanishing race and the vanishing bison were both nostalgic, but as the bison began to make a recovery, these pictures offered at least a modicum of hope that all had not been lost. In addition, focus could be directed toward the recovering bison if not the still-suffering American Indians, offering one way to assuage a national sense of guilt.

At the beginning of the 1700s, artist Mark Catesby documented animals in a scientific effort to record the species of a new continent. By the 1800s, artists had begun depicting the status of the animals with a more Romantic impulse, to show either what had already been lost or what would be lost if wilderness was not protected from the advancing tide of civilization. The early renderings of wildlife featured in this chapter celebrate the fauna of the New World with all the enthusiasm one would expect from artists on the forefront of discovery. Later images lament the loss of habitat and large populations but also set the stage for a new generation of artists who would go deeper into the wilderness to locate and study prime examples of the animals of North America.

MARK CATESBY
United Kingdom, 1682–1749

In Winter their whole Body is covered with long shagged Hair, which in
Summer falls off, and the Skin appears black, and wrinkled, except the
Head which retains the Hair all the Year. On the Forehead of a Bull the
Hair is a Foot long, thick, frizzled, of a dusky black Colour; the Length of
this Hair hanging over their Eyes, impedes their Flight, and is frequently
the Cause of their Destruction. . . . [W]hen wounded they are very furious,
which cautions the *Indians* how they attack them in open *Savanas*, where
no Trees are to skreen themselves from their Fury. Their Hooves more
than their Horns are their offensive Weapons, and whatever opposes them
are in no small Danger of being trampled into the Earth.

Mark Catesby, from McBurney,
Mark Catesby's Natural History, 121

American Bison (figure 1.2) was created by one of the first artists to compile a
natural history of the New World. In addition to this early image of the bison,
Mark Catesby's picture includes a detailed drawing of an acacia branch sprouting
from a truncated tree. The out-of-scale branch creates an arbor over the bison's
head, provides an interesting design element, and allows Catesby to illustrate
two items of interest on a single page. For scientific renderings of the time, this
juxtaposition was not out of the ordinary, particularly for Catesby, whose goal
was not to record the bison in its natural setting but instead to provide a detailed
depiction of American flora and fauna for European audiences to study.

In a 1723 letter, Catesby was born in 1682 and grew up in Sudbury, Suffolk, England. He first
journeyed to America in 1712 to visit his sister, who had sailed to Virginia in 1700.
Catesby remained in Virginia for seven years, studying the plants and animals of the
region with wealthy landowner William Byrd II. Back in England in 1719, Catesby
decided to compile a natural history of the New World. In 1722, he returned to
America under the sponsorship of the Royal Society of London and Colonel Francis
Nicholson, the governor of South Carolina, to continue work on his project. Catesby
also studied in the Bahamas for a year before returning to England in 1726.[11]

In a 1723 letter, Catesby mentions that he had been buffalo hunting
in Carolina but that he did not make a suitable drawing. He later referenced a
drawing by Everhard Kick that he saw in an album of quadrupeds to complete the
plate.[12] Catesby spent the next twenty years composing and selling *Natural History*

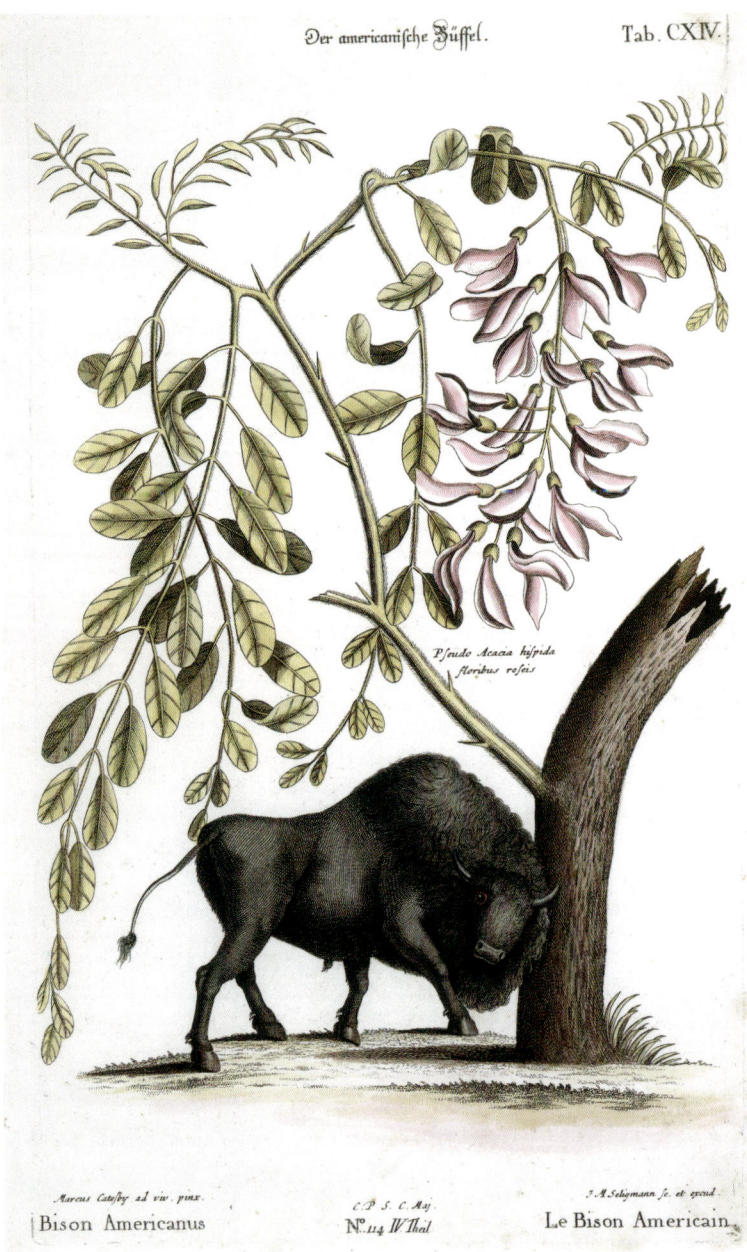

Pfeudo Acacia hifpida
floribus rofeis

Marcus Catesby ad viv. pinx.　　C.P.S.C.Maj.　　J.M.Seligmann fc. et excud.
　　　　　　　　　　　　　　　Nº.114 IV Thal

Bison Americanus　　　　　　　　　　　　　　Le Bison Americain.

FIGURE 1.2.
MARK CATESBY
American Bison, 1749–76.
Hand-colored engraving; 15 × 9 ¼ inches.
Gift of Karl and Mary Wagner.
National Museum of
Wildlife Art Collection.
W1996.069.

in serial chapters (much as Audubon did a century later with *Birds of America*).
From 1729 to 1747, Catesby sold *Natural History* in eleven installments of 20
plates each. In its entirety, the book contained 220 plates of birds, amphibians,
reptiles, fish, insects, quadrupeds, and plants. In 1749, the year Catesby died,
German publisher Johann Michael Seligmann began to reissue Catesby's work
along with that of naturalist George Edwards. Seligmann reduced the size of
Catesby's plates and provided additional nomenclature. He issued nine volumes
of the works of Catesby and Edwards, publishing the final volume in 1776. The
National Museum of Wildlife Art's *American Bison* comes from this later edition.
As a record of natural history, the plate and Catesby's description may not be
completely accurate, but as a historic piece of art, it is just one example among
many that demonstrate European interest in the wildlife and natural resources of
the New World.

JOHN JAMES AUDUBON
Santo Domingo, 1785–1851

John James Audubon is among the most renowned artists in America, acknowledged by both art and natural history museums for his massive portfolio, *Birds of America,* which contains over four hundred hand-colored engravings of North American avian species. Individual prints from *Birds of America* are highly prized today, valued for their accuracy as well as their beauty. Audubon attempted to depict each bird life-sized, in its native habitat. In *Hooping Crane* (which is actually a sandhill crane), Audubon places the bird in Florida, where the species resides year-round (figure 1.3).

Audubon was born in Santo Domingo (which is now Haiti) in 1785. His father was a French sea captain and plantation owner; his mother was a French chambermaid working on the island. The senior Audubon took his illegitimate son back to France, where his wife adopted the boy as her own, giving John James a privileged upbringing. The young Audubon left France in 1803 to escape being drafted into Napoleon's army; he went to America to manage his father's estate near Philadelphia. During the next sixteen years, he enjoyed hunting, sketching, and mounting avian subjects. He also met the famous ornithologist Alexander Wilson, who encouraged him to continue his studies. The family fortunes took a turn for the worse, however, and Audubon was briefly imprisoned for bankruptcy in 1819. In 1820, he moved to Cincinnati and eventually decided to pursue his interest in ornithology by traveling down the Mississippi, collecting and sketching specimens for a portfolio documenting American birdlife. Altogether, the *Birds of America* portfolio took twelve years to complete. When it was finished, it exponentially increased the knowledge of American ornithology. *Birds of America* was both a critical and a financial success, solving Audubon's monetary problems and allowing him to continue his scientific pursuits.[13]

As the avian project drew to a close, Audubon embarked on a companion portfolio for mammals, *The Viviparous Quadrupeds of North America,* which consumed his energies for much of the remainder of his life. In 1843, Audubon traveled up the Missouri River to collect mammal specimens. Robert Peck, of the Philadelphia Academy of Natural Sciences, wrote that John James Audubon "ridiculed what he called 'galloping parties' that had preceded him into the West. These were commercial or military expeditions in which scientists had been included, but which Audubon believed were unable or unwilling to provide

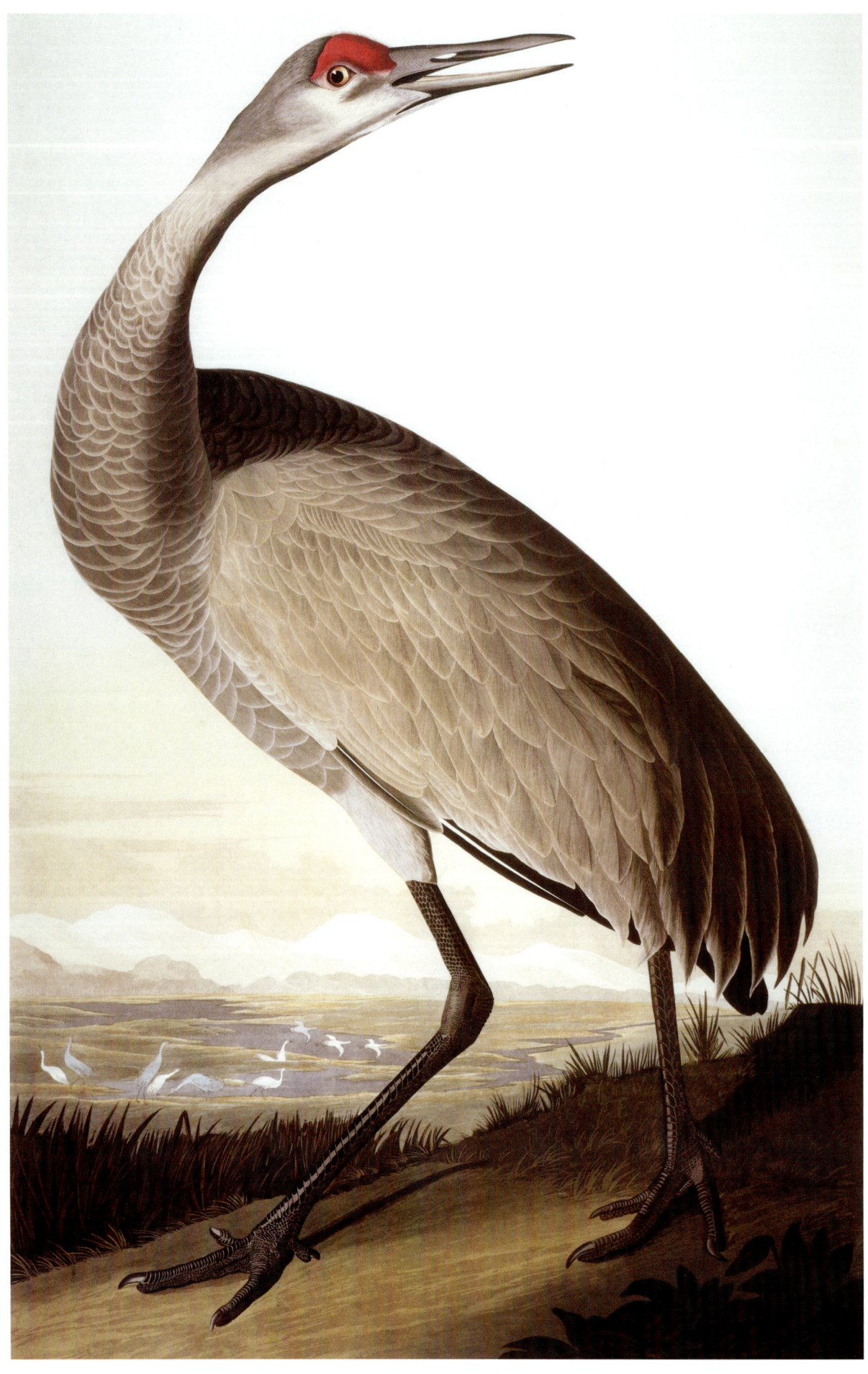

adequate time for collecting or observing wildlife."[14] Expeditions taken by the likes of Titian Ramsay Peale and Karl Bodmer did not venture forth with the express purpose of documenting the nation's mammalian inhabitants; they had a broader interest in topography, American Indians, vegetation, and wildlife. Audubon may have been reacting in particular to journeys such as Sir William Drummond Stewart's of 1837 (which included artist Alfred Jacob Miller) that set out to experience the fabled fur traders' rendezvous and placed emphasis on adventure, not science.[15]

The Viviparous Quadrupeds of North America was to provide subscribers with a complete and accurate picture of the mammalian population of North America, but Audubon did not completely succeed in this venture. His Missouri River journey terminated at Fort Union, and he did not travel far from the safety of the settlement. Peck wrote, "He and his party were seeking new species in a part of the West that had been thoroughly explored and regularly hunted for more than two decades."[16] Even before his expedition, Audubon and coauthor John Bachman realized they would need assistance from other naturalists and collectors, so they put out a call for specimens that they could incorporate into their work. Upon Audubon's return from the West, his health began to deteriorate; his sons, particularly John Woodhouse Audubon, took over the completion of the *Quadruped* series. After the first mammal folio was printed in 1845, Audubon was losing his eyesight and showing signs of senility.

Two Bank Mice (figure 1.4) was never translated into a plate for the *Quadruped* book, though many other small rodents are featured in the compendium. Smaller animals were easier to capture and study than their larger brethren. Because of the difficulty of observing animals (many of which were nocturnal) in the wild, Audubon frequently sketched his subjects using animal skins, taxidermied specimens, or caged animals. Though he had used similar methods for *Birds of America,* the imagery created for the *Quadruped* volumes was less appealing to the general public, perhaps because of either Audubon's inexperience with animals other than birds or his failing health. In the end, Audubon did not meet his goal of depicting the complete range of North American wildlife, but he did depict a broad spectrum: *The Viviparous Quadrupeds of North America* introduced a new audience to many North American mammals, from small rodents to large ungulates. In comparison to the work of Catlin and Bodmer, who depicted animals on occasion, Audubon's two publications brought a wealth of information about America's wildlife to an appreciative public. After Audubon, the next artists to focus primarily on animals would come in the late 1800s. During the middle decades of the century, artists documenting the West depicted a range of subjects, including American Indians, landscapes, and wildlife, all part and parcel of the frontier experience.

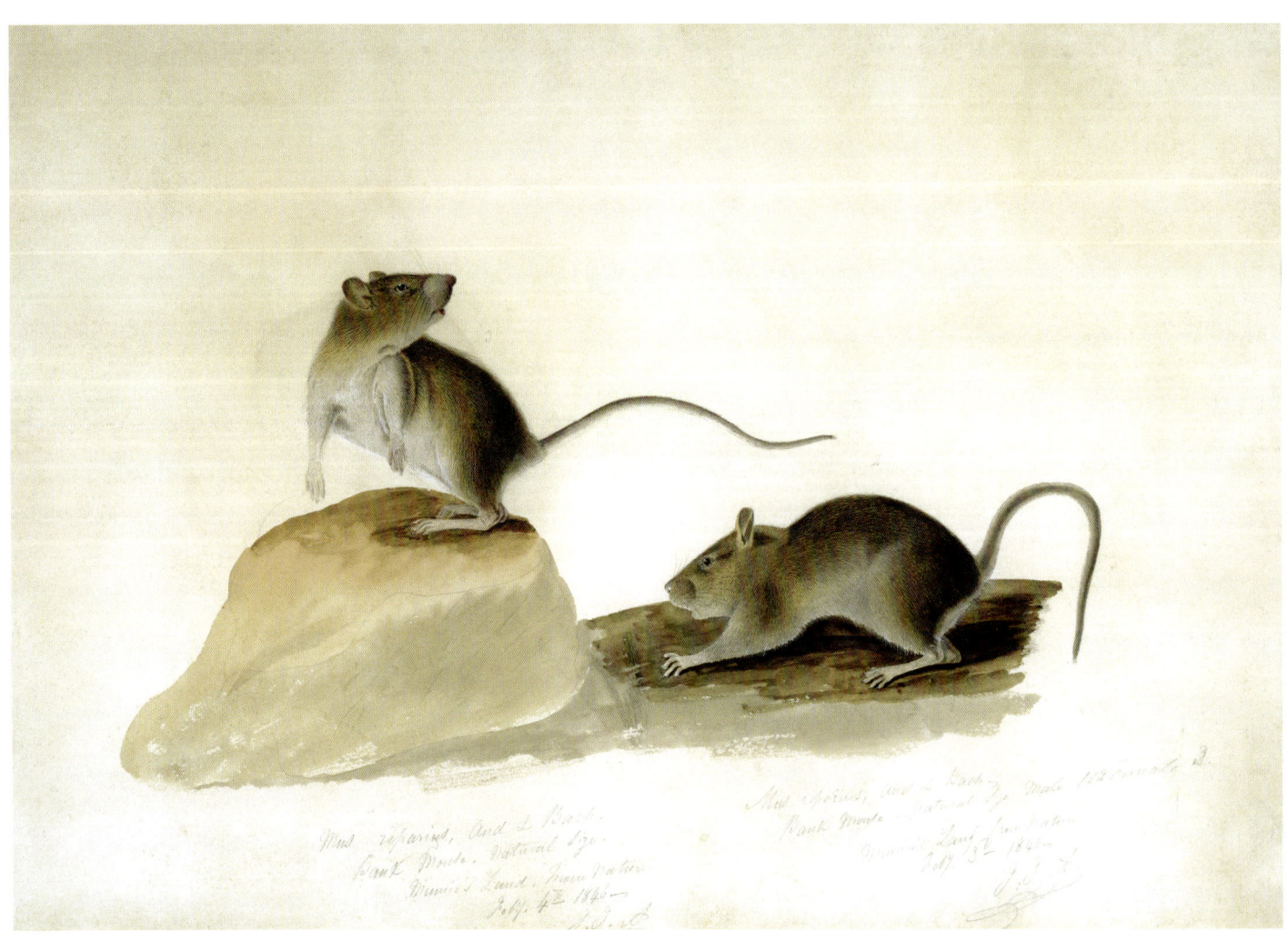

FIGURE 1.4.

JOHN JAMES AUDUBON

Two Bank Mice, 1846.

Watercolor and pencil on paper;

12¾ × 18⅝ inches.

JKM Collection.

JL1997.090.

TITIAN RAMSAY PEALE
United States, 1799–1885

Titian Ramsay Peale, the youngest son of famed artist and museum founder Charles Willson Peale, began his prodigious career as a painter and natural historian under his father's tutelage. He briefly attended the University of Pennsylvania to study anatomy and then, at the tender age of seventeen, became a member of the Academy of Natural Sciences of Philadelphia. In 1817, he accompanied an academy expedition to Florida and Georgia to study fauna and gather specimens. Two years later, Peale set out with Stephen H. Long's expedition to the Rocky Mountains, with the intention of finding the sources of the Red and Arkansas rivers. Though the expedition failed in its stated purpose, it did provide Peale with nearly two years of time in which to study and sketch the West. He returned to Philadelphia with 122 finished drawings of people, wildlife, and plants, as well as hundreds of field sketches.[17]

The museum's *Canis Lupus* (figure 1.5) was one of the earliest illustrations of a western wolf seen on the East Coast. The picture is similar to Peale's *Dusky Wolf Devouring a Mule Deer* (owned by the American Philosophical Society in Philadelphia).[18] *Dusky Wolf* likewise features a canine centered in the composition and displayed in complete lateral profile, so that the majority of its anatomy can be examined in one view. *Dusky Wolf* shows the canine eating its prey, while *Canis Lupus* provides a "before and after" scenario, with a herd of living elk in the background and a jawbone in the foreground—the implied remnants of an animal devoured by the wolf or one of its brethren. The wolf's head is highlighted against a thunderhead in the distance, and its body is set against white clouds hugging the horizon. Peale painted an accurate view of the rolling plains in his division of the landscape, which recedes in clear layers to distant hills far behind the herd of elk. In this one small watercolor, Peale provided a study of the wolf, an indication of its diet, a sense of its habitat, and as an added feature, a dramatic rendering of a gathering storm.[19]

After his return to Philadelphia, Peale held a variety of positions: he served as curator for the Peale Museum upon his father's death in 1827; he journeyed to South America in 1830; and he took part in the Wilkes Expedition to the Northwest Coast, Antarctica, and the South Pacific in 1838. After the Wilkes Expedition, at just over forty years of age, Peale took a position at the U.S. Patent Office in

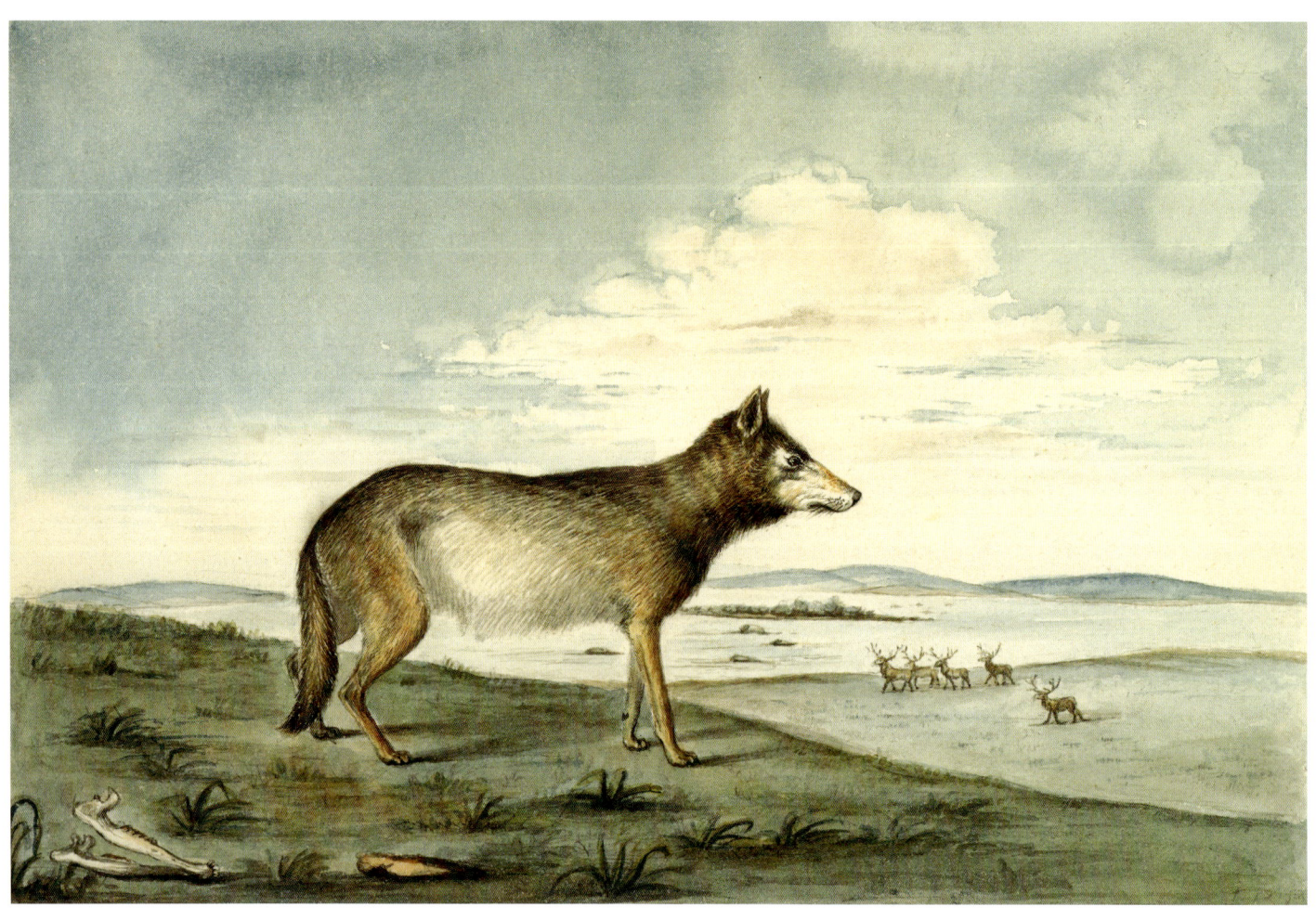

Washington, D.C. Late in life, Peale became interested in photography and formed the Amateur Photographic Exchange Club, America's first organization dedicated to photography. He passed away in his home city of Philadelphia in 1885. Peale's sketches from the Long Expedition and the natural history displays he created in the Peale Museum were seen and studied by both his scholarly circle and the general public. In an era when fine art and natural history went hand in hand, Peale's contributions to the field cannot be overestimated. His work typifies the scientific tradition that sought to bring to the East detailed evidence of the wildlife and wilderness of the West.

GEORGE CATLIN
UNITED STATES, 1796–1872

Though George Catlin is best known for his portraits of American Indians, he also painted wildlife. The museum's *A Group of Deer* (figure 1.6) is a family portrait, with two bucks, two does, and a fawn. Although these are fairly generic-looking deer, the sweeping antlers with tines emanating from a single beam are characteristic of whitetails, which range across North America. Catlin may have seen whitetail deer in European menageries and used those for models, or he may have relied on his sketches from his travels in North America.[20] Regardless of the source, in this work Catlin depicts a full side view of a buck and two contrasting views of the distinctive antlers, as well as profile and frontal views of the does. This allows the painting to be used as a documentary tool, describing the appearance of the animals. In *A Stag and a Doe* (figure 1.7), he painted the elk stag in the same pose he used for one of the whitetail bucks in the previous work but reversed it, so the animal is looking the other direction. Catlin painted the female elk in a convincing, foreshortened three-quarter view. In both paintings, he carefully included details of vegetation, which would have been another source of edification for viewers.

Living in Europe in the middle of the nineteenth century without a reliable source of income, Catlin painted canvases based on his North American experiences and sold them to European patrons eager for renderings of the New World. *A Group of Deer* and *A Stag and a Doe* come from this period. Catlin began his professional career as a lawyer, but he quickly devoted himself to painting. In 1821, he moved to Philadelphia, where he exhibited work (often miniature portraits) at the Pennsylvania Academy of Fine Arts. He befriended artists Thomas Sully and John Neagle, but other influences or art teachers are unknown.[21] In 1826, Catlin saw a delegation of American Indians in Philadelphia and became fascinated by their appearance and culture.[22] Knowing that native tribes of the American West were rapidly losing their historic traditions, Catlin resolved to record their appearance and customs before these disappeared forever. Between 1830 and 1836, he made a series of trips up the Mississippi and Missouri rivers, creating over five hundred paintings of American Indian life. Catlin also recorded the wildlife he encountered along the way, often showing different means of hunting particular animals—most notably the bison. He exhibited his Indian Gallery in major cities on the East Coast and lobbied Congress to purchase it, hoping it would become the

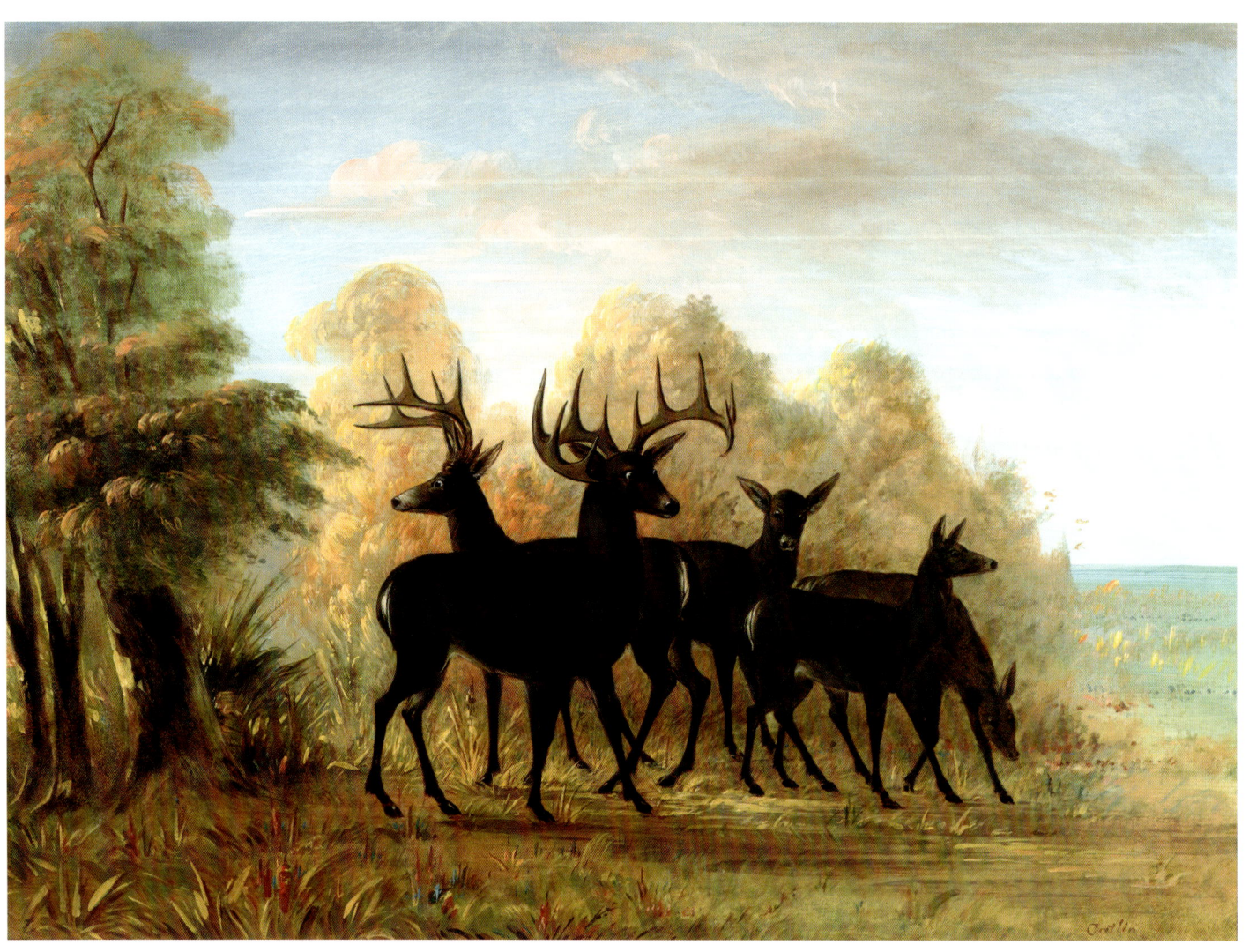

FIGURE 1.6.
GEORGE CATLIN
A Group of Deer, c. 1850.
Oil on canvas; 16 × 19 inches.
JKM Collection.
J1989.002.

nucleus of a National Museum of American Indians. Congress, however, refused to approve the acquisition. Catlin took the Indian Gallery to Europe in 1839 in an effort to generate funds, seeking the same success that had been afforded to Audubon's *Birds of America.*

In England in 1841, Catlin published *Letters and Notes on the Manners, Customs, and Condition of the North American Indians,* which contained simple illustrations adapted from his paintings. According to Ron Tyler, *Letters and Notes* was reprinted as many as twenty times between 1841 and 1860. After his success with *Letters and Notes,* Catlin published a portfolio of hunting scenes and other "amusements" aimed at English sportsmen in 1844. Tyler notes, "Sixteen of the original twenty-five plates depict buffalo, grizzly bear, and antelope hunting scenes or related subjects."[23] The portfolio was issued in at least six European editions as well as one in America, again showing the popularity of wildlife subjects abroad.[24] Neither of these efforts provided Catlin with the financial stability he desperately needed, however.

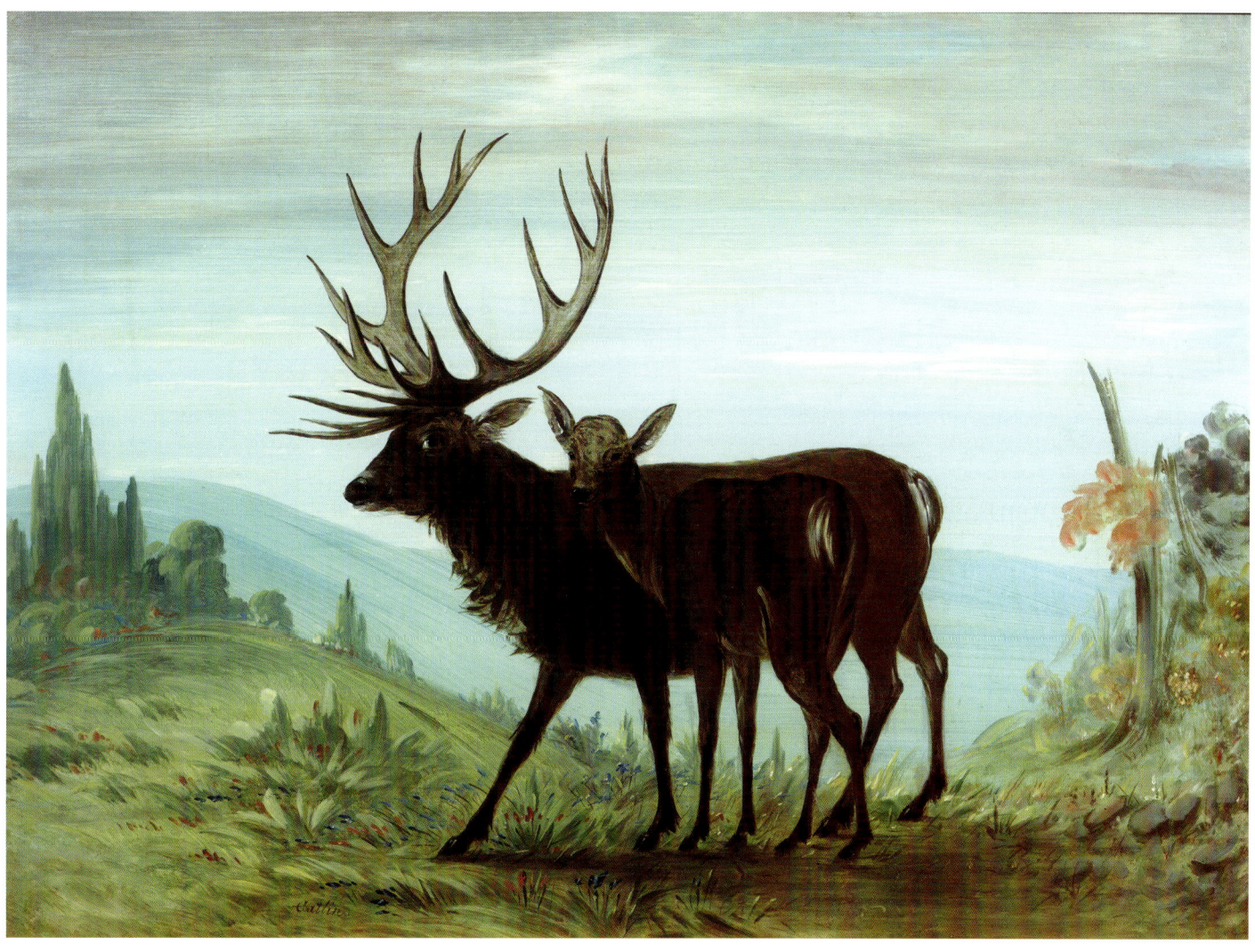

FIGURE 1.7.
GEORGE CATLIN
A Stag and a Doe, c. 1850.
Oil on canvas; 19¼ × 26¾ inches.
JKM Collection.
J1987.131.

In 1851, after a brief period in debtor's prison, he was forced to sell the Indian Gallery to Joseph Harrison of Philadelphia. Catlin passed away in 1872. Seven years later, his original Indian Gallery was presented to the Smithsonian Institution by Harrison's widow. The proliferation and subsequent copying of Catlin's imagery make the vast extent of his influence difficult to gauge. His work was certainly better known in America than that of Karl Bodmer (generally acknowledged as the more accomplished artist of the two). Although Catlin did not sell his Indian Gallery to the United States during his lifetime, he did become internationally known as "the historian of the Indians," and he helped cement a vision of western life in European and American minds that resonates to this day.[25] His gallery now stands as an accomplished historical record of this nation's early inhabitants, both human and animal, and for that he would have been proud.[26]

KARL BODMER
Switzerland, 1809–1893

Not much about Karl Bodmer's early life is known. He was born in 1809 in Zurich and was apprenticed to his uncle, artist Johann Jakob Meier, at the age of thirteen. Meier tutored Bodmer in art for approximately ten years, focusing his lessons on depicting landscapes and nature. In 1831, a book featuring Bodmer's scenes of the Moselle Valley was published. Prince Alexander Philip Maximilian likely saw this publication and arranged a meeting with Bodmer. Known for his natural history research in Brazil, the prince was searching for a professional artist to accompany him on a North American expedition. The two met in January 1832, and Bodmer signed on with Maximilian shortly thereafter. After a few months of preparation, the party set sail in May, landing in Boston on July 4. Bodmer and Maximilian made their way to Saint Louis and traveled up the Missouri River, retracing much of the route taken by Lewis and Clark.[27] During the expedition, Bodmer depicted some of the same people that George Catlin had painted just months before. Bodmer was the last artist to paint the Mandan Indians in North Dakota before the fatal 1837 smallpox epidemic that nearly obliterated them. He sketched portraits of the Sioux, Blackfeet, Hidatsas, and others, while Maximilian studied the appearance, customs, and language of the various tribes. After returning to Europe in 1834, Bodmer completed eighty-one aquatints to illustrate Maximilian's *Travels in the Interior of North America*, which appeared in Germany between 1839 and 1841.[28] Bodmer, who never revisited America, became involved with the Barbizon school outside of Paris, working with the French artists Jean-François Millet and Théodore Rousseau.[29]

Bodmer's considerable artistic talent and European training are evident when his work is compared to that of Peale or Catlin. Hard-pressed to find any direct influences for Bodmer's ability in portraiture, William Goetzmann noted, "He was far more polished in portraiture but no less self taught than George Catlin."[30] Bodmer was primarily interested in depicting American Indians, but like Catlin, he also sketched wildlife. In *Travels in the Interior of North America*, several lithographs—such as *Herds of Bison and Elks* or *Hunting of the Grizzly Bear*—depict the landscape of the West along with its animal inhabitants.

In Europe, Bodmer recalled his time in America with a series of drawings, such as *Une famille d'acrobats* (figure 1.8). These were engraved and appeared in various publications, including the American illustrated newspaper *Every Saturday*

FIGURE 1.8.
KARL BODMER
Une famille d'acrobats, 1863.
Graphite on paper; 20 × 13 inches.
JKM Collection.
M1989.007.

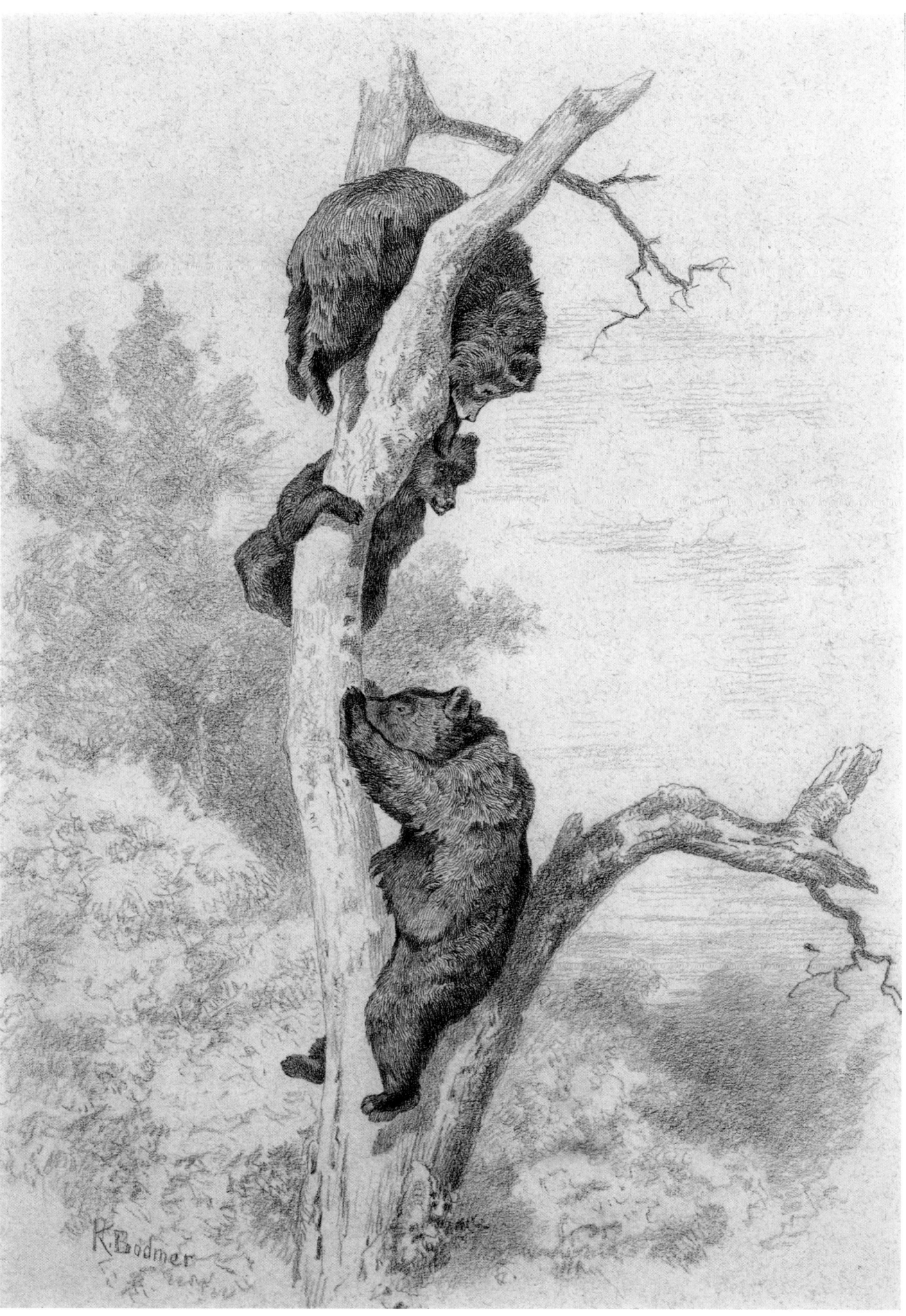

and the French periodical *L'Illustration, Journal Universal. Acrobats* appeared as *Trois oursons dans un arbre* (Three Bear Cubs in a Tree) in Bodmer's *Eaux-fortes: Animaux et paysages* in 1863.[31] A sense of humor, not readily apparent in his documentary work for Prince Maximilian, is evident in this piece featuring a family of bears playing in a tree. Bodmer became well known in Europe as a Barbizon artist, and his animal and landscape paintings appeared regularly in the Paris Salon. Though his images of North American Indians and animals were not copied or distributed to the extent of Catlin's, they were reproduced in the popular press in the 1840s, and their reputation has steadily grown over the course of the twentieth century.[32] Bodmer's work now stands as one of the most accomplished records of native life in the West.

Wildlife in American Art

ALFRED JACOB MILLER
United States, 1810–1874

Pierre and the Buffalo

The incident from which this sketch was made, seems to have had a
fatality about it, as the hero "Pierre," although escaping this, eventually lost
his life in a similar encounter.

His usual practice in hunting the Buffalo was, as he expressed it,
to have "lots of fun"; for this purpose after wounding the animal, he would
commence tantalizing him either by displaying a red cloth or in default of
this, running at him suddenly, whooping and causing the animal to chase
him in rage and agony. All the caution from his elder and more experienced
brother could not induce him to desist, the "hairbreadth 'scape" was a complete infatuation.

Alfred Jacob Miller, from Ross,
The West of Alfred Jacob Miller, note to plate 58

Alfred Jacob Miller was the only eastern artist to witness and record a meeting
of the fabled fur traders' rendezvous in Wyoming. During his youth in
Baltimore, Miller's parents encouraged his artistic talents. He trained with famed
portraitist Thomas Sully in 1831–32. During a European tour in 1832–34, Miller
studied at the École des Beaux-Arts in Paris and the English Life school in Rome.
He subsequently moved to New Orleans and established a studio, where he met
Captain William Drummond Stewart, a wealthy Scottish aristocrat who was about
to depart for an expedition to the Rocky Mountains. After looking at Miller's work,
Stewart invited him along to depict the party's progress. Unlike earlier scientific
expeditions charged with documenting the flora and fauna, this trip was based
solely on adventure. Circa April 1837, the party departed for the rendezvous.[33]
Along the way, they entertained themselves by hunting buffaloes, dashing across
the plains in the midst of the then-great herds. As can be seen in the sketch *A
Wounded Buffalo Overthrowing a Hunter in Pursuit* (figure 1.9), this activity was
not without risk, though from Miller's description above, the hunter in this case
unnecessarily brought much of the pain upon himself.

After reaching the rendezvous, Miller sketched the various trading
activities. Lisa Strong notes in *Sentimental Journey: The Art of Alfred Jacob Miller*
that the party "spent only a week or so at the rendezvous, then headed into the
Wind River Mountains to the source of the Green River. There they spent their

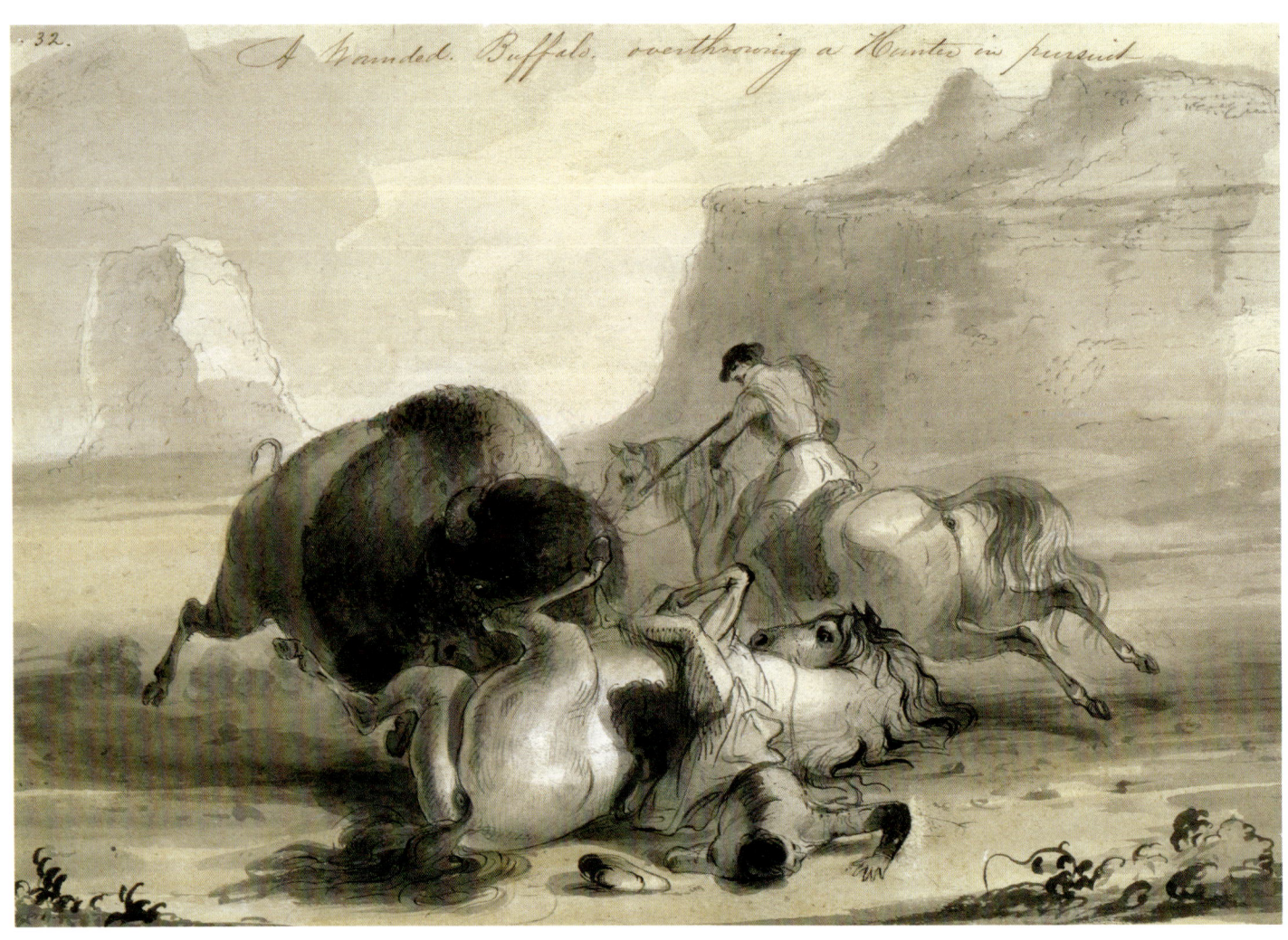

· 32.

A Wounded. Buffalo. overthrowing a Hunter in pursuit

FIGURE 1.9.

ALFRED JACOB MILLER

A Wounded Buffalo Overthrowing a Hunter in Pursuit, c. 1837.

Watercolor on paper;

7¼ × 10⅜ inches.

JKM Collection.

M1990.041.

time hunting moose and elk before returning to Saint Louis in early October."[34] His small works from this period hold a plethora of information about the culture of the time, but each also clearly shows the impact of Miller's European training. The sketches and later paintings were romanticized visions of the rendezvous, not necessarily a record of the facts. William Goetzmann noted that these paintings were among the first comprehensive views of the Rocky Mountains, "a view that was replete with all the charms that high romanticism and emotional energy could bring to them."[35] *Death of the Elk* (figure 1.10) contrasts with the work of Peale and Catlin in that it is not an anatomical study. It depicts, instead, an elk bounding back into the landscape, with hunters emerging above on a ridge. It is a narrative of the hunt, tied to Romantic scenes by the likes of French painter Eugene Delacroix that Miller studied while in Europe. *Death of the Elk* evokes emotion: either the thrill of the hunt or pathos for the elk. In his notes for a series of watercolors produced for William T. Walters twenty years after his return from the West, Miller wrote of the elk, "In comparison with the deer and antelope this animal is a little sluggish, but has a most noble presence, often carrying ten antlers on his head, and is extremely graceful."[36]

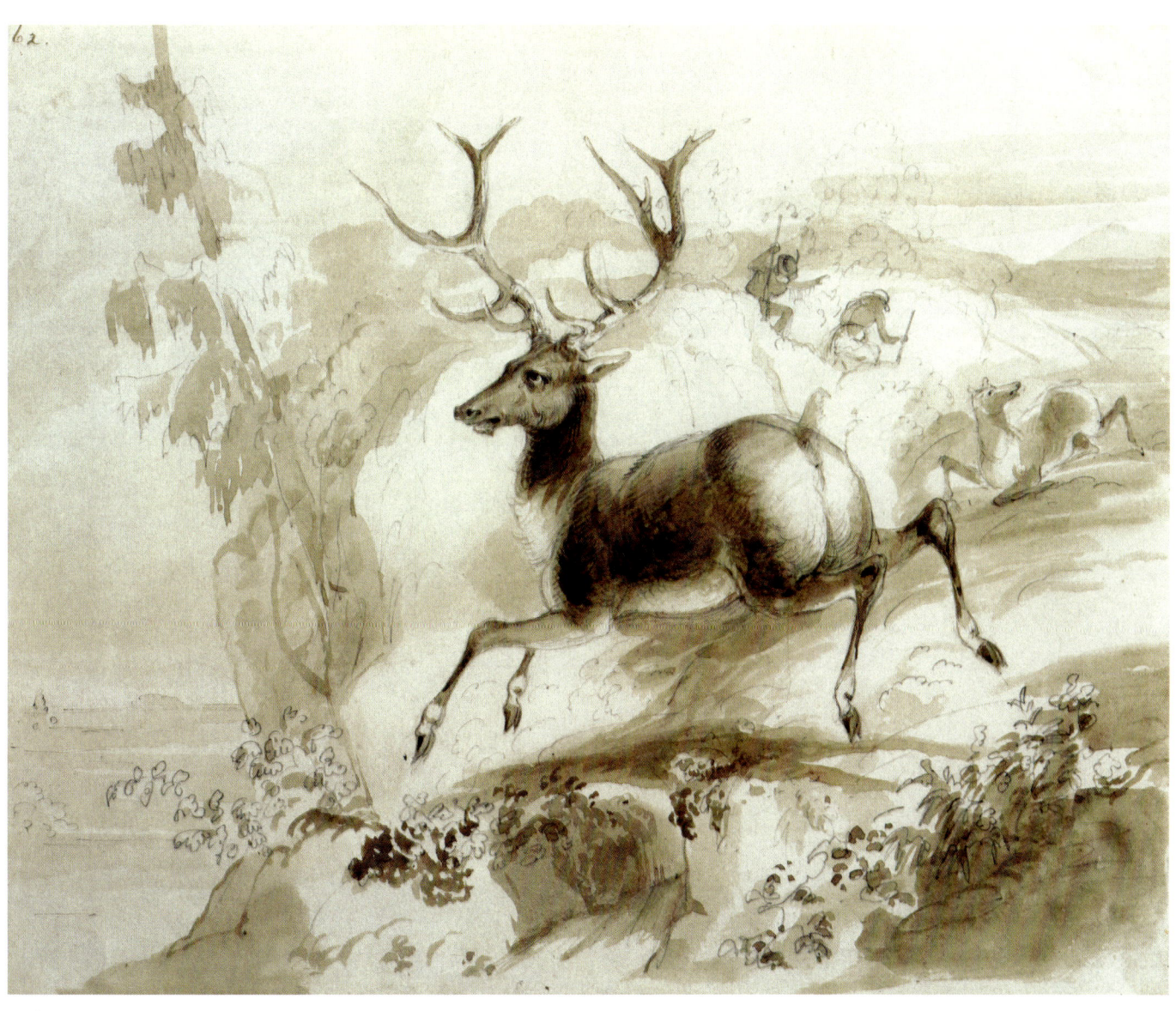

62.

FIGURE 1.10.
ALFRED JACOB MILLER
Death of the Elk, c. 1837.
Watercolor on paper;
8⅞ × 10⅞ inches.
JKM Collection.
JL1993.021.

Miller and Stewart turned east in 1837, after Stewart received news that his brother had passed away and that he would have to return to the family estate, Murthly Castle. Working in New Orleans and then in Baltimore in 1839, Miller created eighteen oil paintings and nearly two hundred finished watercolors based on his field sketches. The paintings were exhibited in New York, receiving rave reviews. Miller subsequently shipped the paintings and his sketches to Murthly Castle, where he lived between 1840 and 1842, creating finished paintings of scenes from the historic trip for Stewart. After completing the commission, Miller returned to Baltimore and spent the rest of his career painting portraits and repainting scenes from his western journey (including a set of two hundred watercolors based on his field sketches for Walters, whose collection became the basis for the Walters Art Museum in Baltimore).[37] Miller's work helped pave the way for the grand, romanticized visions of the West created by master painters such as Albert Bierstadt and Thomas Moran.

JOHN WOODHOUSE AUDUBON
United States, 1812–1862

John Woodhouse Audubon, son of renowned ornithologist and wildlife artist John James Audubon (see figures 1.3 and 1.4), devoted his career to supporting the work of his father. After completing the *Birds of America* portfolio, John James began *The Viviparous Quadrupeds of North America*, which sought to document North America's mammalian population. The project was daunting to begin with, and the elder Audubon's failing health only added to the pressure. After returning from his 1843 Missouri River trip with less-than-satisfying results, the senior Audubon's health began to falter. By 1846, John Woodhouse had been placed completely in charge of rendering the animals, traveling to Texas to collect specimens and then to England to sketch animals in museums and zoos. John Woodhouse painted at least 72 of the 150 plates for the imperial folio edition of *Quadrupeds* and 5 additional plates for the octavo edition. The museum's *Mountain Brook Minks* (figure 1.11) was the basis for one of the additional plates.[38] The figure in *American Grizzly Bear* (figure 1.12) appears behind another bear in the plate of the same name in the imperial folio edition.

Both Audubons often sketched caged or stuffed animals, causing some of their renderings to appear stiff and sinister.[39] In *Mountain Brook Minks*, John Woodhouse combines two color phases of the mink in one image, a pairing unlikely to occur in the wild. Their identical pose suggests that Audubon used a stuffed mink in his studio as a reference, changing the color to show seasonal variation. The younger Audubon often created paintings with a higher degree of finish, including detailed backgrounds, as he found them easier to sell after they had been reproduced for the *Quadruped* series. John Woodhouse Audubon will be remembered in light of his father's accomplishments, in particular for finalizing the elder's last project. Both *Birds of America* and *The Viviparous Quadrupeds of North America* represent an overarching desire to document the fauna of a new nation, a scientific goal that resulted in two incredible artistic achievements.

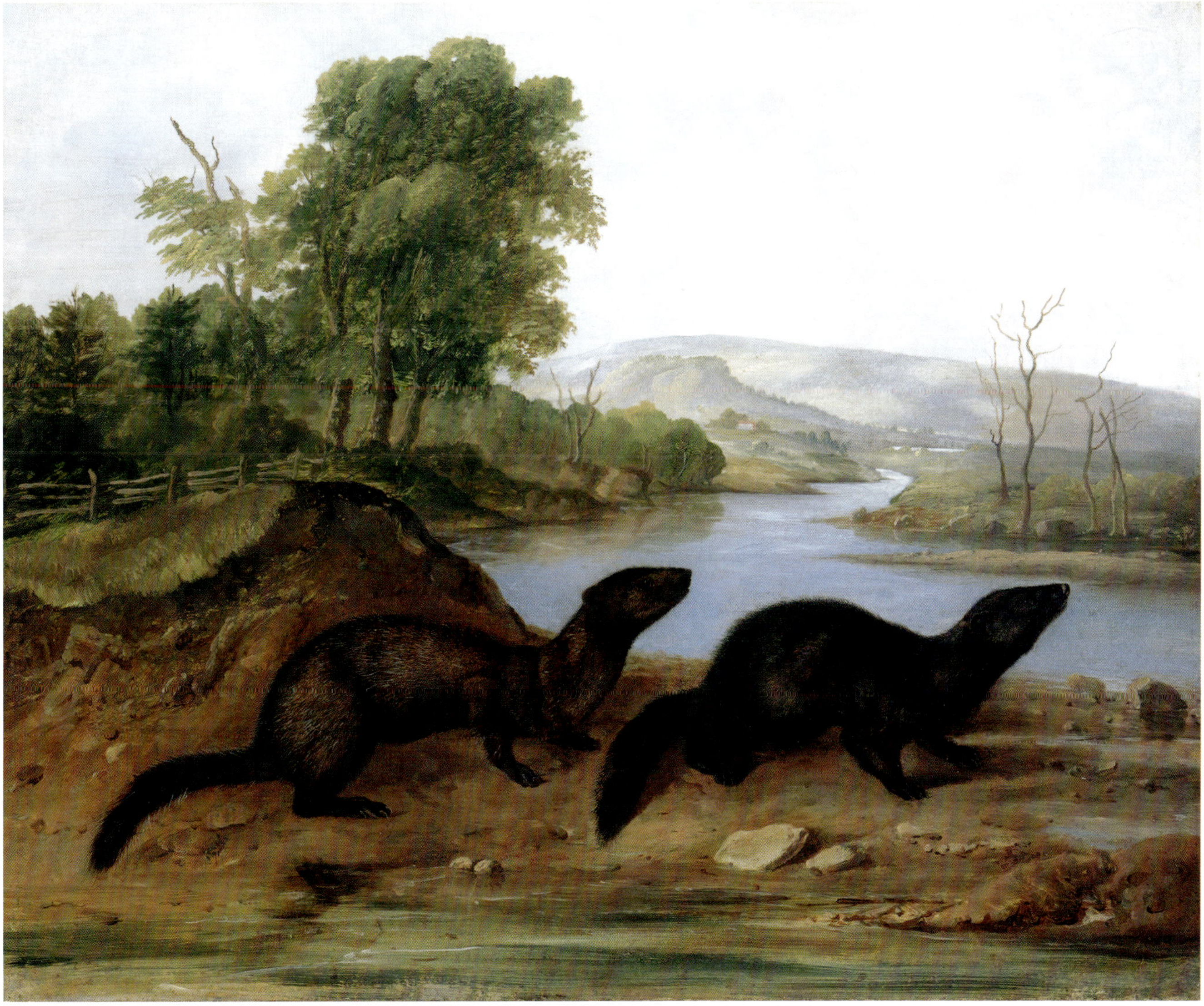

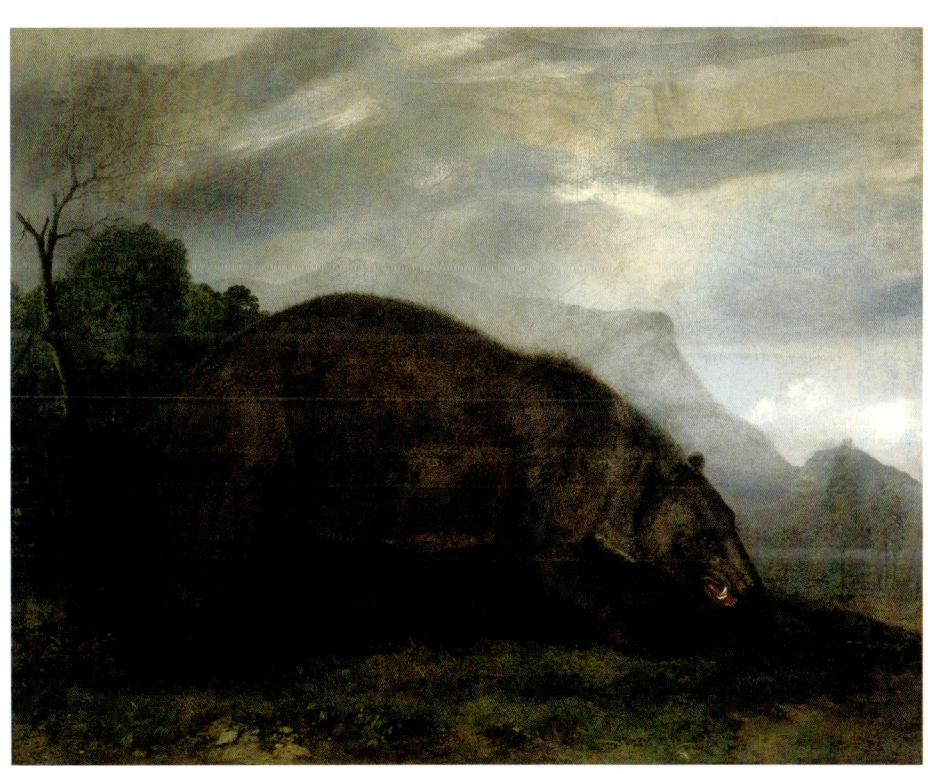

Figure 1.11.
John Woodhouse Audubon
Mountain Brook Minks, 1848.
Oil on canvas; 21¾ × 26¾ inches.
JKM Collection.
M1994.001.

Figure 1.12.
John Woodhouse Audubon
American Grizzly Bear, c. 1840.
Oil on canvas; 22 × 28 inches.
JKM Collection.
J1987.130.

PAUL KANE

IRELAND, 1810–1871

> Towards evening, as we were approaching the place where we were to
> cross the river, I saw some buffaloes idly grazing in a valley, and as I wished
> to give a general idea of the beauty of the scenery which lies all along the
> banks of the Saskatchewan from this point to Edmonton, I sat down to make
> a sketch, the rest of the party promising to wait for me at the crossing place.
> . . . The sleepy buffaloes grazing upon the undulating hills, here and there
> relieved by clumps of small trees, the unbroken stillness, and the approach-
> ing evening, rendered it altogether a scene of most enchanting repose.
>
> Paul Kane, "Wanderings of an Artist"

Paul Kane is the best-known Canadian artist-naturalist of the nineteenth
century. He grew up in York (now Toronto) and started his career as a
decorative furniture painter. After working as a portraitist in Detroit, Kane traveled
to Europe in 1841, and there he met George Catlin. Inspired by Catlin's Indian
Gallery, he returned to Canada determined to paint the indigenous people.
Kane set up a studio in Toronto and took two research trips: his first was a short
excursion to Sault Ste. Marie in 1845; his second was a two-year expedition with
the Hudson's Bay Company to the Pacific in 1846 and 1847.[40]

After his second excursion, Kane had over five hundred sketches of Native
Canadians and wildlife, with portraits of Assiniboines, Blackfeet, Crees, Clallams,
Kwakiutl, and others. Using this material, he completed over one hundred oil
paintings, creating a Canadian Indian Gallery similar to the one George Catlin
had produced of Indians in the United States. Unlike Catlin's, however, Kane's
gallery met with financial success; politician George W. Allan purchased the entire
collection. The Canadian government also commissioned twelve paintings from
Kane. In 1859, Kane published an account of his travels, *Wanderings of an Artist
among the Indians of North America,* to much renown. As Catlin and Bodmer had
done, Kane painted some scenes of the wildlife he saw on his western journey. In
Buffalo at Sunset (figure 1.13), he depicted five buffaloes in a pastoral setting. Four
of the five buffaloes have turned their heads away from the viewer and are looking
back into the canvas, across the river. As Kane described in the above epigraph,
his experience with bison was one of silence and repose; he was neither capturing
the drama of a hunt nor intent on recording details of anatomy. By turning the
bison heads into the painting, the work becomes nonconfrontational. The viewer

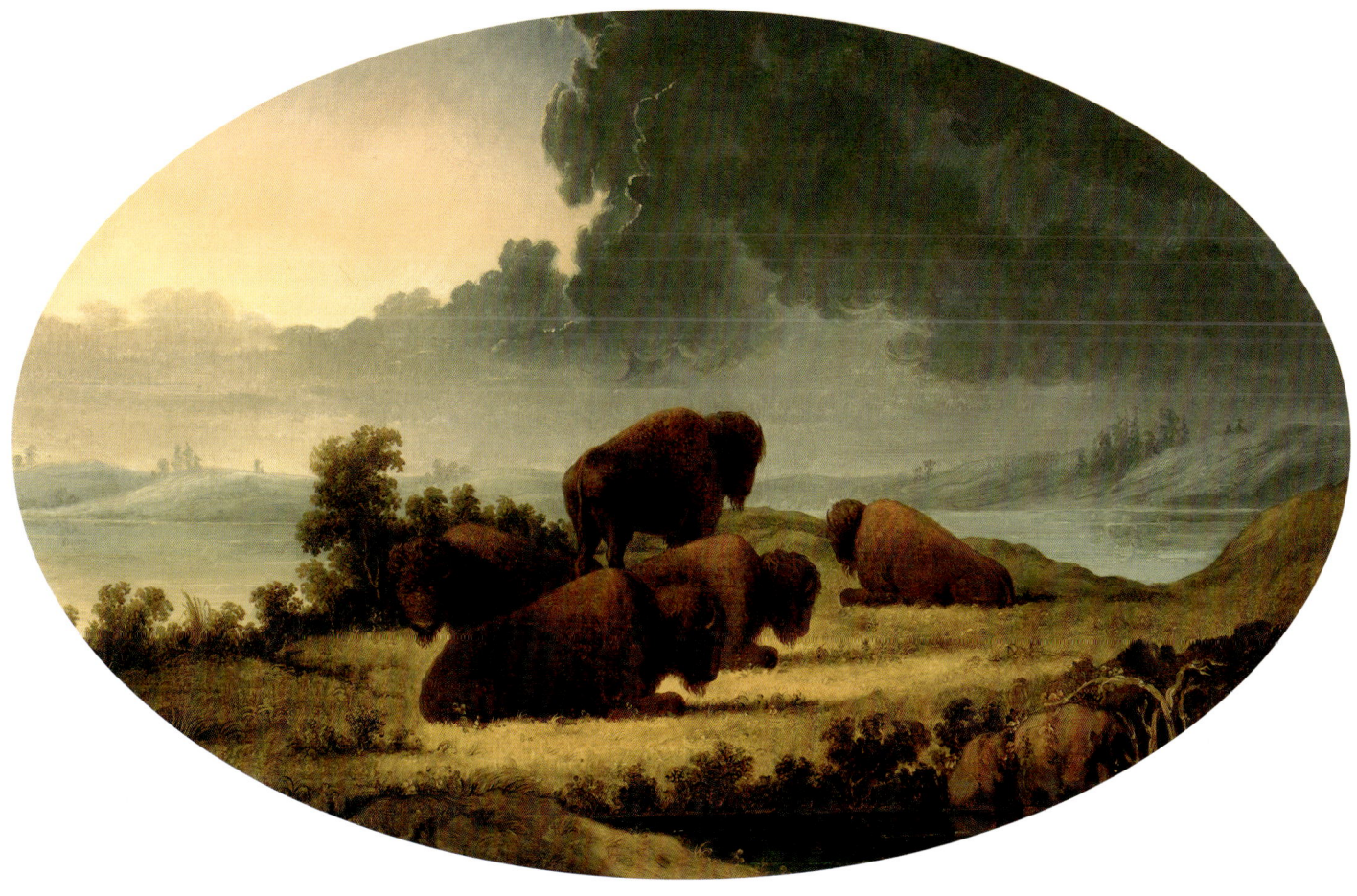

FIGURE 1.13.

PAUL KANE

Buffalo at Sunset, 1856.

Oil on canvas;

16½ × 26¾ inches.

JKM Collection.

JL1992.011.

is positioned not as a threat to the animals but as a participant in the idyllic scene. Kane painted this subject several times; a nearly identical canvas hangs in the National Gallery of Canada, a part of that institution's extensive Paul Kane collection.[41] This composition presents the bison as interesting in its own right, not as food for hunters or as the subject of scientific study but as a distinct part of the untrammeled, Romantic vision of the wilderness that is presumed to exist beyond city streets and cultivated land.

RUDOLPH FRIEDERICH KURZ
SWITZERLAND, 1818–1871

In *Artists of the Old West*, John C. Ewers wrote, "George Catlin and Karl Bodmer visited Fort Union in the early 1830s. John James Audubon, noted artist-naturalist, spent two months there in the summer of 1843. But no other artist knew Fort Union, its resident traders and its Indian customers as well as did a young Swiss, who worked there as a clerk during the winter of 1851–52."[42] The "young Swiss" was Rudolph Friederich Kurz, who came to America from Switzerland in 1846. Entranced with the notion of painting the people and wildlife of the American West, Kurz began to study art in Switzerland before spending three years in Paris perfecting his craft. His compatriot and friend Karl Bodmer cautioned him to continue his studies until he could swiftly record the characteristics of his subject with a few deft strokes.[43] Kurz traveled the Mississippi and Missouri rivers before finding a post at Fort Union. By the spring of 1852, he had become weary of frontier life, however, and his art supplies were dwindling. He decided that he had created enough study material to permit him to return home and concentrate on working up his sketches. Unfortunately, once he was back in Germany, a protracted illness and an inability to combine his sketches into workable compositions prevented him from converting his work into large-scale paintings. He lived out the rest of his life as a master of design at a cantonal school in Berne.[44]

While in the American West, Kurz created hundreds of small sketches and sometimes kept corresponding notes in his journal. On January 26, 1852, he wrote, "Painted a study in still life of a female elk. Observed in detail her shape, color, quality of hair, and proportions, then her movements, in order to get a correct idea, from actual observation, of the beast and its habits."[45] *Herd of Elk* looks like a compilation of studies, with a variety of elk in various poses. Kurz shows a definite interest in portraying the different details of the male, female, and young. When this work is compared to other early depictions of North American wildlife, Kurz's European training clearly shines through. In *Herd of Elk* (figure 1.14), he included a large bull as the central figure, displaying its large antlers and a three-quarter view of its flank. He also shows a cow and calf in motion, bounding back into the landscape. Kurz's competent use of light and shadow heightens the overall atmosphere and effect of the work, leading the eye into the sketch and back toward the distant mountain by using darker tones in the foreground that gradually lighten

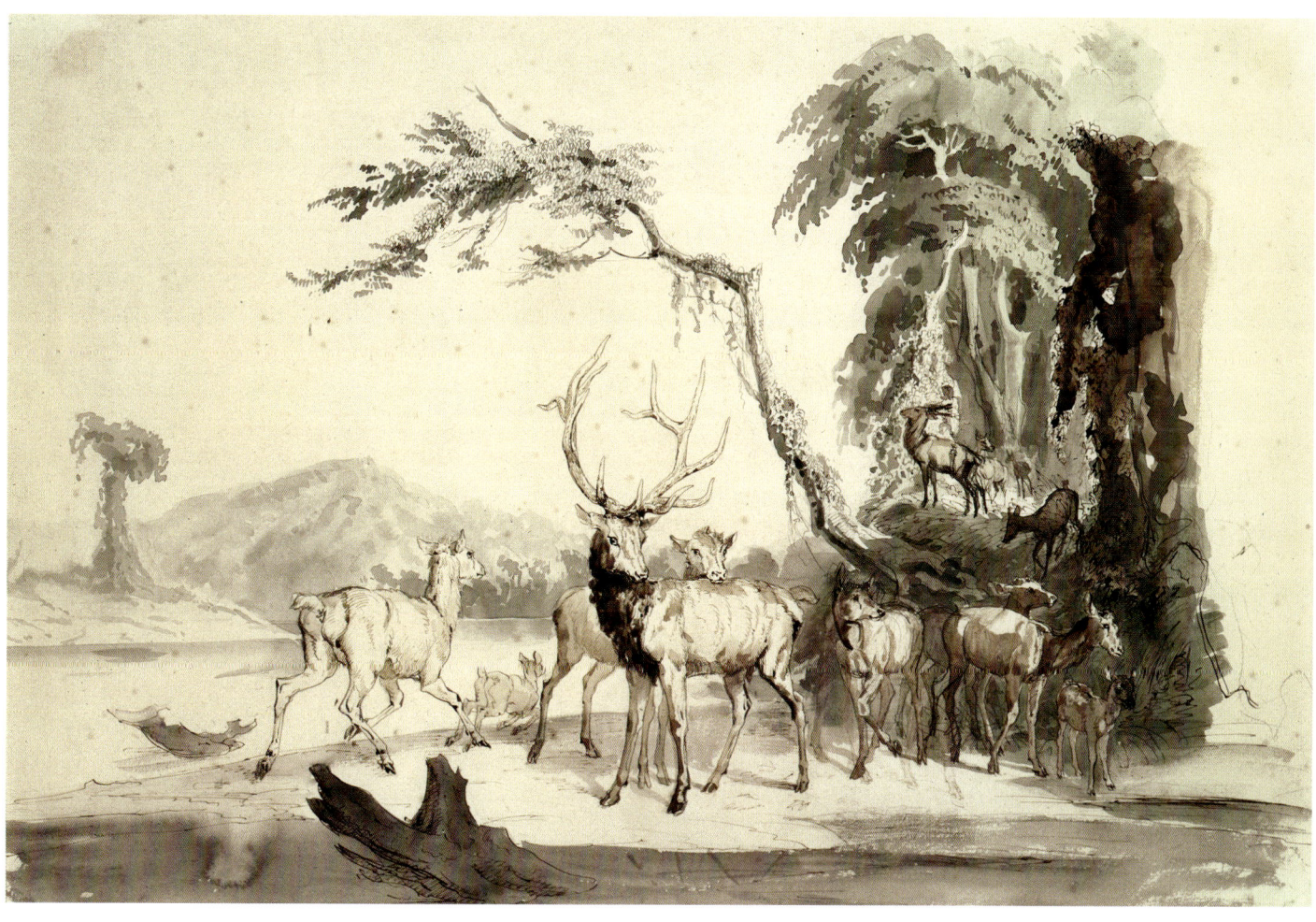

FIGURE 1.14.
RUDOLPH FRIEDERICH KURZ
Herd of Elk, 1851.
Ink and watercolor on paper;
13½ × 20¼ inches.
JKM Collection.
JL1997.072.

as they recede. One can only imagine the canvases Kurz could have painted with working material such as this.

As it stands, Kurz's impact on American art was minimal, but at least five of his compositions appeared in the German newspaper *Die Gartenlaube* in 1862. These pieces illustrated a prairie fire with American Indians and elk in flight, a war party, a buffalo hunt, mustangs, and the condition of American Indians living along the Missouri River. As with other artists who provided a slice of life in the American West, wildlife was featured prominently alongside other subjects.[46] Kurz left behind hundreds of small pencil and ink drawings of early life on the Missouri. His sketchbooks are still in Berne, while many of his individual drawings are owned by the Gilcrease Museum in Tulsa, Oklahoma.

CHARLES FERDINAND WIMAR
GERMANY, 1828–1862

Following the path of some of North America's most noted artists, including George Catlin and John James Audubon, Charles Ferdinand Wimar was among the last artists to travel up the Missouri and witness the wilderness of Montana before it was widely settled.[47] Summing up Wimar's career, biographer William R. Hodges wrote, "A few men of talent have successfully trodden the path blazed by Wimar, but none have surpassed him in the wild free life of the Indian in the trackless West, and his works will enhance in value as the wild Indian and buffalo become a faded memory."[48] American Indians and bison were primary in Wimar's oeuvre; both subjects became increasingly popular among artists and the general public as the two were systematically eliminated from their historic homelands on the plains.

Wimar traveled up the Missouri in 1858 and again in 1859. He died in 1862, four short years after his first trip. Consequently, his work is difficult to find, and most of it is held by museums.[49] *Buffalo Approaching Water Hole* (figure 1.15) is similar in size and media to *Buffalo Hunt* (also done in 1860), in the collection of the National Cowboy and Western Heritage Museum in Oklahoma.[50] Wimar's pastel is similar in feeling to Kane's *Buffalo at Sunset* (see figure 1.13). Both pictures provide a Romantic view of daily bison life, unaffected by human presence. *Buffalo Approaching Water Hole* is related to several earlier paintings by Wimar, such as *Buffaloes Crossing the Yellowstone* and *Buffalo Crossing the Platte* (in the Washington University Gallery of Art and the Gilcrease Museum, respectively). These larger canvases display the vastness of the West, with massive herds of bison extending out to distant horizons. *Buffalo Approaching Water Hole* presents a more focused view, a vignette, of a bison herd descending toward water. Here, Wimar was interested in how the first bison moved as it approached the water and in creating an overall sense of the herd behind. He created depth in the piece with atmospheric perspective, making the trees hazier in the background. The glowing light behind the trees may indicate dawn or dusk or represent the filtered light typical of a prairie fire (also seen in the background of *Buffaloes Crossing the Yellowstone*).

The German-born Wimar immigrated to America with his family in 1844. His stepfather had preceded them, settling in Saint Louis. Wimar apprenticed with a local commercial painter, whose work encompassed everything from signs to steamboats. He then apprenticed with painter Leon Pomarede, who was

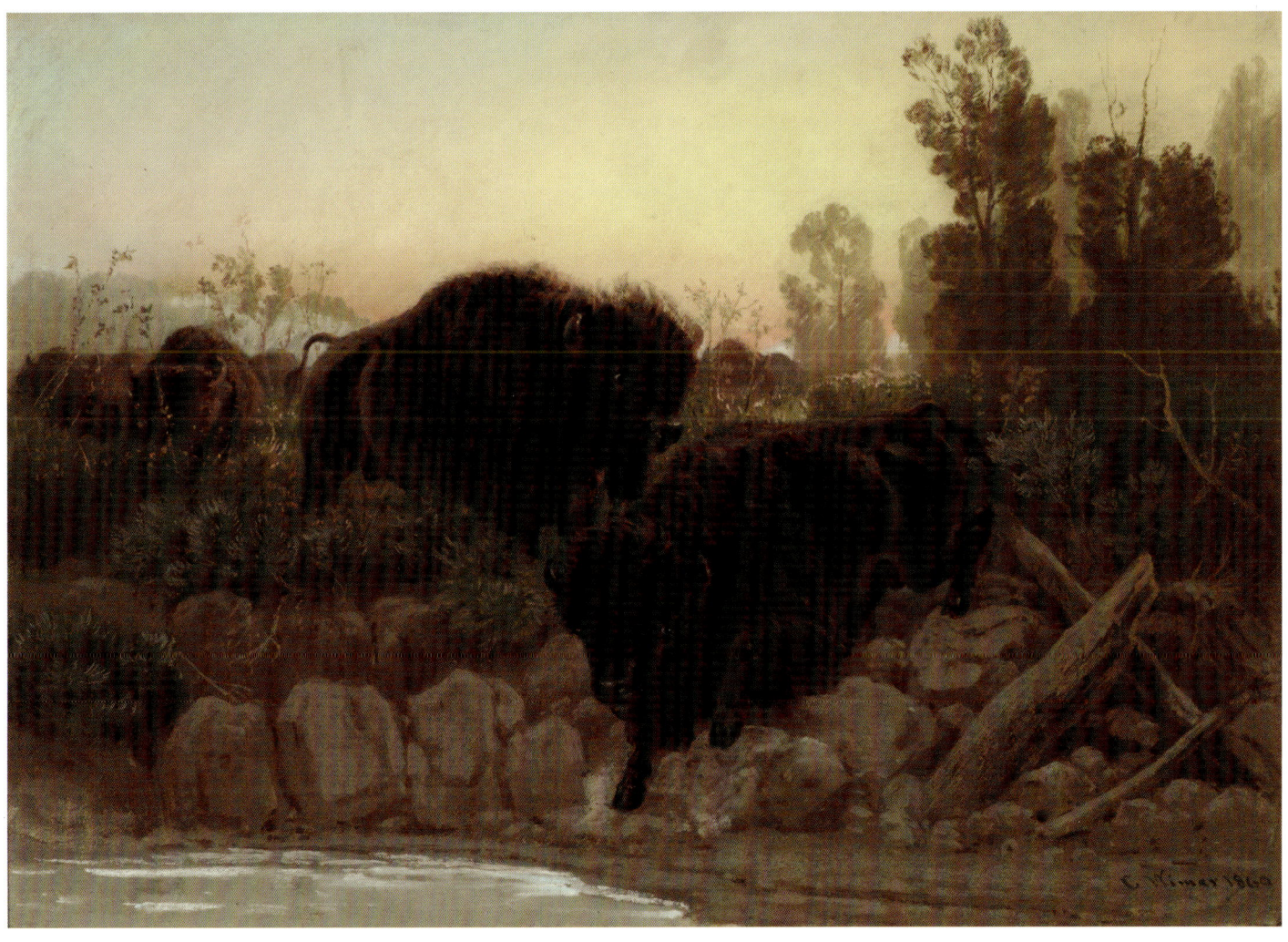

FIGURE 1.15.

CHARLES FERDINAND WIMAR
Buffaloes Approaching Water Hole, 1860.
Pastel on paper; 18 × 24 inches.
This purchase made possible through
previous donations from the Soka'piiwa
Foundation, the P.A.B. Widener
Charitable Trust, and Morton Quantrell,
with additional assistance provided by
the Robert S. and Grayce B. Kerr
Foundation. National Museum
of Wildlife Art Collection.
M2006.034.

working on a panorama of the Mississippi River. In 1850, Wimar opened his own business, painting mostly portraits for Saint Louis locals. He yearned for further training and embarked for Düsseldorf in December 1851 to study with famed painter Emanuel Leutze, who had recently premiered his *Washington Crossing the Delaware* in New York City to rave reviews.[51] Leutze provided the disciplined training that Wimar sought, and Wimar returned to the United States in 1856, an exponentially improved artist, ready to record both the beauty of the upper Missouri and its native inhabitants. Wimar died of tuberculosis in 1862—the same year he finished his biggest public commission, a series of murals for the Saint Louis Courthouse.[52] It is impossible to know what the future might have held for Wimar; his death at the age of thirty-four cut short one of the most promising careers in American art history.

WILLIAM JACOB HAYS

United States, 1830–1875

The prairie dog is, in fact, one of the curiosities of the Far West, about which travelers delight to tell marvelous tales, endowing him at times, with something of the politic and social habits of a rational being, and giving him systems of civil government and domestic economy almost equal to what they used to bestow upon the beaver.

Washington Irving, *A Tour on the Prairies,* 145

The prairie dog's often-massive colonies, consisting of acres of land and riddled with hundreds of holes, were clearly the subject of speculation and interest back east. The pictorial record might seem to suggest that the bison was the only animal subject of ongoing interest. However, tales by Irving and paintings such as *Prairie Dog Village* by William Jacob Hays (figure 1.16) make clear that easterners were interested in a wider variety of animal inhabitants of the West. Looking at Hays's painting through Irving's lens adds a great deal to its interpretation. On its own, the painting is a fine record of an often-overlooked subject in the history of animal art. Add Irving, and the prairie dogs become inhabitants of a thriving community, with different dogs taking on various roles, from mayor to industrialist. This quaint view of prairie dog society ended as settlers began occupying the land. Seen as dangerous to horses and cattle, the colonies were largely eradicated by the twentieth century.[53]

Hays was an accomplished naturalist and took great care rendering the flora as well as the fauna in his paintings. The carefully painted flowers in the foreground of *Prairie Dog Village* are testament to this interest. Mark Catesby's *American Bison* (see figure 1.2) also captured an animal and a particular plant, but Catesby's rendering (made more than one hundred years earlier) was clearly meant as a scientific study and not as a realistic portrait of the animal and plant in a natural setting. By Hays's time, paintings of American wildlife had become more naturalistic, picturing the animal *in* its environment. The *Quadruped* series by John James Audubon and John Woodhouse Audubon represents a stepping stone between Catesby and Hays; the Audubons were interested in scientific rendering and in naturalistic compositions but had a definite natural history impetus. Hays's recordings were accurate, too, but they were more like the canvases of Wimar and Kane in setting the animals realistically within their environment, not singled out as anatomical exemplars.

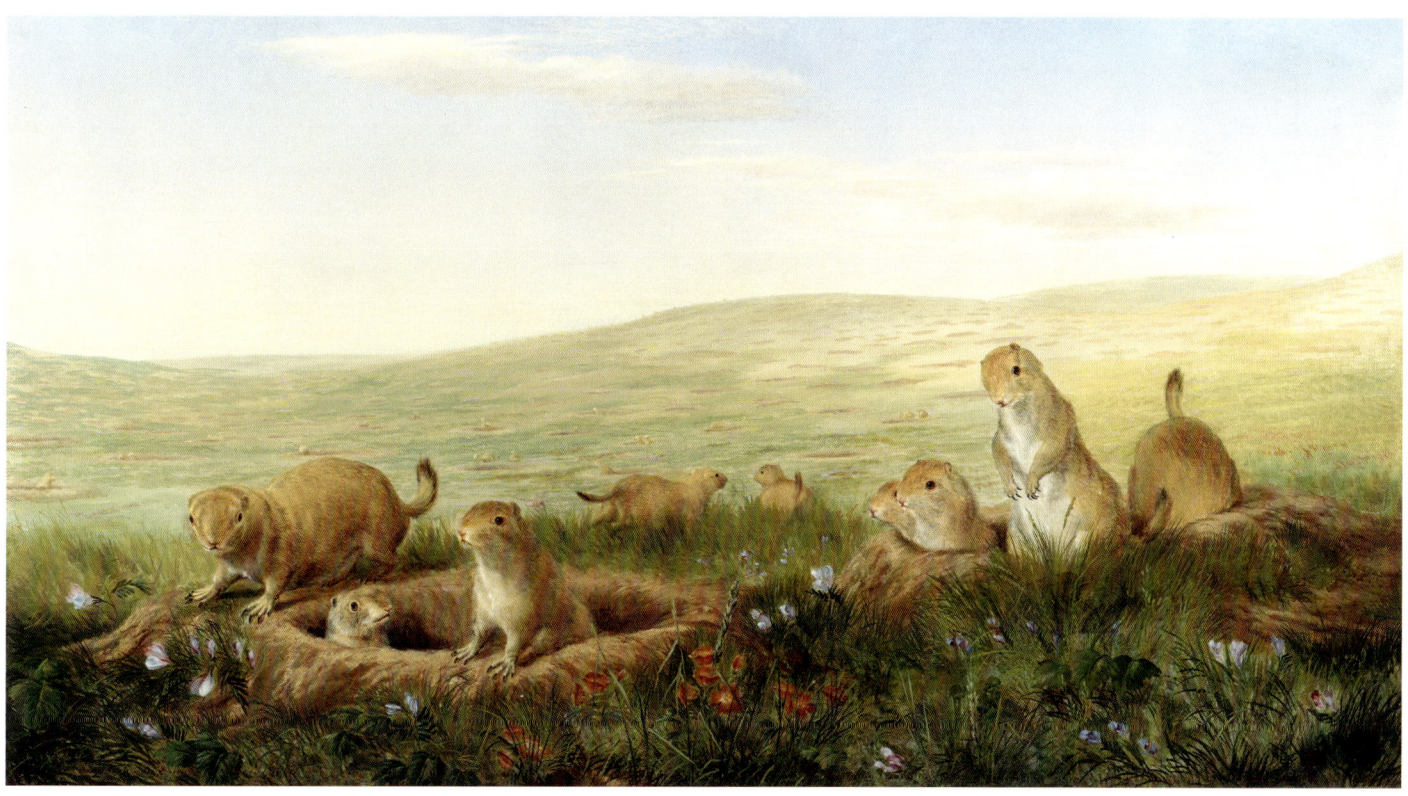

FIGURE 1.16.
WILLIAM JACOB HAYS
Prairie Dog Village, c.1860.
Oil on canvas; 25½ × 47½ inches.
JKM Collection.
J1989.064.

Hays lived in New York City, venturing to the Adirondacks, Nova Scotia, and England on occasion in search of subjects to paint. As a student, he studied with artist John Rubens Smith. In 1858, Hays moved to the famous Tenth Street Studio Building in New York, where he fraternized with Martin Johnson Heade, Frederic Church, and Albert Bierstadt. These accomplished painters greatly influenced Hays, and their support and interest improved the quality of his work. During the summer of 1860, Hays left New York for a five-month expedition up the Missouri River. Hays reached Fort Union but did not encounter any buffaloes, so he went farther upstream to Fort Stewart, where wildlife was more plentiful.[54] After this expedition, Hays returned to his studio in New York to transform his field sketches into Romantic canvases depicting the American West. Hays portrayed wildlife and habitat accurately and with exquisite detail, leaving a lasting legacy of work that did not solely focus on megafauna such as bison and elk but also encompassed the smaller, though no less prevalent, species of the plains, including the spirited prairie dog.[55]

WILLIAM DE LA MONTAGNE CARY
United States, 1840–1922

William de la Montagne Cary's father taught him how to draw, and at age fourteen, he was apprenticed to an engraver. In 1861, one year after William Jacob Hays, he traveled up the Missouri River by steamboat. Cary sketched American Indian activities, ceremonies, and buffalo hunts. He later used these sketches for reference in paintings and magazine illustrations. Cary's illustration career spanned from 1862 to 1892. During those years, magazines such as *Harper's Weekly* and *Frank Leslie's Illustrated Weekly* published his depictions of American Indians, pioneers, and wildlife. *The Lost Buffalo Calf* (figure 1.17) dates from the years after his first journey. The painting could as easily be titled *The Last Buffalo Calf,* as bison populations were in serious decline even at that time. In the background, two tiny figures can be seen; these are likely buffalo hunters who have just slaughtered the calf's mother (and perhaps the rest of the herd). The well-dressed American Indian with the large rifle is also probably a buffalo hunter (a fact that does not bode well for the future of the calf).[56] The bison behavior illustrated by Cary was well known; young calves separated from their mothers would often attach themselves to men on horseback and return with them to camp.

In 1874, Cary made a trip with the Northern Boundary Survey to the upper Missouri. On this journey, he documented the changes that had taken place since his earlier expedition. In his diary from this outing, Cary discussed the diminishing numbers of animals. He wrote, stressing the infrequent nature of sightings: "Sometimes a herd of antelope or deer, occasionally a grizzly bear, a few buffalo. Sometimes a black wolf or two would follow the steamers along the bank for days."[57] The work resulting from this later journey reflected the changes Cary witnessed in the wildlife and the people of the West. While often full of adventure, Cary's depictions also showed eastern audiences the loss of American Indian life and the near-decimation of bison brought on by the railroad, market hunting, and the ongoing encroachment of European settlement. *The Lost Buffalo Calf* is emblematic of those greater themes prevalent in American art during this time.

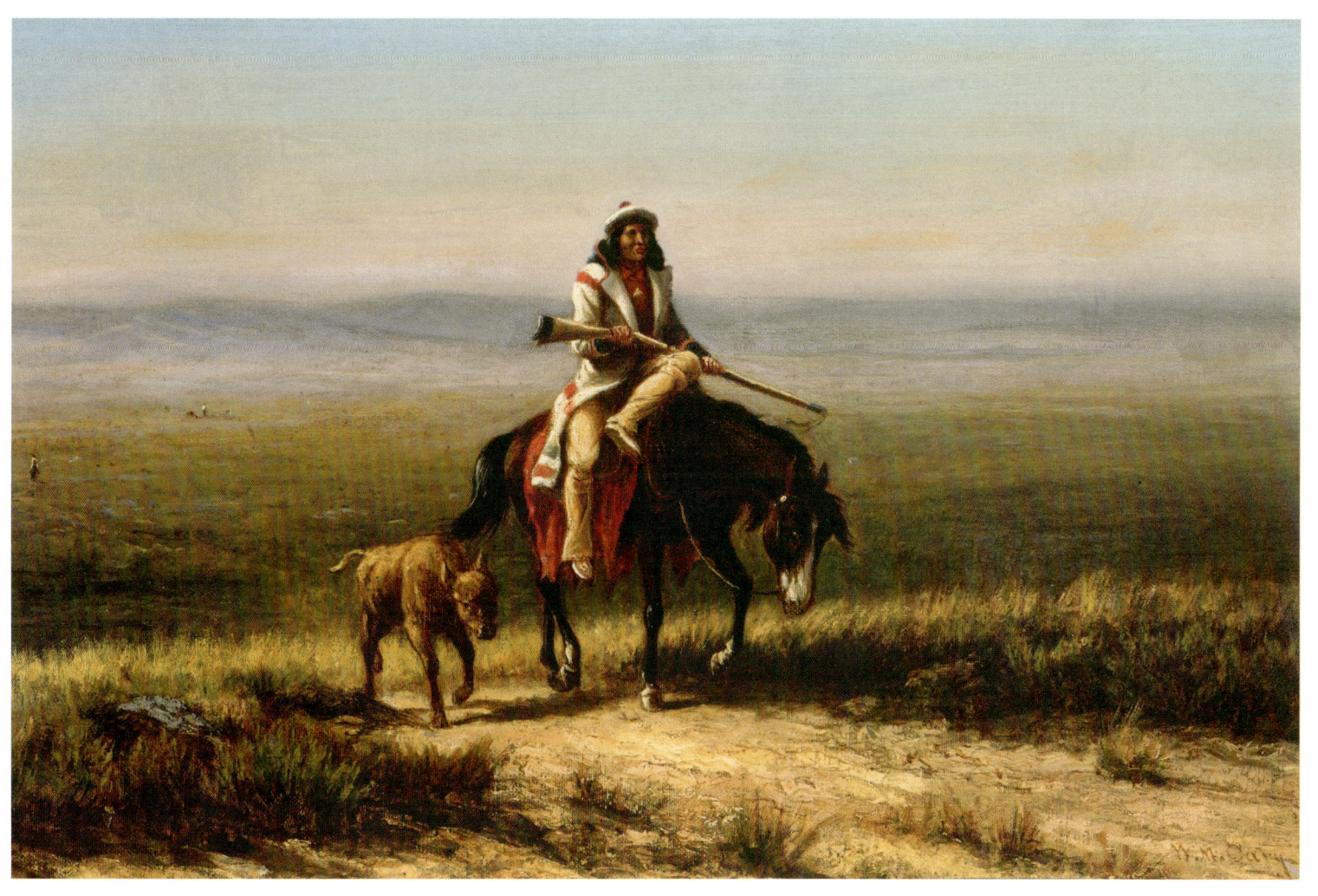

FIGURE 1.17.
WILLIAM DE LA MONTAGNE CARY
The Lost Buffalo Calf, c. 1865.
Oil on canvas; 11 × 16½ inches.
JKM Collection.
JL1998.050.

NEWBOLD HOUGH TROTTER
United States, 1827–1898

Newbold Hough Trotter was a lifelong resident of Philadelphia, taking trips to the West on occasion and making one expedition to Africa. He was mostly self-taught, but he did study briefly at the Pennsylvania Academy of Fine Arts and The Hague in the Netherlands. Trotter worked from nature, painting both animals and landscapes. His work was exhibited at the Pennsylvania Academy of Fine Arts, the Boston Athenaeum, and the National Academy of Design in New York. *Wounded Buffalo Pursued by Prairie Wolves* was displayed at the Philadelphia Centennial in 1876 and was purchased by General William Tecumseh Sherman for the U.S. Army's headquarters in Washington, D.C. Trotter produced artwork not only for the War Department but also for the Pennsylvania Railroad and the Smithsonian Institution.[58]

Not much more is known about Trotter or his career; he is not widely written about or studied. In *Domain Invaded* (figure 1.18), a herd of elk look down from a high plateau toward a campfire in the distance. In this composition, Trotter reversed the typical perspective, which is usually from the human's vantage point looking toward the animal.[59] By changing the point of view, Trotter alters the primary interpretation of the painting, aligning our sympathies with the elk, observing intruding humans. This reversal of perspective anticipates the late-nineteenth-century penchant for wildlife stories that cast the animal as the protagonist and tell tales from its point of view (made most famous by illustrator and author Ernest Thompson Seton). Also noteworthy is the location from which this painting was created. *Domain Invaded* depicts the western slope of the Teton Range in Wyoming. Until the early twentieth century, travel to Jackson Hole—on the eastern and arguably more dramatic side of the Tetons—was extremely difficult. Thomas Moran likewise painted the Tetons from the west on his trip to the region in 1879; because of weather and forest fires, Moran's party was unable to cross into Jackson. Trotter's painting of elk on alert is a harbinger of how wildlife would be depicted in American art in the 1900s: import lies in the accurate representation of an animal's anatomy but equally, if not more so, on creating an overall image of beauty, of wildlife in its natural habitat. Remove the trace of human presence in *Domain Invaded,* and the Romantic vision of nature is complete.

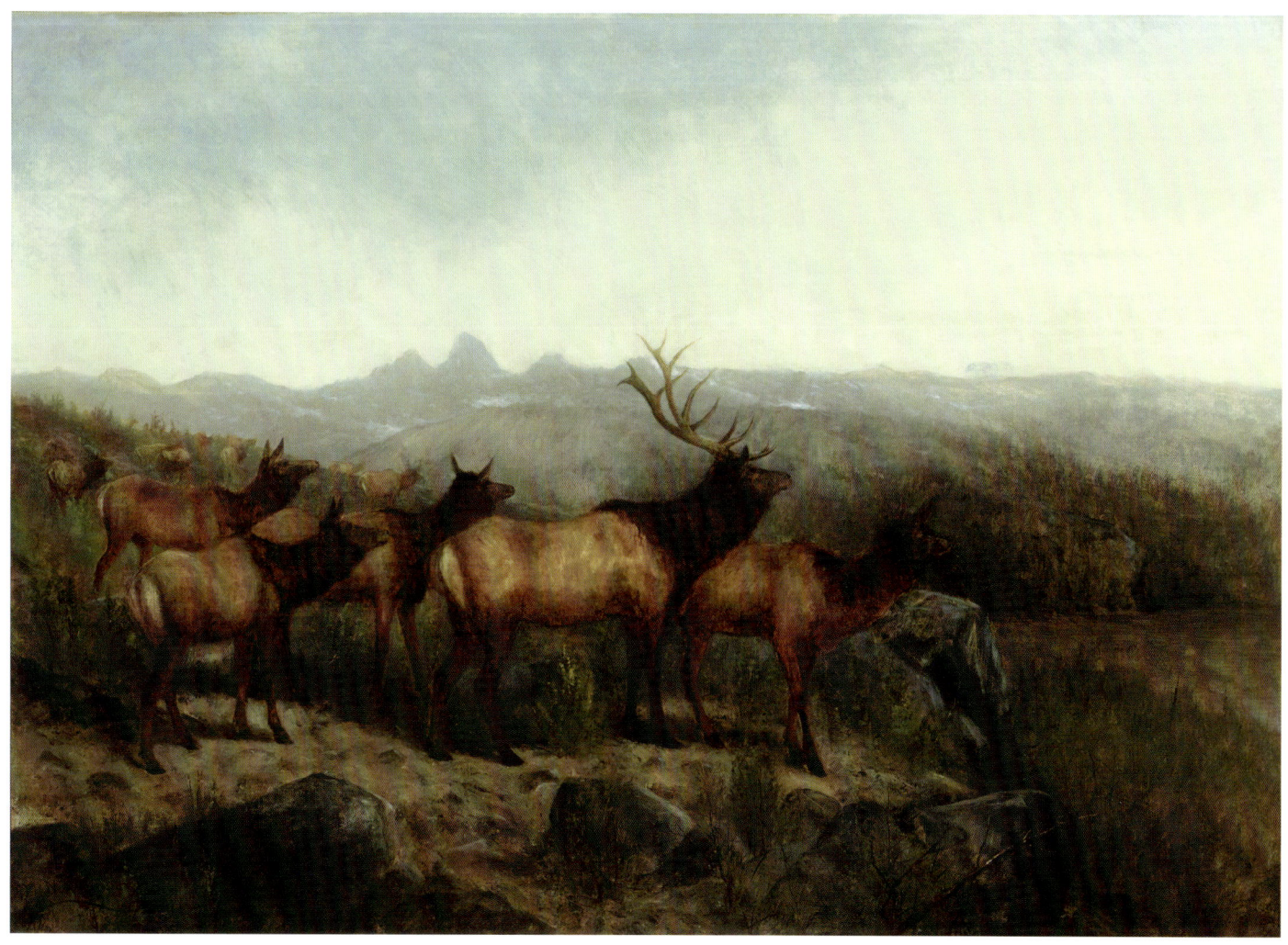

FIGURE 1.18.

NEWBOLD HOUGH TROTTER

Domain Invaded, c. 1870.

Oil on canvas; 28 × 40 inches.

JKM Collection.

M1987.023.

FREDERICK ARTHUR VERNER
CANADA, 1836–1928

Sketching in school and at home, Frederick Verner showed artistic talent at a young age. In 1852, when he was sixteen, he won a prize at the Upper Canada's Provincial Art Exhibition, exhibiting with the revered artist Paul Kane. The young Verner became fascinated with Kane; legend has it that he went to pay Kane a call shortly thereafter, only to have Kane slam the door in his face.[60] Undaunted, Verner continued in his quest for knowledge, traveling to England in 1856, to study at Leigh's Academy. This less-than-prestigious institution likely did little to advance Verner's skills, but the experience of living in England had a lasting effect. Verner returned to Toronto in 1862 after serving in the British Legion. He began working as a photographer and photocolorist until deciding to concentrate on painting full time in 1874. During this period, he became friends with Kane, and his work began to echo Kane's interest in American Indians and native wildlife, particularly the bison. In 1880, Verner moved back to England, where his work sold well. He remained there until his death in 1928. He made several trips back to Canada to gather research material, and he lived in Chicago for a summer during the World's Columbian Exposition in 1893.

Verner often depicted herds of bison in their native habitat, at peace and unaffected by the modern world. This was already in his day a nostalgic vision of bison life, because most of the wild population had been decimated by 1880. Sadness over the loss of the great herds is poignantly depicted in his watercolor *The Last Buffalo,* from 1893 (figure 1.19). According to Canadian art authority Joan Murray, Verner painted a sleeping buffalo in 1888 in a similar pose.[61] In the National Museum of Wildlife Art's painting, Verner changed the theme and sentiment of the piece, adding three birds (one picking at the bison carcass). Twilight marking the end of the day reinforces the theme of the work. As the end of the nineteenth century drew closer, the frontier era in America was also rapidly coming to an end. Though later generations continued to venture out into the wilderness, the days of unexplored territory and vast herds of wildlife were over.

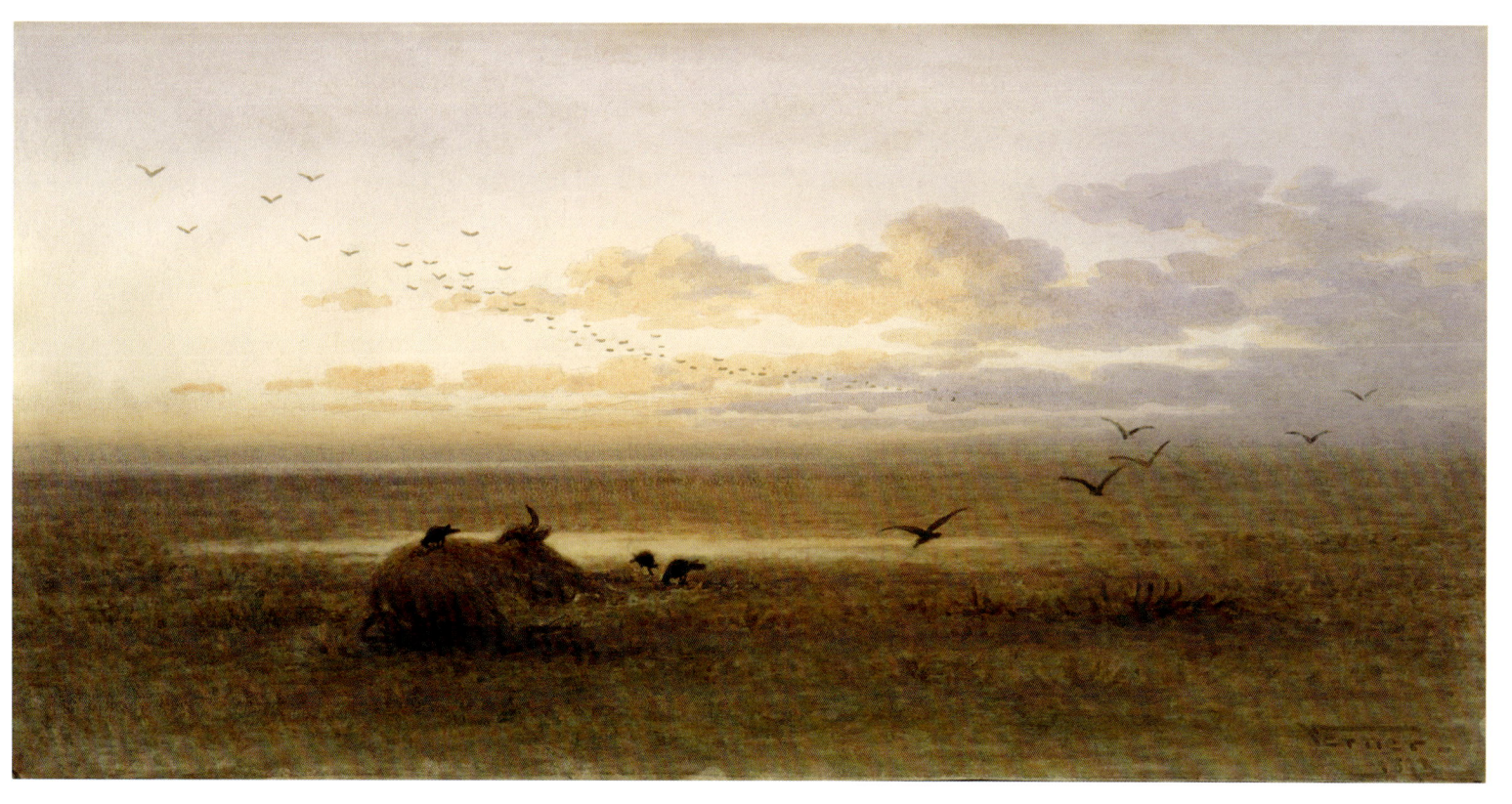

FIGURE 1.19.

FREDERICK ARTHUR VERNER

The Last Buffalo, 1893.

Watercolor on paper; 12 × 23¾ inches

Gift of Joffa and Bill Kerr.

National Museum of Wildlife Art Collection.

W1993.055.

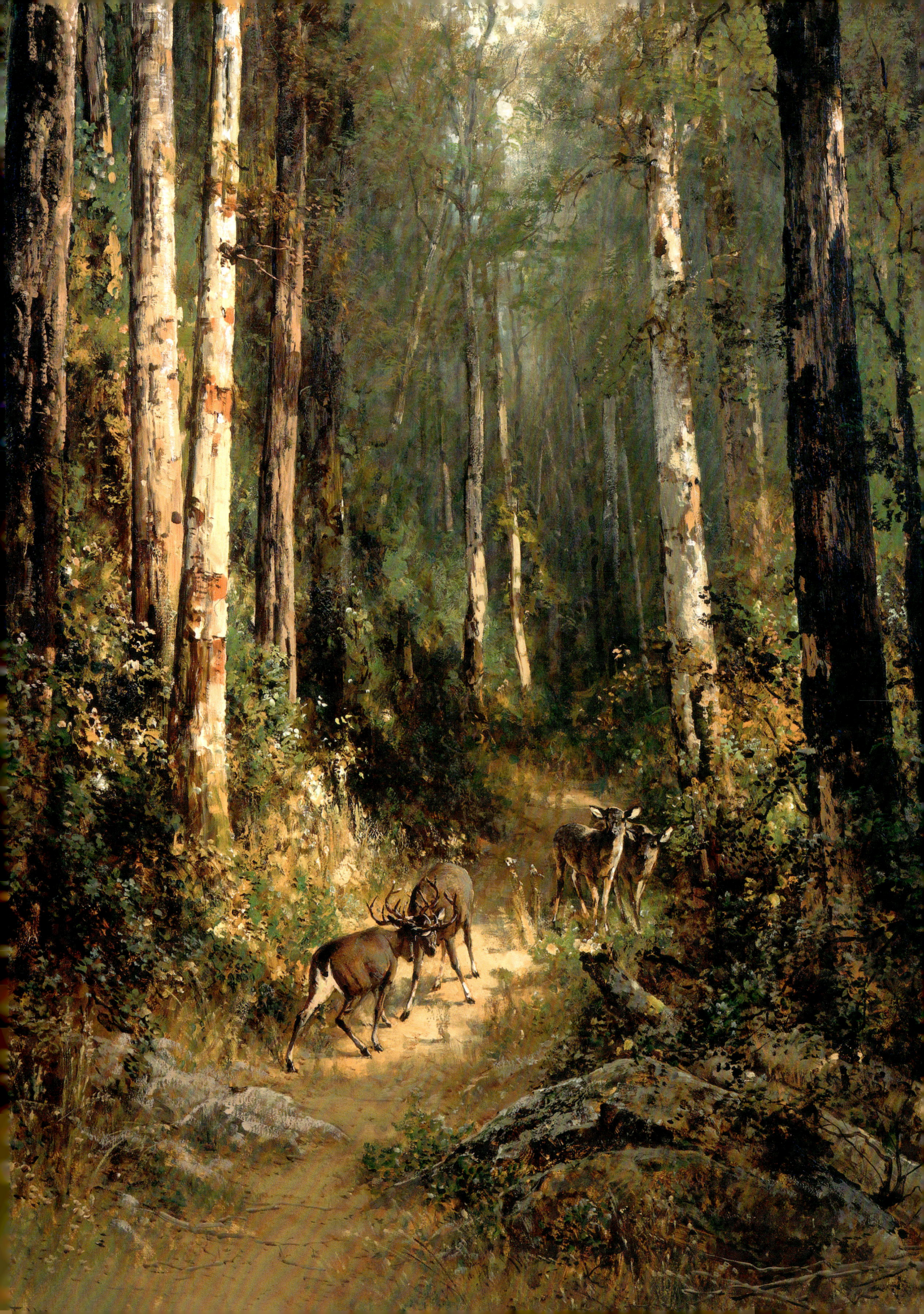

Chapter 2

From Bierstadt to Chase: *Changing Tastes and the Eastern Establishment*

As artists continued to venture west, a new group of landscape painters—including soon-to-be giants in the field such as Frederic Church, Albert Bierstadt, and Thomas Moran—emerged onto the art scene. Their spectacular canvases communicated the grandeur and beauty of America as none of their predecessors had. Church's enormous paintings of the Hudson River valley and South America paved the way for Bierstadt's paeans to the American West. As Robert Hughes noted in *American Visions,* the artists who had ventured west before Bierstadt returned only to create rather small canvases that did not speak for the West as Church had done for Niagara Falls or the Andes. Hughes wrote, "They did not express the idea of a providential mission into the wilderness that was at the heart of Manifest Destiny. Bierstadt set out to do so."[1] Bierstadt's massive paintings presented an epic vision of the wilderness that helped solidify a national sense of identity based on the idea of the American continent as a gift from God, ready to be unwrapped. On the grandest scale, his canvases promoted the West as a national symbol of what America meant. After Bierstadt, Moran's paintings of Yellowstone, in particular, created a sense of the wilderness as something to be proud of, something worth rallying around, and, finally, something worth protecting.

What Bierstadt did for the wilderness he also did, on a smaller scale, for wildlife. In his huge landscapes, animals and detailed vegetation marked the foreground of the painting, which helped set off the towering, misty mountains in the back. On occasion, he painted the animals front and center, as in works such as *Rocky Mountain Goat* (figure 2.1). Here, the goat serves the same function as the tip of the tallest mountain in one of his landscapes; both epitomize the wilderness and speak to humanity's relationship to it. Visually and iconographically, Bierstadt's mountain goat also follows in the tradition of Edwin Landseer's potent male trophy paintings, such as *The Monarch of the Glen* (1851), which display elevated stags as symbols of the wilderness but also connote humanity's power and control over that wilderness. In *The Deer Pass,* Landseer repeats the iconic figure of the proud male stag from *Monarch* in the center foreground (figure 2.2). Bierstadt painted his mountain goat study using a trophy mount in his personal collection.[2] The subjects in these trophy paintings embody the wilderness even as the pictures themselves demonstrate a mastery over it, helping bolster a sense of masculine identity.

In late-nineteenth-century America, still-life paintings of scenes from the hunt became popular, particularly among men. Art historian David Lubin wrote that the typical patron for still lifes was "a certain type of viewer who was for the first time ever dominant in American cultural life, the self-made, geographically mobile, urban middle-class bureaucrat, businessman, or career professional."[3] As life became more centralized in cities, accessing the backwoods became more difficult. But the iconography of the hunt was still a powerful reminder of what it meant to be an American and a man. Art historian Francis Pohl noted, "For the businessman or professional who was now married and seldom trod the backwoods, gun in hand, in search of game, [still lifes] carried a reassuring reminder of the markers of masculinity."[4] Trompe l'oeil paintings of hanging birds or other prey by artists such as Alexander Pope helped define appropriate social roles and identities as the urban middle class rose in prominence. This reading of the still-life genre can be extended to depictions of animals in the wilderness that do not make overt reference to hunting. In the final decades of the 1800s, images of wildlife definitely symbolized the American wilderness, but they took on associated meanings, bolstering a sense of masculine identity for urbanites who rarely had a chance to prove their outdoor prowess.

As urban areas developed and a healthy market for art emerged, a wide variety of artists, painting in an increasingly diverse range of styles, included wildlife in their work. The portrait painter Shepard Alonzo Mount, for example, depicted animals close to his normal haunts, painting a Long Island frog as an addition to his repertoire (see figure 2.4). William Holbrook Beard created humorous, satiric, anthropomorphic pictures of bears and other animals, setting his paintings in New York City or in the not-too-distant eastern wilderness. Arthur Fitzwilliam Tait ventured as far north as the Adirondack Mountains to become that region's principal painter of sporting and wildlife scenes. Tait's relationship with printmakers Currier and Ives resulted in the mass production of Adirondack prints, which helped popularize the region among eastern tourists.

Also painting within easy travel of New York City, members of the Hudson River school depicted the Catskill Mountains and the surrounding region in their quiet, contemplative views of nature. Worthington Whittredge placed wildlife in central positions in his landscapes to express tranquility and harmony; his work also reiterated a sense of the wilderness as a divine gift, untrammeled and pristine. In the last half of the nineteenth century, landscape painting arose as a popular art form, available to more than just elite collectors. In *Hudson River School,* Louise Minks explained, "Landscapes enlightened viewers with the purity of the natural ideal and glorified the often remote and even terrifying grandeur of topographical wonders. Moreover, in transcending the stately art forms of

Wildlife in American Art

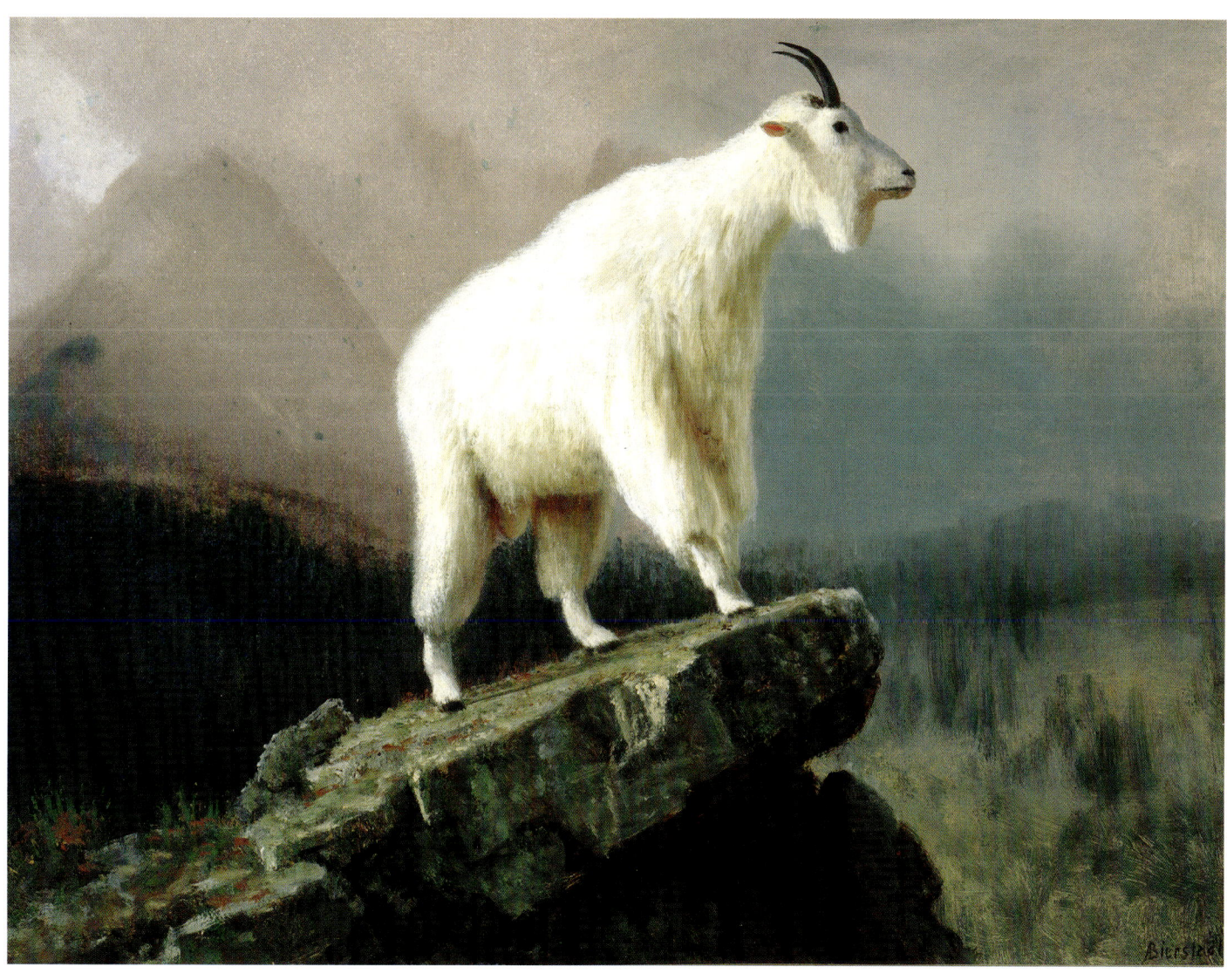

FIGURE 2.1.
ALBERT BIERSTADT
Rocky Mountain Goat, c. 1875.
Oil on paper mounted to linen;
13½ × 19 inches.
JKM Collection.
M1993.025.

portraiture and historical tributes—present only in certain private homes and grand public institutions—these landscapes offered a universal, more democratic artistic expression to be exhibited in any parlor and admired by any viewer."[5]

Before the end of the century, thousands of Americans were traveling to France, many of them to study art. The Barbizon school, in particular, had a significant influence on aspiring painters. Minks noted that, in contrast to the grand studio paintings by the likes of Bierstadt, Barbizon artists "painted directly on site—in the wind, mist or sun—and expressed on canvas their subjective emotional response to nature. Instead of rendering faithful detail, their scenes were more loosely painted and often more simplified."[6] Thomas Hill and Herman Herzog took the Hudson River school and Barbizon aesthetic westward, painting wildlife and landscape in the Rockies and Yosemite. Hard on the heels of the Barbizon painters came the impressionists, who took painting *en plein air* to a completely different level. As tastes changed, prominent artists painting the grandeur of the West, such as Albert Bierstadt, saw their fortunes fall, while artists able to adapt, such as

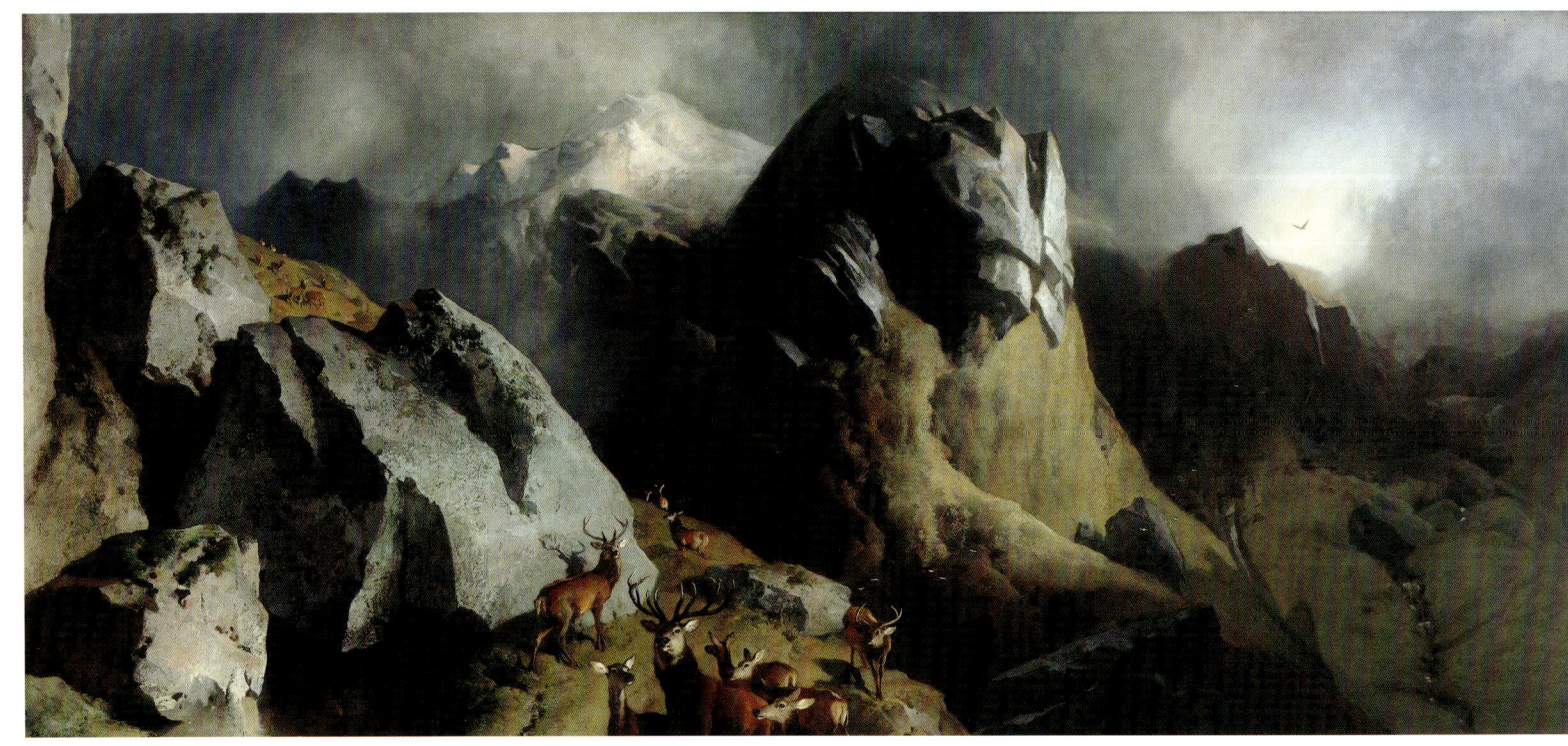

FIGURE 2.2.
EDWIN LANDSEER
The Deer Pass, 1852.
Oil on canvas; 37½ × 83 inches.
JKM Collection.
JL1995.160.

Worthington Whittredge, continued to have successful careers. At the close of the nineteenth century, William Merritt Chase became widely known as *the* American impressionist, in the vanguard of the new art coming over from Europe. His still-life paintings of fish became must-haves for any serious collection, and wildlife (this time of a different, slippery sort) made it into another realm of American painting.

During the course of the 1800s, the wilderness became the wellspring from which a national sense of identity emerged. On a more personal level, it became a place of rejuvenation for a growing urban population that did not experience the wild on a regular basis. Daniel Justin Herman wrote in *Hunting and the American Imagination,* "For every middle-class man who felt encumbered by urban life, the Adirondacks stood as a promise for the renewal of health, manliness, virtue, and Americanness."[7] Simply experiencing the outdoors was an American thing to do. To reflect this patriotic connection to the great outdoors, more and more households found a place for a representation of it on their mantels, in their living rooms, or in their libraries. Art functioned as a reminder of the wilderness and as a way of connecting with it. Images of wildlife—whether in grand panoramic paintings, still lifes of the hunt, or naturalistic renderings of animals at peace in nature—became an essential part of American visual culture.

ALBERT BIERSTADT
Germany, 1830–1902

In *The West of the Imagination,* William Goetzmann wrote, "As the scale and ambition of western exploration increased after the Civil War, so did its pictorial representations; the sublime replaced the pastoral as the predominant image of the West in the American imagination. . . . [P]aintings by Albert Bierstadt, Thomas Moran, and other artists trained in the European romantic tradition pictured a different West, a West of mighty mountains that dwarfed Indian and white man alike, a West of swirling atmospheric forces, of primordial geological drama, of natural—almost supernatural—wonder."[8] In the hands of Albert Bierstadt, the West came to represent something more than it had before, furthering a sense of national identity based not on the age-old history of civilization in Europe but on the vast wilderness that contained a bounty of natural wonders and seemingly inexhaustible resources.[9] Bierstadt's images epitomized the idea of American exceptionalism and provided people with stirring pictures that invoked pride in their nation. That his most famous imagery was painted in places that would become national parks, forests, or preserves (especially Yellowstone and Yosemite) again reinforces the Romantic definition of wilderness as a space apart, a space for rejuvenation, but a space that had to be defended as an essential aspect of what made America great.

In *Elk Grazing in the Wind River Country* (figure 2.3), Bierstadt revisited the landscape painted by Alfred Jacob Miller in 1837, but instead of depicting interactions between mountain men, American Indians, and wild animals, Bierstadt focused on the expanse of landscape, with precisely painted flowers and a herd of elk in the foreground and the towering peaks of the Wind River Range in the background. As he often did, he included a herd of animals not only to give a sense of scale but also to create an Edenic setting, providing a vision of the West that was both wild and pristine.

The skillful combination of these elements was exactly what eastern audiences were looking for, as art historian Nancy Anderson wrote in *Albert Bierstadt: Art and Enterprise:* "Shortly after his arrival in New York, Bierstadt began exhibiting paintings with Rocky Mountain subjects. The pictures drew considerable attention, for they addressed long-standing questions about the western landscape. Although frequently described by government surveyors, travelers, and writers, the West still awaited its visual historian."[10] Bierstadt bridged the gap between the age of the explorer-artist and the gilded age of American art and commerce. His life and career reflect the growing establishment on the East Coast of a fully developed capitalist system, with vast fortunes amassed by industrialists such as Andrew Carnegie. Bierstadt's huge canvases of the mighty American West met the tenor of the times.

Bierstadt immigrated to New Bedford, Massachusetts, with his family when he was two years old. In 1853, he returned to Germany to study in Düsseldorf, where he learned the fundamentals of drawing, plus the compositional design methods found in the romanticized landscapes for which he became best known.[11] He returned to the United States in 1857 and began painting landscapes up and down the East Coast. Bierstadt spent the summer of 1859 on a government wagon-road survey from Fort Laramie, Wyoming, to the Rocky Mountains, sketching his experiences along the way. Shortly after his return, he moved to New York and took a studio in the Tenth Street Studio Building, where his friends Worthington Whittredge and William Holbrook Beard also worked. He began to exhibit large paintings of the West and received rave reviews.[12]

With his huge, dramatic pictures of the Rocky Mountains, Bierstadt presented the glory of the landscape and its inhabitants to an eastern audience eager for imagery of the American West. Bierstadt created the blockbusters of his age, sensational pictures that wowed audiences and brought in large sums of money. However, as is true of the rise and fall of many a Hollywood celebrity, Bierstadt's star began to fade as tastes changed in the late 1870s and critics began to denigrate his work. In the 1880s, Bierstadt was suffering financially and receiving criticism in the press; his large works were rejected as overblown and sentimental.[13] Many of his contemporaries, who had not risen to such great fame as quickly, did not suffer Bierstadt's reversal of fortune but continued to paint the forests, mountains, and wildlife of the West with ongoing success.

Recently, collectors, art museums, and the general public have begun to show a renewed interest in Bierstadt's work. His paintings are undeniably powerful evocations of the wilderness that resonate with contemporary concerns about the environment. From an art historical perspective, Bierstadt's paintings capture a moment in the history of the United States when the West was still the repository for all of America's hopes and dreams about the future, a land ripe with potential, ready for picking.

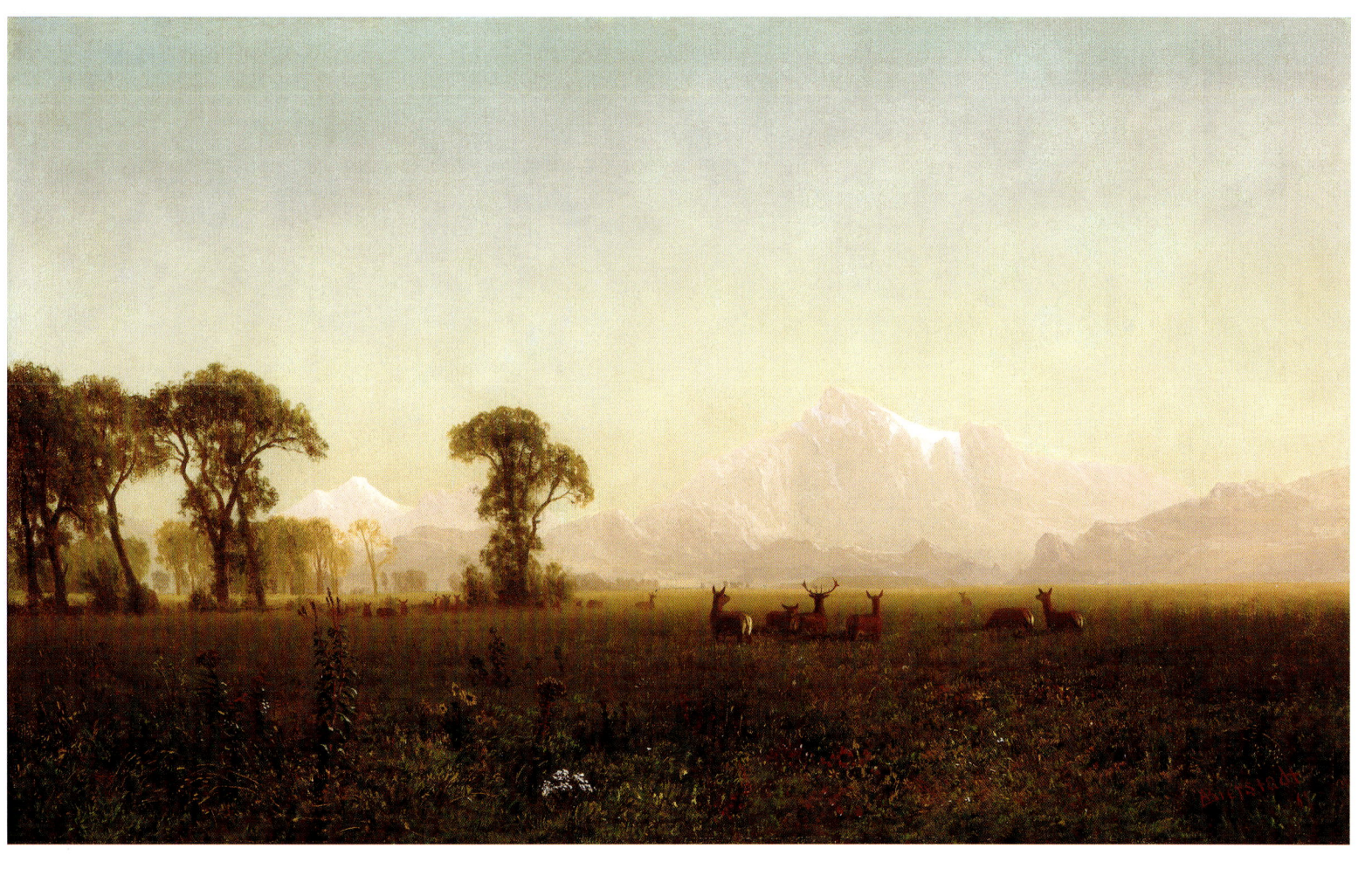

FIGURE 2.3.
ALBERT BIERSTADT
Elk Grazing in the
Wind River Country, 1861.
Oil on canvas; 15⅛ × 25¼ inches.
JKM Collection.
J1990.043.

SHEPARD ALONZO MOUNT
United States, 1804–1868

Shepard Alonzo Mount was the brother of William Sidney Mount, the acclaimed American genre-scene painter. Both brothers grew up on Long Island. Shepard Mount began his career as a carriage painter before attending the National Academy of Design to refine his techniques. After school, the two brothers entered into a portrait-painting business together, but they soon split. Shepard remained a portrait painter, while his brother returned to Long Island and began concentrating on the genre scenes for which he became best known. Centered in New York, Shepard built a business painting portraits of the emerging class of American businessmen. He also found success as an itinerant portrait painter, traveling the county in search of clients. Still-life and landscape paintings such as *Long Island Frog* (figure 2.4; perhaps painted on a visit to see his family back on Long Island) show up in his oeuvre.[14] Mount may have carried this simple, unpretentious painting of a frog in its natural habitat around the country with him to show prospective clients his ability or as additional merchandise that patrons could purchase. As a small and presumably affordable work, *Long Island Frog* represents the democratization of painting in the late nineteenth century, when members of the growing middle class were able to purchase small works to decorate their library or parlor.

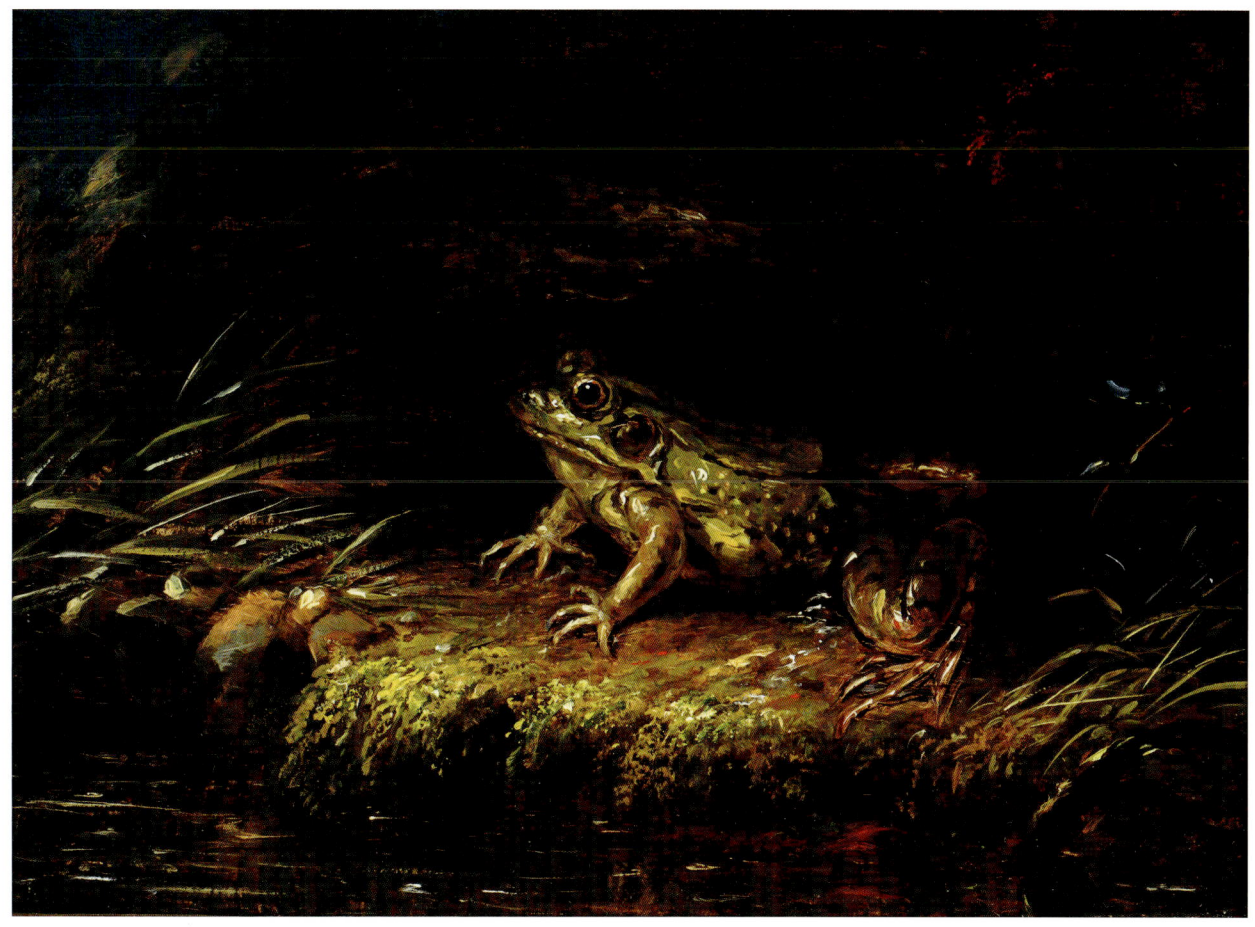

FIGURE 2.4.

SHEPARD ALONZO MOUNT

Long Island Frog, 1860.

Oil on panel; 6½ × 9 inches.

JKM Collection.

JL1999.081.

THOMAS HEWES HINCKLEY

United States, 1813–1896

Sir Edwin Landseer painted his iconic *Monarch of the Glen* in 1851. Familiar to many in the United States as the logo for Hartford Insurance, the image gained popularity in the nineteenth century thanks to a widely distributed print. Thomas Hewes Hinckley may have seen the original in 1851, when he traveled to England to study the art of Landseer; he was undoubtedly familiar with the print by the time he painted *Woodland Prince* (figure 2.5) in 1880. Landseer's and Hinckley's paintings are classic examples of the heroic male portrait, with the stag placed prominently in the center of the composition, elevated from the surrounding landscape (similar to Bierstadt's *Rocky Mountain Goat* [see figure 2.1]). The viewer is positioned below the stag and looks up at him, establishing a clear hierarchy and power dynamic. The regal titles of both paintings also connote authority: the lord of the forest is lording it over the viewer. These paintings are definitely anthems to the power and beauty of nature, but they also say much about the person who displays them. By hanging a picture of a proud stag on the wall, similar to hanging a trophy mount, the owner is demonstrating his power (generally, in this era, the appropriate pronoun is *his*) over the subject of the piece and, by extension, over the natural world. Imagine this painting hanging behind the desk of a captain of industry, the iconography of the painting bolstering the image of the person sitting in front of it—truly intimidating.[15] In a library or hunting lodge, images such as *Woodland Prince* bolster the nature of an already masculinized space. Artists today continue to paint the heroic male, and the iconography remains largely the same. However, given an increased concern with the state of the environment, such works are easily interpreted as symbolizing the power and beauty of nature. In all likelihood, Hinckley was not worried about the environment when he painted this picture in 1880 but was instead concerned with creating his own version of Landseer's iconic stag.

Hinckley was born in Milton, Massachusetts, in 1813. His father, Captain Robert Hinckley, did not approve of art as a career and apprenticed the young man to a Philadelphia merchant when he was fifteen. He managed to attend evening art classes in Philadelphia under the instruction of William Mason. After his father died in 1833, Hinckley returned to Milton and set up a studio as a portrait and sign painter. He later concentrated on animal paintings, studying cattle. He showed two bovine paintings at the National Academy of Design in 1846. After visiting

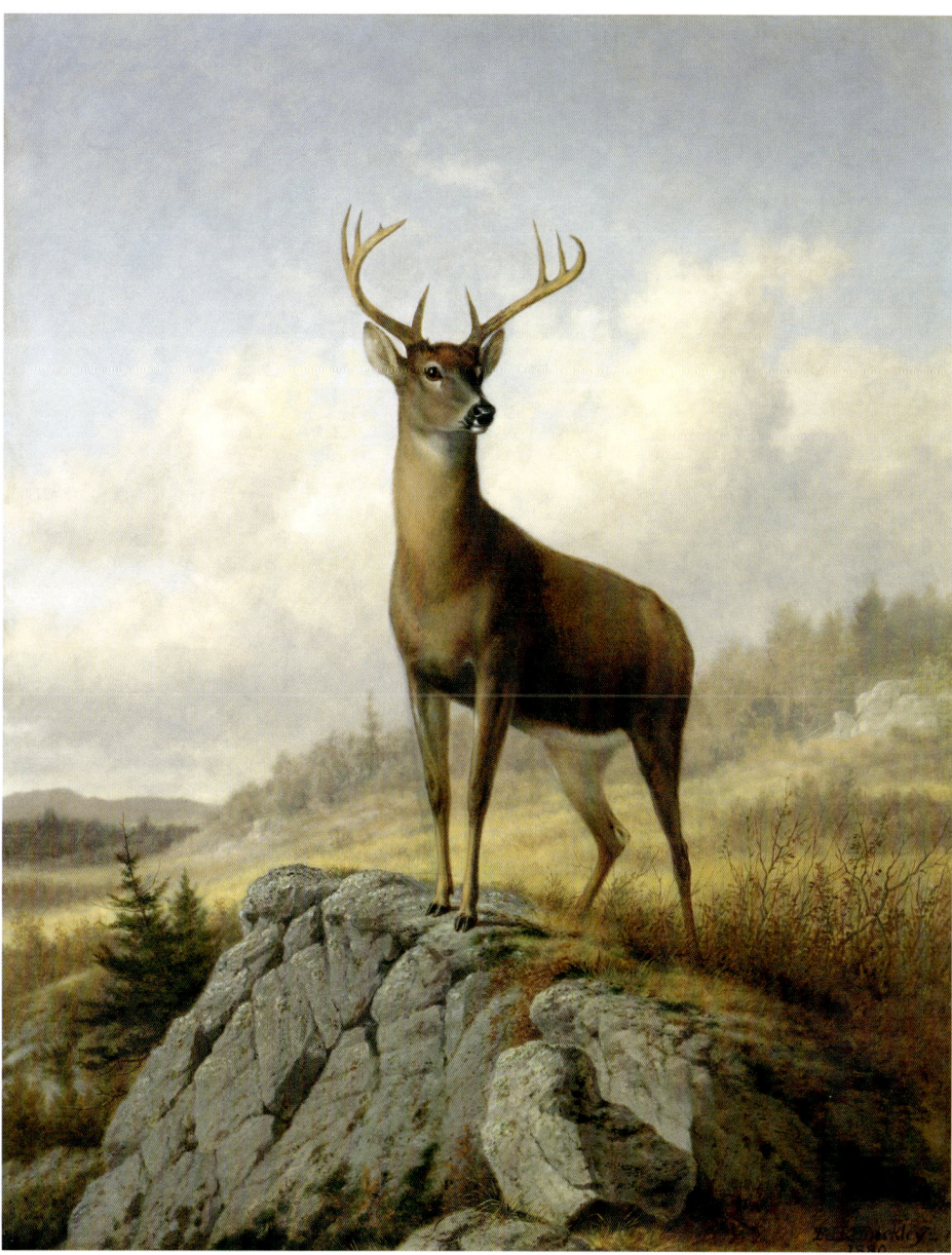

FIGURE 2.5.
THOMAS HEWES HINCKLEY
Woodland Prince, 1880.
Oil on canvas; 36 × 28 inches.
JKM Collection.
JL1992.018.

Europe, he exhibited two paintings of sporting dogs at the Royal Academy in 1858. Hinckley studied deer on Naushon Island in Massachusetts, in the Adirondacks, and at Moosehead Lake in Maine. In 1870, he made a trip to California, where he studied elk.[16] Though a few of Hinckley's paintings were engraved and distributed, his contemporary, Arthur Fitzwilliam Tait, monopolized the interest of popular printmaker Currier and Ives and dominated the sporting print market during the late nineteenth century.[17] *Woodland Prince* clearly differs from earlier depictions of deer, such as Catlin's (see figure 1.6), in that this painting presents a regal icon of the outdoors. It was not created to inform curious easterners or Europeans what a particular species of animal looked like; it speaks much more broadly as a symbol of nature, reflecting the late-nineteenth-century concept of wilderness.

ARTHUR FITZWILLIAM TAIT

UNITED KINGDOM, 1819–1905

For easterners living in increasingly urban environments, Tait's paintings present an idealized vision of the land that existed outside of the city. The Adirondack Mountains—with grand vistas, beautiful foliage, and abundant wildlife—provided an alluring (and attainable) escape for city dwellers. Easily accessible from New York City, the wild and seemingly untouched nature of the area became a favorite of tourists in the late 1800s as members of an increasingly mobile middle class made their way from the city out into the country. The Adirondacks also became a destination for artists who wanted to capture the essence of the outdoors on canvas; Arthur Fitzwilliam Tait was one of the region's most frequent visitors and its most famous chronicler.

Tait was born near Liverpool, England, the son of a maritime merchant. He first became curious about America upon seeing George Catlin's Indian Gallery in Paris in the late 1840s. Intrigued by Catlin's interpretation of the American West, Tait left for the United States in 1850 with the goal of painting the wilderness. Tait settled in New York City but spent much of his time in the Adirondacks painting landscapes, wildlife, and sportsmen. Tait's Adirondack scenes proved popular in both original and print format. Currier and Ives reproduced at least thirty-eight of his paintings in their popular print series; they printed more of Tait's paintings than those of any other artist in their fold. After leaving Currier and Ives, Louis Prang reproduced approximately ten Tait paintings in chromolithograph.[18]

Good Hunting Ground (figure 2.6) emphasizes an abundance of game in a romanticized American wilderness setting and plays into the nation's sense of self as a land full of boundless natural resources. Here, lush vegetation and clean water provide habitat for the rabbits, ducks, and deer. This is a hunter's dream, ready for exploration. In *Arthur Fitzwilliam Tait: Artist in the Adirondacks,* Warder H. Cadbury wrote, "Unlike the private game preserves of Europe, the Adirondack wilderness, still largely unmapped, was a sportsman's paradise, free and open to anyone."[19] North America is celebrated in this work as a land of freedom and plenty where residents (unlike their counterparts in Europe) were free to hunt and where ample game existed to stock the family larder. Tait's unspoiled vision of the wilderness also would have appealed to tourists who visited the Adirondacks, whether they were hunters or not, because it captured the essence of the outdoor experience.

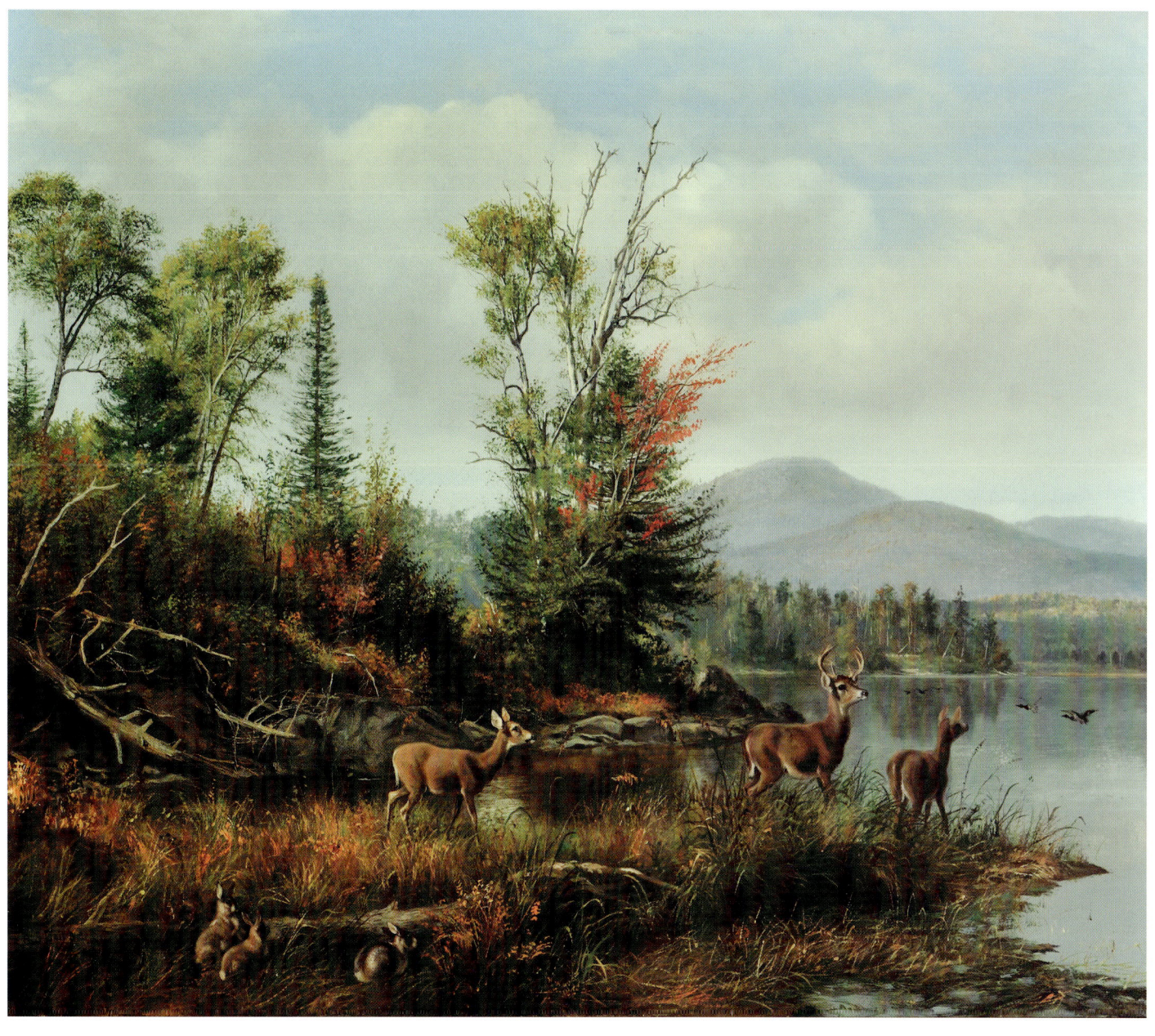

FIGURE 2.6.

ARTHUR FITZWILLIAM TAIT

Good Hunting Ground, 1880–81.

Oil on canvas; 22¼ × 26¼ inches.

JKM Collection.

JL1997.015.

WORTHINGTON WHITTREDGE
United States, 1820–1910

*D*eer Watering (figure 2.7), a luminous painting by Worthington Whittredge, shows deer drinking from a small eastern stream, perhaps in one of his favorite haunts in New York's Catskill Mountains. Whittredge is best known today for his wooded landscape interiors (like this one), characterized by symmetrical compositions, with trees framing either a stream or a pool and gentle light coming in from the back of the canvas. The water featured in this forest scene reflects and diffuses the hazy sunlight, adding a warm glow to the picture. The untroubled deer make the image all the more serene. It is as if the viewer has come across a previously unexplored inlet, an Edenic setting lit by a heavenly source. This work captures the essence of the nineteenth-century idea that God existed in nature and that America's unspoiled wilderness was a sign of the holy presence. As nature fell prey to westward expansion, foresting, and mining, wild places became less common as depictions of them became more popular.

In the 1870s, Whittredge painted many interior woodland scenes like *Deer Watering* that were approximately the same size. Anthony Janson, in *Worthington Whittredge,* wrote that these works were likely painted on site: "All of these canvases are so faithful to the experience of nature as to give the inescapable impression of having been painted outdoors."[20] Whittredge traveled to Europe in 1849, briefly spending time with the Barbizon painters, who advocated painting on site, or *en plein air.* After studying in France, Whittredge moved north to study with Emanuel Leutze in Düsseldorf, Germany. While in Europe, he sketched and traveled with Albert Bierstadt and William Holbrook Beard on occasion and fine-tuned his ability to combine light, landscape, and atmosphere into dramatic and subtle compositions.[21] Returning to New York, Whittredge took a studio in the Tenth Street Studio Building, where Bierstadt and Beard also had space. Given Whittredge's skill at depicting the wilderness, it is no surprise that he became a leading member of the Hudson River school, representing a second generation of artists to take up the mantle. Like other artists of his generation, such as Thomas Hill and Herman Herzog, Whittredge traveled west on several occasions and brought back sketchbooks full of Rocky Mountain material (see figure I.4). Unlike Bierstadt's meteoric rise to fame and subsequent downfall, Whittredge had a quiet but successful career; he was able to change with the times, and his work generally remained in favor with critics.

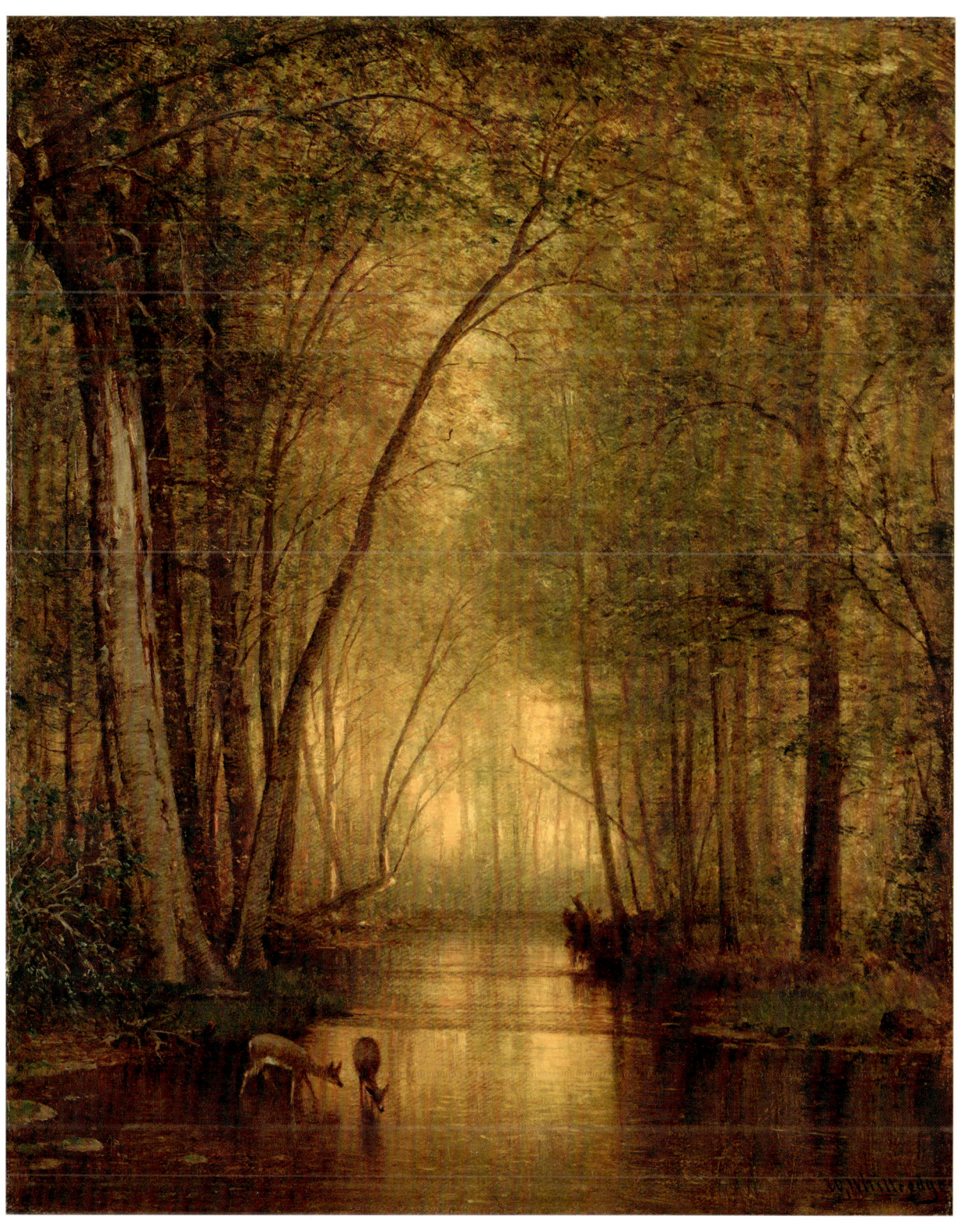

FIGURE 2.7.

WORTHINGTON WHITTREDGE

Deer Watering, c. 1875.

Oil on canvas; 21 × 17½ inches.

JKM Collection.

J1991.007

WILLIAM HOLBROOK BEARD

UNITED STATES, 1824–1900

The Facetious Bear—There is no doubt about the waggishness of bears, who can even laugh at their own jokes; not uproariously, as the laughter of those jolly priests the French artists paint so admirably, but they can assume a well-defined expression of mirth. They are as unmistakably jocose as the most incorrigible jester of our own species, and even harsher than his mortal compeer. In either creature, when jocularity gets a hold, it seems to take full possession of him to the complete subjugation of all else.

William Holbrook Beard, *Humor in Animals*, 65

Artist-naturalists such as George Catlin and John James Audubon often portrayed a male and a female animal in one painting to show both sexes of the species, creating a family portrait without necessarily intending to. In *So You Wanna Get Married, Eh?* (figure 2.8), William Holbrook Beard creates a family portrait without any pretense that he is doing otherwise. Two young bears stand bashfully before the village elder, asking his permission to marry. In the background, the silhouette of another bear, perhaps an anxious mother or another suitor, peeks out from behind a tree. Paintings and stories about animals enacting human customs provide playful ways to think about our traditions, values, and major life decisions. To some extent, every piece of wildlife art is anthropomorphic: artists inevitably put some of themselves into the work, and viewers relate on a certain level by putting themselves into the scene. Paintings such as Beard's bring the anthropomorphic to the fore, providing an easy entrée into looking at other human characteristics inherent in art featuring wildlife.

William Holbrook Beard began his career as a portrait and genre-scene painter. In 1856, he traveled to Italy, Germany, and Switzerland and sketched with Albert Bierstadt and Worthington Whittredge at various points during his journey. In late 1860 or early 1861, Beard moved to New York City and opened a studio in the renowned Tenth Street Studio Building. Unlike many of his counterparts, who were investigating the American landscape, Beard focused on animals almost exclusively. His often-humorous animal paintings, featuring rabbits, cats, monkeys, squirrels, and bears, became immensely popular. William Gerdts wrote that Beard "painted animals of all kinds, from the spider to the elephant, but the bear was his favorite, was painted most often and manipulated with the greatest variety

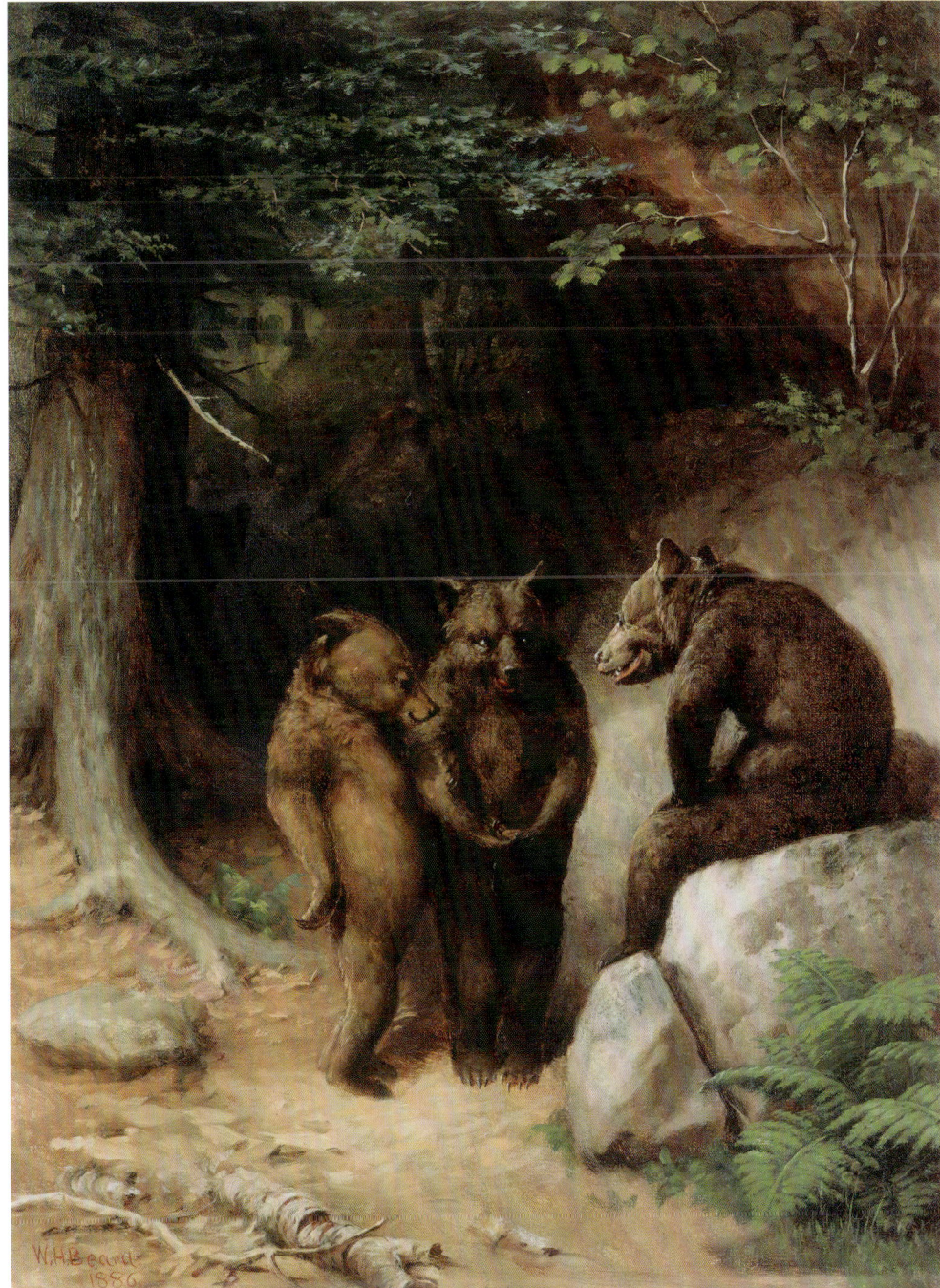

FIGURE 2.8.
WILLIAM HOLBROOK BEARD
So You Wanna Get Married, Eh? 1886.
Oil on canvas; 24 × 18 inches.
JKM Collection.
JL1998.152.

and greatest humor."²² Beard was known for his satirical work, in which he placed animals in situations pointing out the foibles of humankind, but he also used animals in gentler ways with less pointed meanings, as in the rather sweet *So You Wanna Get Married, Eh?*

THOMAS HILL

United Kingdom, 1829–1908

Two Stags Battling (figure 2.9) is overtly theatrical, with tall trees framing the space like curtains and the narrow path fanning out like a stage. One way to read this work is to look at it as a human drama told with animal actors, as two men fighting to win the favor of the women in the background. Though scenes like this take place in nature (bucks do use their antlers for sparring), the implied narrative of the does looking on is the artist's creation. This anthropomorphic reading takes nothing away from the spectacular space represented in the canvas, with its huge trees looming over the protagonists and the soft, filtered light illuminating the scene. Unlike William Holbrook Beard's *So You Wanna Get Married, Eh?* Hill's *Two Stags Battling* is not intentionally anthropomorphic; but one way in which viewers relate to a work is by placing themselves in it or by relating it to a well-known narrative. Here, Hill successfully merges a woodland scene with a common trope, resulting in a canvas that engages on many levels.

Painted in 1883, *Two Stags Battling* was created after Hill moved to San Francisco in 1869. Prior to that, Hill painted in Massachusetts and in the White Mountains of New Hampshire, developing his own take on the Hudson River style of landscape painting. One can easily see the influence of artists such as Worthington Whittredge, who were entranced with the effects of filtered sunlight on interior woodland scenes (see figure 2.7). In 1866–67, Hill traveled to Europe to view the 1867 Exposition Universelle. While there, he studied with German artist Paul Meyerheim in Meyerheim's Paris studio. A noted teacher and painter, Meyerheim encouraged Hill to focus on landscape. According to curator Janice Driesbach in *Direct from Nature,* another principal benefit of Hill's time in France was his exposure to Barbizon painting, which "offered models for treating his canvases more broadly, employing . . . small brush strokes or even daubs of color to effectively signify foliage and figures."[23] The loose brushwork utilized by the Barbizon school had a clear impact on Hill and contrasts greatly with the tight, precise style of the earlier Hudson River school. Hill returned to the United States late in 1867 and returned to California in 1869. Once back on the West Coast, he began to paint extensively in Yosemite, becoming one of its best-known chroniclers. *Two Stags Battling* combines a typical Hudson River school composition with loose brushwork influenced by the Barbizon as it conveys a distinct sense of a densely wooded forest.

FIGURE 2.9.
THOMAS HILL
Two Stags Battling, 1883.
Oil on canvas; 72 × 36 inches.
JKM Collection.
J1991.004.

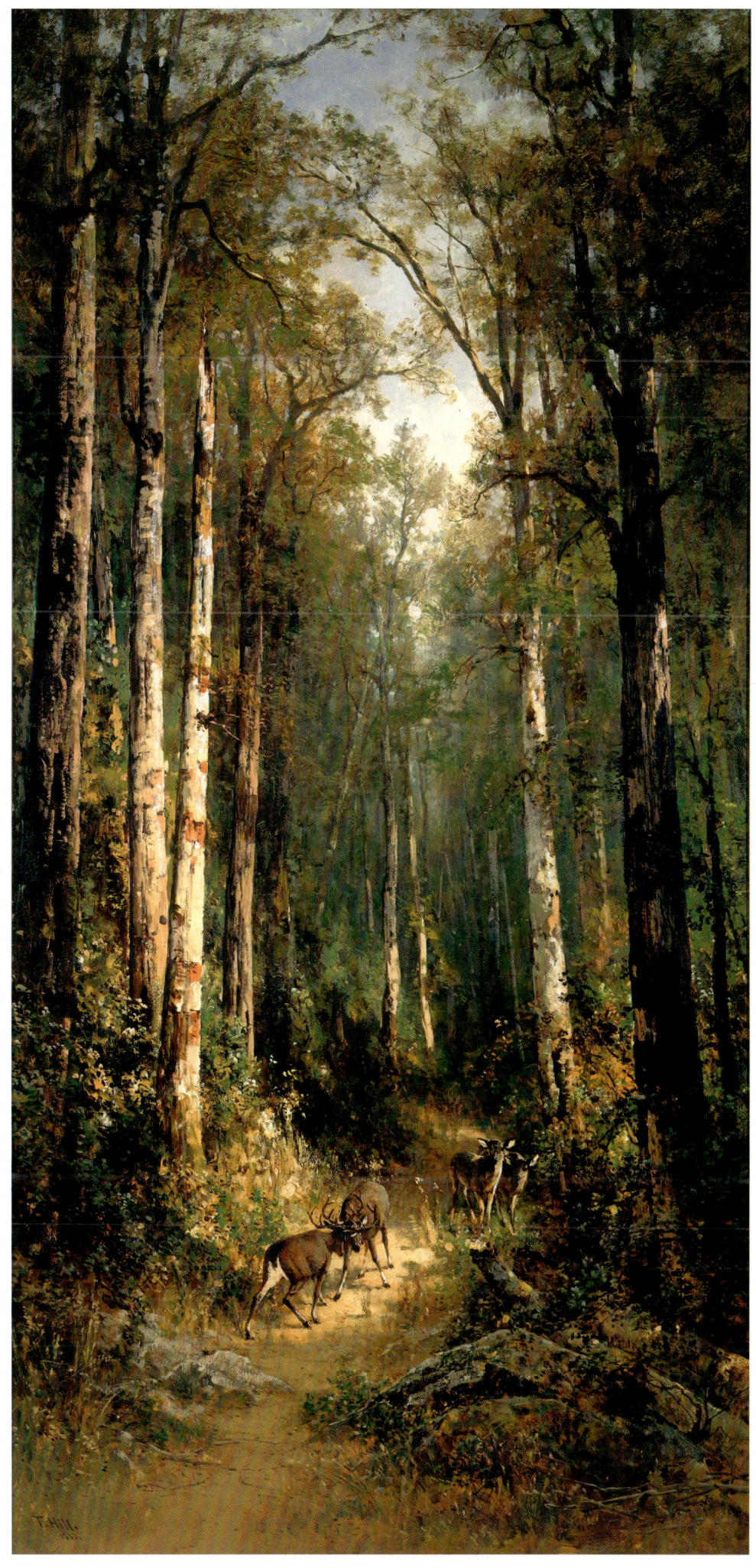

HERMAN HERZOG
Germany, 1831–1932

Well-known émigré Herman Herzog painted in the style of the Hudson River school. *Bears by the Stream* (figure 2.10), however, is set far from the woodlands of the White Mountains or other Hudson River haunts. Grizzlies, even at the turn of the nineteenth century, did not live anywhere on the East Coast. Herzog painted *Bears by the Stream* based on material gleaned from one of the many western journeys he took between 1873 and 1904. According to Donald S. Lewis, Jr., Herzog (in addition to studying the fauna of the regions he visited) often painted waterfalls, which "offered the artist an endless number of visual possibilities. . . . In several scenes, the dynamism of water is juxtaposed with calmer and more pleasing elements in nature, conveying the variety of nature's moods."[24] *Bears by the Stream* perfectly illustrates Lewis's point: if the waterfall symbolizes the power of nature, then the mother bear and her playful cubs on the bank represent the contrasting "calmer and more pleasing elements." Reinforcing the message that this work shows the variety of nature, Herzog includes a brooding sky, which generally signals the sublime drama of nature, but he lets the sun shine through to illuminate the bear family, giving the canvas an uplifting, rather than ominous, feeling.[25]

Born in Bremen, Germany, Herman Herzog entered the Düsseldorf Academy in 1848, where he learned the Old World painting techniques so skillfully applied to his New World subjects. His early paintings depict European mountain landscapes from Norway, Switzerland, Italy, and the Pyrenees. His patrons included Queen Victoria and Emperor Alexander of Russia. In 1869, Herzog immigrated to Philadelphia and began painting landscapes in Pennsylvania and along the Hudson River before branching out and including the American West in his oeuvre. As with Whittredge and Hill, Herzog was painting American nature as a hallowed place, full of potential and as a source of renewal. The animals included by each artist reinforced the idea of the wilderness as untrammeled, a land where wildlife roamed freely, unconcerned with human presence or threat.

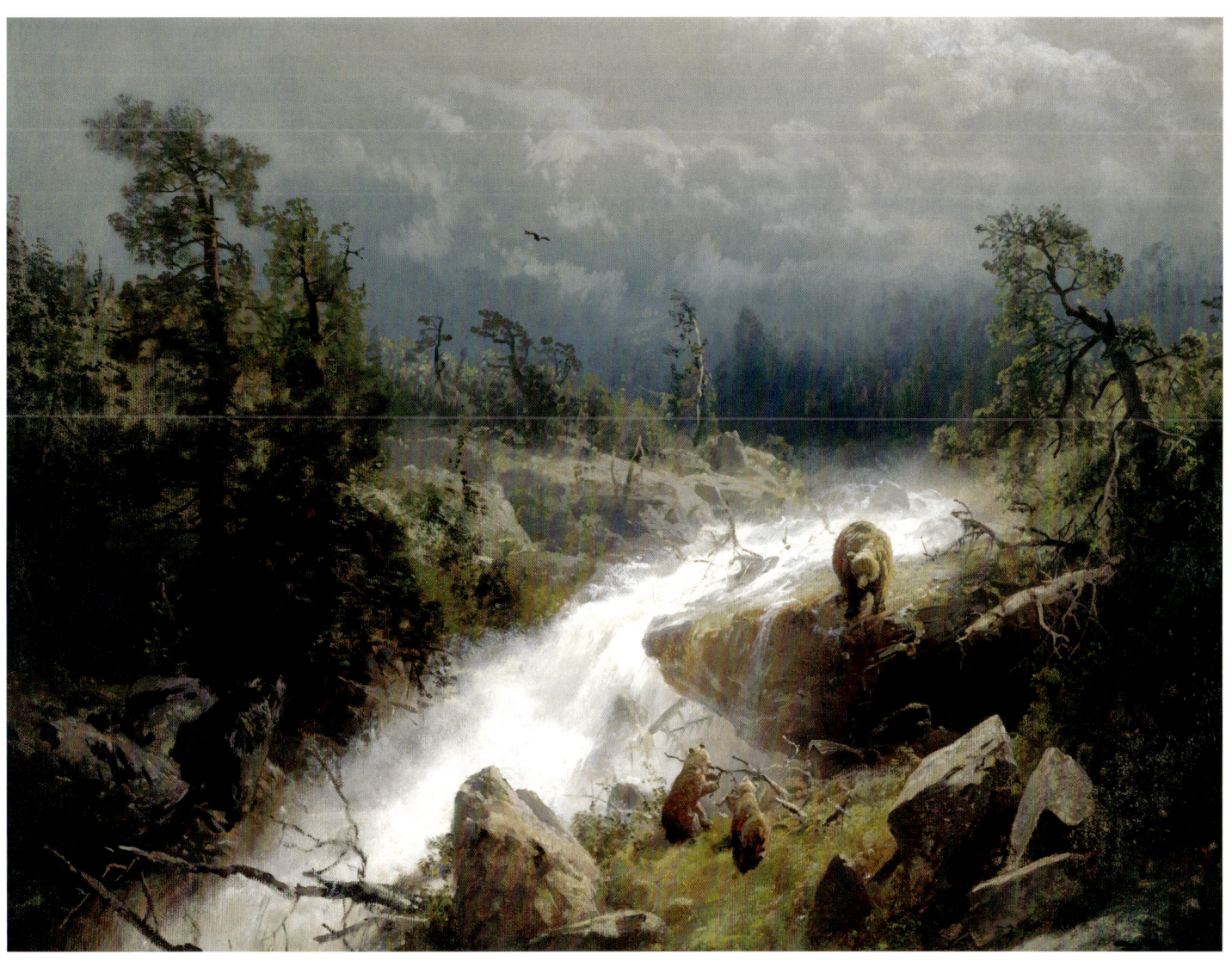

FIGURE 2.10.

HERMAN HERZOG

Bears by the Stream, c. 1900.

Oil on canvas; 22 × 29 inches.

JKM Collection.

M1990.023.

ALEXANDER POPE
United States, 1849–1924

A s a youth, Alexander Pope carved and sketched animals around his home in Dorchester, Massachusetts. In the 1860s, he worked for his family's lumber business, where he learned the qualities of various types of wood. Pope studied carving, painting, perspective, and anatomy with William Rimmer, an influential teacher of many Boston artists. From 1879 to 1883, Pope created many well-received carvings of game (figure 2.11). In 1883, he began painting animals and later pursued a career as a portraitist. Eventually, Pope was considered one of the best Bostonian trompe l'oeil artists of the nineteenth century. The French term *trompe l'oeil* means "fool the eye." Trompe l'oeil paintings appear so real as to trick viewers into thinking they are seeing an actual scene rather than a painted one. In 1902, the *Boston Herald* reported, "It is one of his favorite pastimes to paint birds, rabbits, etc., hanging to a wall and cause them to stand out so as to deceive the sight and to cause many to desire to see the other side in order to be convinced that they are not real instead of painted objects."[26]

FIGURE 2.11.
ALEXANDER POPE
Mallard against a Woven Basket, c. 1880.
Painted wood; 28¾ × 23½ × 4½ inches.
JKM Collection.
JL1999.118.

Pope was known for setting his subjects as if hanging on a slate-colored door, as he did in *Hanging Grouse* (figure 2.12). Still-life paintings such as this emphasize the bounty of the wilderness and the hunt, both of which were available to a broader spectrum of the population in America than in Europe. Even if one took part in bird hunting irregularly or not at all, having a still life of game in the home was a marker of social status and masculinity. Art historian David Lubin observed that "late nineteenth-century American still-life painting made men of its viewers or at least encouraged them to think of themselves as such."[27] In an era when women played increasingly public roles, men sought to more clearly define themselves as men, and objects such as Pope's paintings helped bolster that image.

Many of the wildlife works created during the late nineteenth century and later can be read as masculine markers appropriate to the library or the hunting lodge that gave men a sense of self separate from the feminine. However, the prevalence of wildlife in American art also speaks to greater themes in our culture. Symbolizing more than masculinity, these artworks display an interest in nature as rich in resource and opportunity, a defining aspect of nationhood.

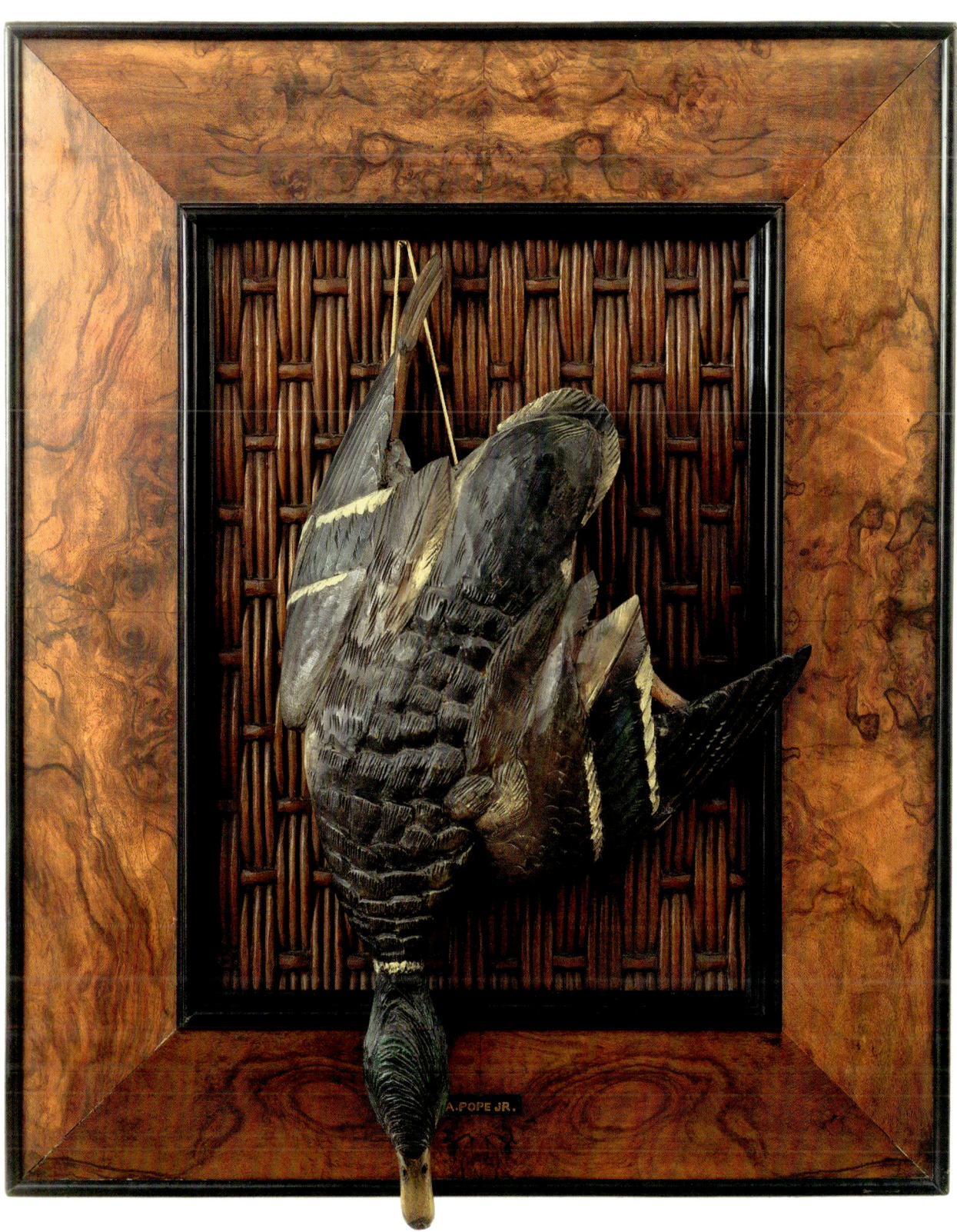

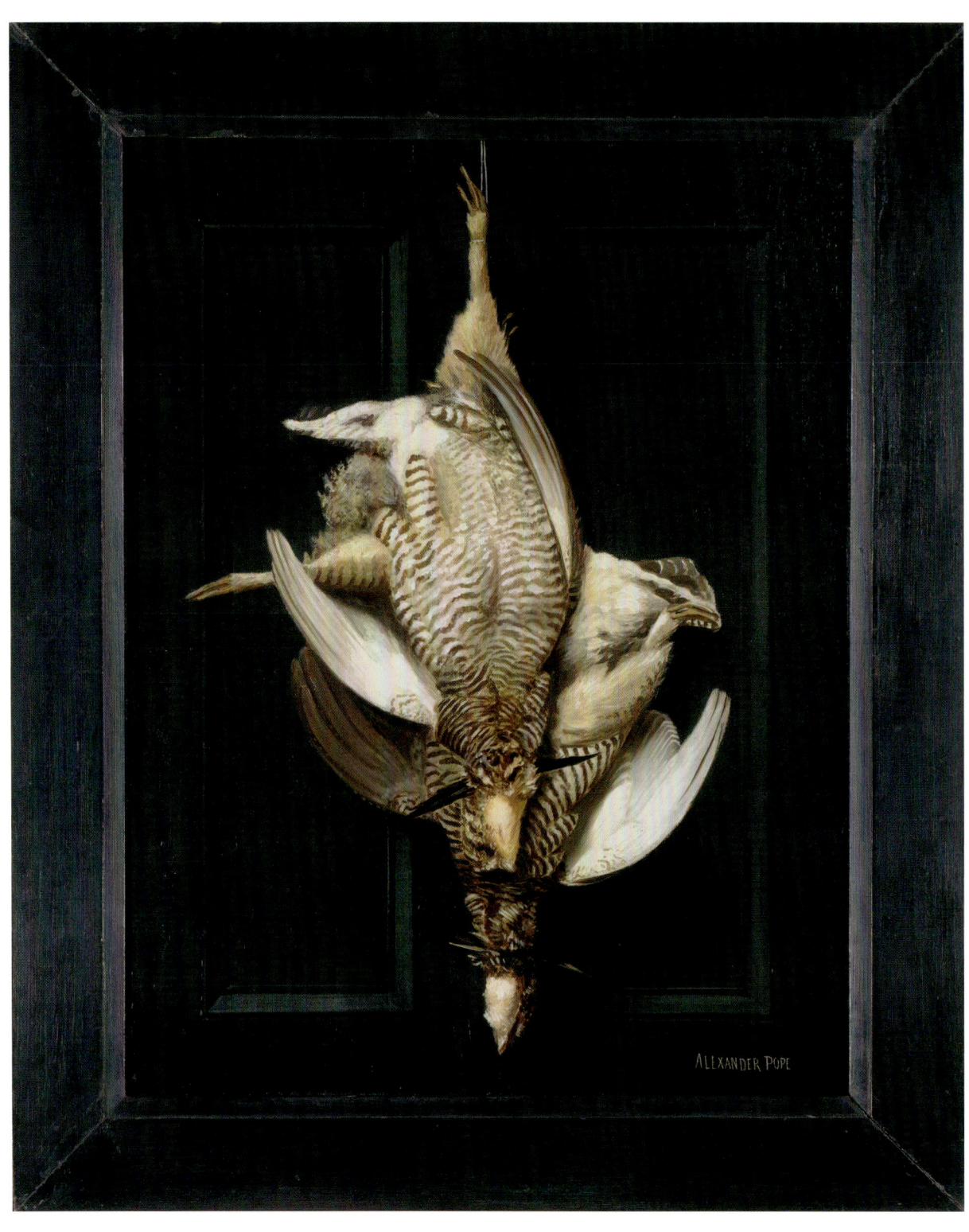

FIGURE 2.12.
ALEXANDER POPE
Hanging Grouse, c. 1890.
Oil on canvas; 28 × 20 inches.
JKM Collection.
JL1999.025.

WILLIAM MERRITT CHASE
United States, 1849–1916

Shortly after William Merritt Chase's death, the critic and collector Duncan Phillips proclaimed him "unequalled by any other painter in the representation of the shiny, slippery, fishiness of fish."[28] Chase in fact feared that his entire reputation would be based on his fish paintings.[29] Around the turn of the nineteenth century, he became fascinated with these animals, commenting, "I take the greatest pleasure in the infinite variety of these creatures, the subtle and exquisitely colored tones of the flesh fresh from the water, the way their surfaces reflect the light."[30] The dark-toned and loosely painted *Still-Life, Cod and Mackerel* (figure 2.13) is a study in light and reflection, with the shiny skins of the smaller fish standing out from the deep reds and browns of the table and the larger cod. Chase portrays the light reflecting off the cod's snout with a few deftly placed dribbles of paint. This work was clearly painted with speed, capturing the essence of the fish without belaboring the details.

Chase began painting fish on a trip to Venice in 1877, after having spent six years in Europe, studying at the Royal Academy in Munich. Exposed to the work of Velazquez and Caravaggio, Chase developed his own admiration for painting in the tenebrist manner, which brings objects out of a darkly painted background with areas of lighter colors. *Still-Life, Cod and Mackerel,* along with most of Chase's other still lifes, uses tenebrism to create depth and richness; dark tones add a warmth to this painting that might otherwise be seen as simply a cold, dead fish. Chase's fish tie into the urban market tradition of still-life painting in Europe, which celebrates the cornucopia available for purchase on the town square, rather than the more rural and American hunting tradition, which celebrates the bounty of the wilderness (such as works by Alexander Pope [see figure 2.12]). But Chase's fish are typically American in their presentation of plentitude without the moralizing undertones of the European still life, which realistically portrayed the robust pleasures of life while warning of the dangers of such indulgences.

Critics and collectors tired of grand landscapes migrated toward Chase's looser, more modern work. In a telling sign of the times, Chase took over Bierstadt's enormous studio in the Tenth Street Studio Building upon his return to the United States in 1878.[31] Chase did not only paint still lifes; he was also renowned as a portrait painter and became widely known for his impressionist canvases of outdoor scenes. He became an incredibly influential force in the

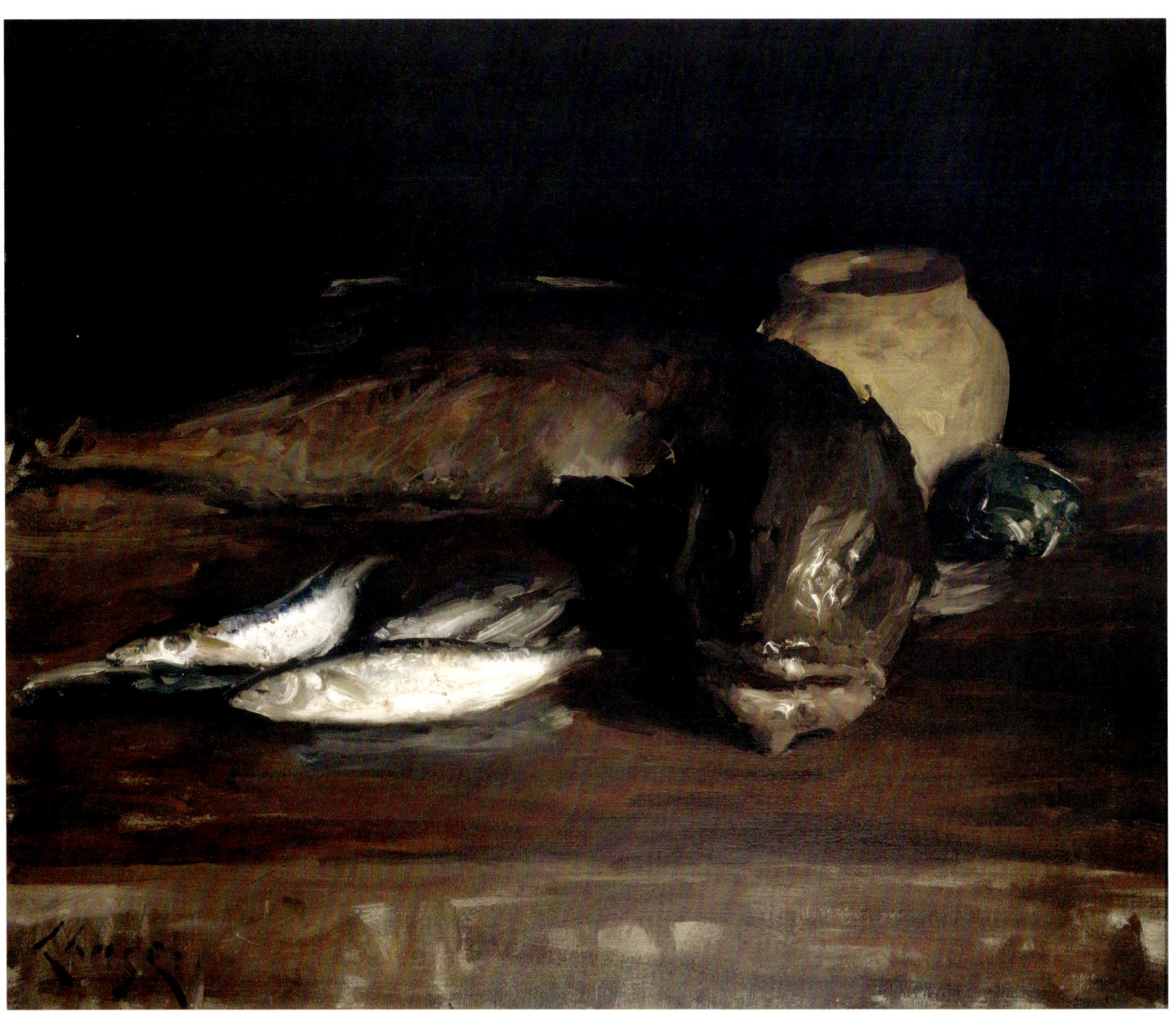

FIGURE 2.13.
WILLIAM MERRITT CHASE
Still-Life, Cod and Mackerel, c. 1900.
Oil on canvas; 25¼ × 30¼ inches.
JKM Collection.
JL1999.006.

American art scene, and his successful career as a painter was coupled with a similarly successful career as an instructor. Chase taught at the Art Students League and at his own Chase School of Art. Some of his more famous students included Georgia O'Keeffe, Edward Hopper, and Rockwell Kent.

During the period between Bierstadt and Chase, American painting went from celebrating the wilderness with huge blockbuster canvases to celebrating certain aspects of it. A quieter, though no less glorious, vision of wildlife emerged, one that fit into urban middle-class homes, reminding the inhabitants of what lay beyond the boundaries of their ever-increasing communities, and that helped instill a sense of pride in American nature and nation.

Chapter 3

American Animaliers: *The Legacy of Barye and Rodin*

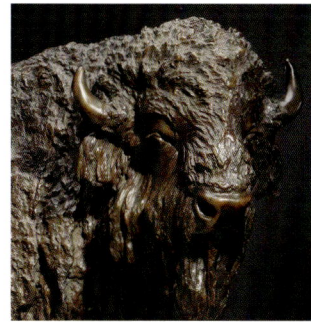

A rt historian Patricia Broder wrote in *Bronzes of the American West* that, until the 1870s, "[t]he choice of an animal as a subject was considered unworthy of execution. How could the representation of mere animals inspire the spirit or enrich the mind? The classical tradition demanded the study and idealization of the human, not the animal, form. It is the Romantic who looks to nature for a subject and chooses an animal, preferably wild or exotic, as worthy of artistic representation and idealization."[1] Animals as a primary subject in American sculpture came to the fore after a generation of artists saw the work of Frenchman Antoine-Louis Barye, the first European sculptor to truly specialize in animal subjects and one of the premiere European Romantic artists. Barye and his followers, known as the animaliers, laid the groundwork for American animal sculpture of the late nineteenth and early twentieth centuries. Another huge influence on American sculptors was one of Barye's best-known pupils, Auguste Rodin (1840–1917). At the forefront of the revolution in French art that began in the late 1800s with impressionism, Rodin's work opened the door to more-personal and more-modern interpretations of individual animals. While Barye and Rodin influenced the style of the American animaliers, an ongoing series of world's fairs gave the animaliers new opportunities to display their art. During this period, the fairs offered many sculptors the chance to share their work with a broad spectrum of the public, either through monumental commissions decorating the fairgrounds or through smaller versions of their work shown inside exhibit halls. Even as art became more modern and more personal during this era, the potent iconography of wildlife and the wilderness remained an essential part of the foundation on which the American animalier school was built.

Why were two Frenchmen so important to the development of American animalier sculpture? Art historian Kathleen Adler noted in *Americans in Paris, 1860–1900* that after the Civil War, American artists and art students began flocking to Paris. At least one thousand were there in 1888 alone.[2] Paris was the center of the art world, and success there was a decent indicator of success elsewhere. In addition, for American animal sculptors, Paris was the birthplace of the animalier movement and the best place to study the work of Barye and his followers. American sculptors could even take a class from one of Barye's pupils, which was almost like learning from the master himself.

Barye began sculpting animals early in his career, but these works initially met with rejection from the elite French Academy. After repeated submissions, his *Tiger Devouring a Gavial* was accepted for the Salon of 1831.[3] From that point forward, animal sculpture gained in popularity, and Barye's influence spread to a group of younger sculptors. One of Barye's students was Emmanuel Frémiet, who subsequently taught classes at Paris's famed animal menagerie, the Jardin des Plantes, and became a professor of drawing at Paris's Natural History Museum. As American artists began to cross the Atlantic for training, many took instruction from Frémiet. For those Americans who could not travel abroad, the work of Barye was easily studied on the East Coast. In 1873, the Corcoran Gallery of Art in Washington, D.C., ordered one of everything Barye had created. Likewise, the private collector William T. Walters opened his doors to visitors in 1874, in part to share his growing collection of Barye bronzes with the public.[4]

Barye's vision was part of the greater Romantic movement in Europe, which evolved as a counterpoint to the ideals upheld during the Enlightenment. In Europe, the Enlightenment stressed the importance of reason and rationality as the way toward a more advanced civilization, and civilization at its peak was seen as the classical era of Greece and Rome. Artists in Europe began to emulate ancient styles, creating a classical revival known as neoclassicism, which was typified by staid allegorical figures carved in marble representing lofty ideals. Romanticism, in contrast, stressed the importance of the imagination and intuition as a way of living in greater harmony with nature, or at least as a way of tapping into the power of the natural world. The Romantics sought a freedom of personal expression that could not be achieved within the strictures of classical forms.

The difference between Romantic and Enlightenment ideals can be broken down into dichotomies: heart versus head, nature versus civilization, emotion versus intellect. Sinuous sculptures of battling animals with muscles bulging, claws ripping, and jaws clamping proved perfect subjects for the Romantics. Other realms of culture also supported a Romantic worldview. Alfred Lord Tennyson's poem *In Memoriam* (1842) included the now-familiar phrase "nature, red in tooth and claw." In 1859, Charles Darwin published *On the Origin of Species*, promoting his theory of natural selection. Economist Herbert Spencer coined the term "survival of the fittest" to describe Darwin's theories in 1864; that phrase quickly took on a life of its own. "Survival of the fittest" along with Tennyson's "nature, red in tooth and claw" came to serve as catch phrases describing the work of Barye and his followers.[5]

Barye definitely broke new ground when his *Tiger Devouring a Gavial* was displayed at the Paris Salon in 1831. However, by the middle of the 1800s,

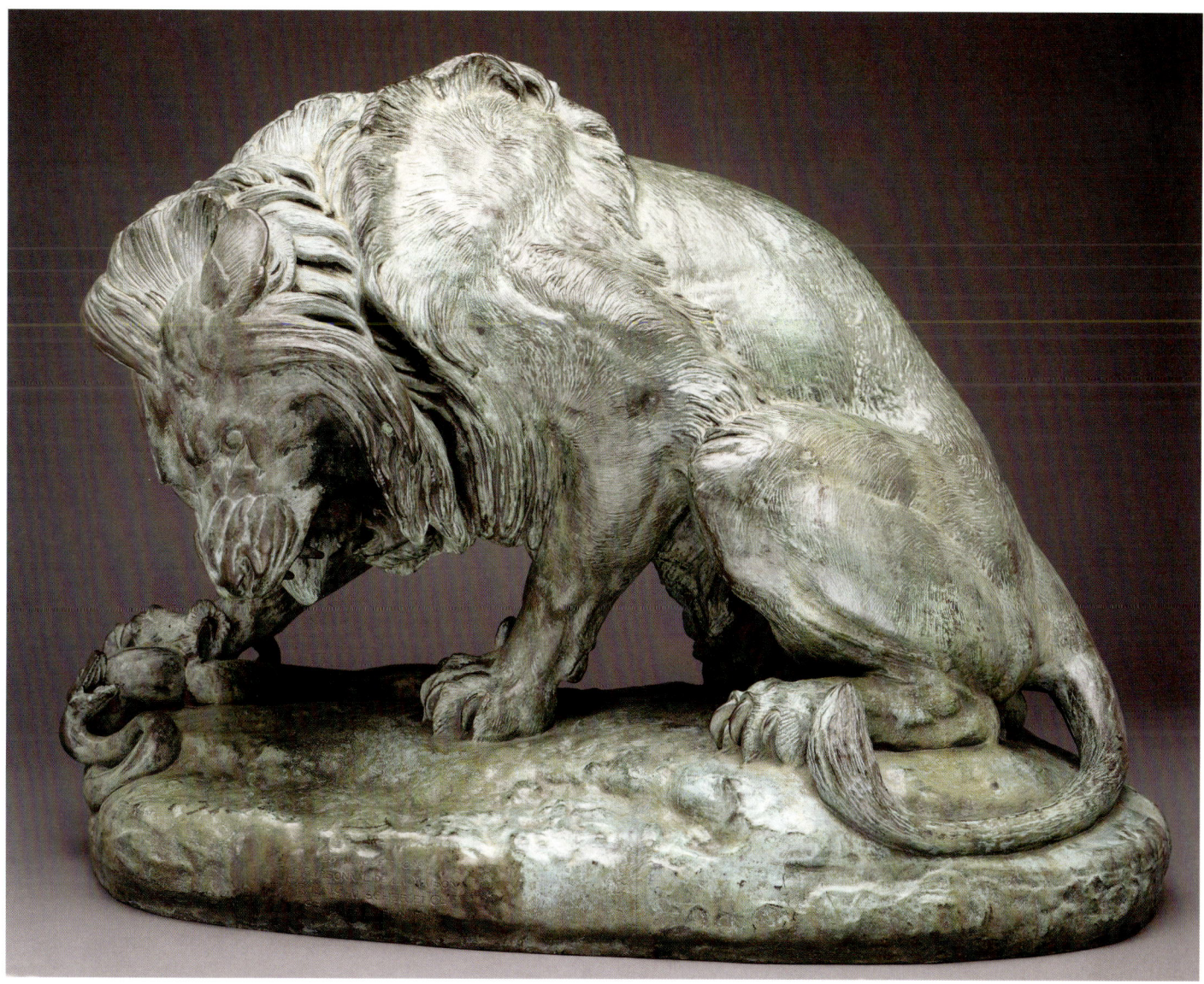

FIGURE 3.1.
ANTOINE-LOUIS BARYE
Lion Crushing a Serpent,
modeled 1832, this cast c. 1899.
Bronze; 15 ¼ × 19 ½ × 10 ⅜ inches.
JKM Collection.
JL1998.027.

he had become a recognized part of the French art establishment, in part because his work had an understood moral underpinning. Displaying the ferocity and violence inherent in nature, which critics at the time cast as evil, was thought to provoke the opposite (virtue and piety) in viewers. Art historian Glenn Benge wrote, "Evil is thus the necessary foil to the monotony of the good and the beautiful."[6] Highly emotional Romantic art can be seen as the necessary opposite to the rigidly sober neoclassical.

Barye's *Lion Crushing a Serpent* (figure 3.1) is a thoroughly Romantic depiction of the power and violence inherent in nature. *Lion*, like Barye's first success, *Tiger Devouring a Gavial*, pits a feline against a reptile: two dissimilar creatures with great contrasts in terms of texture, scale, and form. However, *Lion* also had direct political connotations; the feline was a clear celebration of the newly installed French government, lead by Louis-Philippe, who came to power in 1830 after the July Revolution. Iconographically, the lion represents strength, courage, and fortitude.[7] The snake, in contrast, is a well-known Judeo-Christian symbol of evil. Barye depicted the virtuous lion crushing the wicked snake, or the government crushing its opponents. Louis-Philippe, who was at that time a popular sovereign, ordered a monumental-sized *Lion Crushing a Serpent* for the gardens of the Tuileries, adjacent to the Louvre. This large, public monument not only proclaimed the greatness of the French leader but also provided a ringing endorsement of the animalier genre within the greater art world.

Over the course of a long career, Barye rose to prominence and managed to escape adherence to any single political party or ruler, which helped to ensure his ongoing success. *Lion* was the most overt allegory he created; later sculptures could be read in a more purely Romantic fashion. Adding to his popularity was Barye's pioneering of the serial casting of bronzes, marketed to members of a growing bourgeois class, who began collecting artwork. The serial casting of his work did not end with Barye's death in 1875 but continued into the twentieth century. The *Lion* in the collection of the National Museum of Wildlife Art is a posthumous cast given to the Parisian coach-building firm of Rheims, Auscher, and Company in 1899.[8]

The American animalier movement sprang from the Romantic work of Barye, but it was also influenced by other art movements of the late 1800s. American sculptors began to study Barye's work at the end of his long career; he left a legacy of nearly fifty years of successful animal artwork. His students and followers were legion in France, and many of them continued working in his style. A new generation of sculptors (both European and American) took the then-established animalier tradition and altered it to fit their own more modern concept of what animal sculpture could be. Barye's epic battles gave way to quieter depictions of animals that captured a moment in the creature's life, presenting a certain characteristic gesture or pose; the new sculptures did not always focus on adrenaline-filled action scenes of animals at their peak of exertion. In sculpture, as in painting, a new, more personal vision was taking over as the impact of the impressionists and the postimpressionists rippled across the art world.

Speaking in the 1920s about his own work, American sculptor Frederick Roth said, "Barye did not effect [*sic*] me as much. He looked at the animals as a 'type.' I looked at them as individuals. He was a contemporary of the Romantic era. I was in the psychological era."[9] Roth was sculpting in a time revolutionized by European art movements that stressed as primary the artist's personal point of view, a sea-change that began at the end of the nineteenth century, prompted by the likes of Auguste Rodin. Art historian Stephen F. Eisenman wrote that for artists such as Rodin, Vincent Van Gogh, and Paul Gauguin, "painting and sculpture might as well become as abstract or 'Symbolist' as imagination demanded. . . . Besides, they reasoned, had not an earlier generation of Romantics shown that form alone—line, color, or pattern—was adequate to convey spiritual meaning and personal expression?"[10] The postimpressionists (or Symbolists, as Eisenman calls them) were taking clues from the Romantics as they pushed the boundaries of artistic expression. During the final decades of the nineteenth century, a new generation of artists changed the landscape of art, and American sculptors studying in France took notice.

In 1863, early in his career, Rodin studied anatomy with Barye at the Natural History Museum in Paris. Rodin once stated that of all his influences, he learned the most from Barye.[11] Barye's powerful, twisting forms and graceful compositions made for highly emotional and forceful works. Rodin rarely sculpted animals, but his work echoed Barye's in both impact and emotion. One of Rodin's largest projects was a commission he received in 1877 to create two bronze doors for the planned Musée des Arts Decoratifs in Paris. Inspired by Dante's *Inferno,* Rodin chose to sculpt the Gates of Hell. Many artists before him had chosen this topic, but Rodin broke new ground in studies that surprised contemporary viewers with their frank, personal depictions of various human states. Ruth Butler observed that "Rodin managed to turn his doors into a personal vehicle for some of his most private conceptions in sculpture. When some of the individual figures began to appear in exhibitions in late 1882, both public and critics were shocked by their boldness."[12]

Rodin's work was daring in both subject and style. Like the impressionist painters, he was interested in the effects of light and how it reflected off the different surfaces of his work. Many of his sculptures had rough surfaces and an unfinished appearance that clashed with the smooth modeling found on the work of the previous generation; those sculptures gave no indication of the tool used by the artist, whereas many of Rodin's sculptures celebrated the artist's hand.[13] In addition to experimenting with style, Rodin broke away from the artistic establishment in terms of subject. Instead of conventional depictions of mythological or allegorical subjects, Rodin focused on individuals and feelings, and this placed a focus on the sculpture itself—not solely the story it depicted—as something to be contemplated. For example, his iconic sculpture *The Thinker* was one of the main figures on his *Gates of Hell* commission: a personal, human-centered piece that turns attention away from external forces (God, the devil, angels, saints) and toward internal, mental dynamics.

One of Rodin's only animal sculptures was of a lion, a favorite subject of Barye's. Comparing Barye's *Lion Crushing a Serpent* with Rodin's *Le lion qui pleure* (*The Crying Lion*; figure 3.2), one can readily perceive the shift from an art based on greater civic principals to one based on personal expression. Barye's *Lion* is classically modeled, with a detailed surface that goes to some lengths to show individual hairs on the animal's pelt. Rodin's *Lion,* in stark contrast, is less refined, showing the main form of the lion without giving much surface detail. The subject matter reflects a new exploration of personal emotion. While Barye's *Lion* represented the power of France, Rodin's embodied his sadness over the death of

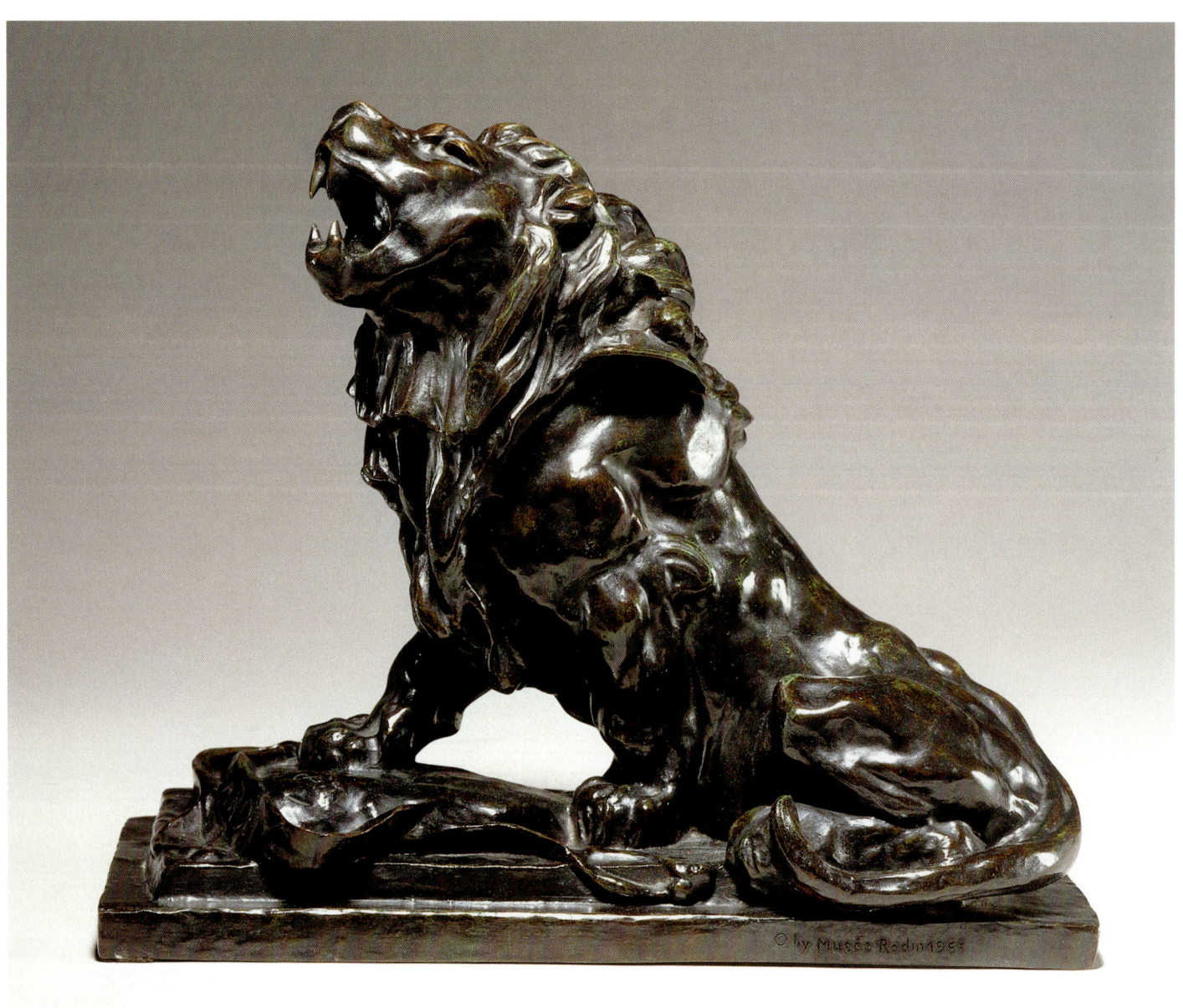

FIGURE 3.2.
AUGUSTE RODIN
Le lion qui pleure,
modeled 1881, this cast 1955.
Bronze; 11¼×13¼×6½ inches.
JKM Collection.
JL1998.076.

a friend, Madame Turquet. Turquet had helped Rodin receive the commission for the *Gates of Hell* (her husband was the undersecretary of state of fine arts), but she passed away in 1881.[14]

Rodin found great success during the 1880s, exhibiting his work at official salons in Paris, Ghent, Brussels, London, Munich, and Vienna. He also displayed his work at the Paris Exposition Universelle in 1889 and in a one-man show adjacent to the second Exposition Universelle in 1900.[15] A cultural phenomenon, world's fairs swept Europe and the United States during the late 1800s and early 1900s. Cultural historian Neil Harris wrote that the American fairs "represented a culture that seemed hopeful, energetic, optimistic. . . . [They] were testaments to the power of an urban dream, the first such dream to emerge in our country, for we still celebrated, rhetorically, the virtues of the countryside. The fairs suggested

Wildlife in American Art

attachment to city living as an emblem of human progress and national greatness."[16] The fairs glorified the modern world but also presented as worthy of reverence the natural resources on which the cities had been built. At fairs such as the World's Columbian Exposition of 1893, the Pan-American Exposition of 1901, and the Louisiana Purchase Exhibition of 1904, exurban subjects decorated the grounds; statues of wildlife were often prominently placed on bridges or at the entrances to exhibition halls. These epitomes of the wild served as reminders of the world outside the fair and bolstered the definition of wilderness as a space intrinsically linked to the development of modern living.

The fairs represented the apex of cultural achievement, and their grounds reflected the overriding ideology of success and progress. In America, the sculptural programs displayed an ongoing infatuation with the West and wilderness. In discussing Alexander Proctor's and Edward Kemeys's sculptures at the 1893 Chicago exposition, Peter Hassrick wrote, "Both figures [the American Indian and cowboy] and several of the species of large animals with which Proctor and Kemeys had decorated the bridges, as well as the frontier itself, had been proclaimed that year by historian Frederick Jackson Turner as prime players in the closing scene of a grand American epoch. For that reason, Proctor and Kemeys, as two men close to the West in their lives and art, were singled out among a legion of sculptors to eulogize a region, its people and their culture, and even nature itself."[17] Instead of sounding a death knell over these quintessentially western topics, the closing of the frontier and the perceived loss of much of what had made America unique spurred even greater interest in the wilderness. In the arts, sculpture representing what had been lost—whether human or animal—became even more popular.

After studying the work of notables such as Barye and Rodin, American animal sculptors began to create distinctly individual bodies of work. Some were more focused on traditional modeling; others, on personal expression. Some relied heavily on studying animals from life, while others created sculptures based on recollection and memory. Edward Kemeys found being out on the open plains and witnessing wildlife firsthand essential to the veracity of his work, while European menageries, with their plethora of available animals, inspired Eli Harvey. Arthur Putnam sculpted slinking felines using his imagination without much reference to living, breathing creatures. Anna Hyatt Huntington combined the external and the internal in works such as *Jaguar* and *Reaching Jaguar,* which evoke the smooth shapes of Putnam's best work but represent an actual jaguar she studied at the New York Zoological Society in the Bronx. Regardless of where each artist found inspiration, and no matter how each artwork appeared, wildlife sculpture captured the essence of the wilderness. As the nineteenth century gave way to the twentieth and open space continued to be eroded by the forces of industry, representations of wildlife proved significant markers of a culture that still upheld its relationship with nature as one of the primary shaping forces in its development.

American sculptors visiting France near the turn of the nineteenth century had the opportunity to see not only the classic animalier work of Barye but also the avant-garde sculpture of Rodin. Wildlife sculptors in the United States absorbed all of these influences, then expressed their own take on the subject in their own way. However, the underlying iconography of what wildlife and the wilderness meant in America remained. American animaliers expressed the ideals, dreams, and history of the culture surrounding them, celebrating western wildlife as a truly American subject.

HENRY KIRKE BROWN
UNITED STATES, 1814–1886

Turn-of-the-nineteenth-century art critic Lorado Taft wrote of Henry Kirke Brown, "With some shadow of justice might the title of 'the first American sculptor' be claimed for him . . . if the emphasis be transferred to the word *American*."[18] Taft was not a great admirer of Brown's work in general but did laud his equestrian statue of George Washington in New York's Union Square and begrudgingly paid him his due as one of the first artists in the United States to cast work in bronze.[19]

Henry Kirke Brown was born in 1814 in Leyden, Massachusetts. At the age of eighteen, he traveled to Boston to study portraiture with Chester Harding. Soon thereafter, he was introduced to sculpting, and that quickly became his passion. With financial help from friends and savings from a civil engineering post on the first Illinois railroad, Brown had enough money to travel to Italy in 1842, staying abroad for four years. When he returned, he began sculpting American subjects, rejecting the neoclassical themes favored by his contemporaries.[20] He traveled to various American Indian settlements in Michigan and made sketches of the people he encountered. As a result of those travels, Brown created a seven-foot-tall sculpture called *Indian and Panther.* Novel for its native subject, this work is also one of the earliest bronzes created in America.

The large cat in *Panther and Cubs* (figure 3.3) is a reduced version of the feline in Brown's *Indian and Panther.* The snarling form, appropriate for a human-panther interaction, lends itself to this grouping as well, in its depiction of a threatened mother protecting her cubs from some unseen danger (possibly the viewer).[21] In the history of wildlife art, depictions of female animals are rare, partly because of market considerations; portraits of proud stags purchased by men for clubs or libraries have dominated the market for many years. When female animals were depicted, they were often cast as part of a herd or as the protective mother. This pose reinforced gender roles, portraying the female as mother, guarding her children from danger.[22]

Brown's *Panther and Cubs* is the first known American bronze to depict a solo wildlife subject; for that reason, among others, it is highly prized at the National Museum of Wildlife Art. Brown's Romantic desire to break away from the more traditional subjects being carved by his contemporaries and his desire to cast

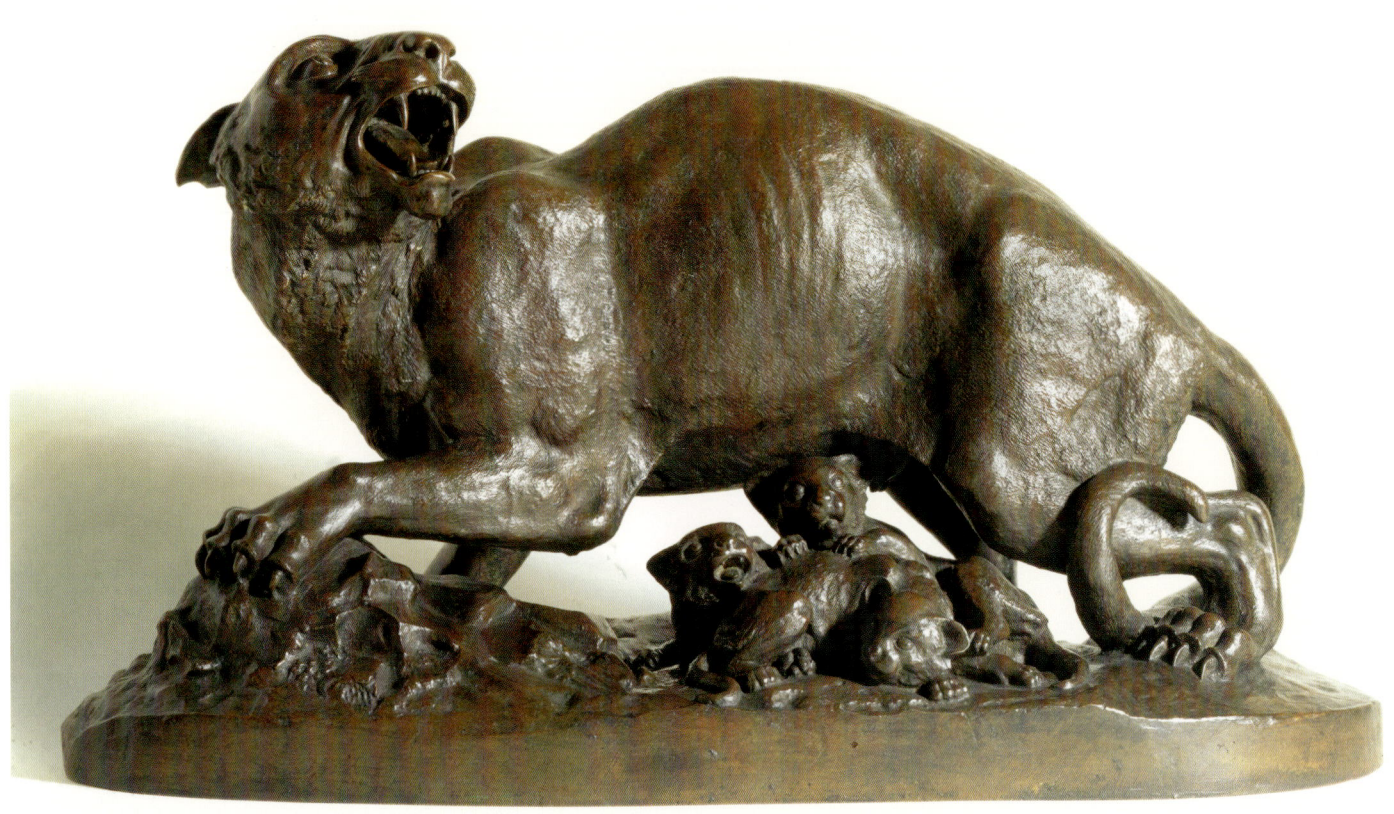

FIGURE 3.3.
HENRY KIRKE BROWN
Panther and Cubs, c. 1850.
Bronze; 9⅞×18⅝×7¾ inches.
JKM Collection.
M1998.013.

in bronze make him a groundbreaking figure in American art. His example would be followed by the first true American animaliers, Edward Kemeys and Alexander Phimister Proctor, who rose to prominence in the years following Brown's death.

EDWARD KEMEYS

United States, 1843–1907

If there were an American counterpart to French animalier Antoine-Louis Barye, it would be Edward Kemeys. Though not as proficient in modeling the motion and diversity of the animal kingdom, Kemeys was the first American to specialize in sculpting animals. Before Kemeys, sculptors such as Henry Kirke Brown and John Quincy Adams Ward included animals as part of greater compositions, only occasionally casting a single wildlife subject (such as Brown's *Panther and Cubs* [figure 3.3]). While Kemeys also sculpted American Indian subjects, animals became his forte and are the subjects for which he is best known. Kemeys said of himself, "The object of my school of sculpture is to perpetuate in enduring form the Indian types and fauna of North America, before they shall have utterly disappeared. . . . I set to work not a moment too soon, hunted the wild animals, and studied them, with the Indians and Trappers for my friends and helpers, and I can say without egotism that I am the pioneer sculptor of the animals of North America."[23] Kemeys focused on the animal life of the American West, in particular. His love of the outdoors began as a young boy spending summers on the Illinois prairie, but he discovered his artistic calling later in life. After returning from duty in the Civil War, Kemeys helped clear trees in New York's Central Park and enjoyed watching the animals in the Central Park Zoo. Legend has it that a chance encounter with a sculptor modeling a wolf at the zoo inspired his first efforts in wax, also of a wolf, in about 1870.[24] Two years later, Kemeys landed a commission from Fairmount Park in Philadelphia for a life-sized group of two wolves contesting over a dead deer. With the proceeds of the sale, in 1873 Kemeys financed a trip to the Rocky Mountains, where he lived among hunters and American Indians while studying wildlife in its natural habitat.

Kemeys traveled to London and Paris in 1877, and there he drew critical acclaim for his distinctive style and subject matter. He disliked the study of caged animals after his experiences in the West, and he condemned the artistic results of such observation as lifeless. Kemeys returned to the United States newly committed to his own artistic vision and practice of studying animals in the wild, and he traveled west whenever funding permitted. In 1883, Kemeys unveiled a large sculpture in Central Park titled *Still Hunt,* which captured a cougar crouching atop a large boulder, giving the illusion that it was about to pounce on unsuspecting passersby.

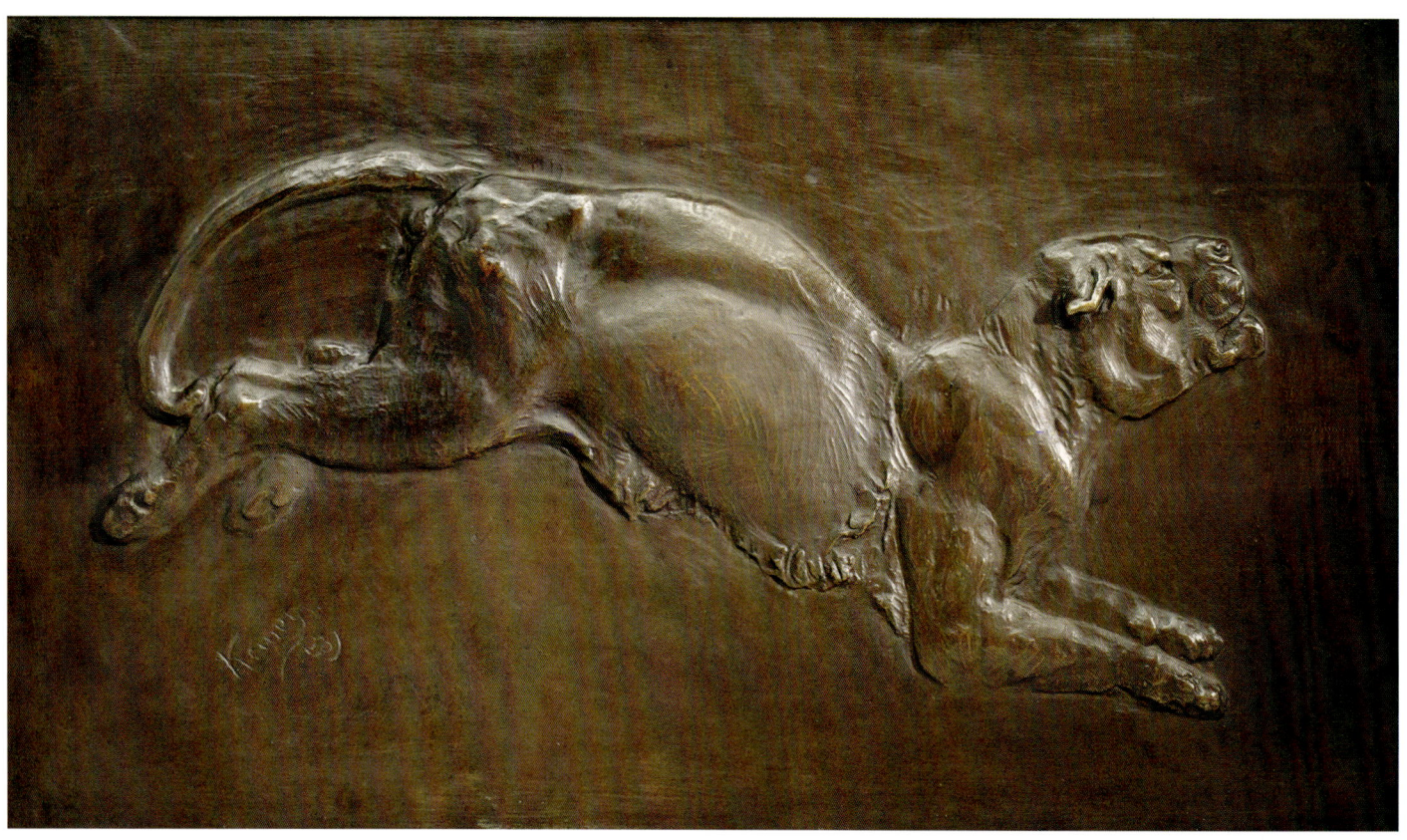

FIGURE 3.4.
EDWARD KEMEYS
At Play, 1894.
Bronze; 13 ¼ × 23 ⅜ inches.
JKM Collection.
JL2001.052.

In 1892, Kemeys moved to Chicago and created twelve life-sized sculptures of grizzly bears, panthers, and bison for the 1893 Columbian Exposition.[25] During this time, Kemeys also modeled the large lions that sit in front of the Chicago Art Institute. Diversifying his output, he cast a line of smaller sculptures and bas-reliefs. An 1894 brochure produced by the Winslow Brothers promoted four reliefs of big cats. One was the well-known *Still Hunt,* a version of the bronze in Central Park. Another relief was *Feeding,* which depicted a jaguar "represented in the act of devouring its prey." The other two reliefs, *At Play* (figure 3.4) and *At Bay* (figure 3.5), are pictured here. Prior to the museum's acquisition of these two, the only known casting of any of these reliefs was *Still Hunt,* in the Metropolitan Museum of Art.[26] The Winslow Brothers brochure states that *Feeding, At Play,* and *At Bay* "were originally designed to take their place in a decorative frieze, and can be most effectively introduced with intervening panels of foliage in like metal." For *At Play,* the brochure notes, "This, with its companion piece, the Jaguar at Bay, shows this beautiful animal at its best under a sportive impulse and with its passions fully aroused. While belonging to the same, the cat family, there are marked differences between the Cougar and the Jaguar, easily traced in the casts."[27]

Early-twentieth-century art historian Lorado Taft said of Kemeys, "It is safe to say that no American artist has more truly epitomized the spirit of the animal. Particularly in rendering the moods of creatures of the cat tribe is he almost epigrammatic."[28] Kemeys's cats indeed captured the essence of the American West

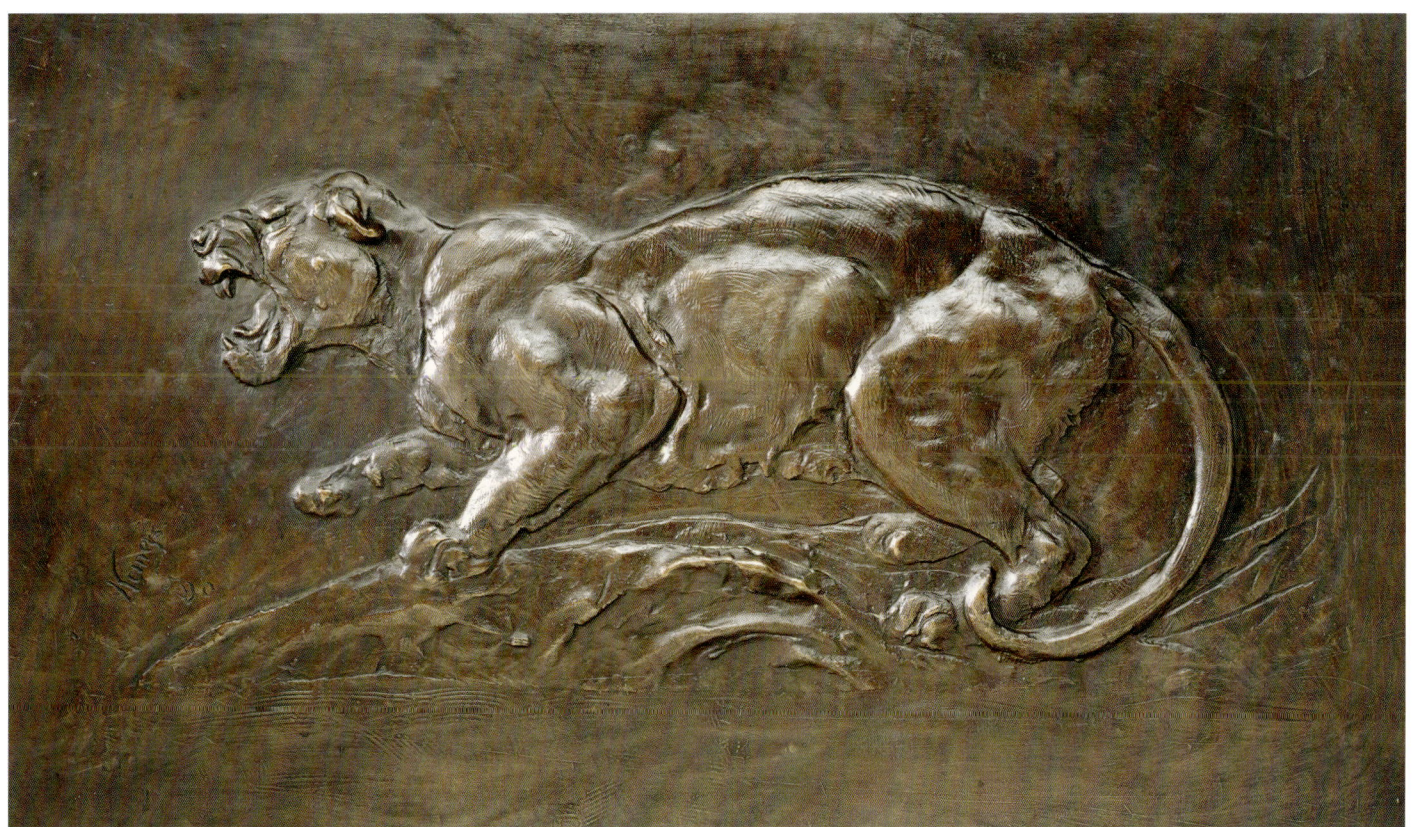

FIGURE 3.5.
EDWARD KEMEYS
At Bay, 1894.
Bronze; 13 ½ × 23 ¾ inches.
JKM Collection.
JL2001.053.

as a wild, untamable place. By 1890, the reality of the West was quite different, but this vision persisted, perpetuated by the work of Kemeys and others who followed him. Kemeys supported himself with his sculpture for the rest of his life, often winning commissions thanks to well-placed acquaintances such as Theodore Roosevelt, who helped him receive one of his last assignments: a set of four bears for the side entrance of the Missouri Building at the Louisiana Purchase Exposition of 1904.[29] Kemeys was awarded a bronze medal at that exposition for fifteen bronzes featured in the art exhibit. After his death in 1907, Kemeys's widow held a retrospective exhibition of his plasters and bronzes at the Corcoran Gallery in Washington, D.C. Kemeys's energetic sculpture captured the essence of American wildlife and inaugurated the proud tradition of animalier sculpture that exists in this country to this day.

ALEXANDER PHIMISTER PROCTOR

CANADA, 1860–1950

Art historian Wayne Craven wrote of Alexander Phimister Proctor, "[W]hile others in his profession were creating robed maidens and assorted neoclassical personifications, Proctor brought to the attention of the world the strength and beauty of the wild animals of America."[30] Following in the footsteps of Henry Kirke Brown and Edward Kemeys, who both returned from Europe dedicated to portraying American subjects, Proctor rose to great fame for his sculptures of wildlife and for his monumental equestrian works, which were among the first to portray American Indians and cowboys.

That Proctor is closely associated with the West is no great surprise, for the West was a central part of his upbringing. As a young boy, he moved with his family from Ontario to Michigan to Iowa, finally settling in Denver, Colorado, where he enjoyed hunting and sketching. Art was also a central part of Proctor's youth. He learned engraving from a local art teacher who had a studio above the *Rocky Mountain News,* and his father encouraged him in his studies. In his autobiography, Proctor wrote, "I can't remember a time when Father didn't have the idea that I should go to Rome or Paris to study art. . . . His ideal sculptors were Phidias and Michelangelo, and he showed me pictures of their work. Raphael was the painter he talked of most, though he liked best the works of the English animal painter Edwin Landseer, and our walls were hung with prints of the latter's paintings. They may have stirred my early interest in wild animals."[31]

The combination of Michelangelo's Renaissance sculpture and Landseer's Romantic painting appears to have had a powerful effect on the young Proctor. In 1885, he traveled to New York to study at the National Academy of Design and the Art Students League. Initially, Proctor studied drawing and hoped to become a painter. But as Peter Hassrick noted in *Alexander Proctor: Wildlife and Western Heroes,* a turn to sculpting came after Proctor saw an exhibition of sculpture by Antoine-Louis Barye in 1889: "Barye's devotion to precise realism and a fidelity of line, combined with romantic themes of wild nature, had obvious aesthetic and practical appeal for Proctor."[32] After sculpting an antelope in wax, Proctor created sculptures of a fawn and a stalking panther.[33] Noting the delicacy with which the fawn was modeled, Frank D. Millet commissioned Proctor to model large-scale animals for the 1893 Columbian Exposition. His animals appeared throughout the grounds alongside those of Edward Kemeys. Praising their work, Lorado Taft

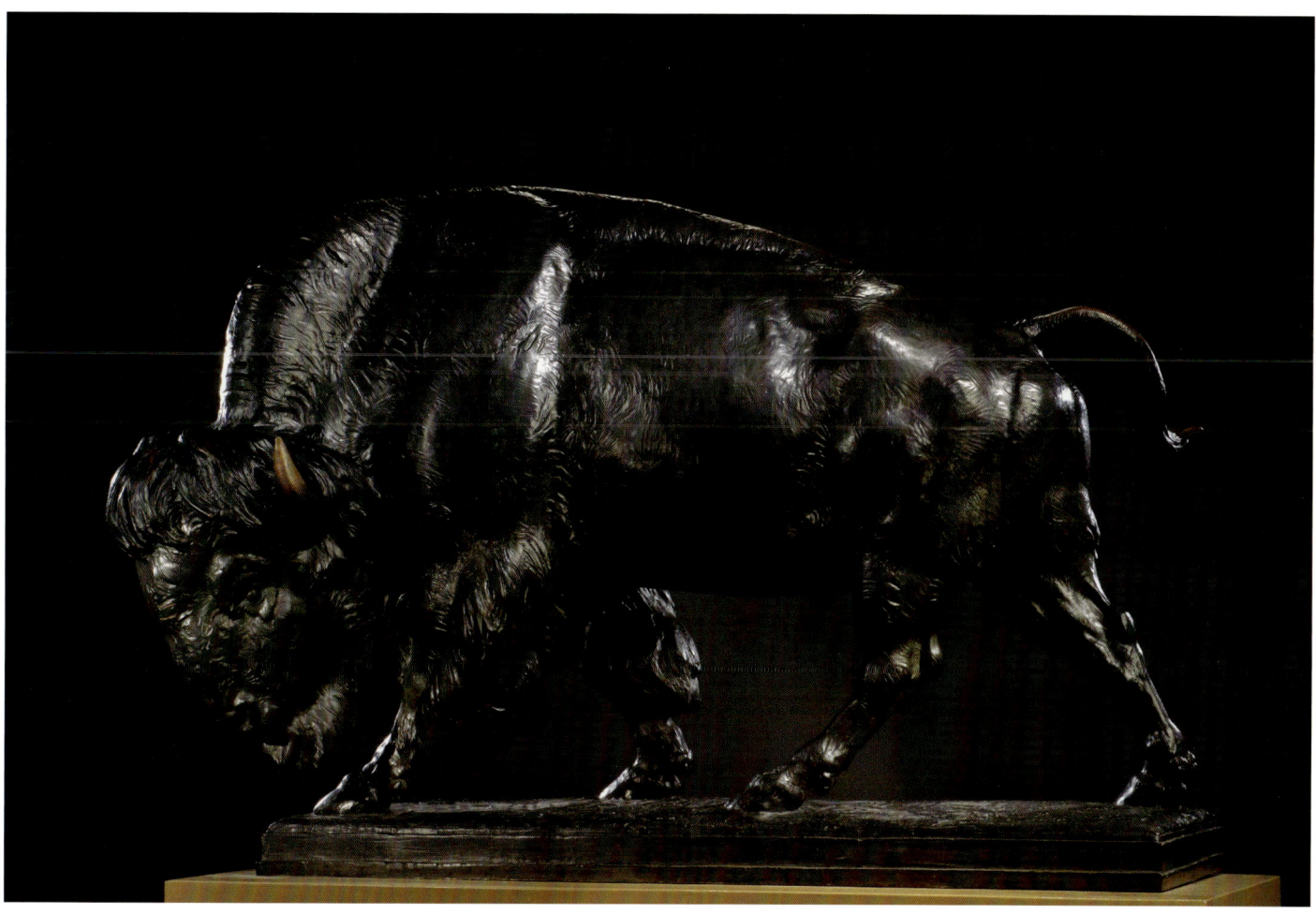

FIGURE 3.6.
ALEXANDER PHIMISTER PROCTOR
Buffalo, 1911.
Bronze; 36 × 56 × 27 inches.
JKM Collection.
J1987.180.

wrote, "Few things, indeed, in the entire Exposition were more interesting and impressive than those great motionless creatures, the native American animals as sculptured by Proctor and Kemeys."[34]

In 1896, Proctor won the Rinehart Scholarship, which enabled him to travel to Paris for further study. Working with noted animalier (and former protégé of Barye) George Gardet, Proctor produced a series of small bronzes, among them a bison with its head down in 1897. Later, he enlarged *Buffalo* for Herbert L. Pratt, who installed it at his Long Island estate. Pratt's unique cast was subsequently acquired by the National Museum of Wildlife Art and is among the most powerful sculptures in the permanent collection (figure 3.6). Instead of sculpting a bison with its head held high, as an epitome of the species, this work displays a particular bison, an individual in midgait, swinging its head to the side, perhaps about to charge or at least move closer to the viewer for further investigation. The implied movement and the dynamic pose single this sculpture out among the many bison produced during this era. Bison proved to be a popular subject for Proctor, who was commissioned to create two monumental ones for the Q Street Bridge in Washington, D.C., in 1911. Proctor continued to garner commissions throughout his life. At age eighty, he completed his last work, *Texas Mustangs*, which stands outside the University of Texas Memorial Museum in Austin.

Although Edward Kemeys was indisputably the first American animalier, Proctor led a slightly younger group of artists who explored the full potential of wildlife sculpture. This next generation took animal sculptures to a whole new level of popularity above and beyond that achieved by Kemeys. Had Kemeys not been followed by these prolific artists, the American animalier movement might never have gotten off the ground. As it stands, however, the wildlife work of Kemeys and that of his immediate followers (Proctor, most notably) laid the foundation for what remains one of the central subjects in American art.

ELI HARVEY
United States, 1860–1957

In his autobiography, Eli Harvey described the genesis of *Lion and Pigeon* (figure 3.7): "During my years in Paris I made just one carving, a lion and pigeon, from a piece of the finest Carrara marble I could obtain. The idea for this composition came from an incident I saw while modeling my study for the Abyssinian lion at the private Ménagerie Pézan. One day the keeper brought a live pigeon for the lion saying, 'It is good for him to have living game sometimes.'" After the keeper tossed the pigeon in the lion's cage, the lion played with it before finally pinning it on its back: "The lion sniffed at the bird but raised his head in apparent disgust at the odor of the feathers. He drew back his head, arched his neck and with ears pricked forward looked at the bird. . . . Though fraught with impending tragedy for the pigeon, nevertheless the attitude of the lion was so natural and the pose so proud that I felt it was worthy to be carved in marble."[35]

Lion and Pigeon won a bronze medal at the Louisiana Purchase Exposition in 1904 and was exhibited along with eight other feline subjects by Harvey. Harvey's marble is executed beautifully, with a gentle sway incorporated into the lion's body, a natural reaction caused by the implied motion of the right paw. Interestingly, the sculptor did nothing to hide the fact that the subject was modeled in a menagerie. Beginning with Barye, other sculptors and painters had gone to great lengths to take the animal out of the zoo and create an impression of true wildness. Harvey's contemporary, the animal painter and teacher Paul Meyerheim, often painted animals as he saw them, cages and all, but this form of wildlife in art never reached the heights achieved by depictions of the same creatures unfettered. Harvey's choice to rely on zoo animals certainly did not hamper his reputation; among many other assignments was a commission to create the sculptures for the New York Zoological Society's Lion House in 1901.

Eli Harvey was born in Ogden, Ohio, in 1860. He studied at the Art Institute of Cincinnati and in the Art Department of MacMicken University, where he took portrait commissions in an effort to raise money to travel to Paris. In 1889, after seven years in Cincinnati, he traveled to France to study at the Académie Julian. At this time, the Barbizon school was in vogue, and Harvey was impressed with the naturalistic style espoused by its members. But as Harvey spent more time at the Jardin des Plantes and private menageries in Paris, he decided to focus on sculpting. He wrote, "As I continued my drawings of the animals which I had

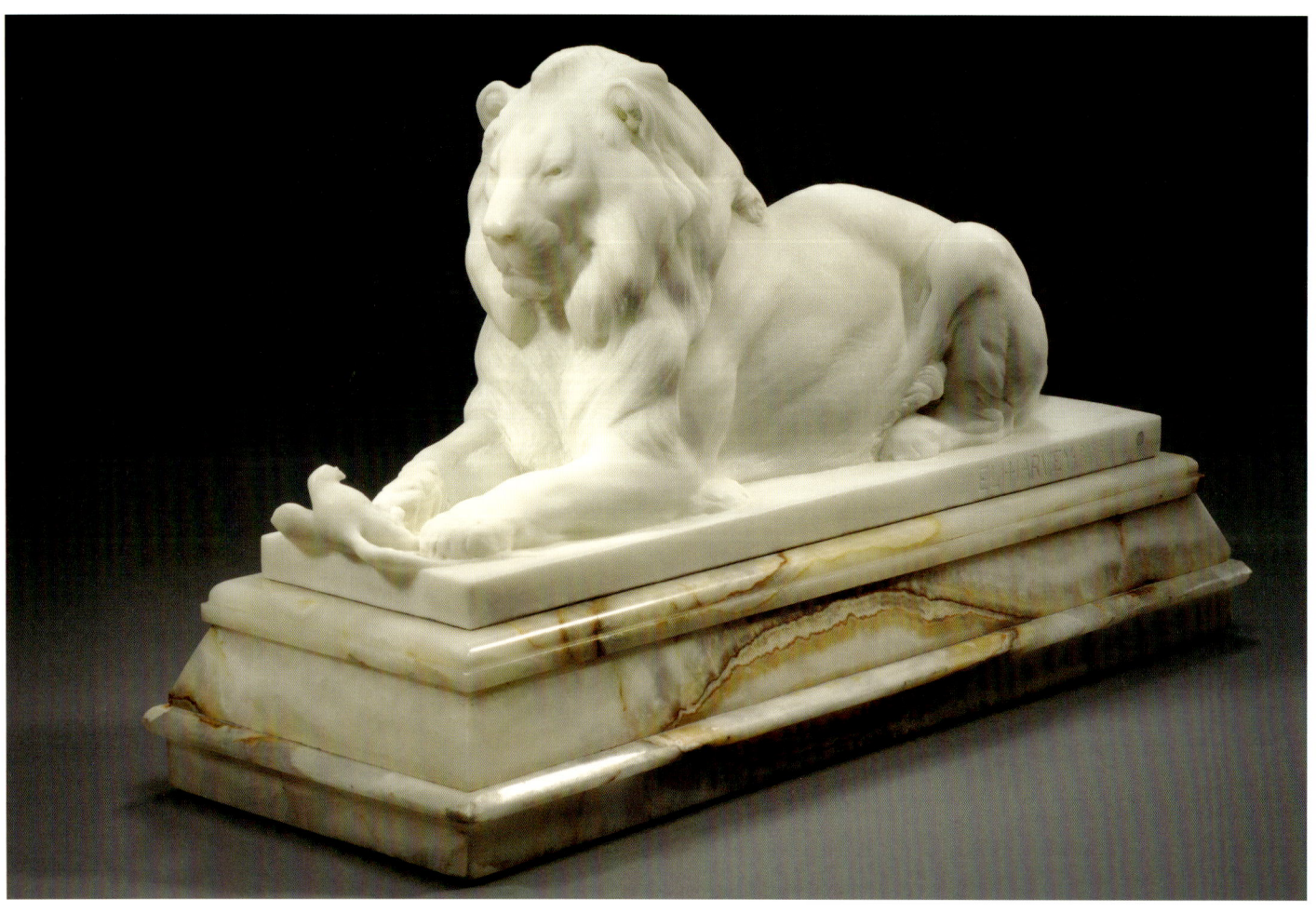

FIGURE 3.7.
ELI HARVEY
Lion and Pigeon, 1900.
White marble and onyx base;
10 ½ × 19 ¾ × 7 inches.
National Museum of
Wildlife Art Collection.
M2003.103.

planned to place in my picture, I discovered before long that to model the animals would not only be just a better way but the best, and indeed only way, thoroughly to know the animals."[36] In Paris, Harvey was mentored by the animalier Emmanuel Frémiet and by the accomplished painter (and the head of the École des Beaux Arts) Jean-Léon Gérôme. Harvey lived and worked in New York City until he moved to Alhambra, California, in the late 1920s. His best-known works include the lions at the Bronx Zoo, an elk for the Order of Elks, and a bear for Brown University (the university's mascot).

EDWIN DEMING
United States, 1860–1942

It is this man and this race, as far as possible uninfluenced by civilization, that I wish to set forth . . . the way of living, customs, decorations of lodges, life in the tipi, transportation, everything that can be told; besides a hundred thing [*sic*] that there is no record of at all, children playing with make-believe travois, animals, tame crows.

Edwin Deming, quoted in Frink, Edward Deming

Deming's art incorporates a broad sense of humor and sensitivity to his subjects, whether American Indian or wild animal. This sense of humor certainly appears in *Mutual Surprise* (figure 3.8). In a work reminiscent of Alexander Phimister Proctor's *Cub Bear and Rabbit* (1894), Deming skillfully models a chance encounter between a turtle and a bear; the cub rears back as the turtle juts its head forward, reacting to one another in a way that is both believable and funny. Art historian Peter Hassrick noted that Proctor and Deming shared adjoining studios in 1887 and that Deming's illustrations of animals and American Indian life may have been an inspiration for Proctor's small bronze.[37] The theme of this piece is echoed also in Charles Russell's later sculpture *Oh Mother, What Is It?* which depicts a mother bear and two cubs eyeing an approaching porcupine with curiosity. William Holbrook Beard described bears as natural subjects for humorous compositions, a sentiment clearly shared by these artists.

Deming was born in Ashland, Ohio, in 1860. He received some education at the Art Students League in New York and spent a year in Paris, where he studied at the Académie Julian from 1884 to 1885 with Gustave Boulanger and Jules Lefebvre. Despite this training, he considered himself largely self-taught. Deming's sympathetic paintings of American Indians came directly out of his long-standing relationships with various tribes; his animal sculptures also emerged from his experiences out west. On one trip, when Deming, his wife, and their six children were visiting friends among the Blackfeet Indians, the tribe adopted the family and gave Deming the name "Eight Bears" to commemorate the size of his family. Deming subsequently named his home and studio in Greenwich Village "The Lodge of the Eight Bears." In addition to his successful painting and sculpting career, Deming collaborated with his wife on a series of children's books and illustrated a children's book written by his daughter Alden. In the 1900s, he began sculpting animals—including bears, bison, and big cats—with

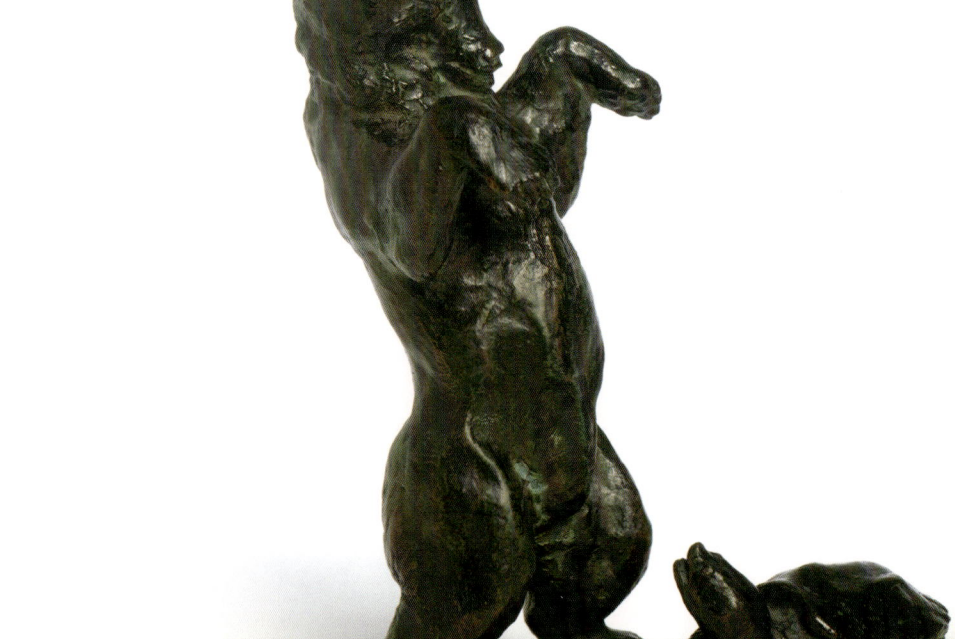

regularity.[38] In comparison to other American animaliers, Deming added a touch of humor and gentleness to his work; he did not always use his sculpture to make grand pronouncements on the state of the nation but instead looked at wildlife in different states, illustrating the range of potential within the subject.

PAUL WAYLAND BARTLETT
UNITED STATES, 1865–1925

In his own Paris studio, at just twenty-two years of age, Bartlett completed *Bohemian Bear Tamer* (figure 3.9), a masterpiece. Lorado Taft remarked, "His skill in the modelling of animal forms is shown in the delightfully clumsy bear cubs of the group in question."[39] Taft was referring to the larger version of *Bear Tamer*, which featured two cubs. For the reduced-size sculpture, Bartlett included just one bear, placing it in front of the tamer. This sculpture depicts a European subject, with a Bohemian (or Czech; the figure is not an American Indian, as is sometimes assumed). holding a whip behind his back, taming a small bear cub The plaster brought Bartlett his first critical acclaim when it was displayed at the Paris Salon in 1887. At the 1889 Exposition Universelle, a bronze cast was awarded a Grand Prix. Later, the plaster was displayed at the Columbian Exposition of 1893, along with Bartlett's more distinctly American Indian sculpture, *The Ghost Dancer.*

Bear Tamer has direct ties to two earlier American sculptures: Henry Kirke Brown's *Indian and Panther* and John Quincy Adams Ward's *Indian Hunter* (two of the earliest pieces to depict American animals). Wayne Craven in *Sculpture in America* noted that Bartlett "demonstrated his mastery of anatomy in the human figure, and his special talent for modeling in lively masses is revealed in the [man's] hair and in the shaggy form of the bear. The liveliness of the surfaces and the suggestion of forms—rather than a literal depiction of them—were characteristics of the art then being taught in Paris."[40] This "new style" in which Bartlett sculpted reflected a more impressionistic sensibility. This sensibility was embodied in the work of Rodin, in whose studio Bartlett served as an assistant.[41]

Bartlett was born in January 1865, in New Haven, Connecticut, to Truman Howe Bartlett, a sculptor, teacher, and author. At age four, his family moved to Paris, hoping that the young Bartlett would benefit from a formal European education. In 1880, when he was fifteen, he entered the École des Beaux Arts and studied with sculptor Pierre-Jules Cavelier and at the Jardin des Plantes with the animalier Emmanuel Frémiet. That year he also exhibited a portrait bust of his grandmother at the Paris Salon. By the time he was twenty-four, he had become a member of the Salon Jury. Bartlett completed several public commissions, including sculptures of Michelangelo and Columbus for the Library of Congress and an equestrian statue of the marquis de Lafayette that was installed outside the Louvre.[42]

FIGURE 3.9. (FOLLOWING SPREAD)
PAUL WAYLAND BARTLETT
Bohemian Bear Tamer,
1887 (front and side views).
Bronze; 26⅞ × 12¾ × 16¾ inches.
National Museum of Wildlife Art Collection.
M2002.001.

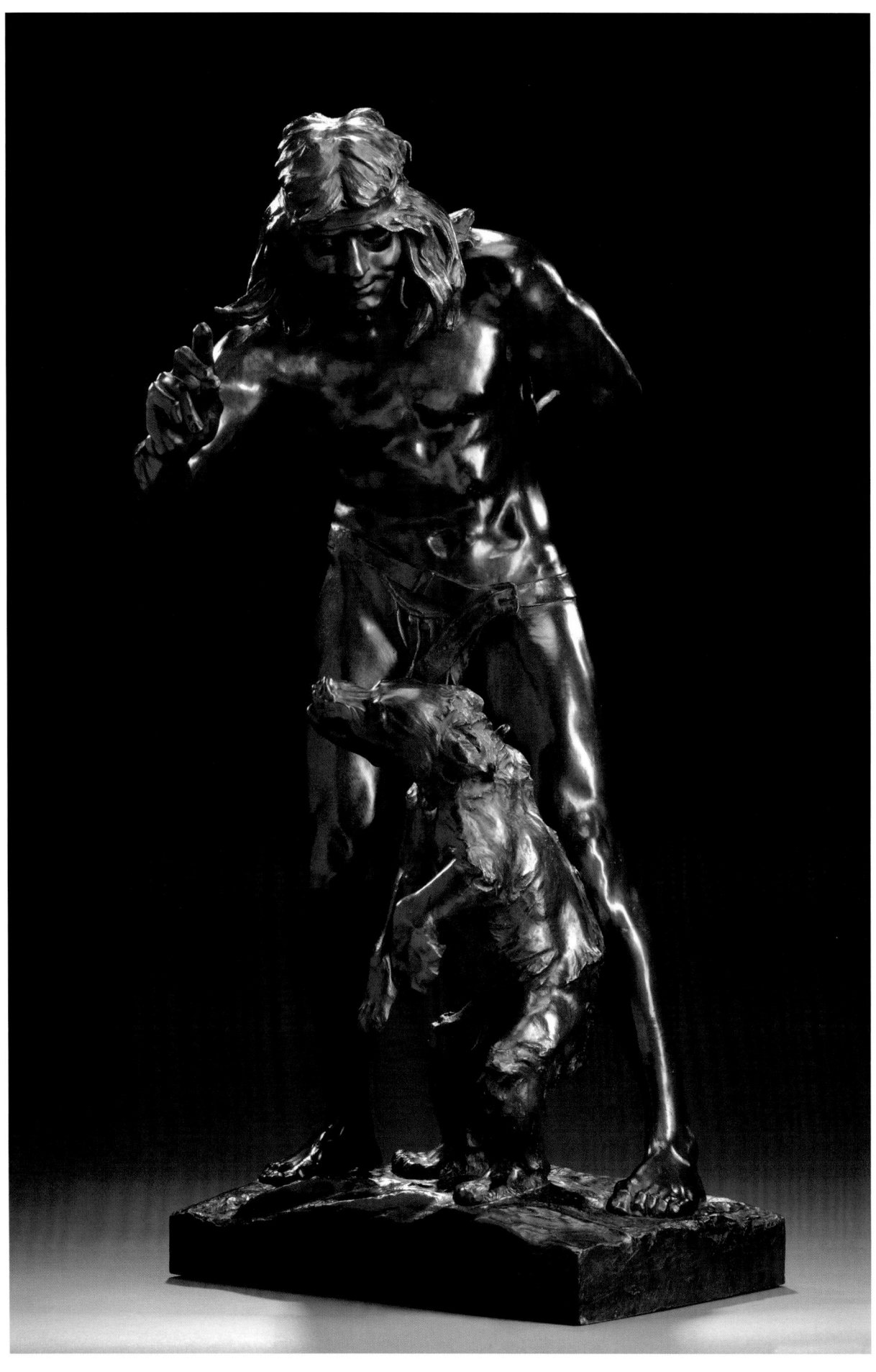

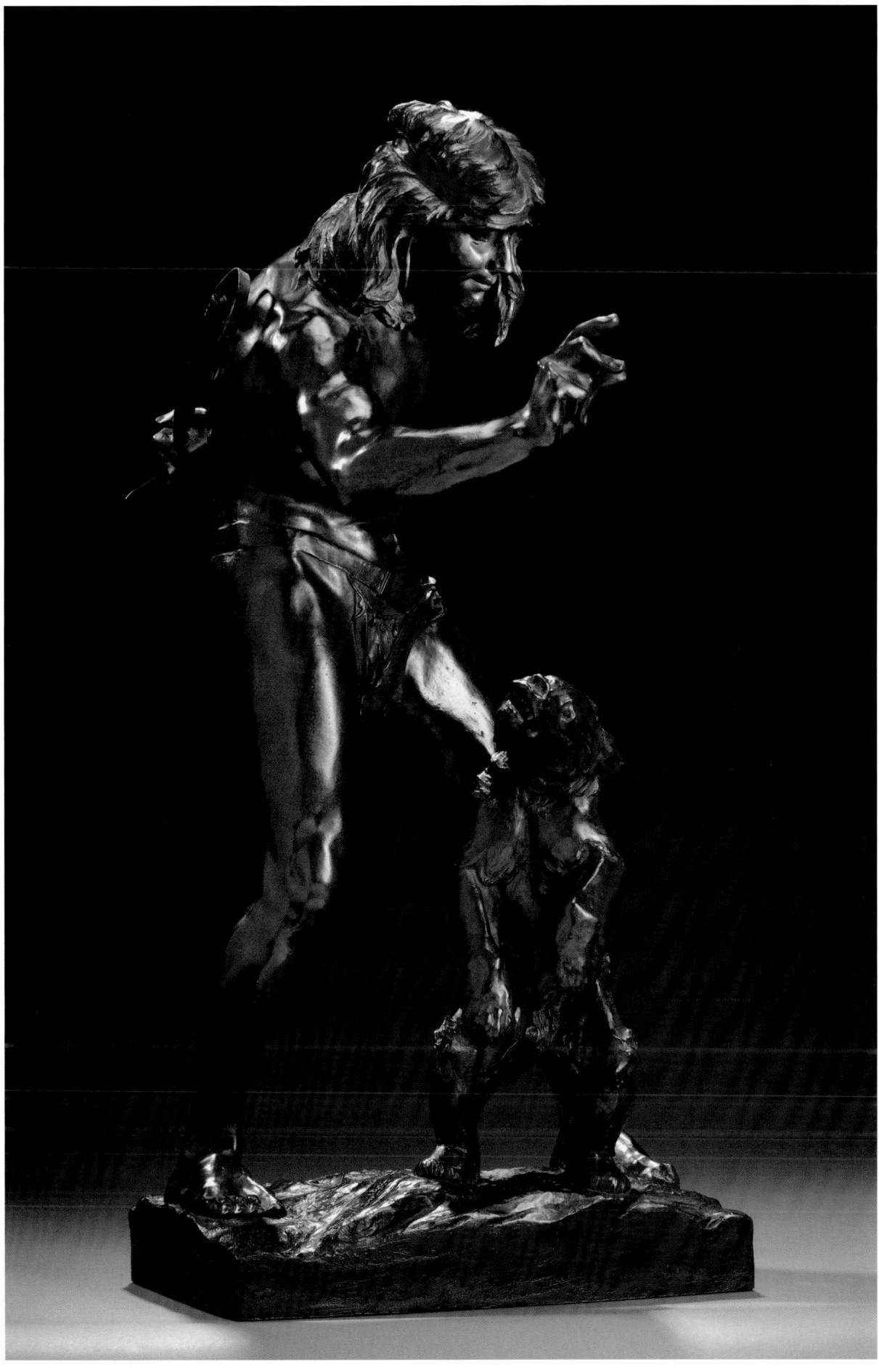

Bartlett's sculpture and career demonstrate the artistic connection between France and the United States, prevalent in an era when notable American artists were studying and working in Paris: John Singer Sargent, James Abbott McNeil Whistler, and Mary Cassatt among them. Bartlett's *Bohemian Bear Tamer* is not only a prime example of this cultural interchange but also a great example of a small but growing segment of the collection of the National Museum of Wildlife Art, one that investigates humanity's relationship with wildlife in a more literal fashion—in art depicting humans and animals interacting. Works such as Bartlett's display an ongoing fascination with wildlife but more directly speak to humanity's power over wildlife: to tame, control, and even train it to fit into our concept of what it should be and how it should act.

HENRY MERWIN SHRADY
UNITED STATES, 1871–1922

Henry Merwin Shrady's rapid rise to fame began with a commission to enlarge two small sculptures for the 1901 Pan-American Exposition in Buffalo, New York. The two bronzes in question were a bison and a moose that Shrady had sculpted using animals at the Bronx Zoo as models. Karl Bitter, director of sculpture at the Pan-American Exposition, saw casts of the sculptures and was impressed. He offered to share his studio and help Shrady enlarge his work. The moose grew to nine feet tall and the bison to eight. In all, Shrady completed eight enlargements to adorn the bridges at the exposition. These wildlife monuments link him to two other preeminent American animaliers: Edward Kemeys and Alexander P. Proctor, who sculpted large animals for the 1893 Columbian Exposition in Chicago. Shrady's career parallels that of Proctor, as he went on to achieve great fame for his monumental work. The viewer can readily see why Shrady's *Bull Moose* (figure 3.10) appealed to Bitter; the upright stance and alert pose looks monumental even in small scale. Pairing it with the similarly proud *Elk Buffalo* (figure 3.11) made for a powerful combination.

As a young man, Shrady had no intention of pursuing art as his occupation. He studied law at Columbia University before serving as president of his brother-in-law's match company. Shrady sketched animals at a pet shop on his way home in the evenings and used his horse as a model for sculpting, dousing it with water to reveal the muscular structure. As Donna Hassler notes in her biographical sketch on Shrady, jeweler Theodore B. Starr was impressed by Shrady's early work and purchased the copyright from him for *Bull Moose, The Empty Saddle,* and *Elk Buffalo (Monarch of the Plains).* Starr featured Shrady's sculptures in his gallery on Fifth Avenue in New York City. Shrady's second major commission came in 1901 (the same year Bitter asked him to enlarge *Bull Moose* and *Elk Buffalo*); the commission was for an equestrian statue of George Washington at Valley Forge, to be placed on the Williamsburg Bridge Plaza in Brooklyn (now Continental Army Plaza). A member of the committee sponsoring the competition for the sculpture saw a casting of Shrady's cavalry horse, *The Empty Saddle,* in the window of Starr's gallery and urged him to submit a design.[43] With his confidence buoyed after receiving the Washington commission, Shrady entered another competition to create the memorial for Ulysses S. Grant in Washington, D.C. Competing

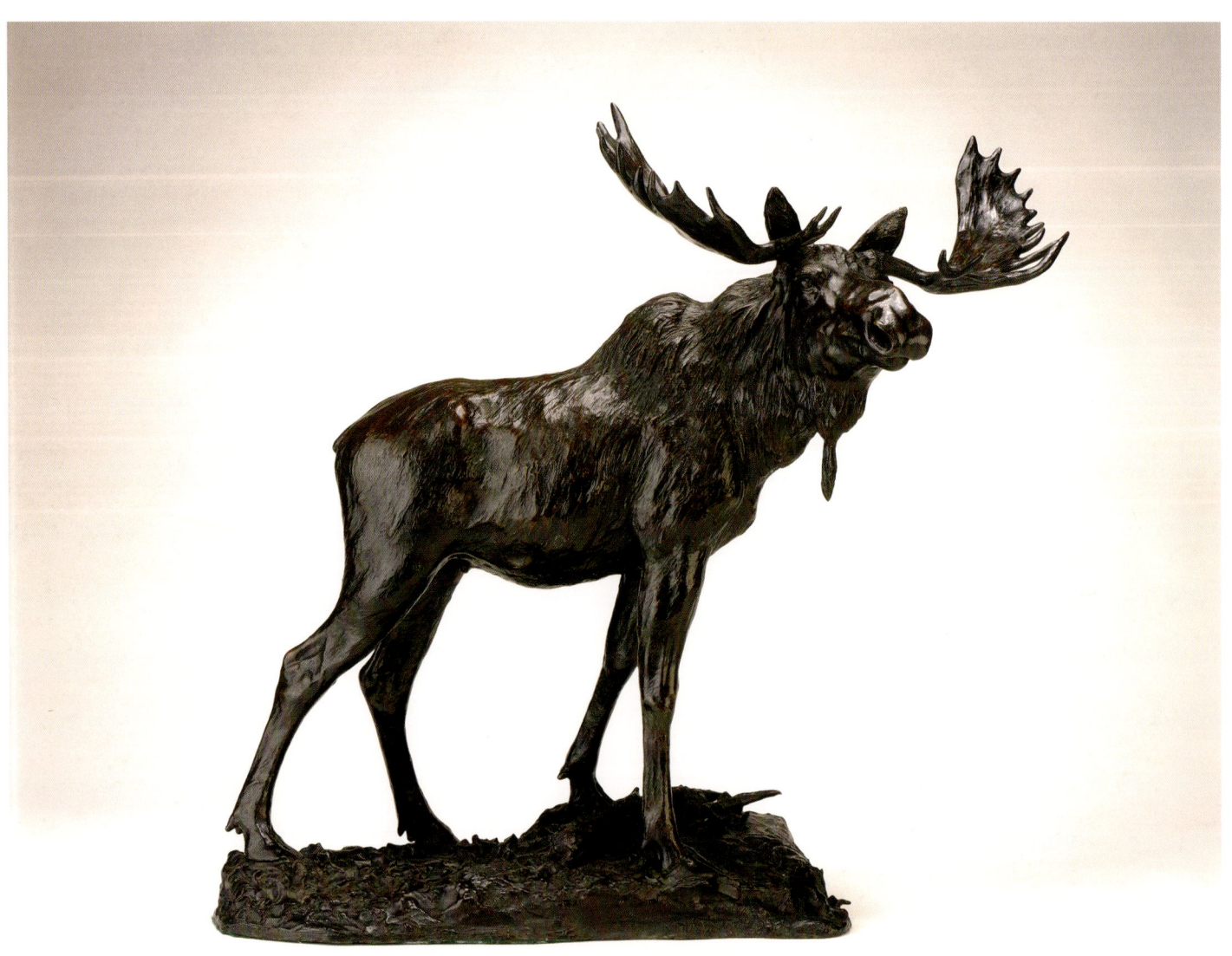

against the top sculptors of his age, Shrady professed with characteristic modesty, "I had no expectation of winning; but there is always a chance of your doing so in a competition."[44] He did win and spent the next twenty-two years of his life on the commission, dying just weeks before the memorial was unveiled.[45]

Similar to Kemeys's and Proctor's monumental mammals at the Columbian Exposition, Shrady's *Bull Moose* and *Elk Buffalo* exemplify the powerful ideology of the wilderness that continued to impact America's sense of self. By 1901, the bison, in particular, had come to symbolize both the great loss and the squander of natural resources while simultaneously representing the success of easterners settling the West. Great animals such as the moose and the bison, represented in such urban contexts as an exposition, reminded Americans of the wilderness on which the nation had been built—a wilderness that was growing increasingly segmented into national parks and preserves, places in need of protection from the ongoing incursions of commercial interests.

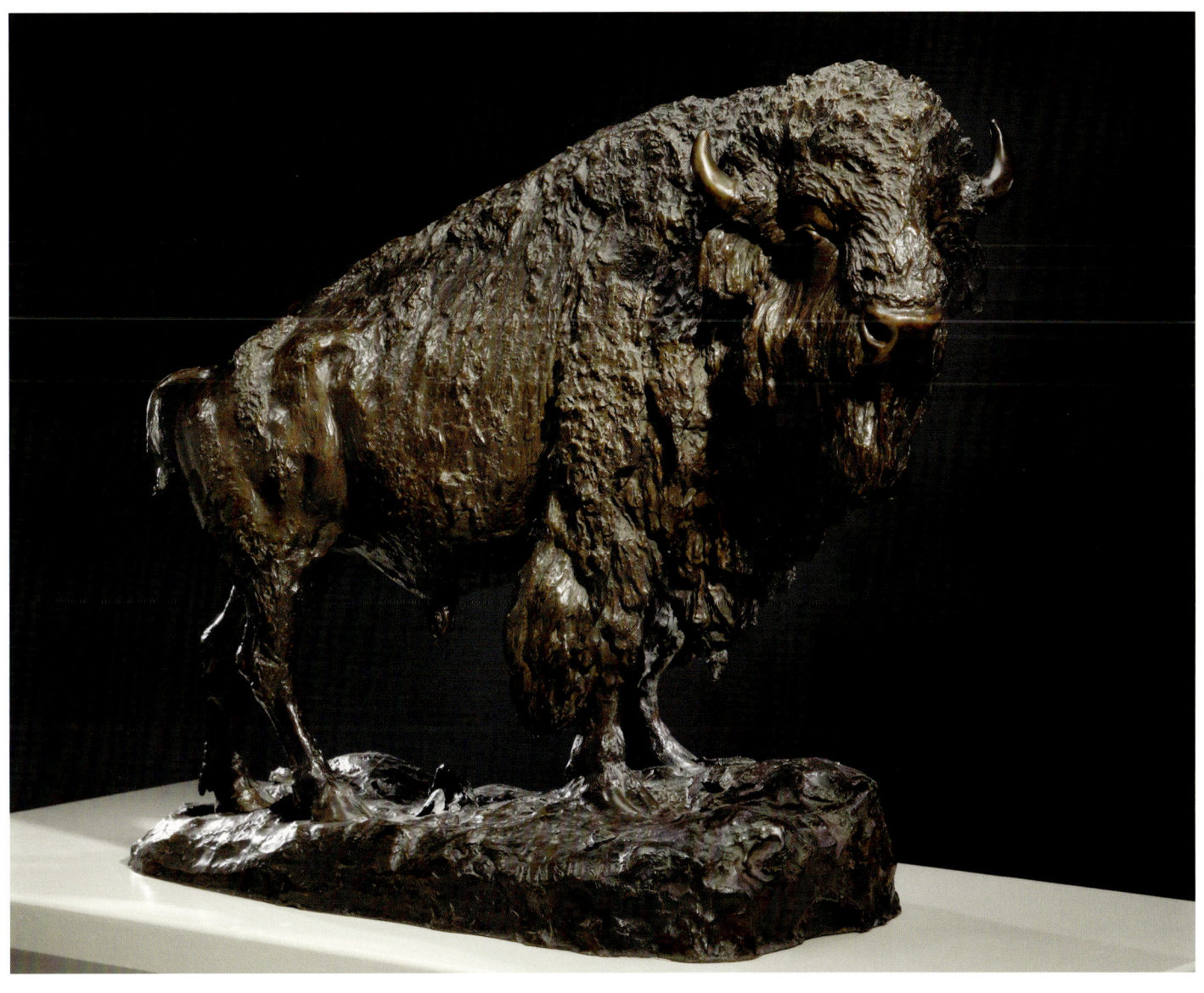

FIGURE 3.11.

HENRY MERWIN SHRADY

Elk Buffalo, 1900.

Bronze; 23 ¾ × 28 × 10 ¾ inches.

JKM Collection.

JL1993.030.

FREDERICK GEORGE RICHARD ROTH

United States, 1872–1944

Working decades after Barye, Frederick Roth focused on subjects reflecting a new sensibility that did not cast animals in battle, metaphorically representing good and evil, but cast them instead in a more impressionistic fashion, capturing a fleeting moment in life. Roth's works present the animals more naturalistically, posed as he saw them in the various zoos around New York City. Like Henry Shrady, Roth became a favorite of Karl Bitter, director of the 1901 Pan-American Exposition in Buffalo. Bitter went on to become director of sculpture at both the 1904 Louisiana Purchase Exposition in Saint Louis and the 1915 Panama-Pacific International Exposition in San Francisco; in both cases, he involved Roth in the overall sculpture program. At the 1904 exposition, Roth exhibited a polar bear sculpture, for which he won a silver medal. He modeled another group of polar bears in 1905, and this was instrumental in his election to the National Academy of Design.[46]

Clearly, one of Roth's favorite subjects was polar bears. His first bear sculpture presented a single subject, striding leisurely along a flat plinth, head swaying to the side. Soon thereafter, Roth sculpted the polar bear group featured here (figure 3.12), displaying two bears in motion: one standing atop an icy outcropping, perhaps sniffing the air for the scent of seals; the other climbing over a small ledge. This composition is particularly powerful, as it rises to a crescendo in an inverted triangular form, widening from the bottom to the top, with the gently curving back and neck of the top bear leading the eye back around and down the sculpture. Roth's polar bear works were popular in his time; the Bowdoin Class of 1912 commissioned a striding bear sculpture from Roth to commemorate its lost members and as a tribute to the school's long history of sponsoring polar exploration. One of Bowdoin's most famous graduates was Rear Admiral Robert E. Peary (class of 1877), who, in 1909, led the first team to reach the North Pole.[47]

Before Roth was commissioned to create his famous works at world's fairs, he attended the Academy of Fine Arts in Vienna and the Royal Academy in Berlin, receiving instruction from Edmund von Hellmer and Paul Meyerheim, respectively. At the Pan-American Exposition of 1901, his sculpture of a racing chariot, with one wheel off the ground and many horse hooves in midair, received acclaim but also prompted controversy; some critics felt that this composition was too dynamic for sculpture.[48] Roth is best known today for the work he created in New York's Central Park. *Balto,* his sculpture of an Eskimo dog, is among the most

FIGURE 3.12.
FREDERICK GEORGE RICHARD ROTH
Polar Bears, 1910.
Bronze; 15 ½ × 13 ½ × 10 ½ inches.
JKM Collection.
JL1994.053.

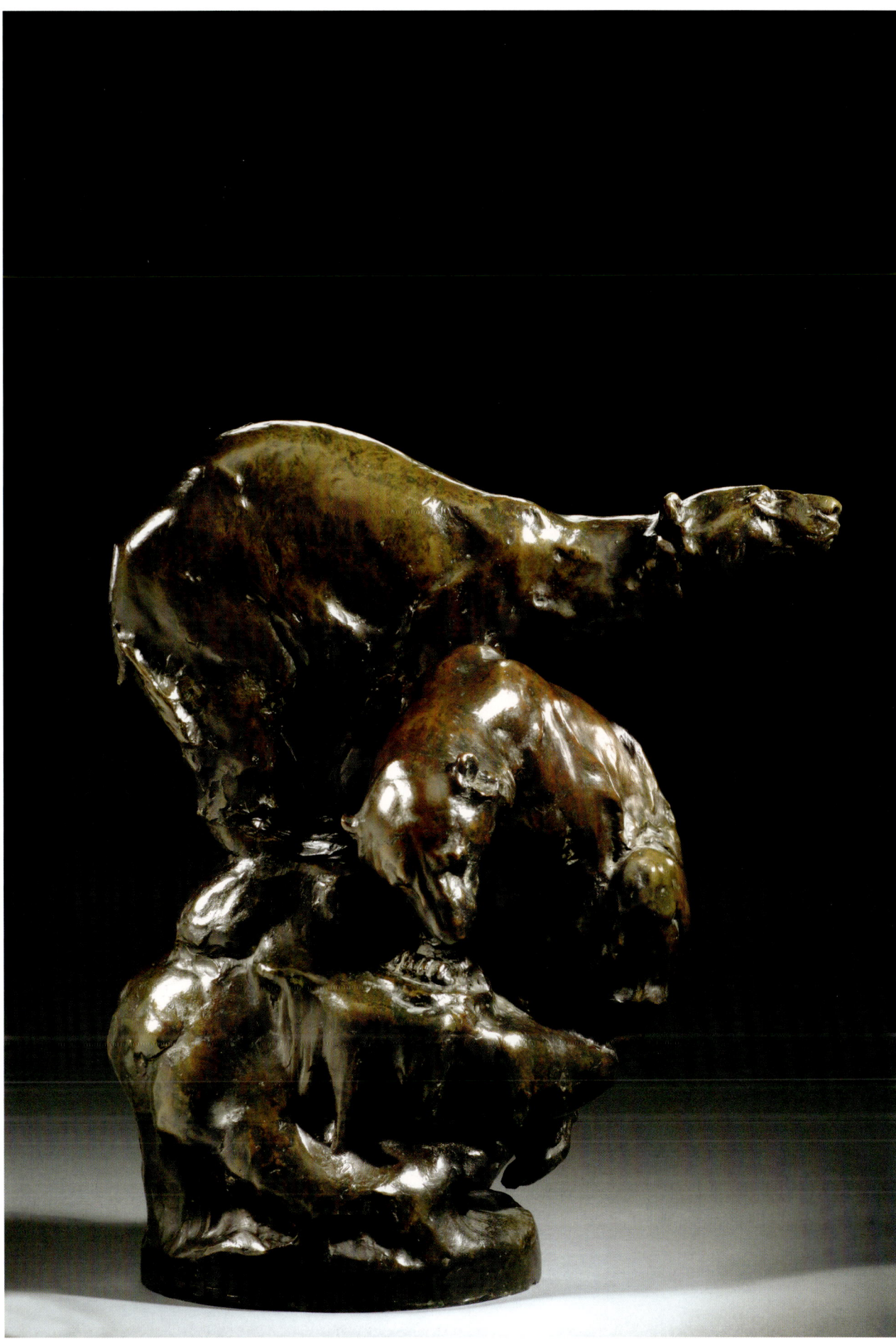

popular. Balto died leading a sled-dog team that raced antitoxin to Nome, Alaska (the inspiration for the Iditarod), during a diphtheria epidemic in 1925. During the Great Depression, Roth acted as chief sculptor for the New York City Parks Department and installed *Dancing Goat* and *Honey Bear* near the Central Park Zoo cafeteria. In 1938, he and a team of other artists created a whimsical homage to Mother Goose. As noted in the introduction to this chapter, Roth said that he sculpted during a more psychological era, when animals were not cast as types but sculpted as individuals. This often resulted in quieter and more contemplative work than that of his predecessor, Barye, but also led to pieces that were more lighthearted and humorous, such as the sculpture he created while working in Central Park.[49]

ARTHUR PUTNAM
United States, 1873–1930

The subject of Arthur Putnam's *Puma and Deer* (figure 3.13) has a strong lineage in animalier sculpture. Antoine-Louis Barye sculpted *Panther Attacking a Stag* in 1836, and Edward Kemeys tackled the subject in 1876. Barye's work displays an epic battle with the feline about to emerge victorious. Kemeys's version displays a moment at the peak of battle, but which animal will win is unclear. In Putnam's sculpture, the altercation is clearly over, won by the puma. Straining under the deer's weight, the predator carries the prey slung over its back. A principal quality of Putnam's work is the smooth modeling of his figures. He did not attempt to render hair or other texture with fidelity but instead gave a sense of the shapes of his animals without delving into detail.

According to biographer Julie Heyneman, Putnam often sculpted from memory, finding the study of live animals distracting. Putnam remarked, "The damn thing disturbs me by thrusting his individual peculiarities between my conception and the work I am doing."[50] On the basis of a strong knowledge of anatomy and a clear sense of how an animal looks in certain poses, Putnam created sculptures that were based on the internal workings of his mind rather than the external appearance of a particular animal, creating sculptures that said as much about him as they did about the wild kingdom. Not without a sense of humor, Putnam sometimes deflected compliments with a wry turn of phrase. Upon seeing a freshly modeled puma, for example, a wealthy client remarked, "You were thinking of some great event in the early history of mankind—a cataclysm, perhaps. And when the tumult reigned supreme, out of chaos came this animal, silent, snarling. Tell me, Mr. Putnam, was it not such a thought that inspired you to make this darling little panther?"

After a brief pause and with a slight smile, Putnam replied, "Started to make a cow and this thing just evolved itself."[51] Putnam's deflating response indicates his discomfort at taking the lofty critique from his visitor. However, by sculpting free-form from his imagination rather than by rigorously studying and rendering any animal in particular, he opened himself to such a reading, whether he intended to or not.

Putnam's upbringing began in Omaha, Nebraska, where he spent more time outdoors than at his studies. He was sent to Kemper Hall Military Academy in Davenport, Iowa, but was expelled soon after. He then worked in various

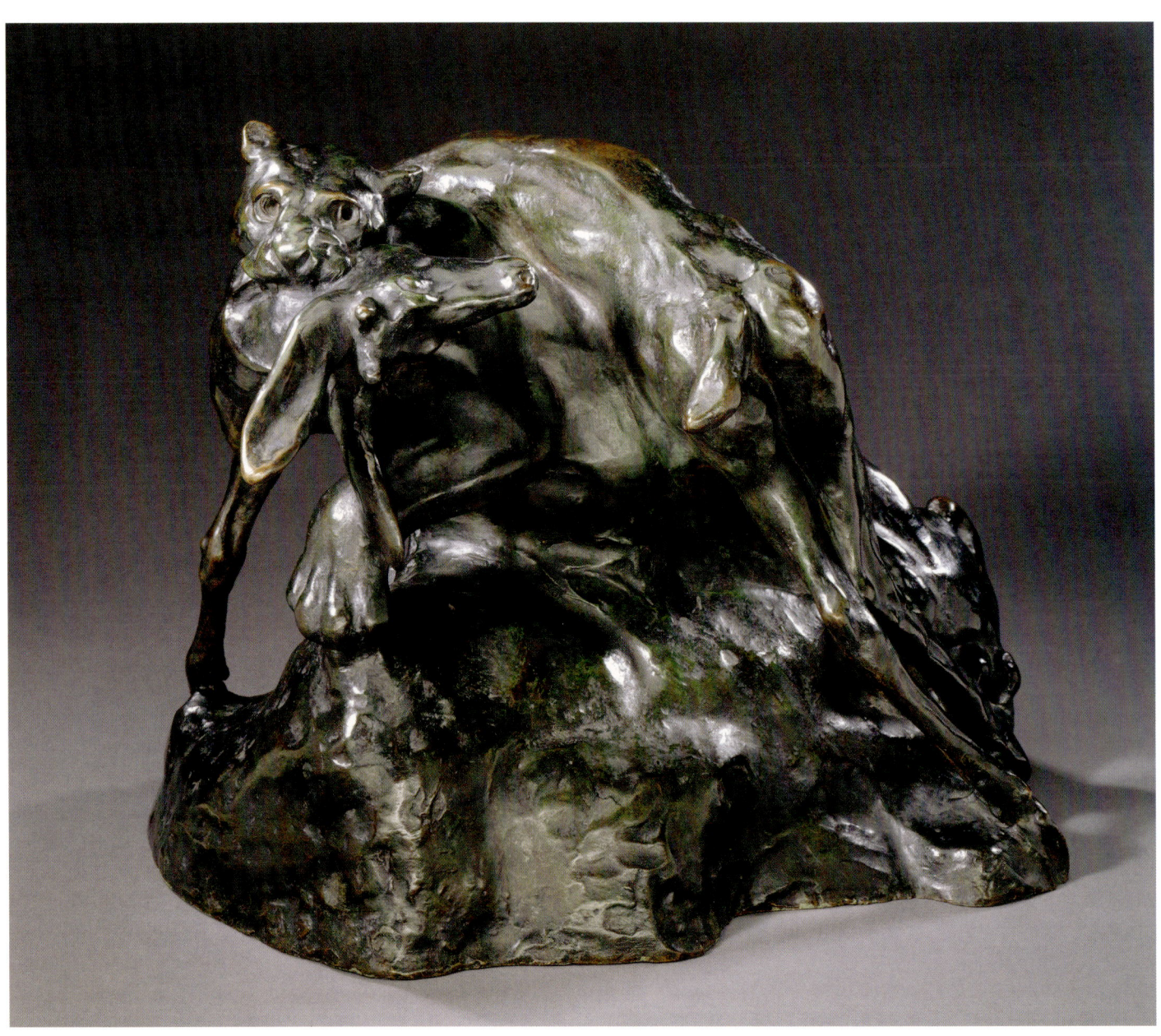

FIGURE 3.13.
ARTHUR PUTNAM
Puma and Deer, 1902.
Bronze; 11½ × 15 × 11½ inches.
JKM Collection.
JL1995.003.

places, ranging from a photoengraver's office to an iron foundry. In 1894, he moved to San Francisco and enrolled at the Art Students League, taking lessons from Julie Heyneman. Putnam assisted sculptor Rupert Schmidt and worked at a slaughterhouse, which undoubtedly helped him learn about animal anatomy. He also apprenticed with Edward Kemeys in 1897 in Chicago. He traveled to Europe in 1905 and exhibited work at the 1906 Salon in Rome and the 1907 Salon in Paris. In Paris, Putnam saw the work of Rodin, whose groundbreaking sculpture clearly influenced the younger American's style. Putnam returned to San Francisco after the cataclysmic earthquake and fire had destroyed most of the city in 1906. He began sculpting architectural elements to aid reconstruction efforts, modeling everything from bank friezes to street-lamp bases.[52] Putnam's career came to an effective end in 1911 when an operation to remove a brain tumor resulted in partial paralysis and left him subject to severe mood swings. His work continued to be exhibited, however. Most notably, it was included in the famous New York Armory Show of 1913, where modern work such as Marcel Duchamp's *Nude Descending a Staircase* changed the course of art in the twentieth century. One can imagine the smoothly modeled forms of Putnam's pumas (not too far removed from the impressionistic forms of Rodin) striking a chord of moderation in the midst of the cacophony that accompanied the exhibition. The strength and grace of Putnam's sculptures are undeniable, whether they came from a deep primordial place within him or simply evolved as he worked with the clay.

ANNA HYATT HUNTINGTON
United States, 1876–1973

In art featuring wildlife, the individual biography of the subject is rarely known. In the case of Anna Vaughn Hyatt Huntington's *Jaguar* and *Reaching Jaguar* (figure 3.14), however, quite a bit is known about the sitter. His name was Señor Lopez, and he was the first feline inhabitant of the Lion House at the New York Zoological Society (now known as the Bronx Zoo). Señor Lopez was imported from South America, making an arduous journey across the Atlantic to England, then crossing again to the United States. In the midst of his travels, he began to lose weight owing to a broken tooth. Trying to ease Señor Lopez's pain, his caretaker suggested putting some cocaine on the end of a stick and rubbing that onto Lopez's gums. Before this cure was attempted, the caretaker tried feeding Señor Lopez some finely cut beef, which appeased him.[53]

After being safely delivered to New York, Señor Lopez took up residence in the Lion House. Novel in its construction, the building was designed with artists in mind, incorporating a studio room with a glass enclosure through which an animal could be viewed. In 1903, Huntington took advantage of this space when modeling Señor Lopez in both crouching and reaching positions. She applied the finishing touches to the sculptures in Paris in 1907. Cats often appeared in Huntington's work; these two sculptures stand out as masterpieces, representing the peak of her considerable artistic achievements. Casts of the jaguars are in the collections of the Metropolitan Museum of Art and Brookgreen Gardens. Stone versions can be found at the Bronx Zoo and at the Mariners Museum in Newport News, Virginia. The National Museum of Wildlife Art's jaguars, the first in the edition, were purchased by George W. French of Davenport, Iowa. They were installed outside for many years, resulting in the green patina (which occurs when bronze is left exposed to the elements). As gateposts, these works are powerful signifiers, looking down from their perches at approaching visitors. As sculptures, seen on a less imposing level, they are fluid, sinuous works that capture the lithe feline character with incredible acuity.

Huntington was a remarkable figure in the world of art. Her father was a professor of paleontology and zoology at the Massachusetts Institute of Technology and Boston University, so she grew up in an atmosphere that embraced a wide spectrum of animal life. Her mother was a painter; her elder sister, a sculptor. Her family encouraged her artistic endeavors, and she collaborated on a few works

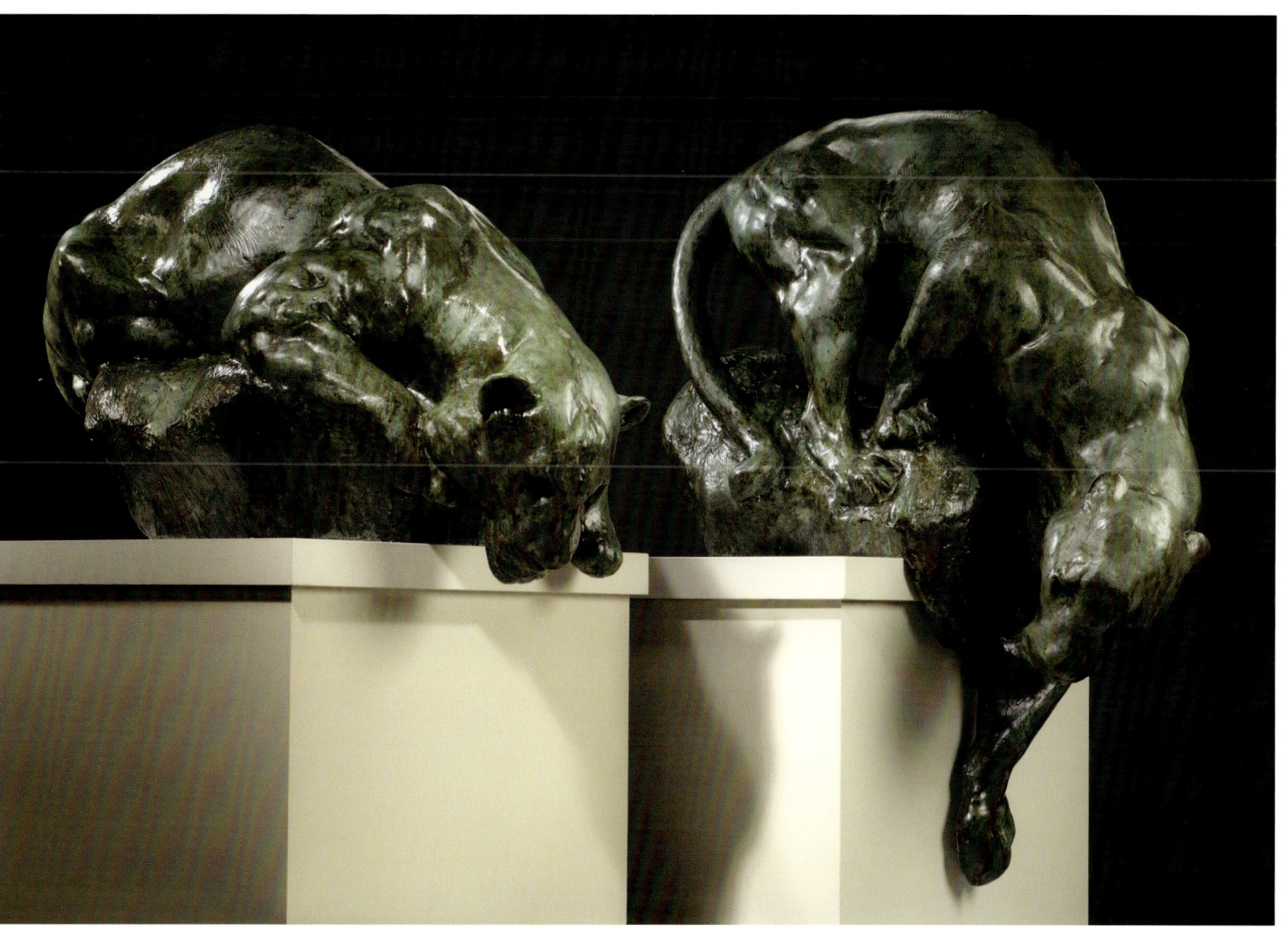

FIGURE 3.14.

(left)

ANNA HYATT HUNTINGTON

Jaguar, 1906–07.

Bronze; 27×43×25 inches.

JKM Collection.

JL2003.110.002.

(right)

ANNA HYATT HUNTINGTON

Reaching Jaguar, 1906–07.

Bronze; 44½×37×20½ inches.

JKM Collection.

JL2003.110.001.

with her sister. She studied with sculptors Henry Hudson Kitson in Boston and, after moving to New York in 1902, with George Grey Barnard and Hermon Atkins MacNeil at the Art Students League. She also worked for sculptor Gutzon Borglum and shared a studio with Abastenia St. Leger Eberle. She and Eberle collaborated on numerous sculptures, including *Men and Bull,* which won a bronze medal at the 1904 Louisiana Purchase Exhibition in Saint Louis. In 1915, she won a silver medal at the Panama-Pacific International Exposition in San Francisco for a group of ten animal pieces. In conjunction with her husband, Archer Milton Huntington, she opened America's first public outdoor sculpture garden, Brookgreen Gardens, on their private estate in South Carolina in 1931. Huntington was the first female to be elected to the American Academy of Arts and Letters (in 1932). In 1940, the couple opened Stanerigg Farm in Connecticut, where they raised deer and birds. During her career, she was awarded numerous commissions, including an equestrian statue of Joan of Arc in 1915, placed on Riverside Drive in New York City. Another *Joan of Arc* casting sits next to her sculpture of El Cid at San Francisco's Legion of Honor. In addition to her remarkable accomplishments as an American animalier, Huntington paved the way for other American female sculptors, offering budding artists such as Katherine Lane Weems her time and instruction. Huntington's legacy can be seen at Brookgreen Gardens, which hosts exhibitions of American sculpture on a regular basis and supports the work of contemporary animalier artists.[54]

ALBERT LAESSLE
United States, 1877–1954

Albert Laessle was born in 1877 in Philadelphia. He studied art at the Drexel Institute and then at the Pennsylvania Academy of Fine Arts (where his instructors were Thomas Anshutz and Charles Grafly). His sculptures were rendered in a highly realistic manner that caused some controversy during his lifetime. Laessle sculpted birds and reptiles, which appeared so lifelike that some critics accused him of casting his models from life. Laessle's first successful sculpture featured a snapping turtle and a crab fighting over a dead crow. It was exhibited in 1901, and critics insisted it was a life-cast. Knowing that Antoine-Louis Barye had faced similar accusations, Laessle refused to respond in writing. Reportedly, he harassed one of the critics in the street, thanking the critic for the free advertising.[55] His next creation, equally realistic, was a small sculpture in wax called *Turtle and Lizard.* This piece silenced his critics for the time being. He sent a bronze casting of *Turtle and Lizard* to the Louisiana Purchase Exposition. The Pennsylvania Academy ordered a casting of it for its permanent collection.

Laessle won the Cresson Scholarship in 1904 and traveled to Paris, where he stayed until 1907. In Paris, he studied at the Jardin des Plantes and sculpted another turtle. This one, called *Turning Turtle,* was in the midst of righting itself; this poignant piece met with skepticism from critics, who again accused him of casting from life. Laessle returned from Paris and began a prestigious career centered in Germantown, a suburb of Philadelphia. He was an instructor at the Pennsylvania Academy of Fine Arts from 1921 until 1939. In 1915, he won a gold medal at the Panama-Pacific International Exposition in San Francisco for a group of twenty small animal bronzes. Among the pieces exhibited was likely *Frog and Katydid* (figure 3.15), which depicts a frog that has just captured a katydid. Sculpted "warts and all," this piece is a good example of the naturalism that Laessle imparted in his small, meticulously rendered works. The detail, however, does not distract from the overall effect of the artwork. Laessle knew how to use modeling effectively to further the artistic impression, also evident in *Victory* (figure 3.16) of 1918.

The streamlined *Victory* depicts an aggressive, forward-moving eagle with wings cocked up and head lowered, in a stance that is both challenging and confident. The striding figure is placed on an ovoid base rimmed with stars (a detail that reinforces the patriotic theme of the sculpture). This work is one of the only

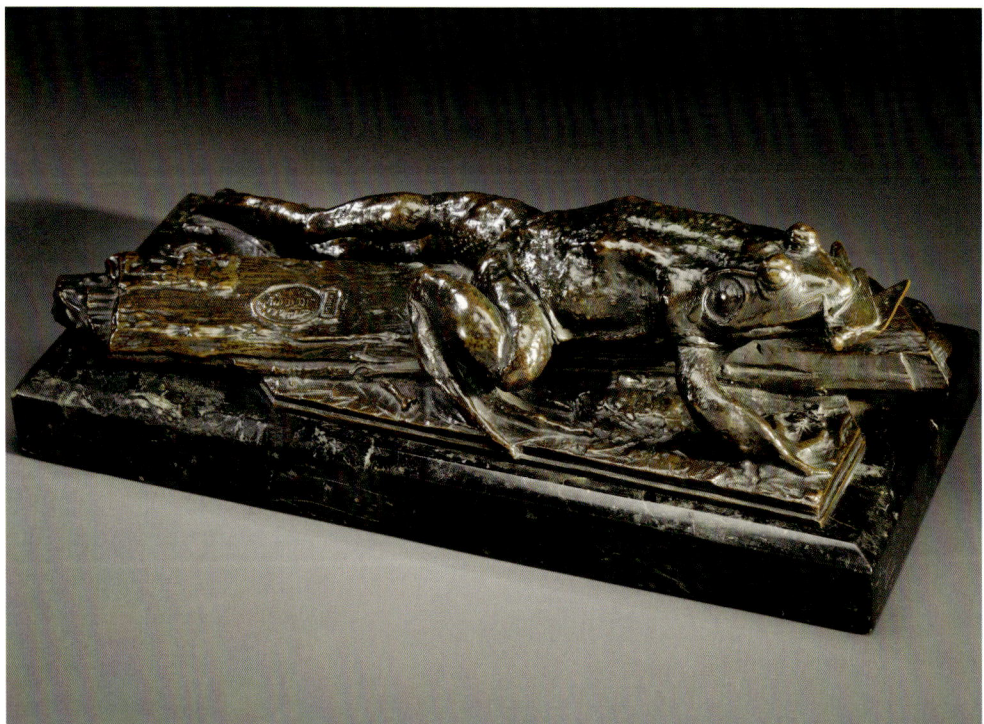

pieces Laessle created that was overtly allegorical, representing victory for the allies in World War I in 1918. Laessle modeled the eagle as precisely as he had his turtle sculptures, but in this case, no critics accused him of casting from life.

Although he typically sculpted his animals life-sized, he did create some larger works, including a billy goat, installed in Philadelphia's Rittenhouse Square, and a penguin group, installed at the Philadelphia Zoological Gardens. Comparing Laessle's work with that of his slightly older contemporary, Arthur Putnam, proves instructive. Whereas Putnam created smoothly modeled figures based as much on his imagination as on observation, Laessle created highly detailed models that involved a great deal of precise anatomical study as well as a good sense of design. Putnam's sculptures are not necessarily more imaginative than Laessle's, but their slightly more abstract forms can lead interpretation in that direction. The success of each artist during his lifetime indicates the ongoing diversification of the American animalier movement, a trend that continues to this day; the contemporary field consists of an incredible number of artists sculpting subjects from fruit bats to grizzly bears, in styles ranging from super-realistic to almost abstract.

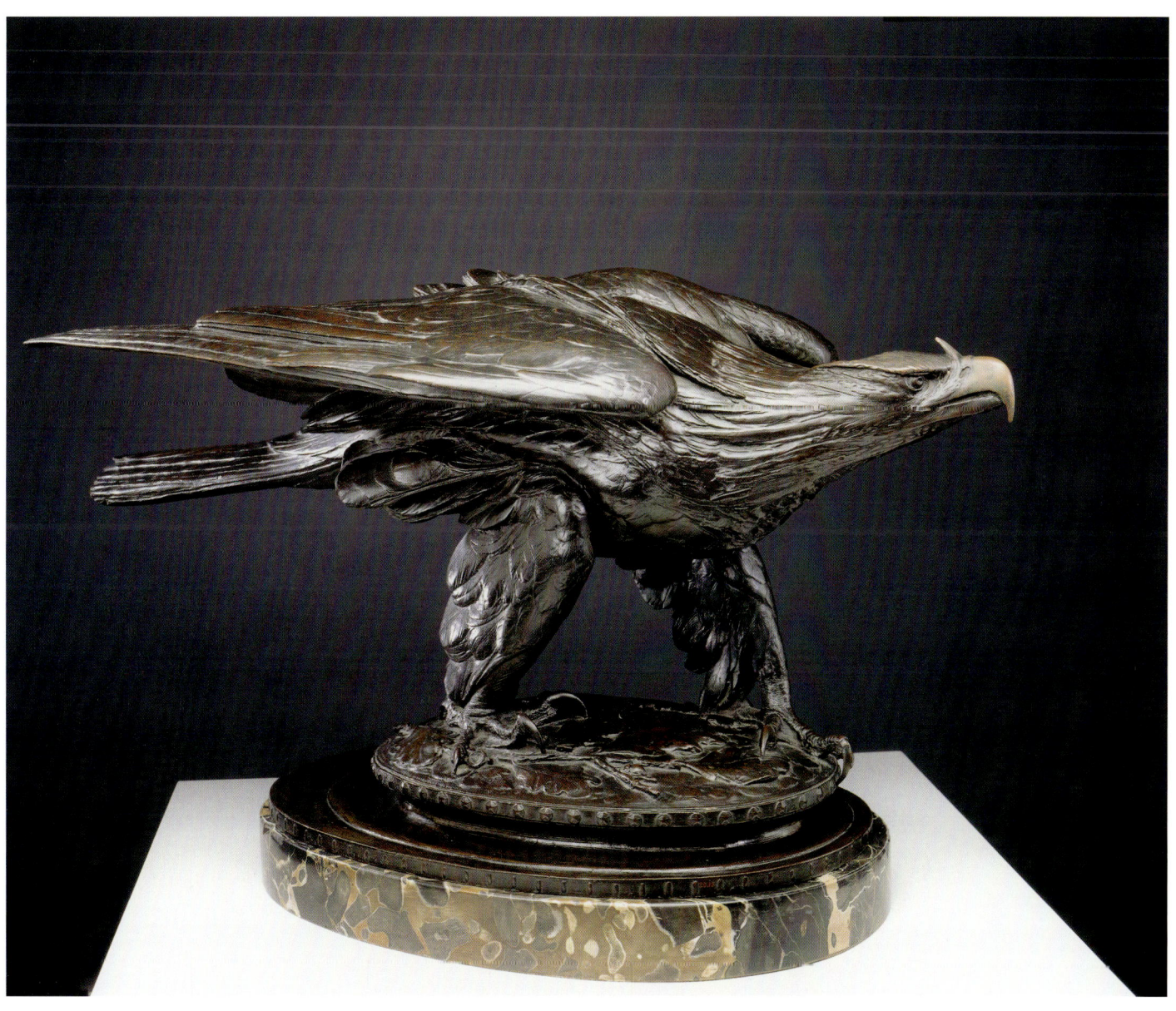

FIGURE 3.16.
ALBERT LAESSLE
Victory, 1918.
Bronze; 18½×38×23 inches.
JKM Collection.
JL1998.014.

HARRIET WHITNEY FRISHMUTH

United States, 1880–1980

In 1911, the employees of the Ruppert Brewery in Manhattan commissioned an eagle for their boss.[56] Although a well-known brewer, Jacob Ruppert is perhaps better remembered as a long-time owner of the New York Yankees (1915–39). The eagle request came early in Harriet Whitney Frishmuth's career, before she had hit upon the lyrical, outstretched female form that would become her trademark. Frishmuth had been honing her skills, however, sculpting small bronze bookends, letter openers, ashtrays, and relief portraits. She had also apprenticed with sculptor Gutzon Borglum and assisted him on an eagle sculpture. In the recent catalogue raisonné of Frishmuth's work, American sculpture expert Thayer Tolles wrote, "During her stint in Borglum's studio, Frishmuth recalled that she remedied the flaws in his version of the iconic American symbol." Frishmuth said, "I helped him . . . with modeling an eagle. I happened to know a little bit about eagles because I'd modeled one on my own. And I had a very good model because my uncle, in his office, he had a large golden eagle, that he had shot on one of his hunting trips out West. And I was able to study the way the feathers went. And Gutzon Borglum's eagle's tail feathers were put on wrong."[57]

Frishmuth modeled a smaller version of *Ruppert Eagle* in 1911 and then enlarged it for the commission. *Ruppert Eagle* (figure 3.17) closely resembles the logo for Jacob Ruppert's Knickerbocker beer, which is thought to have served as a model for the sculpture (although the logo also may have been altered to match the form of the eagle, after it was presented to Mr. Ruppert). In either case, the form of Frishmuth's eagle is a clear indicator of things to come. The gracefully extended wings and outstretched head speak to her interest in exploring taut anatomical lines. Frishmuth's later sculptures often display the female form in a state of reaction, pulling back from chilly water or cresting the top of a wave, frozen at the peak of an intense emotion. The 1911 eagle is modeled in a similar manner; it is not a staid, regal eagle but one full of fire, in the midst of an interaction.

As a child, Frishmuth moved with her divorced mother and sisters to Europe. In Paris, she was fortunate enough to have briefly studied at the Académie Rodin, where Rodin would regularly visit and offer critiques. Frishmuth later recalled that Rodin told her "a figure in action shouldn't be too correct. There should be a little of the action that was passed and a little of the action to come, and that way you get the illusion of . . . motion. And that I really felt I was doing

FIGURE 3.17.

HARRIET WHITNEY FRISHMUTH
Ruppert Eagle (Large American Eagle), 1911.
Bronze, inscribed "Presented to
Jacob Ruppert by his employees as
a token of regard and esteem, 1912";
40×46×41 inches.
JKM Collection.
JL1997.060.

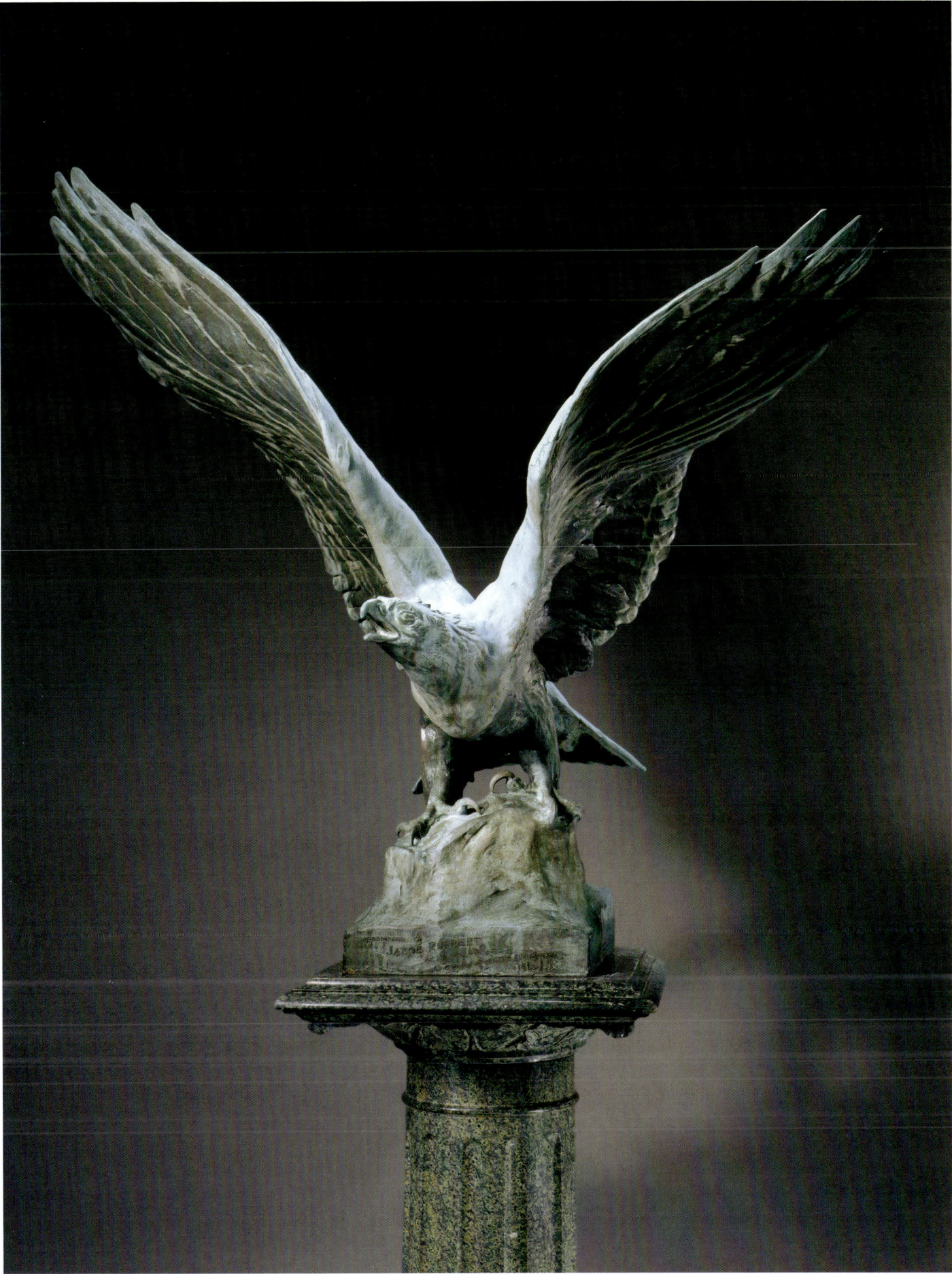

when I started making these figures in motion."[58] Rodin saw potential in Frishmuth and encouraged her to continue her studies. She spent the following two years at the Académie Colarossi and exhibited in the Paris Salon of 1903 before moving to Berlin, where she served as an assistant to Cuno von Uechtrizt-Steinkirch on several monumental commissions.[59] Around 1907, she returned to the United States and studied with Hermon Atkins MacNeil and Gutzon Borglum at the Art Students League; she also worked with Karl Bitter as an assistant. Her career began to gain momentum with small decorative bronzes and portrait commissions cast by the Gorham foundry. In 1913, she purchased a converted stable in the Murray Hill district of New York City, making it her home and studio.[60] Frishmuth exhibited with the National Sculpture Society, the National Association of Women Painters and Sculptors, the National Academy of Design, and the Pennsylvania Academy of Fine Arts. She continued casting her work until the early 1970s, living in Connecticut during her final years.[61]

KATHERINE LANE WEEMS

United States, 1899–1989

Animals do not talk back, they do not bring their relatives to see how you
are getting along and say "there is something wrong about the mouth."
Katherine Lane Weems, quoted in Ambler,
Katherine Lane Weems, 101

As a child growing up in Boston, Katharine Lane Weems was exposed to a wide
array of art, thanks to her father, the president of the board of the Museum
of Fine Arts. On a family trip to Europe when she was fourteen, she wrote down
twelve of her favorite paintings. Her list indicates a budding interest in animal art,
as it included work by Edwin Landseer and Rosa Bonheur, as well as Jean-Louis-
Ernest Meissonier and Antoine-Jean Gros, who often painted battle scenes with
multitudes of charging horses. She also recorded notes on various animals and
sketches of sheep.

Weems's father passed away in 1914, leaving her mother in charge of the
family estate, which she managed well. Weems had a privileged upbringing, even
in the midst of World War I. She took drawing classes at the Museum of Fine
Arts and practiced etching and pottery. In *Katherine Lane Weems: Sculpture and
Drawings,* art historian Louise Todd Ambler noted that on July 15, 1918, Weems
went to visit Anna Hyatt (later Anna Hyatt Huntington). Ambler quotes Weems's
diary, describing the visit: "Of course it was a red-letter day for me and when we
found her in trousers like my beloved Rosa Bonheur, my joy was complete." After
Weems proclaimed her interest in animal sculpture, she wrote that Hyatt "seemed
much interested and almost took my breath away by asking me to come over some
morning round 10, next week and she would show me how to set up the wires to
make something."[62] Tellingly, there are no diary entries for the next month; Weems
seems to have been too busy sculpting. When Weems brought a sculpture of a
cow for critique, Hyatt responded favorably and encouraged Weems to continue
sculpting. After a few more lessons, Weems enrolled in the art school at the
Museum of Fine Arts, where eminent portraitist Charles Grafly critiqued her work
every other Wednesday.

In 1920, Weems visited Hyatt's New York studio, and the two went to
the New York Zoological Society (now the Bronx Zoo) to study and sketch. At
the zoo, Weems expanded the range of her subjects from domestic animals to
wilder varieties. She began showing her work at art galleries and expositions soon

thereafter. In 1926, she received the George D. Widener Memorial gold medal, as well as a bronze medal, at the Sesquicentennial International Exposition in Philadelphia.[63] From that point on, she received a steady stream of accolades. In 1930, Weems received her first commission: a carved brick frieze and sculpture for the biological laboratories at Harvard University. For the frieze, she created bas-reliefs of pelicans, elephants, tigers, and bison. For the sculpture component, she modeled two giant Indian rhinoceroses to flank the entry doors, plus gilt-bronze panels inserted into the doors, representing earth, air, and sea.

Two crowning achievements came relatively late in Weems's life. In 1965, a gallery at the Museum of Science in Boston was created to showcase her sculpture. It was named the Emma Gildersleeve Lane Gallery, in memory of her mother. In 1973, she began to work on a large sculpture of swimming dolphins playing in the waves. The managing director of the New England Aquarium saw the piece and was intrigued. Weems entered into a contract with the aquarium, and in 1979, an over-fourteen-foot-long bronze of swimming dolphins was installed outside the aquarium. The National Museum of Wildlife Art owns a reduction of this large-scale bronze, which captures the same smooth, undulating forms and sense of motion (figure 3.18). This sculpture is typical of Weems's oeuvre in many ways, though she did not often depict marine mammals. Her sculptures were typically quiet portraits of a favorite pet or domestic animal. When she sculpted wildlife, she did not depict battling masses but instead modeled character studies full of dignity. Weems continued creating realistic sculpture in an era when abstract art had become a dominant force.

Ambler concluded her book with the following passage about the dolphin sculpture:

> The interest of art critics has long since moved to sculpture whose only subject matter is its own form in space, whose ideas are conveyed without the representation of familiar objects in a realistic way. . . . But like much of the work [Weems] produced during the previous sixty years, it is a fine example of the traditional sculpture that is understood by a wide public. Its subject matter, marine life, announces the purpose of the aquarium it enhances, just as the animals that flank the entrance and range across the façade of the laboratories at Harvard declare the activity that takes place within those walls. More than would any sign or logo, the presence of these sculptures engages the imagination of the passerby.[64]

Weems's career is a prime example of the often-overlooked and ongoing history of representational art. The legacy of Kemeys, Proctor, Putnam, and Huntington lives on in younger generations of sculptors who have taken up the animalier mantle.

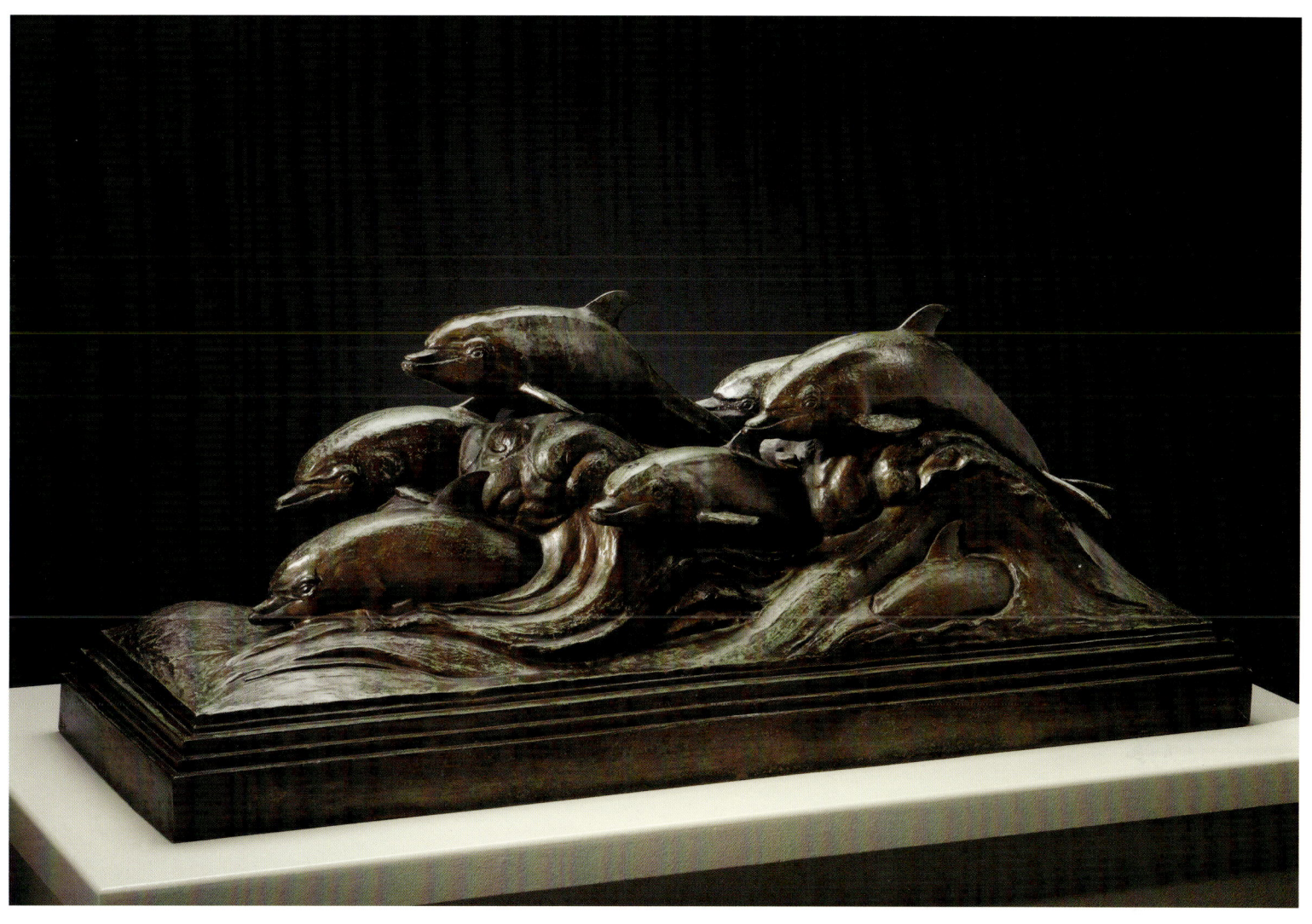

FIGURE 3.18.
KATHERINE LANE WEEMS
Dolphins of the Sea, 1977.
Bronze; 15¾ × 35¾ × 11½ inches.
JKM Collection.
JL1992.049.

From Weems and her contemporaries of the twentieth century to the leading artists of the twenty-first, wildlife sculpting continues to be a rich and dynamic field—one that looks back at the long legacy of animalier sculpture in America as it stretches the boundaries of artistic expression with innovative, meaningful work that resonates with contemporary audiences.

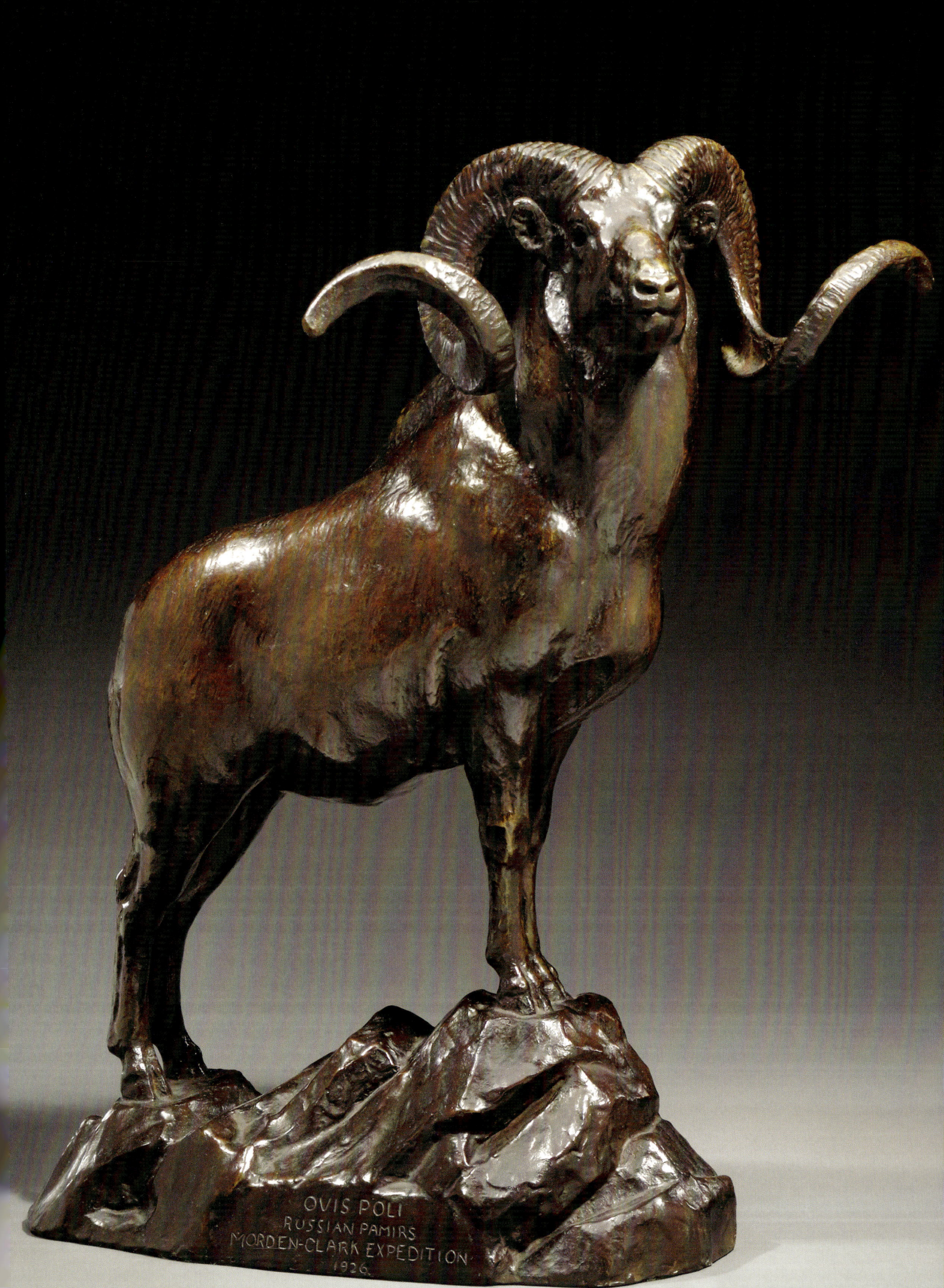

OVIS POLI
RUSSIAN PAMIRS
MORDEN-CLARK EXPEDITION
1926.

Chapter 4

Carl Akeley and a New Breed of Artist-Naturalist

> Africa is an unexampled storehouse, a marvelous virgin reservoir of incomparable inspiration for painters, poets, dramatists, novelists, sculptors, and composers. It is today the world's most sublime theater for romance and adventure.
>
> William R. Leigh, *Frontiers of Enchantment*, xi

Substitute "The West" for "Africa" in the above epigraph, and it would aptly describe eastern sentiments about the American frontier prior to its closing in 1890 (as reported by historian Frederick Jackson Turner). Leigh wrote that passage in 1938, many years after the West had become much like the rest of America; its luster as an unexplored space, rife with adventure, had faded (though its powerful allure as subject matter in the arts and popular media remained vivid). Easterners who might have traveled west during the early twentieth century began looking elsewhere for adventurous places to visit. Africa became a "new west" for naturalists, who found new specimens to study; industrialists, who found new resources to exploit; sportsmen, who found an abundance of game to hunt; and artists, who found wide-open territory, beautiful scenery, and amazing animals to paint and sculpt (figure 4.1). Scholars Peter Hassrick and Rick Stewart noted that Carl Akeley's *Stung* (figure 4.2) is like an African version of Frederic Remington's *Rattlesnake* (the dynamic bronze of a cowboy struggling to hold his seat as his mount rears away from a snake on the ground). Given the new interest in Africa in the early 1900s, the two sculptures have much more in common than a surface-level similarity of serpentine subject.[1]

African animals have been subjects in art for millennia, the Egyptians being the most well-known ancient chroniclers of their beauty. In the middle of the 1800s, an interest in Africa and other exotic locales emerged in Europe. At the forefront of this movement were orientalist painters such as Jean-Léon Gérôme, who traveled abroad to depict the people, lifestyle, animals, and architecture of the Ottoman Empire (see figure 5.7). The first European-trained artist to spend lengthy amounts of time studying African wildlife in its natural habitat was

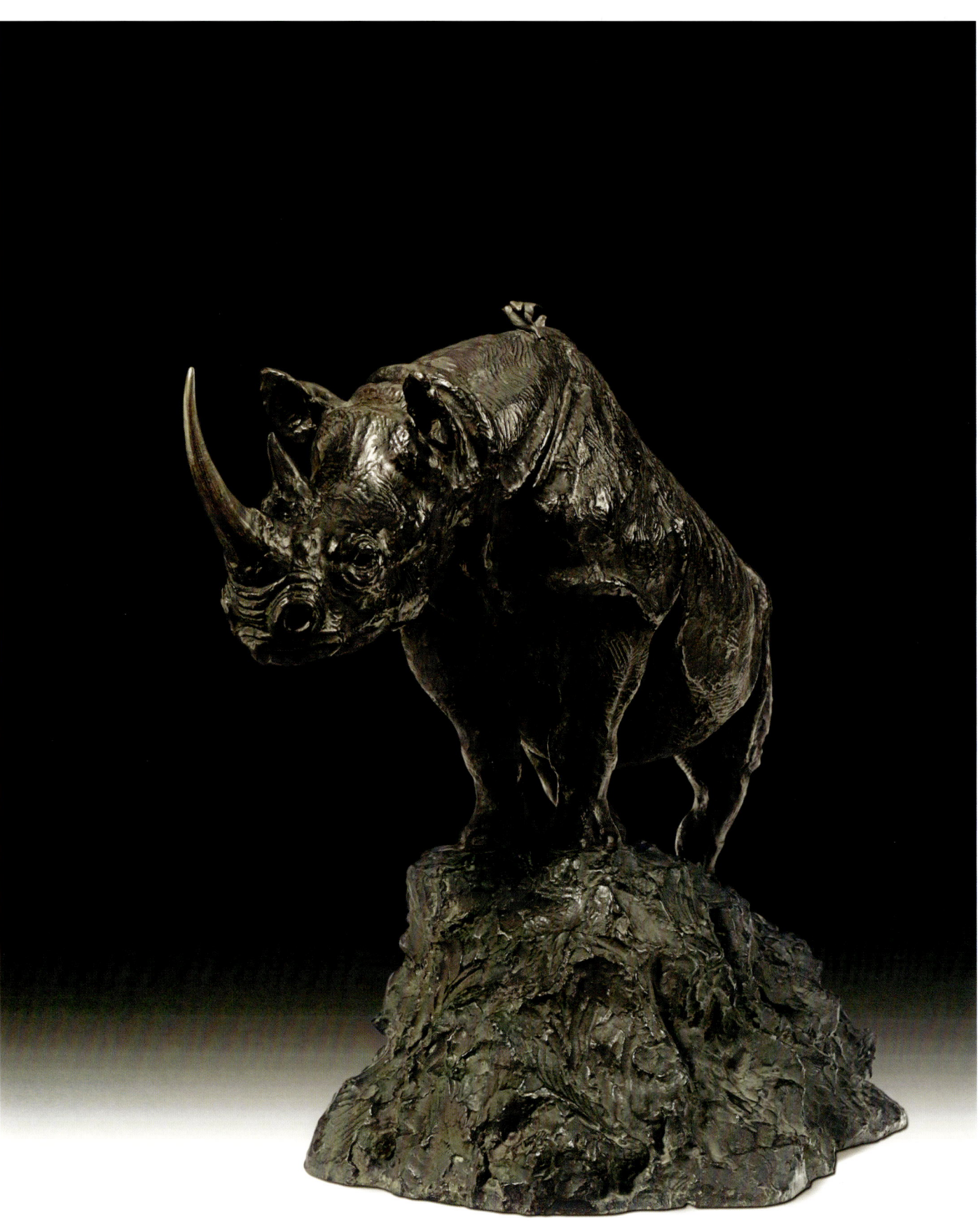

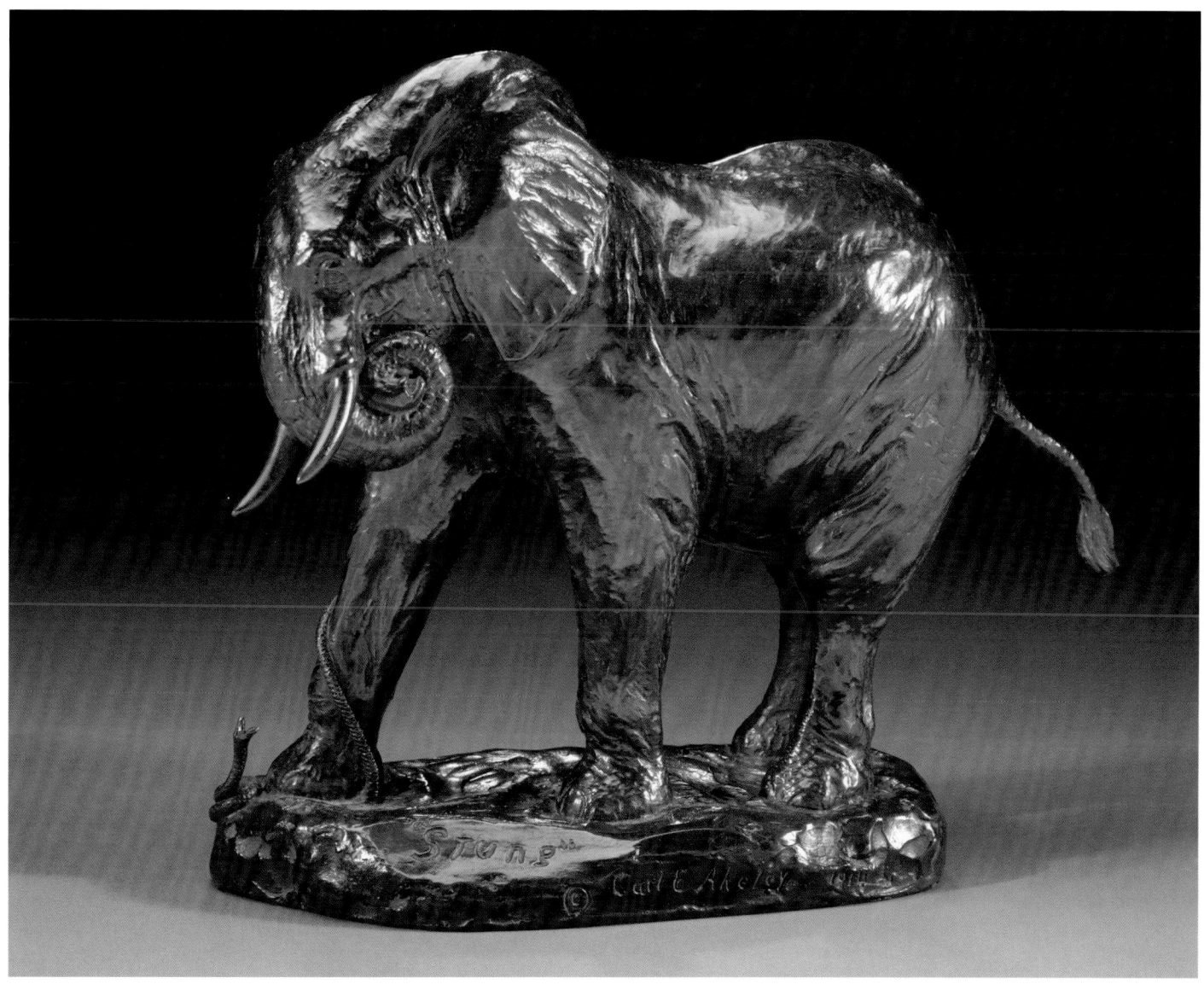

FIGURE 4.1.
JAMES LIPPITT CLARK
African Black Rhino with Tick Birds
(aka *The Battleship of the Plains*), 1912.
Bronze; 27¾ × 38 × 17½ inches.
JKM Collection.
JL2008.004.

FIGURE 4.2.
CARL ETHAN AKELEY
Stung, 1914.
Bronze; 9¼ × 11 × 4½ inches.
JKM Collection.
JL2007.015.

Carl Akeley and a New Breed of Artist-Naturalist

German-born Wilhelm Kuhnert, who took extended safaris in 1891, 1905, and 1911 (see figure 5.4). Kuhnert's journeys coincided with the colonization of various areas of the African continent, just as artists had followed the settlement of various areas of North America.

The first artist-naturalists to venture into the American West accompanied government surveys to record the landscape, people, and wildlife they encountered in a scientific fashion. During the first decades of the twentieth century, a new group of artist-naturalists emerged, centered on the American Museum of Natural History in New York City. Working with famed taxidermist and natural historian Carl Akeley, artists, naturalists, and taxidermists James Lippitt Clark and Robert Rockwell traveled to Africa to help bring Akeley's vision for a new mode of natural history display to the public. While the impetus behind their expeditions and exhibitions was scientific, there is no denying the Romantic underpinnings of their adventures. Their trips were exciting forays into the unknown; Akeley and his companions were at the forefront of discovery, like their artist-naturalist forebears, bringing back information about a new continent largely unknown to American audiences. Later, Louis Paul Jonas joined the museum's faculty, working under Clark, as Akeley's scientific and artistic legacy continued.

The artists working at the American Museum of Natural History shared a belief that the great mammals of their age in both Africa and North America—the rhinoceros, elephant, lion, moose, elk, and deer—were being pushed toward extinction with little chance of survival. Their goal was to preserve specimens of these charismatic creatures for future generations to see. Clark wrote, "Quite regardless of what we may do now, the animals are doomed. The best for which we can hope is that a wider appreciation of them, and a greater sympathy for them may stave off the day when they will no longer range abroad as they have ranged since before mankind first appeared upon the earth."[2] To a certain extent, Clark's best-case scenario has come true; by gaining a wider appreciation of wildlife, we have prolonged the decline of various populations. In some instances, we have improved upon his dire predictions and now hope to never lose the populations ranging across the vast plains of both Africa and North America. However, dwindling numbers of wild tigers in Asia (which may never range across their natural habitat as they once did) show that Clark was prescient in his estimation of the decline of certain species.

In the early 1900s, the conservation movement in America was growing in strength and popularity. In addition to prompting a concern for North American animals, the movement fostered an interest in Africa and its wildlife population. Scientists and artists, fearing that hunting and human incursion would soon decimate the vast populations, began to take expeditions to Africa to study the animal inhabitants. Part of the goal of these expeditions was to collect specimens for natural history museums back home. Today, reading some of the accounts of these travels proves difficult, because the scientists seem to have been killing at least as many animals as the hunters were. However, the rationale at that point was much different than it is today; the emphasis was not on preservation of the creatures, because their situation was assumed to be hopeless. On collecting specimens, Clark wrote:

> A hundred years ago there were very, very few careful observers of animals. A hundred years from now there will be very, very few animals to be observed. Now is the time to become acquainted with those interesting and appealing creatures which have inhabited the earth for so many thousands of years, but which, unfortunately, are rapidly giving way before the inexorable advance of civilization. Before many years have passed, the animals will be gone, or the pitiful remnants will be so trifling and scattered as no longer to be typical. Only in the museums of natural history and in books and motion pictures on the subject, will information concerning them be found. The work, then, is not merely for the present—it is for the future.[3]

Despite his ethnocentric claim that there were few other careful observers of animals before his generation came along, Clark writes a sensitive account of why natural historians thought it necessary to collect specimens.

The natural historians and taxidermists of the early 1900s shared much in terms of technique with the animal sculptors working at the same time. New developments in the practice of mounting animals meant that naturalists needed sculpting skills or needed to hire sculptors to assist with their projects. Equating the new taxidermy to a fine art, Akeley brought together a talented team of artists to help him create the African Hall at the American Museum of Natural History. After fulfilling Akeley's vision, Clark led the team, which produced similarly awe-inspiring displays in the halls dedicated to the animals of Asia and North America. Another artist closely associated with the American Museum was Charles R. Knight, who pioneered the art of reconstructing the way extinct animals might have looked. His paintings and sculptures of prehistoric creatures brought a new vision of dinosaurs and prehistoric humankind to visitors eager for more than the standard display of fossils and early tools. Knight could also sculpt living creatures with great acuity.

By the 1950s, travel to Africa was becoming increasingly affordable, and a growing number of safari companies stood ready to take visitors into the bush to view wildlife. The subjects of film and literature, Africa and its animal inhabitants also grew popular in painting and sculpture and remain so today. The early efforts of artist-naturalists such as Akeley broke trail into new territory blossoming with economic, scientific, and artistic potential. Africa was an unexplored continent containing a similar allure as the American West had had at its peak in the 1800s, an allure that spoke to adventurous painters and sculptors eager to investigate this new artistic territory.[4]

CARL ETHAN AKELEY

United States, 1864–1926

I had a dream of a great African Hall of forty groups of animals with all the
ingenuity, all the technique, and all the art the country could boast of. By
that time I had come to feel that taxidermy could be great art. I felt that
a beautifully modeled animal required at least as much knowledge, taste,
skill and technique as a bronze or stone animal. But I knew this conception
was not common. . . . It was a recognized thing to support art. Taxidermy
had no such tradition. The only way out of the dilemma that I could see
was to prove that whether or not taxidermy was an art at least a taxidermist
could be an artist.

Carl Akeley, *In Brightest Africa,* 176

Carl Akeley began his taxidermy career at the tender age of sixteen, going
to the extent of having business cards printed up that stated his chosen
occupation. During these years, he also studied painting, to create realistic
backgrounds for the specimens he had mounted. Though he would not see the
fruition of this vision at the American Museum of Natural History in New York
City for many years, the genesis of great things to come was visible in Akeley's
small dioramas. While still a teenager, Akeley began working at Ward's Natural
Science Establishment in Rochester, New York. Taxidermy was a crude art in
the 1880s, and the finished models were basically cured skins stuffed with straw,
resulting in less-than-lifelike results. As Akeley grew older and continued to
practice, he developed a method of taxidermy that relied on many facets of the
sculptor's art, including anatomical study, modeling, and casting. From 1895 to
1909, Akeley worked at the Field Museum in Chicago. He then took a position at
the American Museum, where he spent the rest of his storied career.

In his late forties, Akeley cast his first bronze, *Wounded Comrade* (1913;
figure 4.3). To drum up financial support from patrons who normally gave money
to art museums, he set out to show that a taxidermist could also be an artist. After
seeing Akeley's model of *Wounded Comrade* in clay, sculptor Alexander P. Proctor
convinced his friend and patron George Pratt to order a casting of the sculpture.
Financier J. P. Morgan also saw the model and went one step further, agreeing to
help finance the African Hall.[5]

Wounded Comrade depicts two young elephants helping an older bull walk
to safety after being shot by a hunter. Akeley did not witness this scene himself,

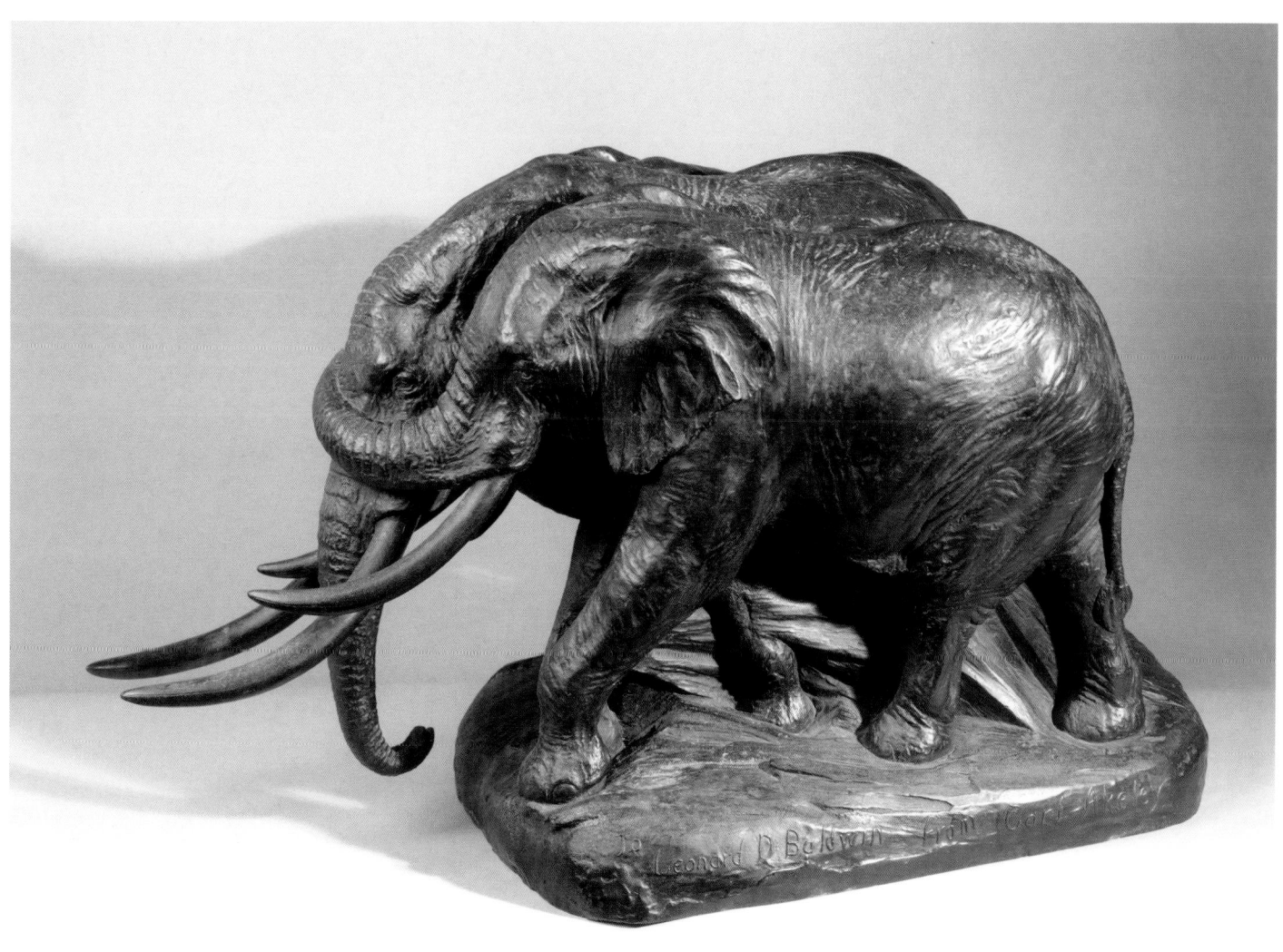

FIGURE 4.3.
CARL ETHAN AKELEY
Wounded Comrade, 1913.
Bronze; 12 × 23 × 12½ inches.
Gift of the 1999 Collectors Circle.
National Museum of Wildlife Art Collection.
M1999.112.

but he had heard the story and it stuck with him. The quality of the finished bronze—in technique, modeling, and overall impression—backs up Akeley's statements about the shared skills of the taxidermist and the sculptor. This is not "bronze taxidermy," a derogatory term applied to uninspiring sculptures today, but a fully realized work of art that speaks to both the animal and the human condition. The financial and artistic success of *Wounded Comrade* did not prompt Akeley to switch careers, though he did cast several other sculptures during his lifetime.[6] His passion continued to be collecting specimens and mounting them for the African Hall. Akeley spread his enthusiasm for taxidermy and art to James Lippitt Clark, Robert Rockwell, and Louis Paul Jonas. Believing that the backgrounds should be as accurate as the foregrounds, he employed artists such as William Leigh to create paintings for the dioramas. Akeley's last expedition to Africa was in 1926; he perished while in the Congo collecting gorilla specimens. He was buried in Albert National Park (now Virunga National Park), which he helped establish as central Africa's first wildlife preserve.

CHARLES R. KNIGHT
UNITED STATES, 1874–1953

Charles Knight's casting of an Asian elephant (figure 4.4) closely resembles a model for an imperial mammoth he created in the early 1900s. The main difference is in the size of the tusks; these appear to be much smaller than the ones appended to Knight's mammoth model.[7] How could a mammoth and a contemporary elephant look so similar? The imperial mammoth became extinct about 11,000 years ago, at the same time as the saber-toothed tiger, the woolly rhinoceros, and the giant sloth. Before this, mammoths ranged from Canada to Honduras. Closely related to the Asian elephant, North American mammoths came in two distinct varieties, the wooly and the nonwooly. The imperial mammoth was of the nonwooly variety; because of this, it is speculated to have closely resembled the Asian elephant. In February 1914, Charles R. Knight held an exhibit of his work at the American Museum of Natural History, where he exhibited both his imperial mammoth and his Indian elephant sculptures, along with a host of other artwork depicting contemporary and prehistoric creatures.

The multitalented Knight was well known for his work as a natural history painter, bringing prehistoric animals to life in museums from New York's American Museum of Natural History to the Natural History Museum in Los Angeles. Knight also excelled at sculpting, working on the sculpture program at the New York Zoological Society (now the Bronx Zoo) with greats such as Alexander Proctor, Anna Hyatt Huntington, and Eli Harvey. At age fifteen, Knight took drawing classes in the basement of the Metropolitan Museum of Art and then enrolled at the Art Students League. In 1890, J. and R. Lamb, a firm specializing in church decoration, hired him to paint vegetation and animals for stained-glass window designs. By 1893, he was creating animal illustrations for children's books and magazines such as *McClure's* and *Harper's*. For reference material, he often studied at the Central Park Zoo and at the American Museum, where he became a well-known fixture. One day, a member of the paleontology department wanted someone to draw an interpretation of a prehistoric animal. Because of his familiarity with the collection, Knight was an obvious choice for the assignment. Soon after this initial foray into prehistory, Knight embarked on a European tour, beginning in Paris. Much like Edward Kemeys, he found the atmosphere at the Jardin des Plantes stifling and preferred to spend his days in the Louvre or one of the city's other cultural institutions. Knight met and received a friendly critique

FIGURE 4.4.
CHARLES R. KNIGHT
Elephant, 1909.
Bronze; 29⅛ × 35 × 12½ inches.
Gift of the 2002 Collectors Circle.
National Museum of Wildlife Art Collection.
M2001.163.

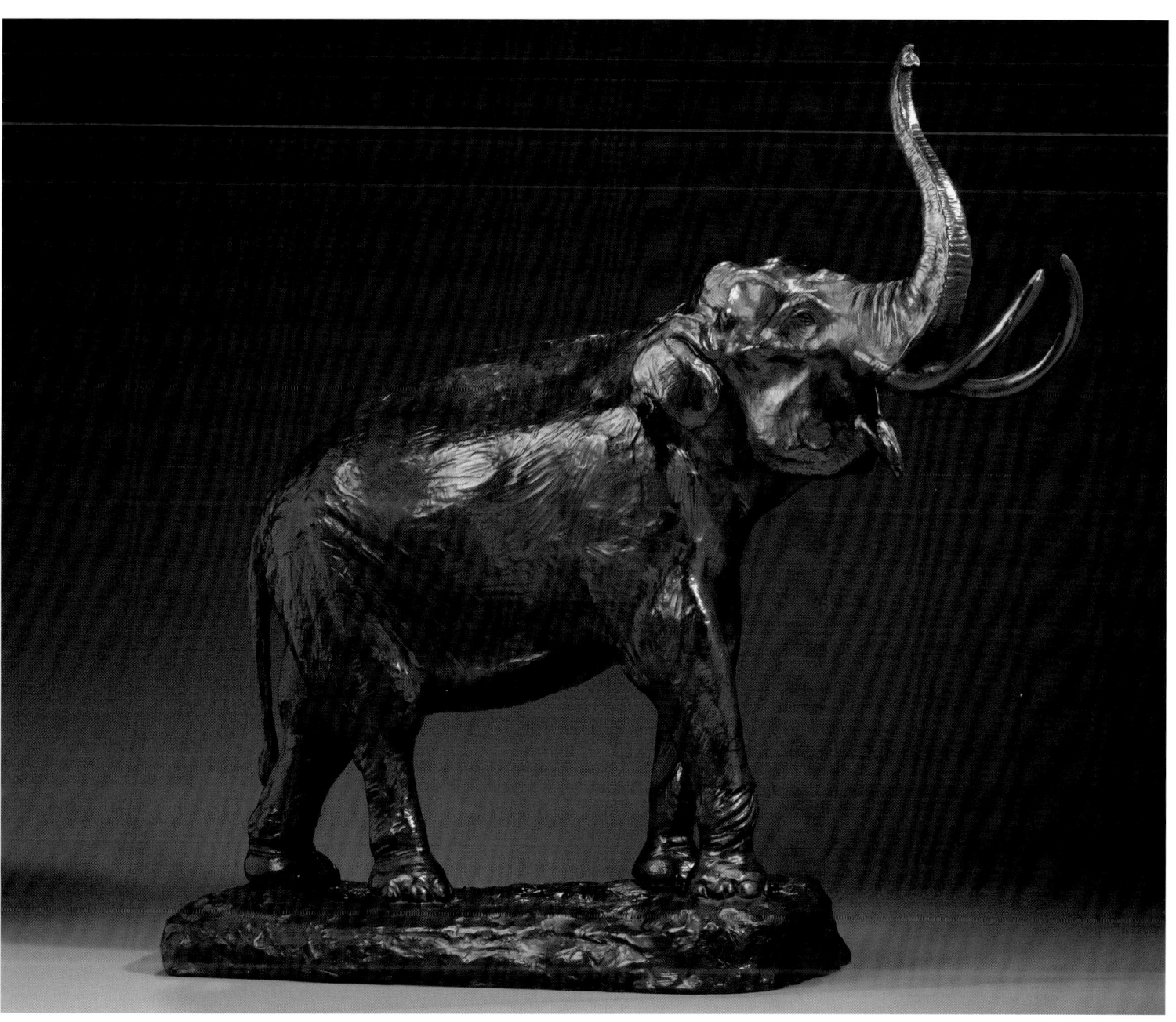

from animalier Emmanuel Frémiet and painter Jean-Léon Gérôme. He also visited Antwerp and found the zoological gardens there much more conducive to study. Before returning to New York, Knight visited Amsterdam and London, studying at the zoos and museums in each city.[8]

Upon his return to the United States, Knight quickly resumed his work with the American Museum, working with Professor Henry Fairfield Osborn. Osborn, unlike previous generations of paleontologists, was interested in bringing fossil skeletons to life, both by mounting them in realistic poses and by displaying artists' renderings of how they likely appeared in the wild. Part of Knight's painting method was to sculpt a three-dimensional model of the animal to use as a basis for sketching. These models became the basis for some of his later works cast in bronze.

JAMES LIPPITT CLARK
United States, 1883–1969

Patricia Broder, in *Bronzes of the American West,* wrote, "Although Carl Akeley was the undisputed founder of modern taxidermy, James Lippitt Clark has been described as 'its major prophet.'"[9] Clark completed Akeley's African Hall at the American Museum of Natural History after Akeley perished in Africa; Clark oversaw the creation of the museum's Asian and North American halls. He traveled the globe in search of wildlife, hoping to preserve an accurate picture of how these animals lived in their native habitats. As noted in the introduction to this chapter, however, Clark's vision for the future of the world's wildlife was a dark one, as he feared that extinction for many was close at hand. He hoped his dioramas would show future generations how animals used to live.

Clark began his artistic career at the Gorham Silver Company in Providence, Rhode Island, where he first became interested in sculpting. From there, he went to the Rhode Island School of Design. In 1902, the director of the American Museum of Natural History spotted Clark's work while he was still in school and asked him to join the staff, hoping that he could apply his artistic abilities to the museum's taxidermy program. Clark wrote, "It was as a sculptor, then, not at all as a taxidermist, that I entered the Museum."[10] Clark went to Chicago to study modern taxidermy with Akeley soon after he was hired. Clark was an avid student of the animal form, stopping at the Central Park Zoo most mornings to sketch its inhabitants and venturing out to the Bronx Zoo on weekends for more study. Hearing Akeley and others describe adventures in Africa, Clark longed to go on an expedition. The opportunity arose in 1908, when wildlife photographer A. Radclyffe Dugmore went on safari to take pictures of African wildlife for a series of stories about Theodore Roosevelt's African travels. Clark went as Dugmore's protector, guarding him as he shot some of the earliest film and photographs of African wildlife.

Upon returning to New York in 1909, Clark rejoined the American Museum. During that same year, Carl Akeley also joined the staff. Clark worked for the American Museum until 1949. During that time, he traversed the globe on museum expeditions. He wrote, "I have hunted and studied in Nova Scotia, Wyoming, Alberta, British Columbia, and Alaska. I have visited Africa three times. I have crossed Asia from India and the borders of Afghanistan to Siberia and China. Always, on these journeys, I have had animals principally in mind."[11]

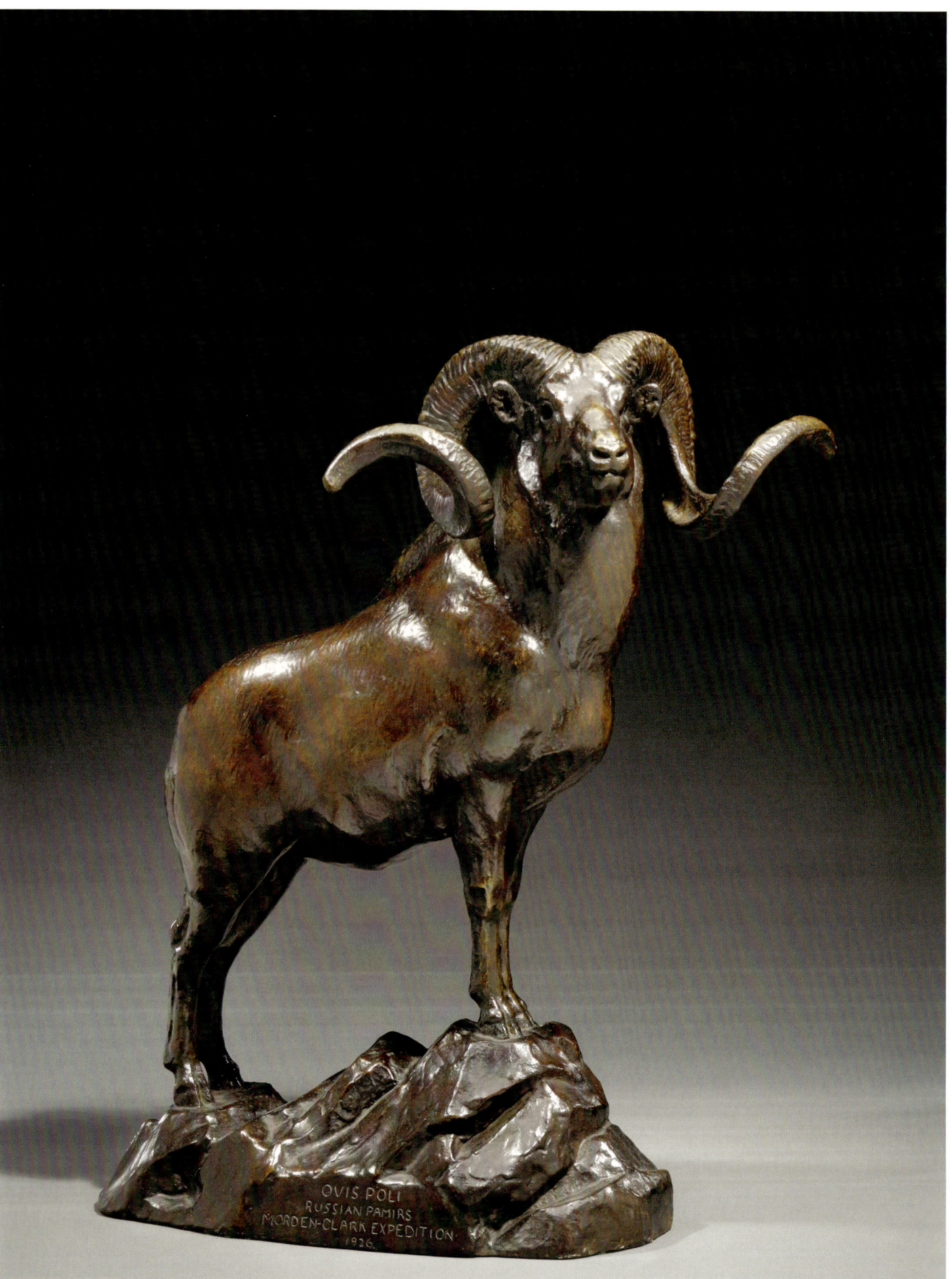

OVIS POLI
RUSSIAN PAMIRS
MORDEN-CLARK EXPEDITION
1926.

Clark's sculpture covers ground similar to that of his travels. Because of his wide-ranging experiences, Clark remains one of the only sculptors to have produced a body of work spanning North America, Africa, and Asia. Notable in his oeuvre are the bronzes *Wapiti Bull, Bighorn Ram, Townsend's Seal, Ovis Poli, Penguin, African Cape Buffalo,* and *Black Rhinoceros.* Although he did occasionally sculpt animals in movement, the majority of his work depicts the subject in a static pose, simply posed on a bronze plinth, or standing atop a rocky outcropping, such as the Asian wild sheep, *Ovis Poli* (figure 4.5). The natural history influence is clear in these works, which are finely detailed and realistic, showing his intimate knowledge of animal anatomy. Clark was recognized as an artist outside of the natural history world, receiving the National Academy's Speyer Prize in 1930 for a wild horse group. His career exemplifies Akeley's theory and practice of incorporating the best skills of the artist to create the best results in taxidermy.

FIGURE 4.5.
JAMES LIPPITT CLARK
Ovis Poli, 1930.
Bronze; 17 × 15 × 7⅛ inches.
JKM Collection.
JL1996.046.

ROBERT HENRY ROCKWELL

UNITED STATES, 1885–1973

Of the artists working with Carl Akeley, Robert Henry Rockwell is best known for his taxidermy, though he did cast significant sculptures during his career. Brookgreen Gardens in South Carolina owns castings of his *African Elephant, Black African Rhinoceros,* and *Survival of the Fittest. Survival of the Fittest* features two bull moose fighting, posed similarly to his moose group at the American Museum of Natural History. (Carl Rungius painted the background of this diorama, one of the most painterly scenes in the North American Hall.)

Rockwell's *Moose* in the NMWA collection holds a more static pose than the fighting moose at the American Museum, but it still retains a sense of motion (figure 4.6). Rockwell was known for his ability to create lifelike poses in his taxidermy that suggested imminent movement. Stephen Christopher Quinn wrote in *Windows on the World: The Great Habitat Dioramas of the American Museum of Natural History,* "Few museum taxidermists can match him for creating a dramatic pose and achieving an effect of arrested motion."[12] Rockwell's taxidermy talent translated to his sculpture. His moose looks as if it has just raised its head to sniff the air, looking neither alarmed nor frightened, but alert. The moose is sculpted naturalistically, similar to the work of Akeley and Clark. The antlers show a particular degree of care in the precise modeling of the various tines.

Rockwell spent some time as a youth on a farm in Ireland, which may have contributed to his later interest in animal life. He began his taxidermy career at Ward's Natural Science Establishment in Rochester, New York. Rockwell continued at the Smithsonian Museum of Natural History in Washington, D.C., working on Theodore Roosevelt's African collection. He served as the chief taxidermist at the Brooklyn Museum of Arts and Sciences for twelve years before joining the staff of the American Museum of Natural History. Rockwell became Akeley's chief assistant and accompanied Akeley on his last African expedition. Upon his return, Rockwell worked on the exhibits for the African Hall. He subsequently assisted Clark in the completion of the North American and Asian halls. Throughout his career, he experimented with sculpture, creating several fine models, which he cast in bronze. After his retirement from museum work in 1942, Rockwell cast about fifty animal and bird figures in ceramic.[13] His greatest contributions to the world of animal art are his beautifully posed specimens at the American Museum: one in particular, the Alaskan brown bear, has become an icon for the entire institution.

FIGURE 4.6.
ROBERT HENRY ROCKWELL
Moose, 1939.
Bronze; 19 × 19½ × 11½ inches.
Gift of Joffa and Bill Kerr.
National Museum of Wildlife Art Collection.
W1998.141.

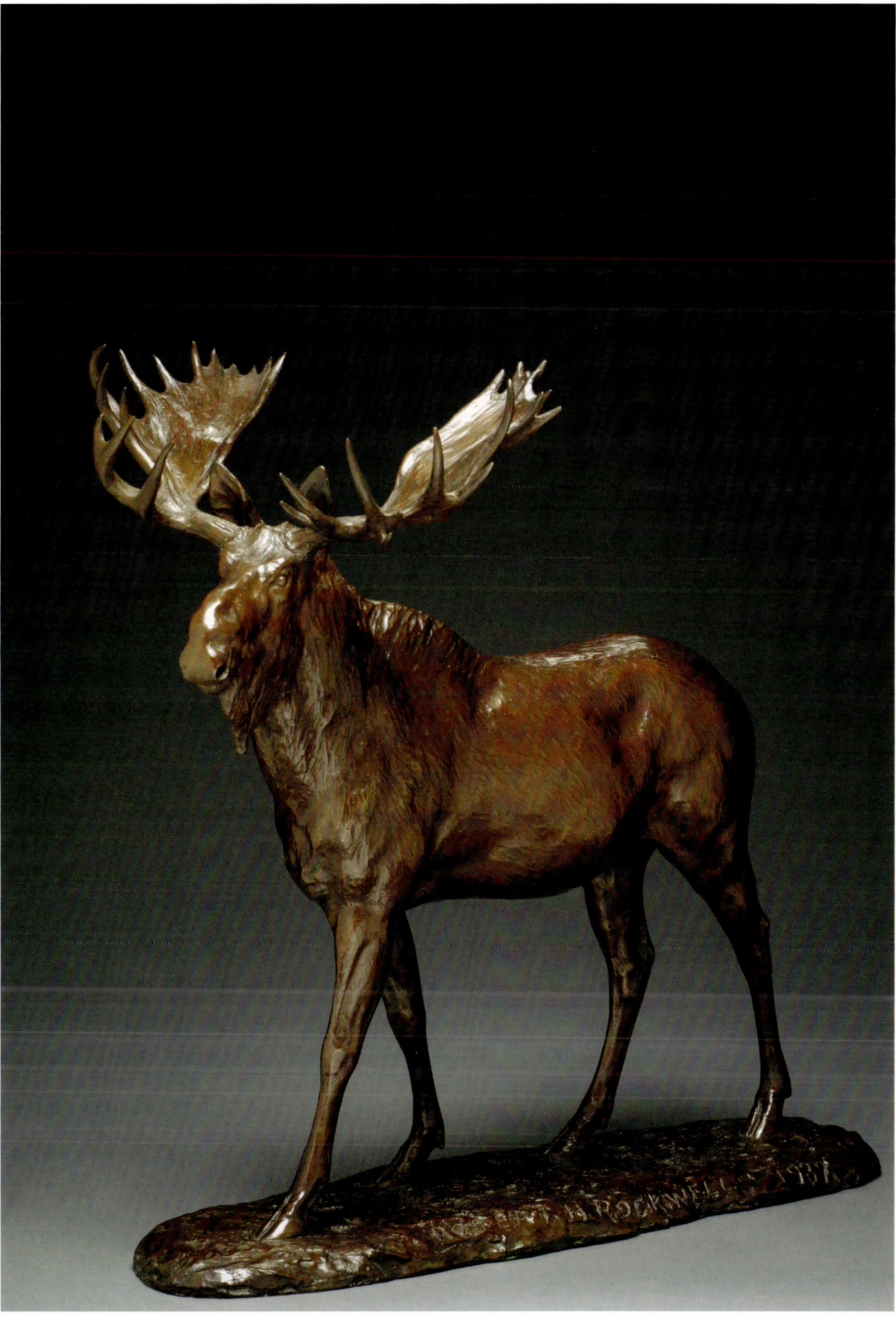

LOUIS PAUL JONAS
Hungary, 1894–1971

In contrast to the static realism of James Lippitt Clark, Louis Paul Jonas often sculpted animals in dynamic poses, while incorporating an art deco sensibility. Born in Hungary, Jonas attended art school in Budapest before immigrating to the United States at the age of fourteen. He settled in Denver, where his brother owned a successful taxidermy studio. In his later teenage years, Jonas met Carl Akeley and eventually went to New York to work at the American Museum of Natural History. He studied at the National Academy of Design under Hermon Atkins MacNeil and George Bridgeman. During World War I, Jonas designed camouflaged blinds for artillery installations. After the war, he returned to Denver; then, in 1926, he went to work at the American Museum, assisting Clark with taxidermy in the Asian Hall. During the late 1920s and early 1930s, Jonas created two of his best-known sculptures, *Giant Sable Antelope* (figure 4.7) and *Zebra Surprised by a Cobra* (figure 4.8). These bronzes represent Jonas at his most stylized, with sweeping swirls forming bases from which the animals emerge. Upright manes on both resemble the plumes on a Trojan helmet. The bold, smooth planes of the bodies complete each sculpture, creating a uniform whole.[14]

Jonas worked in both taxidermy and sculpture throughout his life, sometimes combining the two in novel ways. According to Beatrice Gilman Proske in *Brookgreen Gardens Sculpture*, "Jonas's admiration for Barye resulted in several action groups in taxidermy which he calls 'sculptodermy,' one of them an African lion attacking a Cape Buffalo, and another a lion slapping a coiled python, adapted from Barye's bronze" (see figure 3.1).[15] Jonas had always wanted to collaborate with Charles Knight on a dinosaur installation, but Knight died before the two had a chance to work together. Jonas did, however, help create nine life-sized dinosaurs for the New York World's Fair in 1964–65. Another crowning achievement was a series of over 350 animals sculpted in one-tenth scale, which he and a team placed into miniature habitat dioramas. These were made available to museums and schools that could not afford full-scale dioramas or did not have the space. Jonas was also commissioned to create a seal fountain for the Denver Zoo and a life-sized female grizzly bear with two cubs for Denver's City Park. Titled *Grizzly's Last Stand,* the statue was donated by John A. McGuire, founder of *Outdoor Life* magazine, in 1930. A plaque appended to the base offers a quote from McGuire and sums up the tenor of the times, as appropriate now as it was

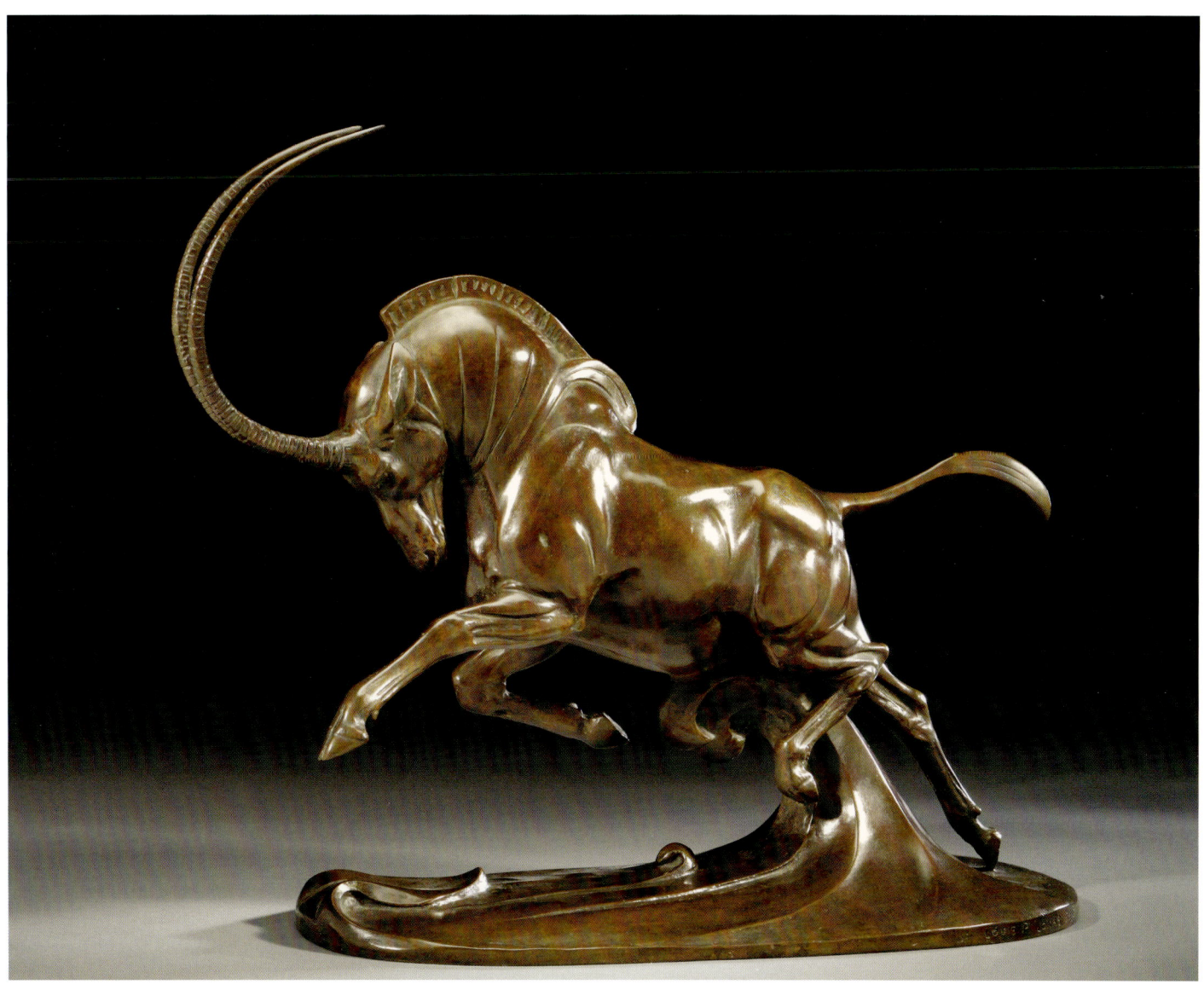

FIGURE 4.7.
LOUIS PAUL JONAS
Giant Sable Antelope, 1927.
Bronze; 14⅜ × 17¾ × 6¾ inches.
JKM Collection.
JL1995.049.

then: "When the grizzly is gone we shall have lost the most sublime specimen of wild life that exalts the western wilderness."[16]

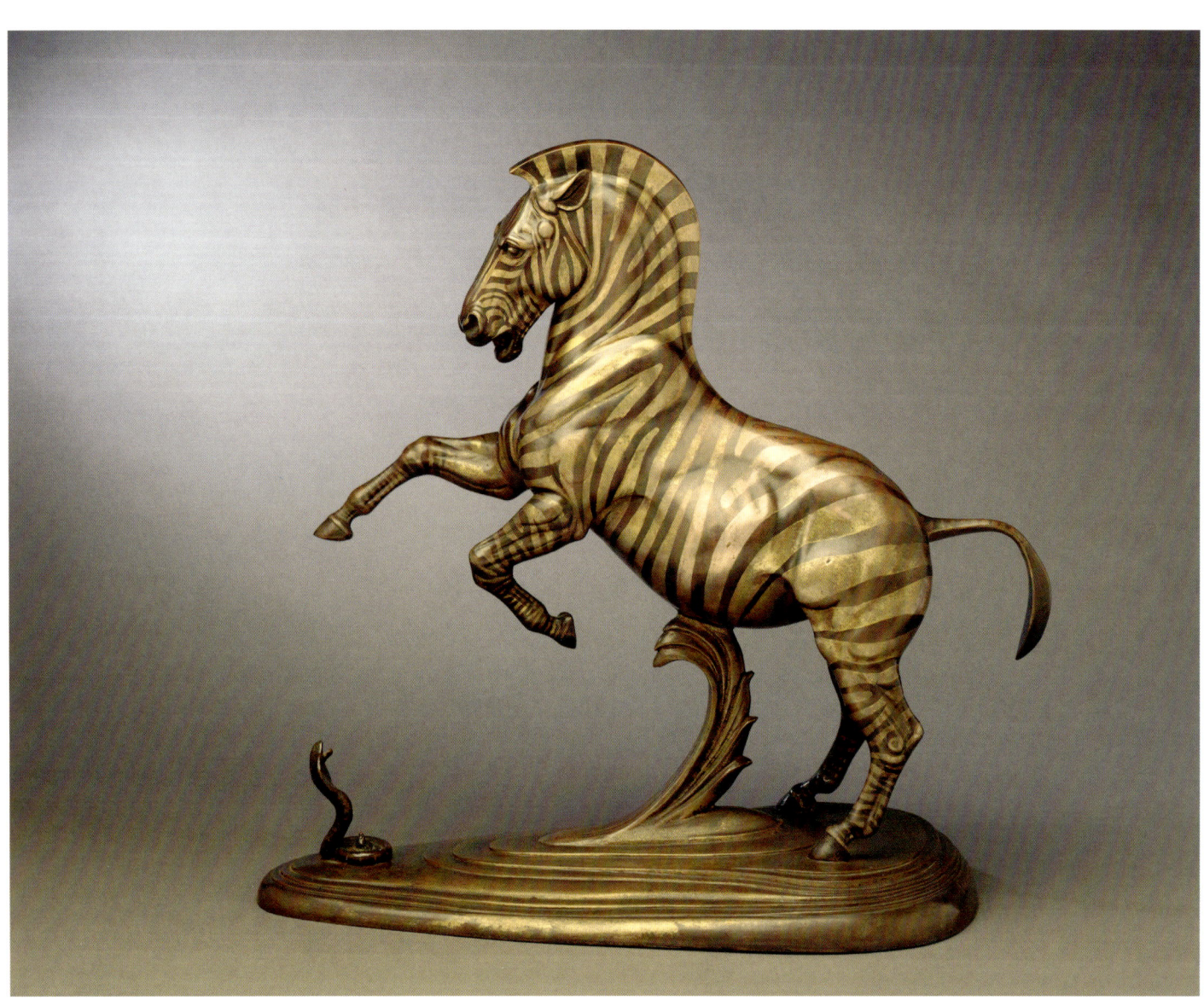

Figure 4.8.
Louis Paul Jonas
Zebra Surprised by a Cobra, 1935.
Bronze; 15¼ × 16½ × 8 inches.
JKM Collection.
JL1996.059.

Chapter 5

Carl Rungius and His Contemporaries: *Wildlife, Western, and Illustration Art*

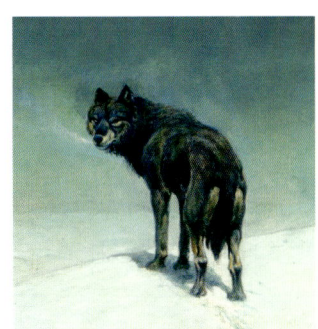

Carl Rungius is widely acknowledged as the premiere painter of North American wildlife; he is an icon in the field with a body of work that few others have approached in terms of quality, quantity, and influence. He is the modern forefather of what became a burgeoning American wildlife art movement in the twentieth century. Rungius's success is attributable not only to his ability and his longevity but also to a confluence of cultural concerns that came together in the early 1900s in America. Rungius was creating art in an era of increasing affluence and in an age of growing interest in the world's wildlife population. Also during this time, the impact of modern European art moments continued to have a profound effect on American art; many of the avant-garde stylistic innovations pioneered by French impressionists and postimpressionists became part of the everyday artistic vocabulary of painters who were more conservative. Using impressionistic techniques became an established and popular way of painting the great outdoors. This era was also in the midst of the golden age of illustration, an era that fueled a demand for artists to fill the pages of mass-market periodicals with alluring and dynamic imagery. Western art as a distinct subject became popular, as did wildlife; the two were often intertwined. Many prominent artists known for their American Indian and cowboy work also painted or sculpted animals, an integral part of the western experience.

The development of wildlife as a popular subject in art coincided with an increase in concern about wildlife in general. After Europeans disempowered indigenous populations in the American West and colonized regions of Africa, travel to these destinations became increasingly popular as the perceived threat of violence at the hands of native inhabitants diminished. The same cultural concern that propelled Carl Akeley and his group at the American Museum of Natural History to create dioramas of various exotic species from around the globe (discussed in the previous chapter) led the imagination of the general population farther afield, to wilder regions in their own country and abroad that had been previously inaccessible. Art historian Wayne Craven noted:

In the late 19th and early 20th centuries zoologists, sportsmen, photographers, and even artists were roaming the remote parts of the world in search of wild animals. Zoos were growing in number and size, and museums of natural history were displaying stuffed animals of the wilderness in their natural surroundings. Wealthy hunters and business tycoons, and even an American President, were traveling to the far-off jungles of Africa and to the still-wild areas of the American West for the thrill of stalking big game. The "stay-at-home" sportsmen contented themselves with Sunday afternoon family trips to the zoo.[1]

From illustrated magazines to fine art paintings and from natural history displays to zoo exhibits, wildlife was on the minds of a broad spectrum of the population. The potent iconography of American wildlife and wilderness extended internationally as Americans explored remote regions of the globe, either in person or from their armchairs.

Concomitant with this growing popular interest, advancing commercial enterprises continued to make damaging incursions into wilderness areas. A bittersweet nostalgia formed surrounding the loss of wildlife and wilderness at home and abroad. In a 1905 article about the presumed extinction of the bison in the *Saturday Evening Post,* Emerson Hough wrote, "Continually we make war upon the wilderness, its people, its creatures; yet, having done so, we covet again the wilderness, yearn for it, depend on it, and ape it even in our clothing. We may abolish the wilderness from the land and from the map, but we cannot abolish it from our blood."[2] Hough's quotation reiterates the contradictory position that Americans valued the wilderness because it was wild and free but also found self-affirmation in conquering and taming it.[3] The bison came to symbolize this contradiction, representing the quality of the wilderness Americans admired while at the same time expressing a lament over their role in its destruction. Newell Convers Wyeth illustrated Hough's article with a series of images, one titled *How Many Millions, One Can Only Guess,* a title that alludes to the massive numbers of bison that had once roamed the plains (see figure 5.25). In addition to articles such as Hough's, bison were the subject of sorrow in many mournful paintings from the early 1900s (picking up where William Cary and Frederick Verner left off at the end of the 1800s [see figures 1.17 and 1.19, respectively]). Rungius painted this subject in an early masterwork titled *The Last of the Herd* (figure 5.1), which focuses on a single bison standing away from a small group on a rolling plain near the Wind River Mountains. He revisited the topic in *The Days of Bison Millions* (figure 5.2), which pictures a plain full of bison, stretching as far as the eye can see.[4]

Images of bison and other animals were in demand, thanks to a developing fine art market. The growing middle class that began collecting art in the late 1800s continued to develop in the early 1900s. Art historian David Lubin wrote, "The

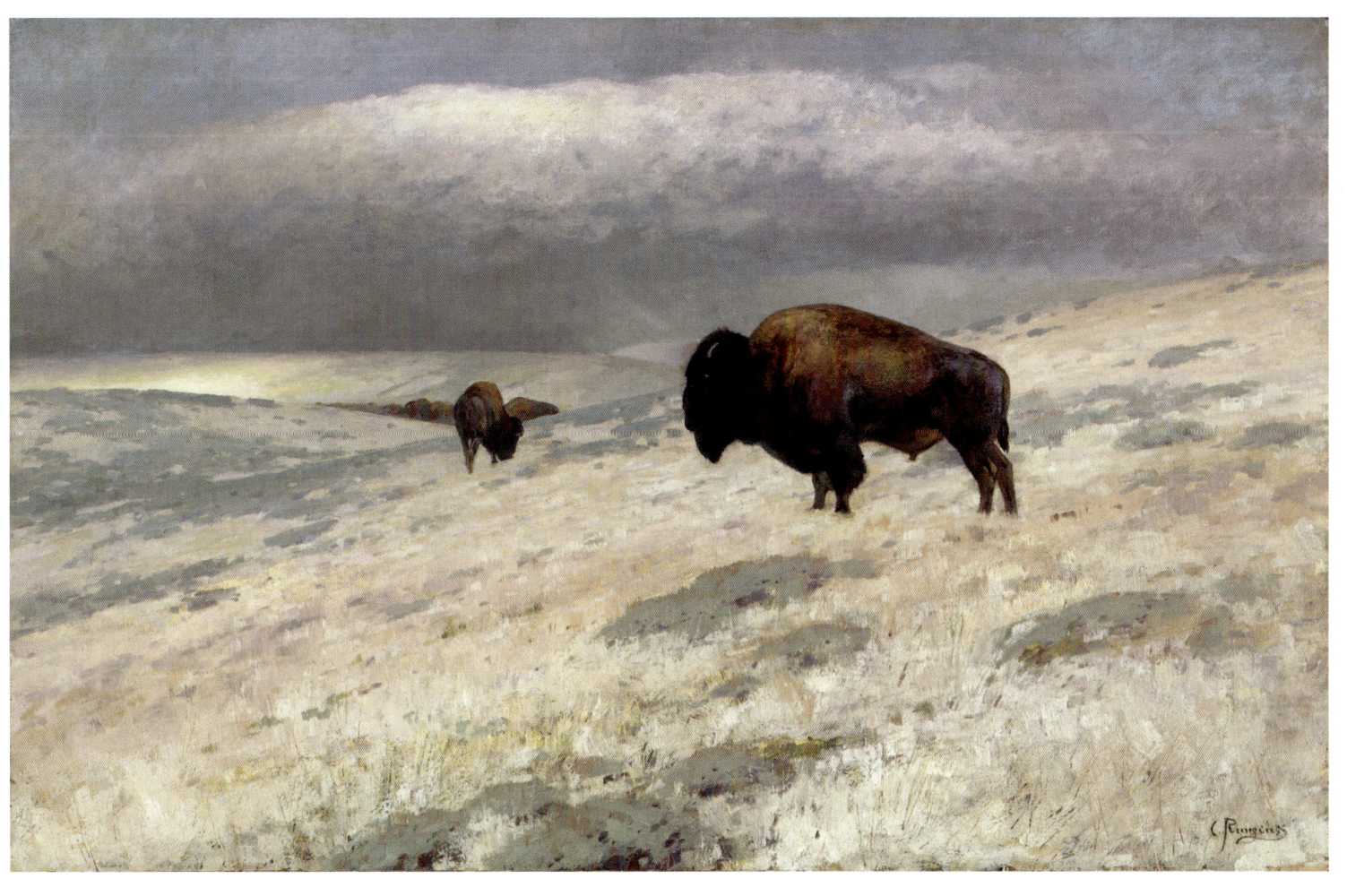

FIGURE 5.1.
CARL RUNGIUS
The Last of the Herd, 1900.
Oil on canvas; 28½ × 45½ inches.
Gift of Pete Widener, Jr.
National Museum of Wildlife Art Collection.
W1998.094.
© Estate of Carl Rungius

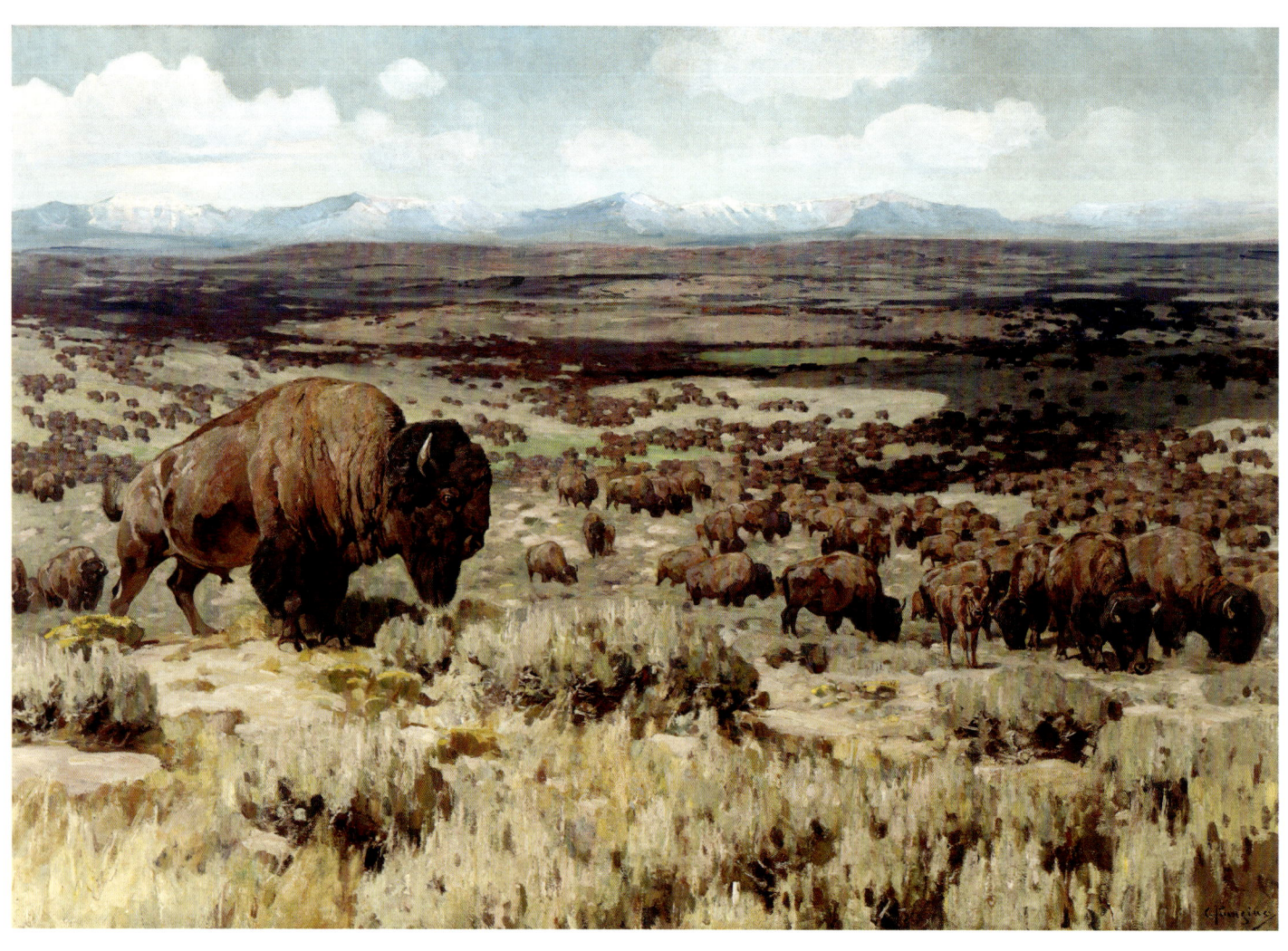

FIGURE 5.2.

CARL RUNGIUS

The Days of Bison Millions, 1917.

Oil on canvas; 69 × 90 inches.

Gift of Jackson Hole Preserve/

Laurence S. Rockefeller.

National Museum of Wildlife Art Collection.

W1994.081.

© Estate of Carl Rungius

public's appetite for art had indeed become enormous. Fine-art painting and sculpture were sought by men's clubs catering to [a] wealthy clientele who wished to mix leisure and commerce in culturally refined settings."[5] This trend evolved in part in reaction to the growing number of female patrons and artists. Lubin continued, "As never before, women entered the marketplace as art makers, art students, art instructors, art critics, art purchasers, and, simply, art viewers. Certain branches and sub-branches of painting that had traditionally been looked down upon by high-minded guardians of culture were now able to thrive: among them, for instance, flower painting and sentimental genre painting. At the same time that these 'feminine' branches of painting sprung onto the market, so too did certain reinvigorated 'masculine' branches: the hunt scene, for example; the provocative depiction of coy, fair-skinned, rustic maidens; and the *trompe l'oeil* still life."[6] If a still-life of flowers was hung in the parlor, then a proud moose painting might be found in the library, where men would retire from mixed company at the end of an evening. In painting masculine subjects that recalled the American wilderness, Rungius and his cohort flourished in the early twentieth century as the art market grew and the wilderness continued to play a symbolic role in the identity of the nation.

As wildlife subjects grew in popularity, so did masculine western subjects, spurring a camaraderie among the artists in these areas. In 1908, Frederic Remington (1861–1909) paid a visit to Rungius's New York studio. Unfortunately, the younger painter was not there, but Remington later wrote a complimentary note:

> My dear Mr. Rungius:
> I was disappointed in not finding you in, but Mrs. Rungius was kind enough to let . . . me see the elk and bear and the new moose pictures, all of which I like very much.
> For a long time I have said "This man Rungius knows our big game animals and he knows their backgrounds, and he paints it so it looks all right to me; and I am going to own one sooner or later." . . . There is not likely to be another fellow who will have the opportunity to study big game as you are doing, and I think records of us fellows who are doing the "Old America" which is so fast passing will have an audience in posterity, whether we do at present or not.[7]

Both artists have definitely gained an audience in posterity, as Remington hoped they would. Remington died a scant year after writing to Rungius—before Remington's reputation reached the height it has today and before he had a chance to acquire a Rungius painting. Rungius's reputation grew steadily during his lifetime, with people such as Theodore Roosevelt and William Temple Hornaday becoming his patrons and admirers. In addition, Rungius's reputation has grown since his death in 1959, as interest in wildlife art has followed a rising interest in western art among collectors, museums, and scholars. Remington's assertion that he and Rungius were painting the "Old America" provides a clear link between the two subjects and points out the nostalgia that was inherent, even then, in much western and wildlife artwork. Subjects seen as being truly American in nature—such as American Indians, cowboys, and wildlife—were of genuine interest to artists and audiences of the era; this interest expanded as those subjects began to fade into history, prompting some sense of urgency to record them before they disappeared forever from the increasingly populated West.

Wildlife and western art are often connected (as Remington did in his letter to Rungius), and many western artists included wildlife as part of their repertoire. In addition to Remington, well-known western artists such as Charles Russell and William Leigh contributed to wildlife art, painting the animals that were part and parcel of the outdoor experience (figure 5.3). Russell's wildlife paintings and sculptures make up a significant part of his oeuvre. Leigh traveled to Africa with Carl Akeley, and his designs for diorama backgrounds made their way into the permanent displays at the American Museum of Natural History in New York. Similar to the evolution of American animalier sculpture, a painting movement developed in the early 1900s that focused exclusively on wildlife: Emil Lenders was known as the finest painter of bison in Oklahoma; Belmore Browne painted the animals of the Canadian wilderness; Louis Agassiz Fuertes focused on American birdlife. All of these artists found a niche within wildlife art and explored it, producing powerful images that continue to resonate with art lovers today.

Popularizing the work of many painters during the early 1900s, the publishing industry proved an eager patron. Illustrated magazines were a major source of imagery for early-twentieth-century Americans and a major source of income for emerging artists. Illustration art is often compared unfavorably with fine art, with some justification. However, many highly regarded artists used illustration to support themselves as they began their careers. Several then broke away from illustration and built their legacies on painting subjects of their own choosing, not on assignment-driven art. Rungius and others in this chapter, such as William Leigh and Gerald Delano, followed this path. In contrast, Philip Goodwin never left illustration and has only recently received critical attention for the artistry of his oeuvre. As their reputations grew, some illustrators became known for particular subjects. Two artists who have yet to receive their critical due are Charles Livingston Bull and Paul Bransom: known for their animal art, both inspired a generation of younger artists such as Robert Kuhn to put pencil to paper and begin drawing wildlife.

As more artists began to depict animals, the specialized field of wildlife art emerged. By the end of the twentieth century, wildlife art had become a

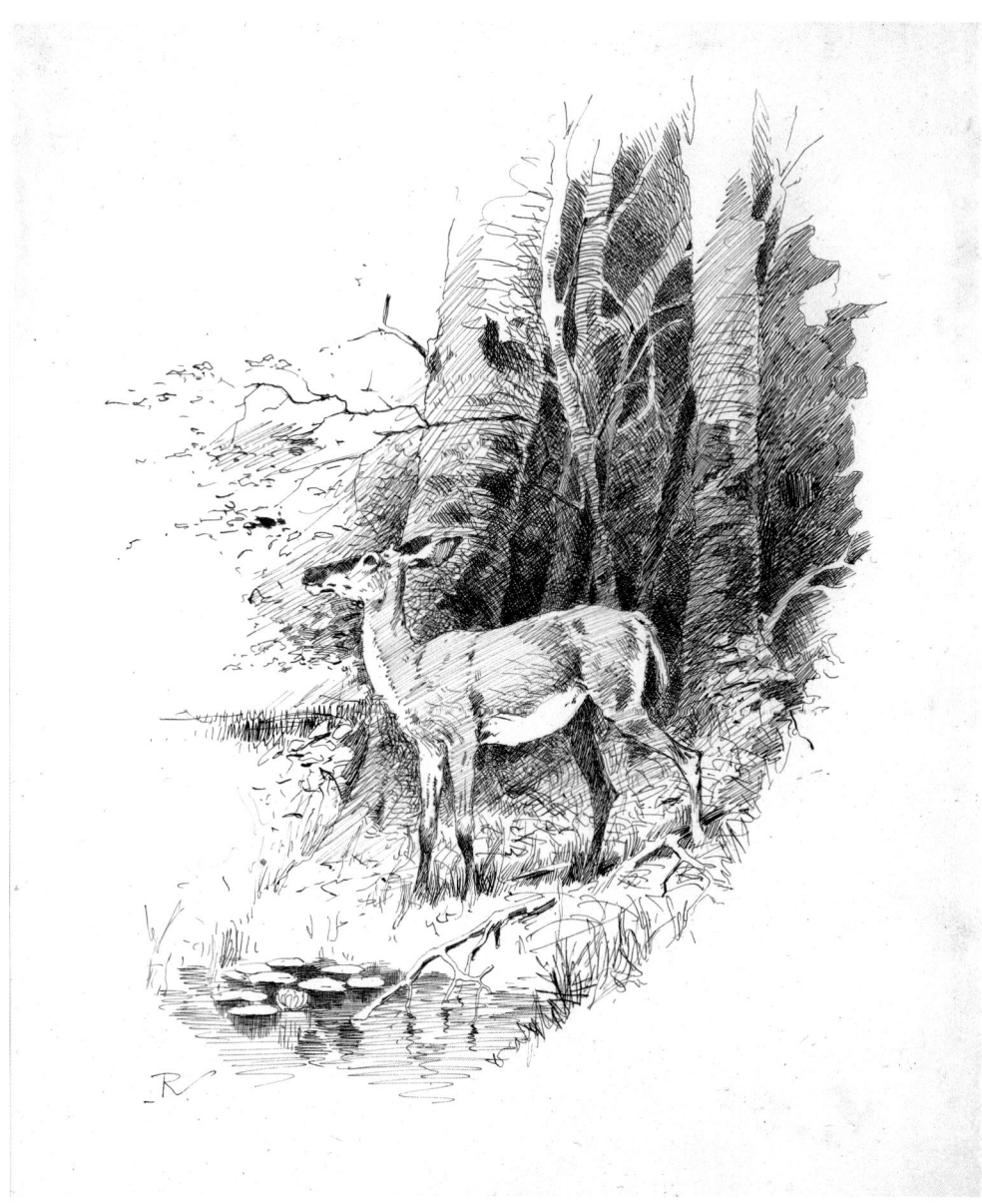

FIGURE 5.3.
FREDERIC REMINGTON
Deer in Forest, 1890.
Ink on paper; 14¾ × 12 inches.
JKM Collection.
JL1994.005.

major force in the art world, with associated fairs, exhibitions, and organizations. The field's popularity has also opened it to a great deal of criticism, some vehement.[8] Unfortunately, some critics retain a one-sided view of wildlife art, a view Rungius railed against relatively early in his career. In 1913, he told a reporter from the *New York Times,* "For me, my pictures are simply pictures . . . and I can't help deploring the insistence with which the general public looks upon animal pictures as illustrations of natural history."[9]

As recently as 2007, a reviewer for the *Toronto Globe and Mail,* in commenting on a retrospective of the work of artist Robert Bateman, wrote that Bateman describes the animals "in terms that are essentially those of illustration. There is no way in which his handling of paint, or his understanding of what painting is, pushes that medium forward, or even gives it a personal inflection. There is no way in which his paintings reveal interesting thinking about the relationships between man and nature; his environmentally themed paintings, for example, have all the sophistication of *Reader's Digest* illustrations."[10] Almost one hundred years after Rungius argued against judging wildlife painting as illustration, the practice continues. The main reason for this point of view in contemporary times is simple ignorance of the ongoing history of realism in the broader scope of art history. After the abstract art movements of the twentieth century, labeling anything representational as illustration comes all too readily; it is the simplest and easiest critique one can make. Labeling Bateman's paintings as lacking personal inflection reveals the reviewer's clear lack of knowledge of the specific history of wildlife art. Even a rank amateur can spot a Bateman painting a mile away based on his distinctive style: a style so popular that it has produced a string of imitators.

While wildlife art is often still prejudged and misunderstood by naïve reviewers, a trend among scholars and museums to look seriously at wildlife in art is emerging. *Fierce Friends: Artists and Animals, 1750–1900*, an exhibit shared between the Carnegie Museum of Art in Pittsburgh and the Van Gogh Museum in Amsterdam, opened in 2005. *Oudry's Painted Menagerie*, an exhibit shared between the Getty in Los Angeles and the Houston Museum of Fine Art, opened in 2007.[11] These exhibitions examine the place of animals in art within the greater realm of art history in an effort to understand the ongoing relevance and interest in the subject. They are not looking at the genre of wildlife art per se but at wildlife *in* art, a broader playing field that opens the door to a greater variety of imagery and artists. This wider perspective aligns with the mission and collection at the National Museum of Wildlife Art. One of the most interesting things about wildlife is the nearly universal attraction it has for artists across generations, working in a variety of styles, in a variety of places. Just this small survey from the museum's permanent collection includes artists ranging from George Catlin to Georgia O'Keeffe: two artists painting a century apart with different motivations, styles, and influences. Displaying this kind of diverse history is pivotal to the museum's mission.

Central to the history on display at the museum is the work of Carl Rungius. He and his cohort (including Wilhelm Kuhnert, Richard Friese, and Bruno Liljefors) broke new ground around the turn of the nineteenth century with their environmentally conscious paintings of wildlife in natural habitats. At the end of the 1800s, Germany gained a strong reputation for its school of animal art. Painter Paul Meyerheim (1842–1915) led classes in animal drawing at the Royal Academy of Arts in Berlin, teaching his students to study animals carefully at the zoo.[12] Friese was a student at the academy and later became a professor. Meyerheim's students also included Rungius and Kuhnert. After honing their artistic skills in urban menageries, Friese, Rungius, and Kuhnert took wildlife art into the field, pioneering the discipline of studying and sketching animals in the wild and then returning to the studio to create finished canvases. At the same time, artist Bruno Liljefors was accomplishing similar things in his home country of Sweden.

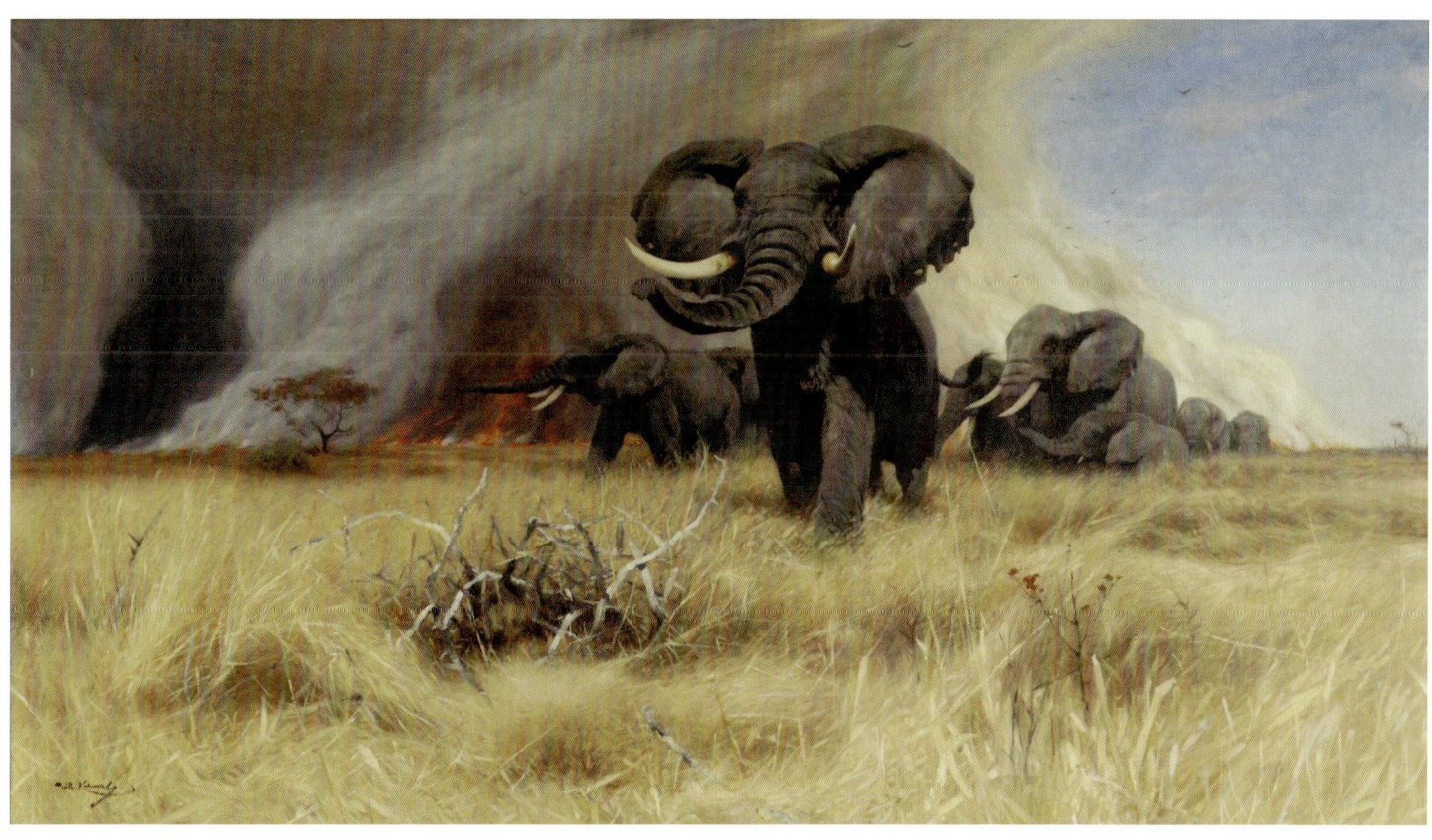

These artists are known as the "Big Four," the acknowledged masters of late-nineteenth and early-twentieth-century wildlife painting, and each had his own area of specialization: Kuhnert is best known for his paintings of African wildlife (figure 5.4); Friese focused on the animals of the Arctic and northern Germany (figure 5.5); and Liljefors depicted wildfowl as well as foxes, hares, and eagles in his own environs (figure 5.6). Rungius claimed the large mammals of North America as his domain; he ventured out and studied these animals in the wild as no one before him had done. The Big Four tended to concentrate on natural habitat and natural behaviors. Gone were the imagined battles between felines and serpents of Antoine-Louis Barye (see figure 3.1) or the fantastical renderings of artists such as Jean-Léon Gérôme (1824–1904 [figure 5.7]), whose *Tiger Observing Cranes* is masterful for what it is, an evocation of the exotic aimed at wealthy urbanites that in no way is meant to record the specific behavior of a tiger in its natural habitat. The Big Four produced magnificent canvases of animals in the wilderness, beautifully conceptualized, composed, and rendered. They shared a dedication to careful observation and field sketching. Back in their respective studios, they combined their research into breathtaking compositions and had the skill to alter and adjust their material to create canvases of lasting impact.[13]

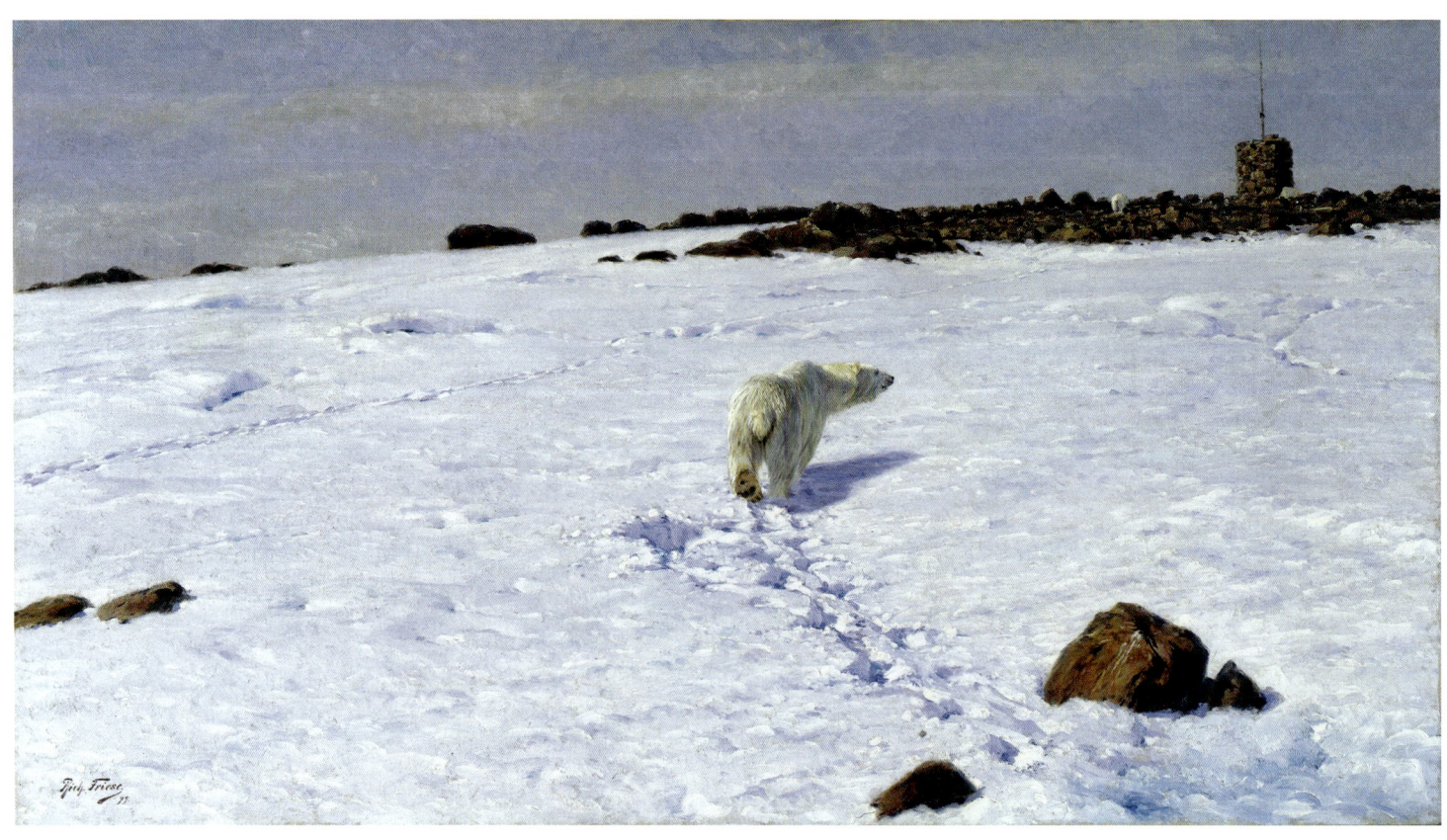

FIGURE 5.5.
RICHARD FRIESE
Arktikwanderer, 1899.
Oil on canvas; 36 × 56 inches.
JKM Collection.
J1991.033.

The style of the three youngest artists in the Big Four also developed along similar lines. Early works by Kuhnert, Liljefors, and Rungius are tightly rendered and employ a relatively dark palette. As each spent more time out in the wilderness, his painting became looser and his colors became brighter. The influence of impressionism and postimpressionism and the rapid acceptance of those styles among the art-buying public certainly had something to do with this change. However, the practice of rapidly recording animals in nature or capturing specific effects of passing light on a hillside trained these artists to work quickly, laying in shape, color, and value with confident, swift strokes. Their later work did not rely on fussy details to create an impression but conveyed an essence of the animal and the landscape with bravura brushstrokes that aptly completed the scene.[14]

Friese, Kuhnert, Rungius, and Liljefors ushered in a new era in wildlife art, reflecting a shared vision of the importance of wildlife and habitat—a vision that was fully in line with the Romantic definition of the wilderness as untrammeled and pristine. Of this group in this survey of wildlife in American art, Rungius plays the most important role. In addition to his undeniable skill, Rungius lived a long life and produced paintings of high quality for most of it. His career occurred during an era when wildlife painting was of growing interest across a broad spectrum of the art-buying public. From wealthy men's-club-goers to individuals concerned with

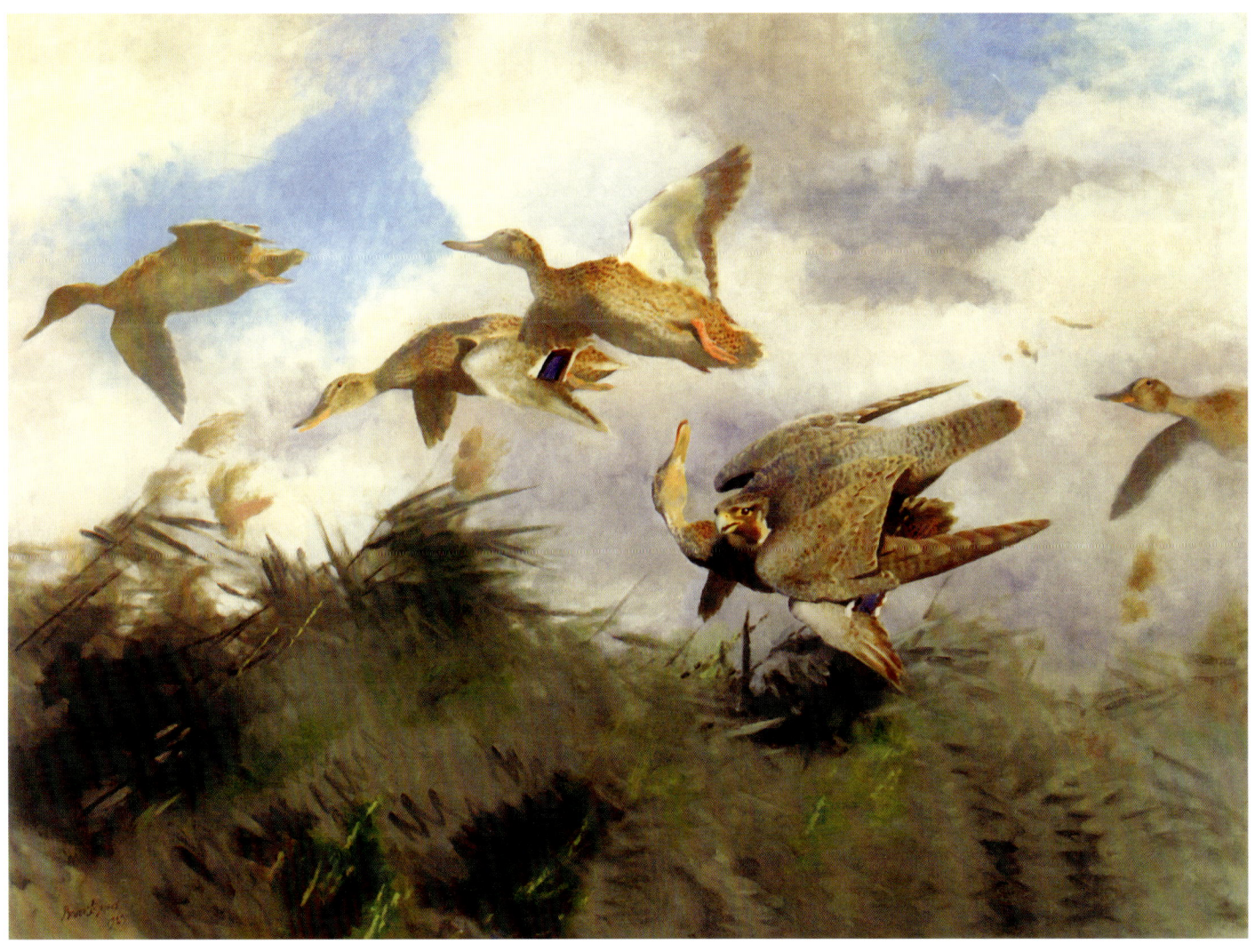

conservation, Rungius's work spoke to patrons leading increasingly urbanized lives who longed for outdoor adventure. These patrons were also concerned with the loss of wilderness and wildlife and wanted some representation of it in their homes. Rungius's success set the benchmark for his contemporaries and for a generation of later artists who painted the wildlife of North America. The works in this chapter display the ongoing interest in North American wildlife among Rungius's contemporaries and the next generation, across a spectrum of diverse artists, including painters of the Old West, illustrators, and naturalists.

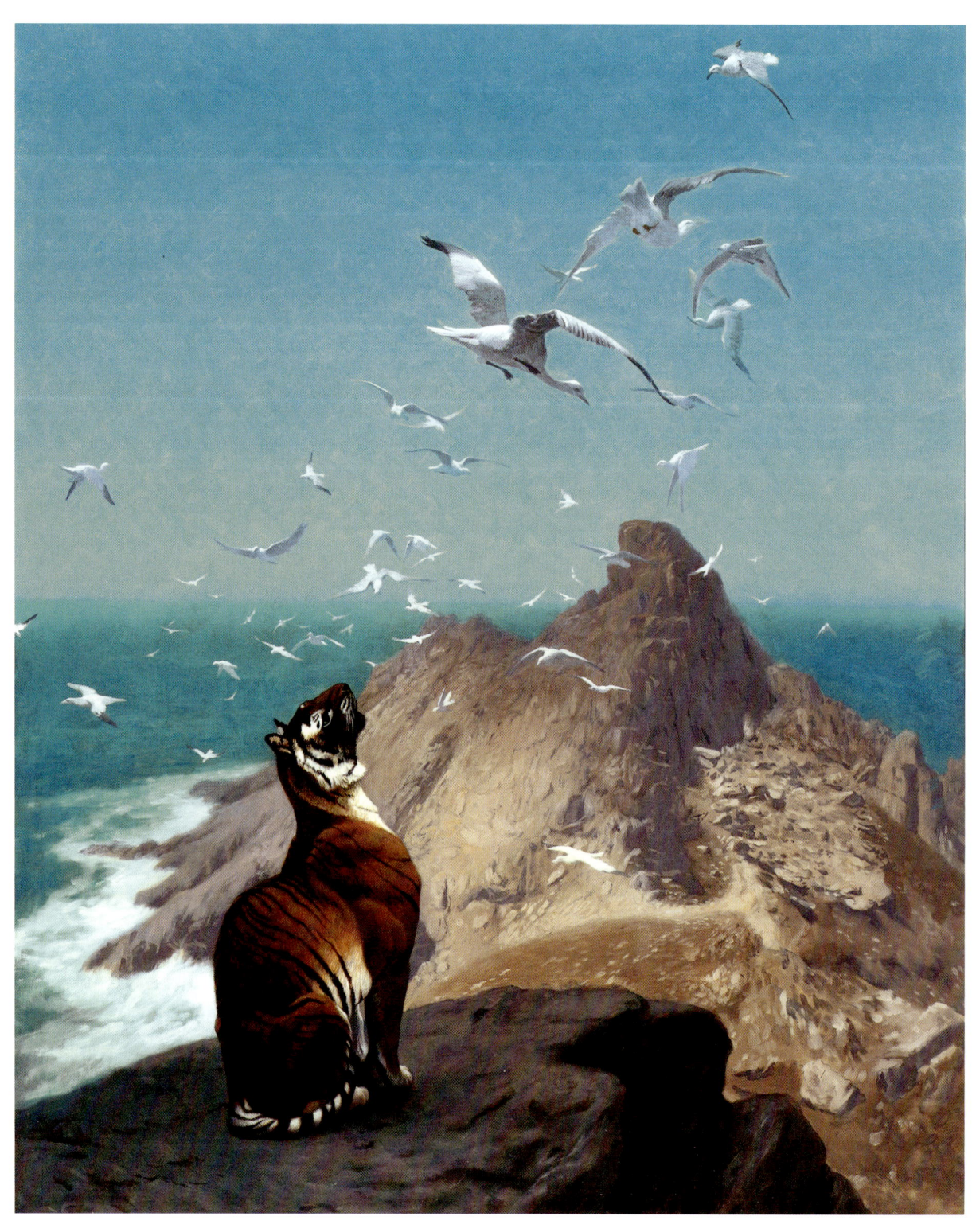

FIGURE 5.7.

JEAN-LÉON GÉRÔME

Tiger Observing Cranes, c. 1890.

Oil on canvas, mounted on panel;

32 × 25¼ inches.

National Museum of Wildlife Art Collection.

M2001.159.

CARL RUNGIUS
Germany, 1869–1959

Of the many mammals of North America, the moose most clearly appealed to Carl Rungius. In fact, he was worried that in perpetuity he would be known as "the man who paints moose."[15] Rungius excelled at painting other animals, of course: elk, bear, deer, mountain goats, and mountain sheep were among his favorites. He was also unequalled in his ability to convey a sense of the vast and rugged landscape that made up his subject's natural habitat. *Northern King* (figure 5.8) is atypical for its lack of a mountainous background, but Rungius communicates a sense of the wide western sky with a brilliant expanse of blue and pink paint that extends across the upper two-thirds of the canvas. Another particular strength of his was painting the intricate patterns of crossing trunks and broken branches of the deadfall that lie below the moose. As he became more confident in his abilities and became freer with his brushwork, Rungius laid-in densely wooded foreground with bravura strokes that made for both a perfect representation of moose habitat and a masterly demonstration of painting prowess.

In 1894, the German-born Rungius accepted an invitation from his uncle to travel across the Atlantic for a Maine moose hunt. Their first foray was unsuccessful, prompting Rungius to stay in New York and try again the following season. During the spring of 1895, Rungius met outfitter Ira Dodge, who had a ranch in Wyoming at the base of the Wind River Mountains. That summer, Rungius traveled west and fell in love with the wide open spaces and the abundant elk and pronghorn antelope. He also experienced a freedom to hunt and explore that was unavailable in Germany. That trip changed the course of Rungius's life. He remarked to biographer William Schaldach, "Returning to New York in December, I painted from the collected material and later, in the spring of 1896, I went back to Germany for a few months. My decision to cut all ties with the Old World and to live in America for good was due in no small part to this first Wyoming trip. For my heart was in the West."[16]

In 1910, Rungius traveled to Banff in Alberta, Canada. The magnificent wilderness and plentiful wildlife of the region appealed to him; he was always on the lookout for new territory to explore and new wildlife to paint. He spent most of the summers thereafter in Banff, building a studio and home there in 1922. By 1915, Rungius had broadened his subject matter to include scenes of ranch life, pack trains, and landscapes. Rungius remarked, after spending time in

Alberta, "I felt strongly the urge to paint straight landscape—that is, landscape for its own sake. Until then I had considered landscape only as a setting for big game animals. But the grandeur of the mountains with the marvelous atmospheric conditions in Alberta and consequent color effects changed all of that."[17] After submitting landscape paintings of the Canadian Rockies to the National Academy of Design, Rungius was elected as an associate member in 1913. He was elected a full academician in 1920 for a round-up painting called *On the Range,* which was based on material collected on a 1915 trip to Wyoming. During that stay, Rungius encountered little wildlife. He remembered, "Since there was no big game left there for studies, I painted horses, cattle and landscape. . . . I rode with a couple of round-ups, making sketches and photographs from the saddle."[18]

In his forties, Rungius began using a broader brush and was able to handle his paint and colors with greater confidence. The change in his style can be seen by comparing *The Last of the Herd,* from the early 1900s, with *Northern King,* from the middle 1920s (see figures 5.1 and 5.8). In *The Last of the Herd,* Rungius was experimenting with ways of handling the atmosphere, using predominantly pastel tones. He also was using a thinner brush and included finer details in both the animals and the vegetation. By the time he painted *Northern King,* Rungius had migrated to bolder colors applied with thicker brushstrokes. He often used a wet-on-wet technique, which allowed paint from different layers to intermingle and create distinct colors on the canvas. Rungius did not paint his masterpieces all in one sitting, however. He was a meticulous craftsman and would set work aside to let it rest, picking it up later to add finishing touches. This method let him build up certain areas with many layers of paint, which adds to the substantial feeling of each canvas. Individual elements in *Northern King* such as tree trunks, vegetation, and even the moose's coat are composed of blocks of color that seamlessly integrate to create a cohesive, dynamic whole.

The head of the New York Zoological Society, William Temple Hornaday, was an admirer of Rungius's work and commissioned him to begin a series of paintings of North American mammals for the society's headquarters in the Bronx. Although the commissions provided Rungius with a steady income over the middle period of his career, they were difficult for him at times because of the society's stipulation that each painting had to be a full and accurate representation of the animal, limiting his artistic freedom. However, the works of art that he completed for the society, particularly *American Black Bear* and *The Days of Bison Millions* (see figure 5.2), have stood the test of time and rank as some of his most accomplished paintings.

American Black Bear (figure 5.9) is one of the most impressive pieces commissioned by the society, combining vibrant colors, bold brushstrokes, and a loose painting style. Hornaday, however, did not necessarily regard these as positive aspects; he preferred the carefully delineated animals that Rungius had produced

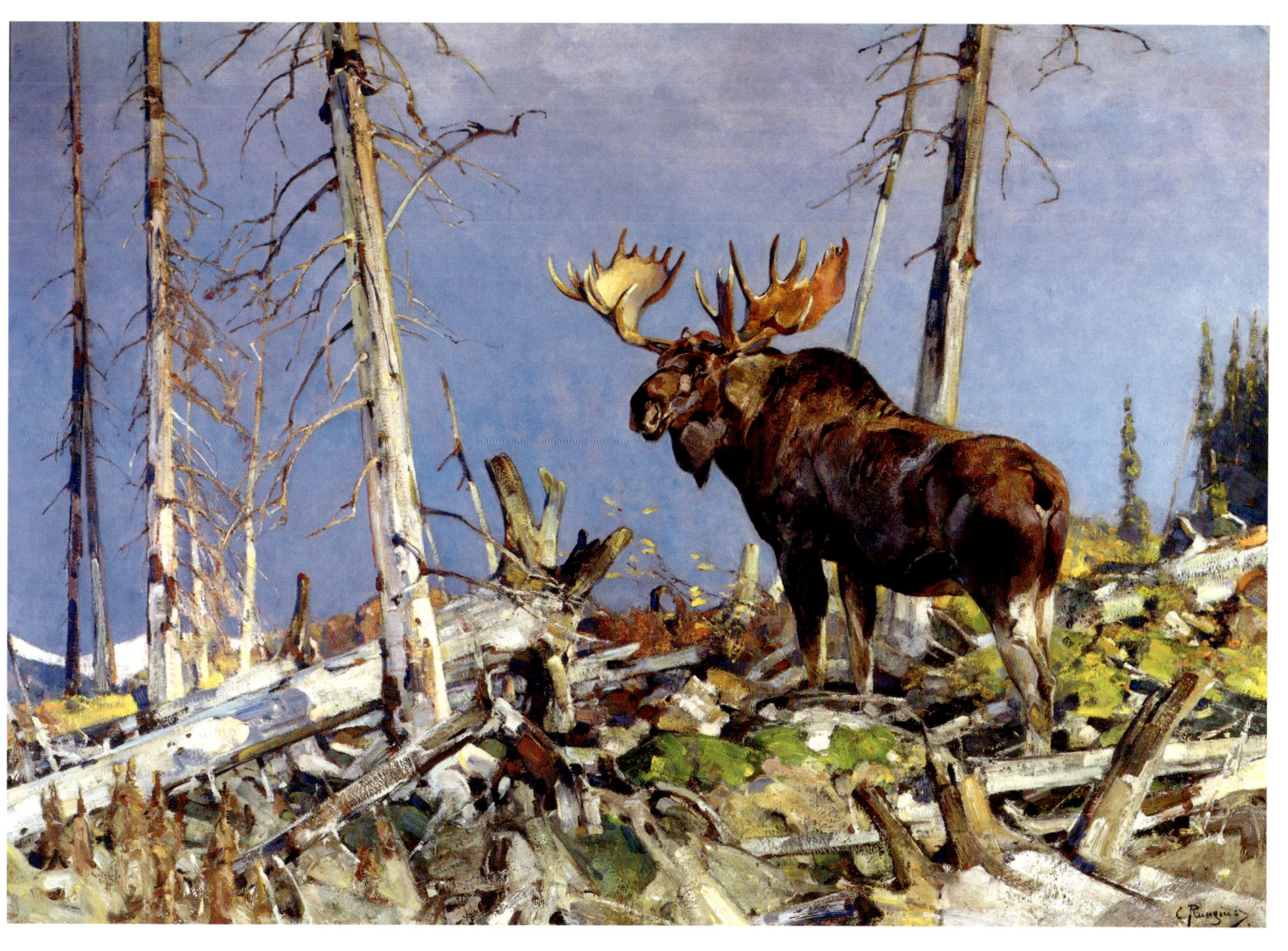

FIGURE 5.8.
CARL RUNGIUS
Northern King, 1926.
Oil on canvas; 42 × 60 inches.
JKM Collection.
J1987.024.

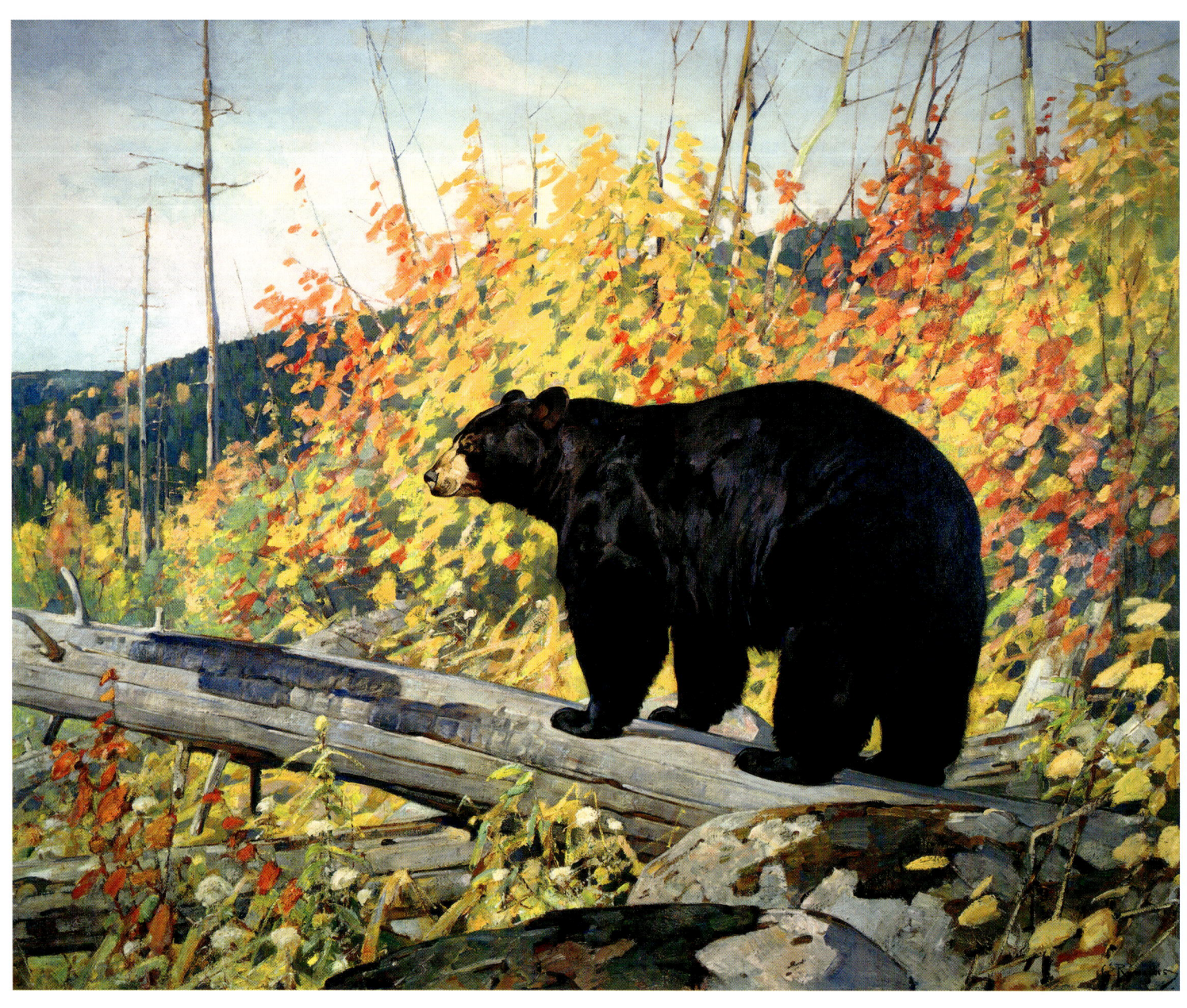

FIGURE 5.9.

CARL RUNGIUS

American Black Bear, 1929.

Oil on canvas; 61½ × 76½ inches.

Gift of the Jackson Hole Preserve/

Laurence S. Rockefeller.

National Museum of Wildlife Art Collection.

W1994.082.

© Estate of Carl Rungius

earlier in his career. In 1925, dissatisfied with the direction in which Rungius was heading, Hornaday wrote, "Your letter and your latest pictures clearly indicate that you have greatly changed your technique, and that you are now an out-and-out impressionist."[19] Despite Hornaday's misgivings, however, the society continued to commission paintings from Rungius until the middle of the 1930s, and Rungius continued to develop his impressionistic style.

The years between 1925 and 1945 were Rungius's peak period. He was painting with great passion, confidence, and knowledge. Rungius had grown from a young sportsman into a mature painter, remaining eager to explore new territory and study different animals until his final days. His undeniably moving and beautiful work envisions the wilderness as a place apart from everyday life, apart from human habitation. Rungius's paintings of lone moose, standing amidst deadfall with sunlit peaks towering in the background, embodied the essence of what the wilderness meant to many people; his popularity during his lifetime is in no small part due to his ability to depict this shared vision of the wild (his postmortem popularity can be similarly attributed). Rungius's reputation continues to grow as art lovers see and study his art. His paintings can be admired for their realistic representation of wildlife and nature; for their dynamic composition, colorful palette, and impressionistic sensibility; or for their distinct evocation of the wilderness ideal. American wildlife painting would not be what is today without Rungius; he set the standard for artists of his generation and continues to be studied, copied, and admired.

JOHN FERY
HUNGARY, 1859–1934

For the majority of his life, John Fery devoted himself to painting grand mountain vistas. He is best known for his large paintings set in Glacier National Park, most of which were commissioned by the Great Northern Railroad.[20] *Red Eagle Lake* (figure 5.10) is a prime example of Fery's work, both in composition and in style. His training in the classic European manner of the Vienna Academy of Art is apparent in his clear ability to negotiate the transitions from the atmospheric heights of the Rocky Mountains to the forested middle ground to the two moose in the foreground. He was not a meticulous painter, picking out every detail, but painted with relatively broad strokes, capturing the essence of a scene. Fery first traveled to the United States in 1883 and began painting panoramas, the entertainment rage of the late 1800s. A panorama was a very long canvas or series of canvases painted with a battle scene or historic tableau displayed in a circular arrangement, to provide an all-encompassing visual spectacle. After his stint at panorama painting, Fery returned to Europe and married, then took his wife and firstborn daughter to America in 1886, settling first in New Jersey and later in Cleveland, Ohio. Throughout the next several years, Fery often left his family to go on sketching trips, exploring the great American outdoors.

Fery was among the first artists to depict the Tetons in Jackson Hole, Wyoming.[21] He first traveled through the area in 1891 en route to Seattle. On this trip, he made arrangements to lead upscale hunting trips through the region, which he did in 1892 and 1895. Fery had hoped that these adventures would provide a base of financial security for his family, but they did not prove profitable. The strain of being away from his family also took its toll, and Fery decided to bring his wife and three children with him to Jackson in 1900. They took up residence in a cabin on Jackson Lake in the fall, remaining through the long winter and into spring. Fery reveled in the freedom to sketch the surrounding landscape, but his family suffered from the isolation and the cold. During these years, Fery completed thirty-five known canvases of the region, including *Jackson Lake and the Tetons* (figure 5.11). In this painting, he combines elk with a view of Jackson Lake and a striking silhouette of the Teton Range. The Tetons were not often painted, particularly from the east, until the middle of the 1900s, when artists such as Conrad Schwiering, John Clymer, and Paul Bransom began to focus artistic attention on the region.

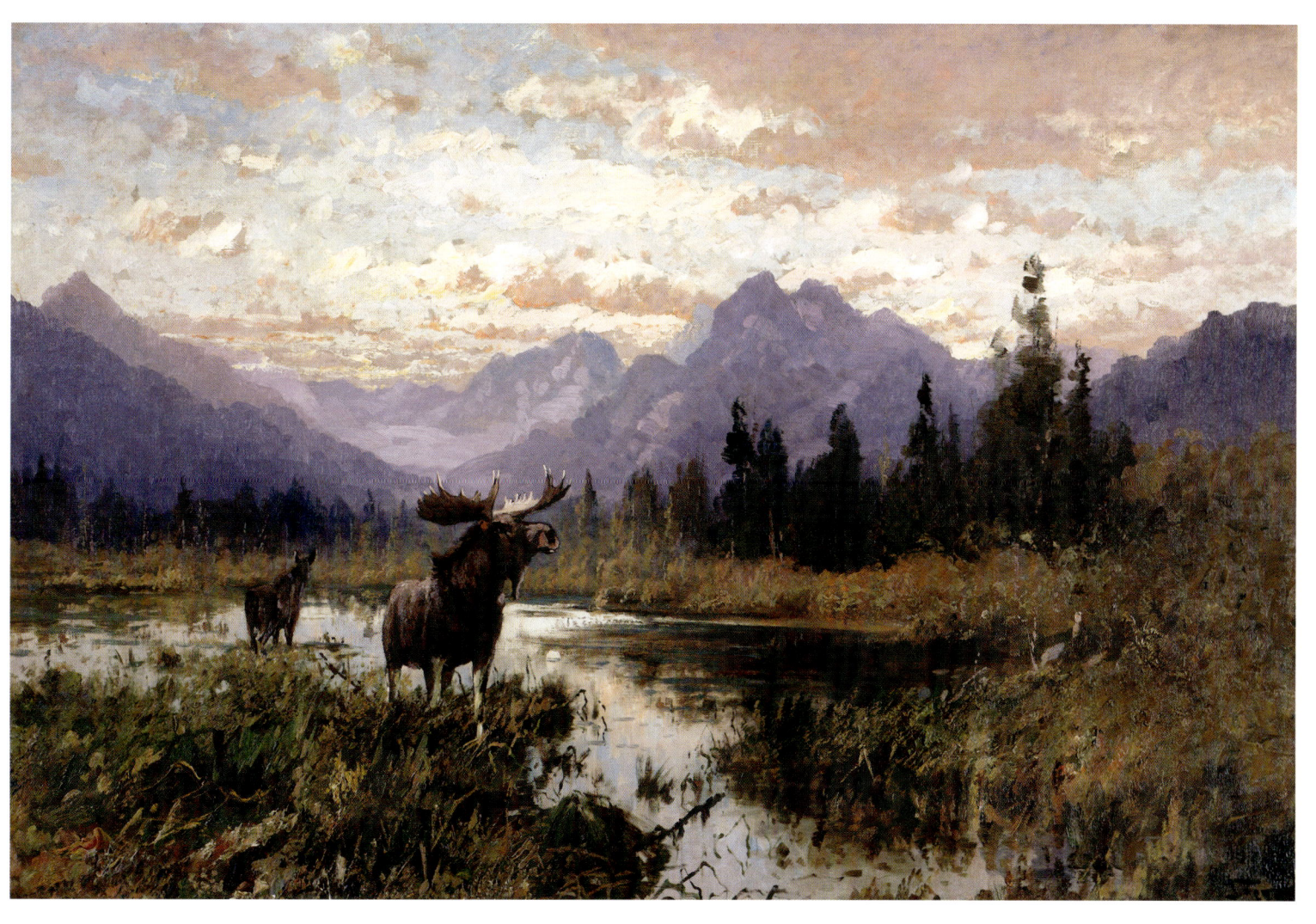

FIGURE 5.10.

JOHN FERY

Red Eagle Lake, Glacier National Park, 1915.

Oil on canvas; 40 × 60 inches.

JKM Collection.

M1990.036.

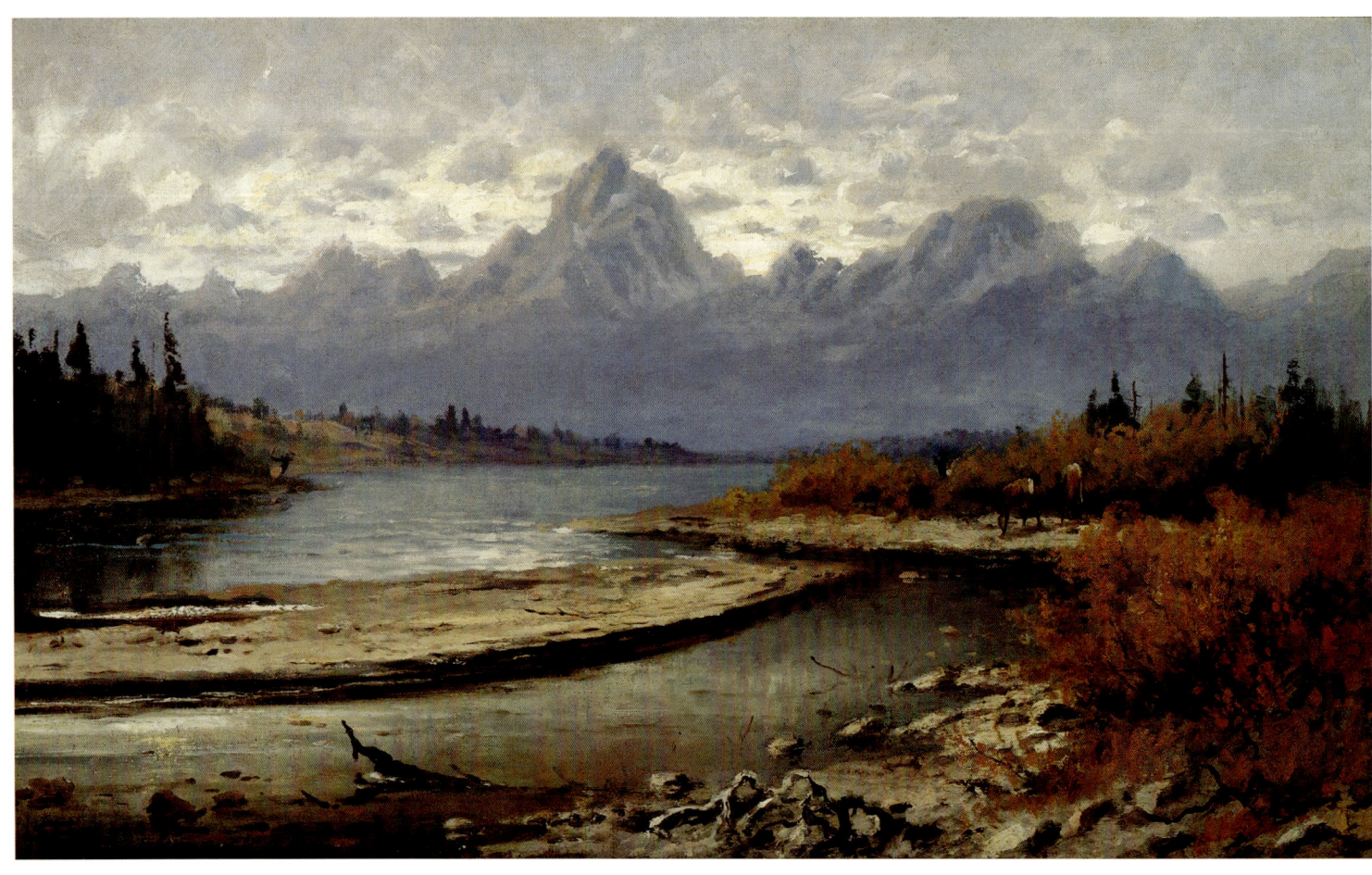

After their stay in Wyoming, the family moved to Milwaukee, where Fery established a studio with eleven other German artists. In 1911, Fery moved to Minnesota, where the Great Northern Railroad commissioned him to create large paintings of the scenery en route to and within Glacier National Park. The paintings served as advertisements for rail travel and for the Great Northern's hotel inside the park. In 1920, Fery moved to Salt Lake City and painted more landscapes, concentrating on Zion's canyon. He eventually settled on Orcas Island, near Bellingham, Washington. In 1929, a fire destroyed his cabin and all his possessions, including many of his paintings and sketches. After the death of his wife in 1930, he moved to Everett, Washington, where he died four years later. Fery's canvases celebrating the beauty of Glacier National Park inspired many to take a trip on the Great Northern. After his death and after the railroad changed advertising strategies, however, Fery's work fell into relative obscurity. Though he was painting in many of the same places as artists such as Thomas Hill, his reputation has not attained the same heights. Recent interest in the artwork of Glacier National Park and a traveling exhibit of Fery's work have begun to bring him back into the spotlight.[22]

EMIL W. LENDERS
England, 1864–1934

E mil Lenders was born in England, the child of an English father and a German mother. His father died when he was four, and his mother moved the remaining family to her father's home in Stuttgart, Germany. There, Lenders's mother became an antiques dealer, and as Emil grew older, she hoped he would open an antique store of his own. However, Lenders's interest in American Indian culture, spurred by reading the adventure novels of Karl May, led him in a different direction. Despite his mother's disapproval of art study, Lenders attended art school in Berlin and began a painting career. He immigrated to the United States sometime in the late 1880s, becoming a U.S. citizen in 1906. About this time, Lenders encountered Buffalo Bill's Wild West show; he soon became a regular fixture around their camp, studying the animals, cowboys, and American Indians as the troupe traveled across the country. He was befriended by Buffalo Bill, who convinced him to settle in Oklahoma. On the Miller Brothers' 101 Ranch, Lenders was able to study and sketch resident buffaloes, as well as individuals from the Wild West show. As a measure of esteem, Buffalo Bill gave Lenders a saddle with an inscribed silver plate:

> Emil William Lenders
> *The best painter of buffalo in the world,*
> *From his admiring friend W. F. Cody*
> July 1910   Buffalo Bill[23]

In an article for *Gilcrease Journal*, Joan Carpenter Troccoli wrote, "Although [Lenders] never enjoyed the renown of such contemporary painters of the West as Charles Marion Russell or William Robinson Leigh, Lenders was, at his death in 1934, one of Oklahoma's most prominent artists. . . . Gordon W. 'Pawnee Bill' Lillie called him 'the best painter in the world of our national animal, the buffalo.'"[24] *The Challenge* (figure 5.12) provides ample evidence of Lenders's skill as a bison painter. The painting depicts a large bull, head raised in a pose that suggests imminent action. The bison is either sniffing the wind for sign of a challenger or warning off other bulls in the herd. In the middle ground, another big bison approaches, perhaps looking for a fight. Spread out in the background, a vast herd of bison reaches to the horizon, but the main emphasis here is not on

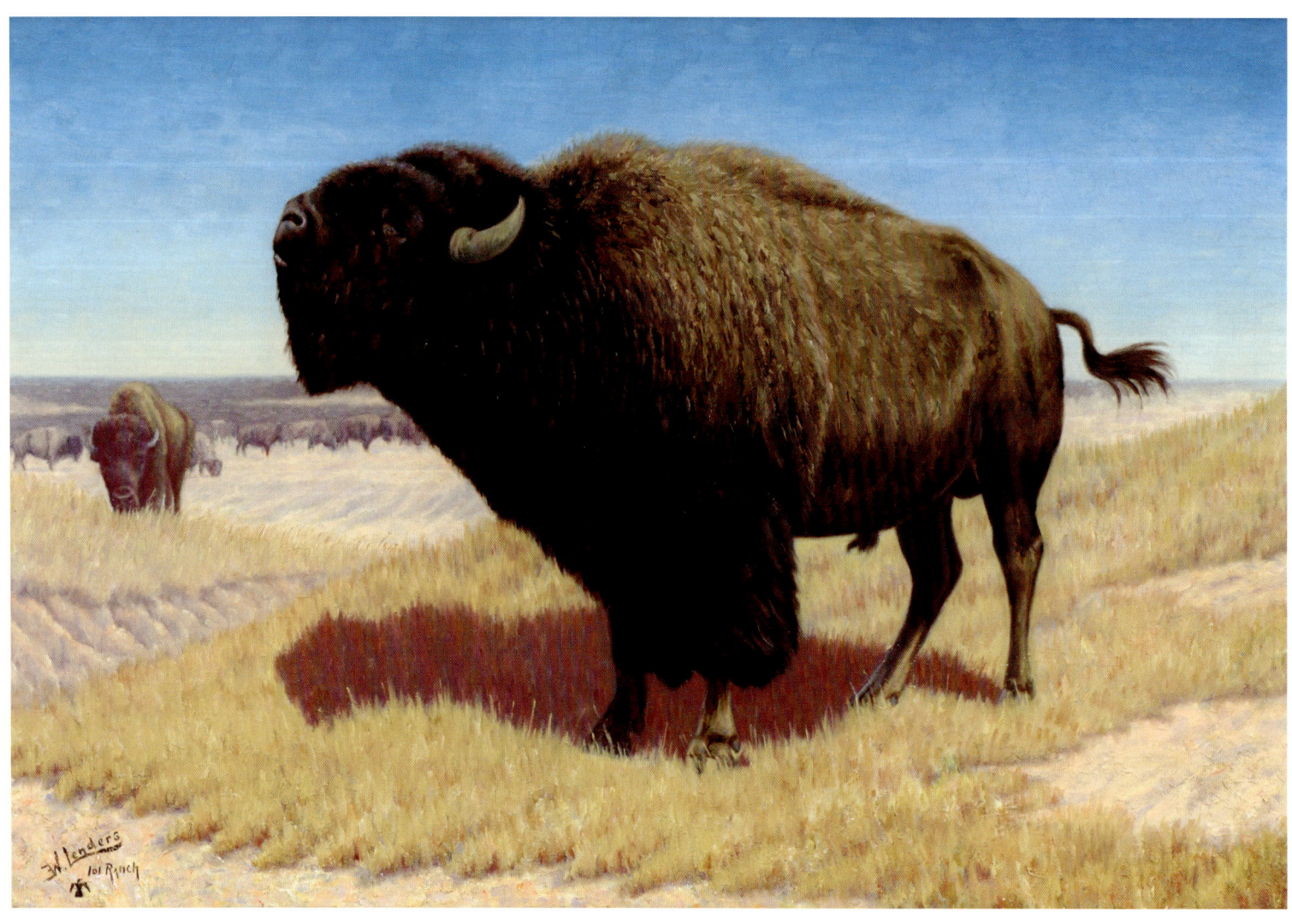

FIGURE 5.12.
EMIL W. LENDERS
The Challenge, c. 1925.
Oil on canvas; 24 × 36 inches.
JKM Collection.
JL1994.045.

the many but on the one (unlike N. C. Wyeth's *How Many Millions, One Can Only Guess* [see figure 5.25], where the overall tone is sadder and more nostalgic).

Lenders said of the bison, "Buffalo should be designated the king of beasts. . . . The buffalo is the American animal; this was his only home; he was found nowhere else. He should be preserved just as he is for all future generations."[25] Lenders's work elevated the bison to heroic status, a symbol of what was most impressive about America. Ironically, Lenders lived in an age when many of the remaining bison were living on private ranches in small, protected herds. Their existence was not ensured, and their daily life more closely resembled that of domestic cattle than that of wild, free-roaming denizens of the plains.

CHARLES M. RUSSELL
UNITED STATES, 1864–1926

In *To the Victor Belong the Spoils*, a pack of wolves circles a grizzly bear standing over a deer (figure 5.13). Unanswered questions provide narrative drama. Did the wolves or the bear kill the deer? Who will end up with the spoils? Do we sympathize with the bear as the individual besieged by the wolf pack? Or do we sympathize with the wolves, who may have had the fruits of their collective labor stolen by the big bully of the forest? Typical of many of Charles Russell's works, this piece lays out the elements of a story and prompts viewers to imagine a conclusion.

Russell is known primarily as a cowboy artist; along with Frederic Remington, he cemented a distinct image of the American West in the minds of many people in the early 1900s. However, a close comparison of Russell's and Remington's oeuvres reveals that the two had very different visions of the West. Russell's view was, in general, kinder, more sympathetic, and more humorous; Remington's West was harsher and more serious. Another key difference is that Remington did few major wildlife pieces, while about a quarter of Russell's work incorporated wildlife. *To the Victor* has little humor, but it does not present the animals in the heat of battle; the conflict is still in the reconnaissance stage, where anything is possible. Many of Russell's bronzes, particularly those that depict animal interactions, display his broad sense of humor. *The Bluffers* (figure 5.14), for example, compares the aggressive posturing of one wild animal confronting another, each putting on a great show of strength meant to intimidate the opponent. The title indicates that both may have a bark in mind rather than a bite.[26]

Russell was self-taught and began drawing and sculpting at an early age. When he was fifteen, he left his hometown of Saint Louis and moved to Montana to work as a cowboy. The western lifestyle became the focus of his sketches and paintings. His first patrons were local merchants and salon proprietors who paid modest prices for his work. In 1896, he married Nancy Cooper. She became his business manager, and her influence had a direct, lucrative impact on his career. After 1919, the Russells spent their winters in southern California, where they found a new group of western art collectors who soon became Russell enthusiasts. Fittingly, Russell passed away in the place that had inspired him throughout his career; he died in Great Falls in October 1926.[27] Unlike the work of other western artists who painted wild animals only on occasion, Russell's oeuvre cannot be fully appreciated without examining his wildlife work. From charismatic "predicament"

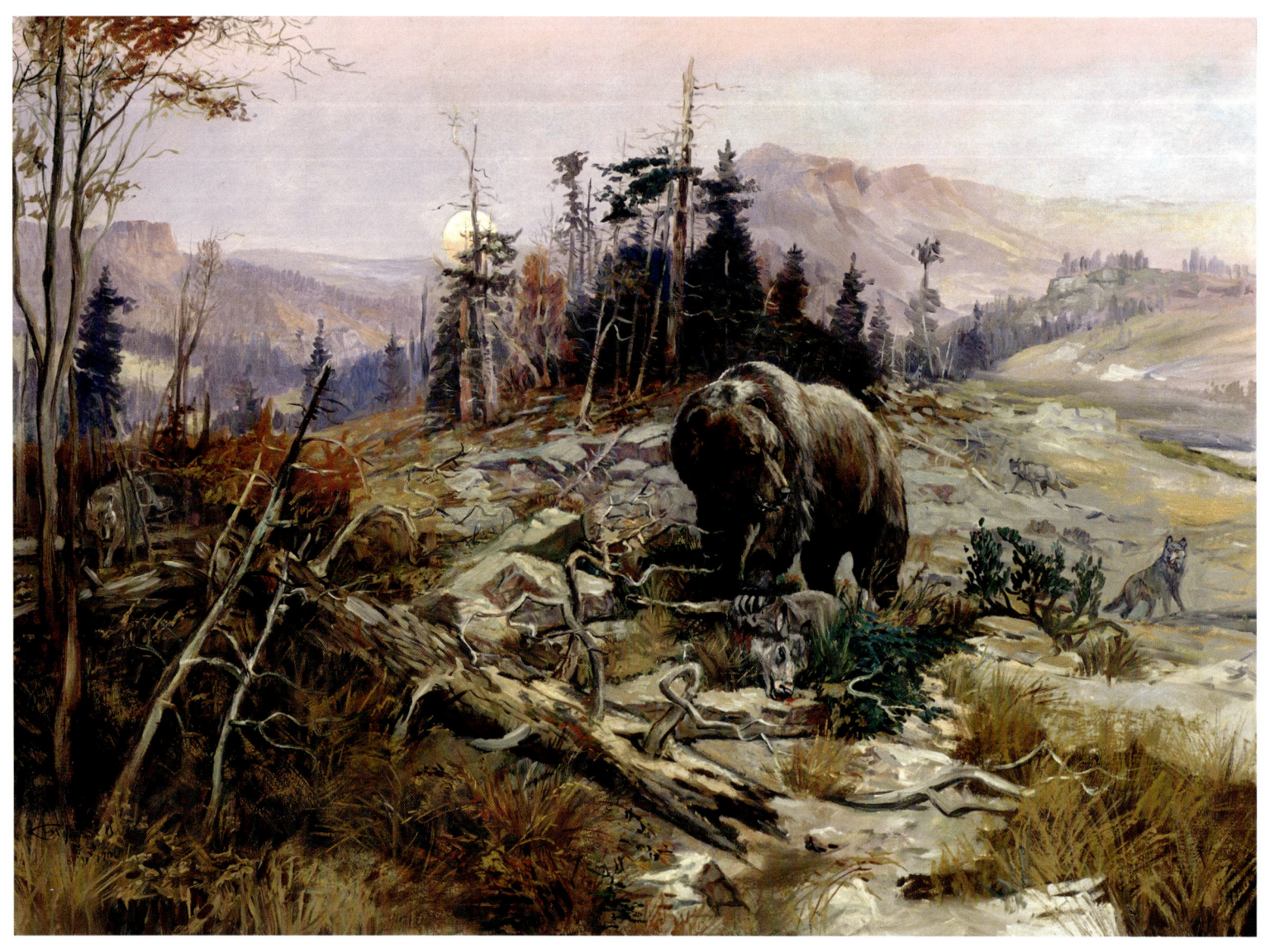

FIGURE 5.13.
CHARLES M. RUSSELL
To the Victor Belong the Spoils, 1901.
Oil on canvas; 31½ × 44½ inches.
JKM Collection.
J1987.126.

pieces, in which two creatures (sometimes human and animal) find themselves in the middle of dicey situations, to the more traditional depictions of healthy wildlife in glorious settings, Russell ably captured a diverse range of subjects and paved the way for a generation of younger artists who incorporate narrative, humor, action, and drama in their work.

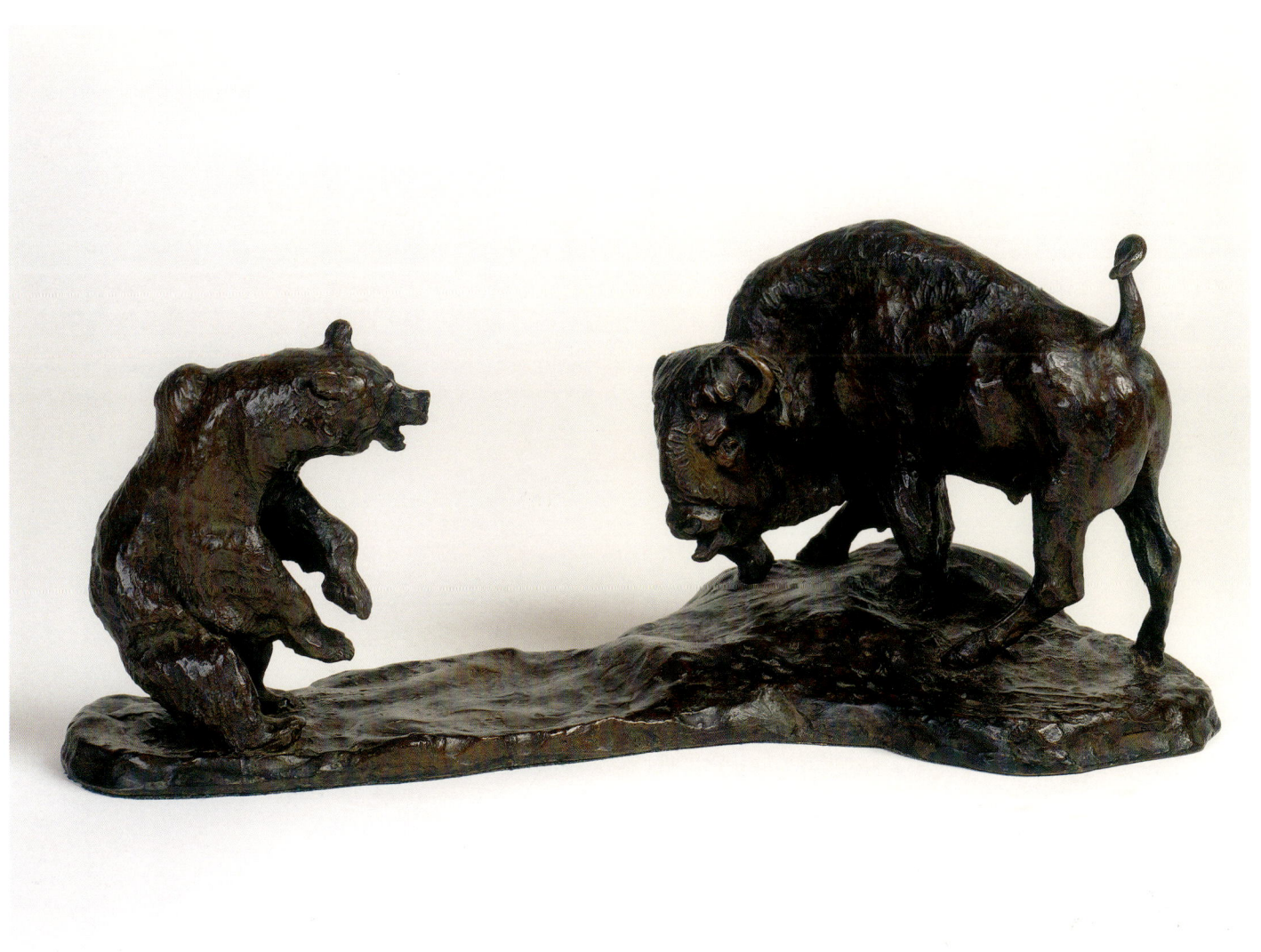

FIGURE 5.14.
CHARLES M. RUSSELL
The Bluffers, 1924.
Bronze; 7⅝ × 18 × 9 inches.
JKM Collection.
J1987.204.

GRACE CARPENTER HUDSON

United States, 1865–1937

In *Boy with Fox* (figure 5.15), Grace Hudson paints a quiet moment between a young American Indian and a fox. On a symbolic level, this painting depicts the poignant relationship between the Pomoan culture and surrounding nature, subjects that Hudson pursued throughout her career. Hudson's sweet portrayal of the boy, Shaili, playing the lute to the wild fox brings to mind William Congreve's line "Music has charms to soothe the savage breast," which in common parlance often becomes "Music tames the savage beast."[28] Lutes, children, and animals were frequent subjects in Hudson's work and were always depicted as coexisting in harmony. The few scenes of strife she painted were pictures of crying babies, often too cute to be judged as displaying any real discord.

Grace Hudson's oeuvre focuses on the Pomo Indians, a group of American Indians who lived near the town of Ukiah in northern California. Her sensitive portraits of individual tribal members spoke to her close relationship with the community and her interest in depicting specific people, not stereotypes (though the paintings may look like stereotypes through modern eyes). Most of the more than six hundred oil paintings she completed focused on children. If these portraits are looked at through a contemporary lens, they may appear overly sentimental. However, in their day, they were lauded as honest pictures and praised for the skill with which they were rendered. Hudson had good art training, obvious natural talent, and an abiding interest in the American Indians who lived around her. In 1880, she enrolled at the California School of Design in San Francisco, after spending two years studying at the San Francisco Normal School. The School of Design featured traditional lessons in drawing, landscape, and portraiture. After finishing her studies, she returned to Ukiah and continued painting.

Not until 1890 did Hudson begin to focus on the Pomoans. She married John Hudson, a local doctor interested in archaeology, ethnology, and the local tribes. Hudson's first notable painting, called *National Thorn,* depicts a native baby on a cradleboard, asleep, with a puppy sitting next to him. This work was exhibited at the Minneapolis Art Association. Receiving favorable reviews, she painted several additional portraits that also garnered national attention. The mildly political nature of her title, *National Thorn,* seemed not to cause a stir. She usually titled her later work in simple terms, using the name of the sitter or a description of the action portrayed. About this time in her career, she also began doing magazine illustrations.

FIGURE 5.15.
GRACE CARPENTER HUDSON
Boy with Fox (aka *Shaili with Fox*), 1922.
Oil on canvas; 20 × 16 inches.
JKM Collection.
JL1998.063.

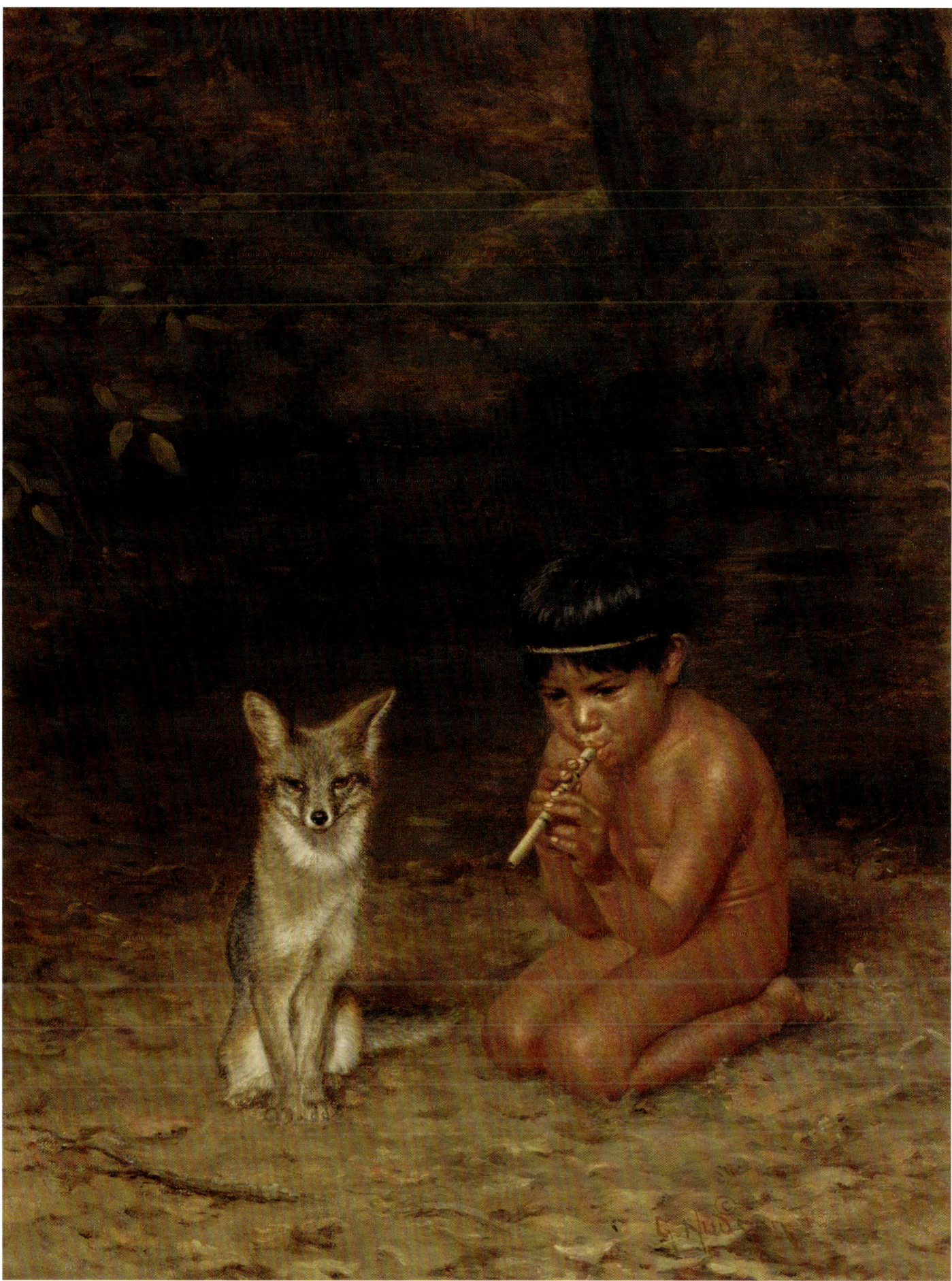

In 1893, she painted *Little Mendocino*, which proved to be a breakthrough for her career. The painting was first exhibited at the San Francisco Midwinter Fair and garnered rave reviews before traveling to the Columbian Exposition in Chicago. A forgery of the painting caused an uproar in the San Francisco press, creating even more interest in the original and in Hudson, whose success with American Indian portraits continued after *Little Mendocino* for the rest of her career. *Boy with Fox* is typical of her oeuvre; she often used an interior wooded setting as a backdrop for her subjects and employed a fox or dog as a companion to her subject.[29] In an era when artists were searching for authentic, American subjects, Hudson's gentle renderings of the Pomoan people and the animals they kept provided a sensitive record of indigenous culture.

WILLIAM R. LEIGH
UNITED STATES, 1866–1955

Even late in life, William Leigh's canvases were full of energy. *Female of the Species,* created when he was eighty years old, depicts a mother mustang chasing a prairie wolf away from her colt (figure 5.16). Despite its relatively small size, this work is replete with hallmark Leigh elements, such as the broad but colorful desert, the excellent sense of depth and atmospheric perspective, and, of course, the perfectly executed subjects, in medias res, legs flung out, at the peak of emotion. *Swans,* in contrast, depicts a serene moment as two swans mingle on a quiet lake (figure 5.17). Arranged in a heart-shaped pose, this painting is a valentine to nature. Leigh painted *Swans* in an almost pointillist style, combining dots of subtle color encircling the nuzzling birds that anchor the composition. Like Carl Rungius, Leigh was aware of European modern art movements and embraced all of the possibilities they offered.

Leigh has been grouped with Charles Russell and Frederic Remington as one of America's greatest painters of the West. Though Leigh's paintings of cowboys and bucking broncos are superlative, he had an amazing range, spanning from gentle scenes of American Indians to action-filled encounters between predator and prey. Biographer June Dubois noted, "In his autobiography and other writing Leigh has given his reasons for his consuming desire to paint Western subjects: his love of animals, his fondness of nature and the unpretentious, a childhood infused with Indian folklore, and above all, his certainty that the West represented the intrinsically authentic America."[30]

In 1883, after studying at the Maryland Institute in Baltimore, Leigh attended the Royal Academy in Munich, where he studied until returning to the United States in 1896. For ten years, he worked as an illustrator for magazines such as *Scribner's, Collier's, McClure's,* and *Harper's.* Ensconced in the New York commercial art scene, Leigh could have lived his life carrying out assignments for other people, but he yearned to go west. At age forty, he decided that if he did not act quickly, he would lose his chance. Leigh offered to trade a painting of the Grand Canyon with the Santa Fe railroad if they would provide him passage. Railroad officials agreed but said they would prefer a painting in Pueblo country of the Zuni or Laguna areas. So Leigh was off to the desert, a place he would revisit in person and in paintings for the rest of his life. After that fateful break from

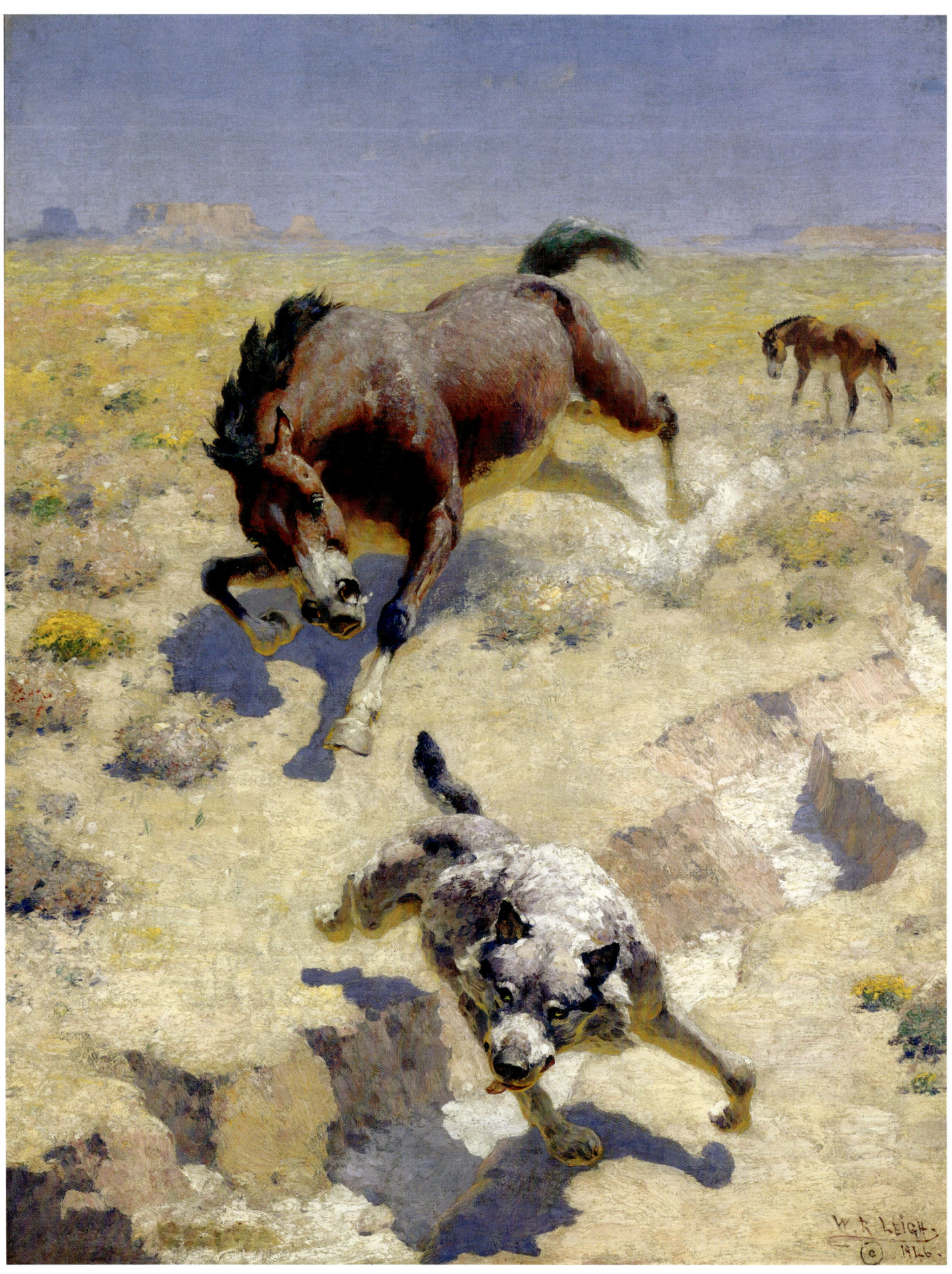

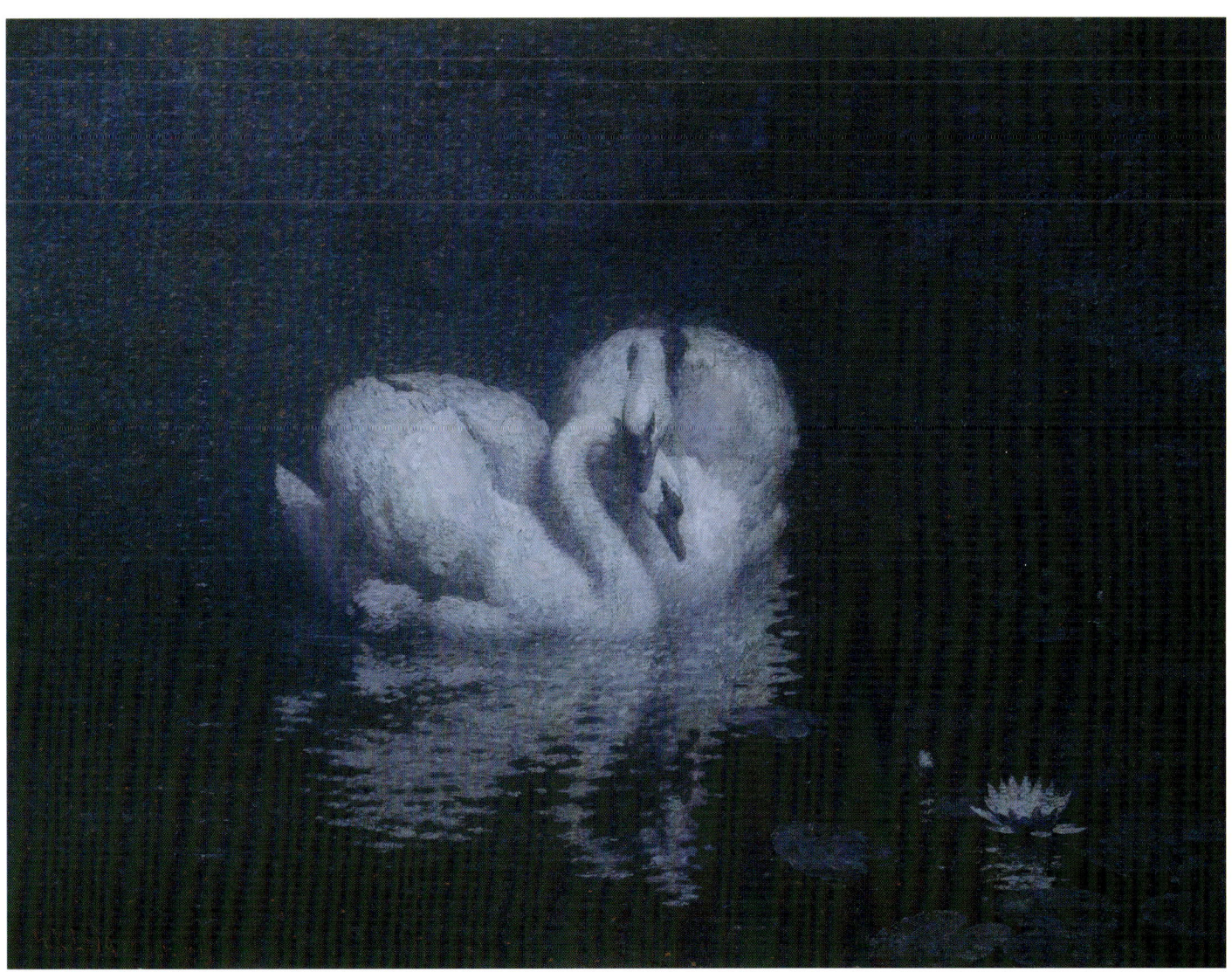

illustration, Leigh established a fine art career, becoming known for his vibrant canvases, which often reached nearly panoramic proportions.

Leigh's travels were not limited to the American West; when the opportunity arose in 1926 to travel with Carl Akeley to Africa and prepare background studies for diorama murals, Leigh jumped at the chance. His paintings of the vast African plains form an integral part of dioramas in the African Hall at the American Museum of Natural History. Leigh felt strongly that artists were best able to convey the beauty of the continent to the general public and that, by doing so, they might help preserve some of Africa's wildlife. Leigh's dual interests in the American West and Africa represent a larger cultural concern of the era, a concern over the world's wild places and wild animals. Though Leigh was not primarily an animal painter, animals make up a significant portion of his oeuvre. Living long after Remington and Russell had passed away, Leigh painted into his eighties and along the way received countless awards and accolades. He died two weeks after being elected into the National Academy of Design. His widow, Ethel Traphagen (founder of the Traphagen School of Fashion in New York), gave his entire studio collection to the Gilcrease Museum in Tulsa, Oklahoma.

FRANK TENNEY JOHNSON
United States, 1874–1939

In 1931, reviewer Everett Carroll Maxwell wrote the following about Frank Tenney Johnson: "Many of his best canvases are enlivened by horses and figures, and perhaps suggest a story, yet are in themselves superb landscape renderings. For example, one of the best moonlight mountain landscapes I have seen in any exhibition serves as the background for a big-horn sheep which stands on an overhanging ledge of rock in the foreground."[31] Though Johnson is best known for his scenes of western life, portraying cowboys on horses with regularity, wildlife was definitely part of his repertoire. *Coyote Moonrise* (figure 5.18) shows Johnson's talent for nocturnes, with the last light of day illuminating the slopes in the background as the moon rises on the horizon. The coyote in the foreground is cloaked in shadow, looking back, inviting the viewer into the scene. The landscape before him is easily read as his territory and, by association, also the viewer's. This differs from a work such as Russell's *To the Victor Belong the Spoils* (see figure 5.13), which sets up a tableau to contemplate but does not so clearly offer a direct invitation into the scene.

Johnson was born in Big Grove, Iowa, and spent much of his childhood there. His family moved to Milwaukee, Wisconsin, in 1888, and there he apprenticed with F. W. Heine, a watercolorist, then studied under Richard Lorenz, a European-trained artist who painted panoramas. Lorenz had spent two years traveling around the West before beginning to teach at the Milwaukee School of Art. His experiences and instruction greatly influenced the young Johnson, who said, "Nothing better could have happened. Lorenz was imbued with the spirit of the West. . . . I determined that I too would someday go out west and soak up its atmosphere."[32]

Johnson did go west, but not until many years later. He first traveled east, to study at the Art Students League in New York City under landscape painter John Henry Twachtman. Johnson returned to the Midwest and married Vinnie Reeve Francis on December 31, 1896. In 1902, the couple moved back to New York, where Johnson studied briefly with Robert Henri and William Merritt Chase. He finally received an opportunity to visit the West in 1904, courtesy of *Field & Stream* magazine. He spent five months journeying through Wyoming, Colorado, and Texas, gathering reference material for his illustrations and paintings. Increased interest in the Southwest led him to visit the Navajo region

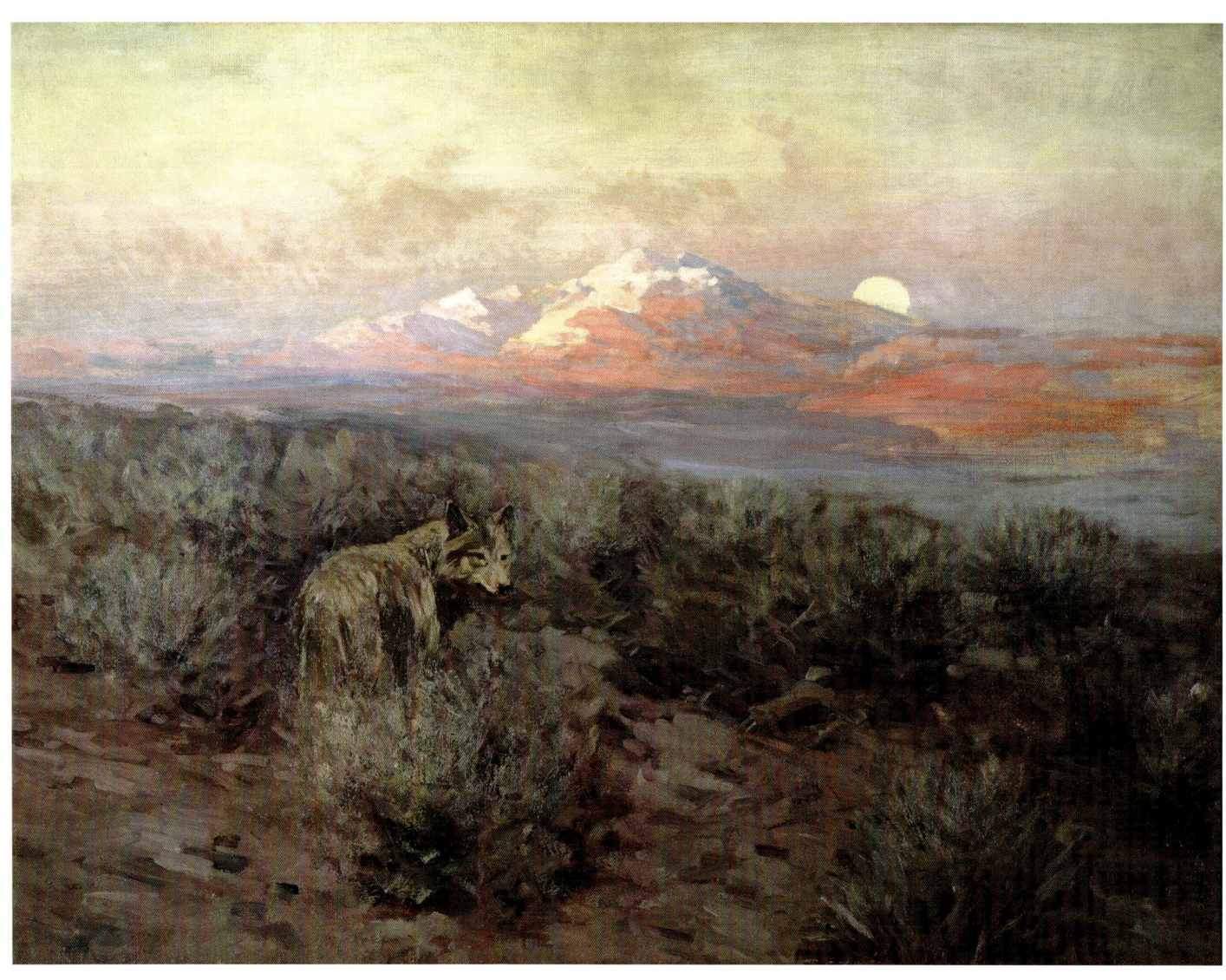

FIGURE 5.18.
FRANK TENNEY JOHNSON
Coyote Moonrise, c. 1920.
Oil on canvas; 30 × 40 inches.
JKM Collection.
JL1997.093.

in 1906. These formative journeys cemented his interest in western subjects. He and his wife erected a summer studio in Alhambra, California, in 1922. In 1932, he built a studio at Rim Rock Ranch between Cody, Wyoming, and Yellowstone National Park. Johnson spent his summers at the ranch until 1938. In 1939, he died in Los Angeles, California, from spinal meningitis.[33] Johnson's career illustrates the confluence of cultural concerns that engendered an ongoing interest in the inhabitants of the West; his mighty nocturnes mythologized their subjects, human and animal alike, into larger-than-life icons of the western experience.

CHARLES LIVINGSTON BULL
United States, 1874–1932

Prolific illustrator Charles Livingston Bull was known for his accurate depictions of wildlife from all over the globe; he was a great fan of zoos and studied foreign creatures whenever the opportunity arose. Anice Page Cooper wrote of Bull's wife that while traveling, "all she ever learns of a city is the location of its zoo and print shops."[34] The accuracy of his work did not lead to static compositions, however. Instead, his pieces show a strong design sensibility, using the curvilinear elements of art nouveau and the bold outlines characteristic of the arts and crafts movement. Bull also tightly cropped his compositions, focusing attention on the principal subject, be it a cat ready to pounce or a fight between predator and prey. *Caracal* (figure 5.19) shows many of these trademark elements, with its focus on the feline and the dynamic diagonal composition. As with many artists of his time, Japanese prints strongly influenced Bull. His work is often composed of flat planes, with a shallow depth of field and clearly delineated subjects.

Early in life, Bull showed a propensity for drawing and a keen love of animals. In his teens, he worked for Ward's Natural History Establishment (the same place that introduced Carl Akeley and William Temple Hornaday to the world of natural history). He also took classes in the evenings at the Rochester Athenaeum and Mechanics Institute (now the Rochester Institute of Technology). For the 1893 World's Columbian Exposition in Chicago, Bull helped mount approximately five hundred birds native to Guatemala for their national exhibit. Soon after, he moved to Washington, D.C., to work at the Smithsonian Museum of Natural History as head taxidermist. After installing the Philippines exhibit at the 1901 Pan-American International Exposition in Buffalo, New York, Bull decided to investigate a career change, taking a portfolio of sketches to publishers in New York. From *Frank Leslie's Illustrated Magazine* to *McClure's* to *Outing*, Bull's sketches were a hit. He is perhaps best known for his illustrations in Ernest Thompson Seton's *Kingdom of the Wild* and Jack London's *Call of the Wild* (1902 and 1903, respectively).

Bull died in Oradell, New Jersey, in 1932; he and his wife had settled there in 1910.[35] Though he provided countless illustrations for magazines and illustrated more than 125 books during his career, he died leaving his wife in relative poverty. She was forced to sell what work remained in the studio to keep herself afloat

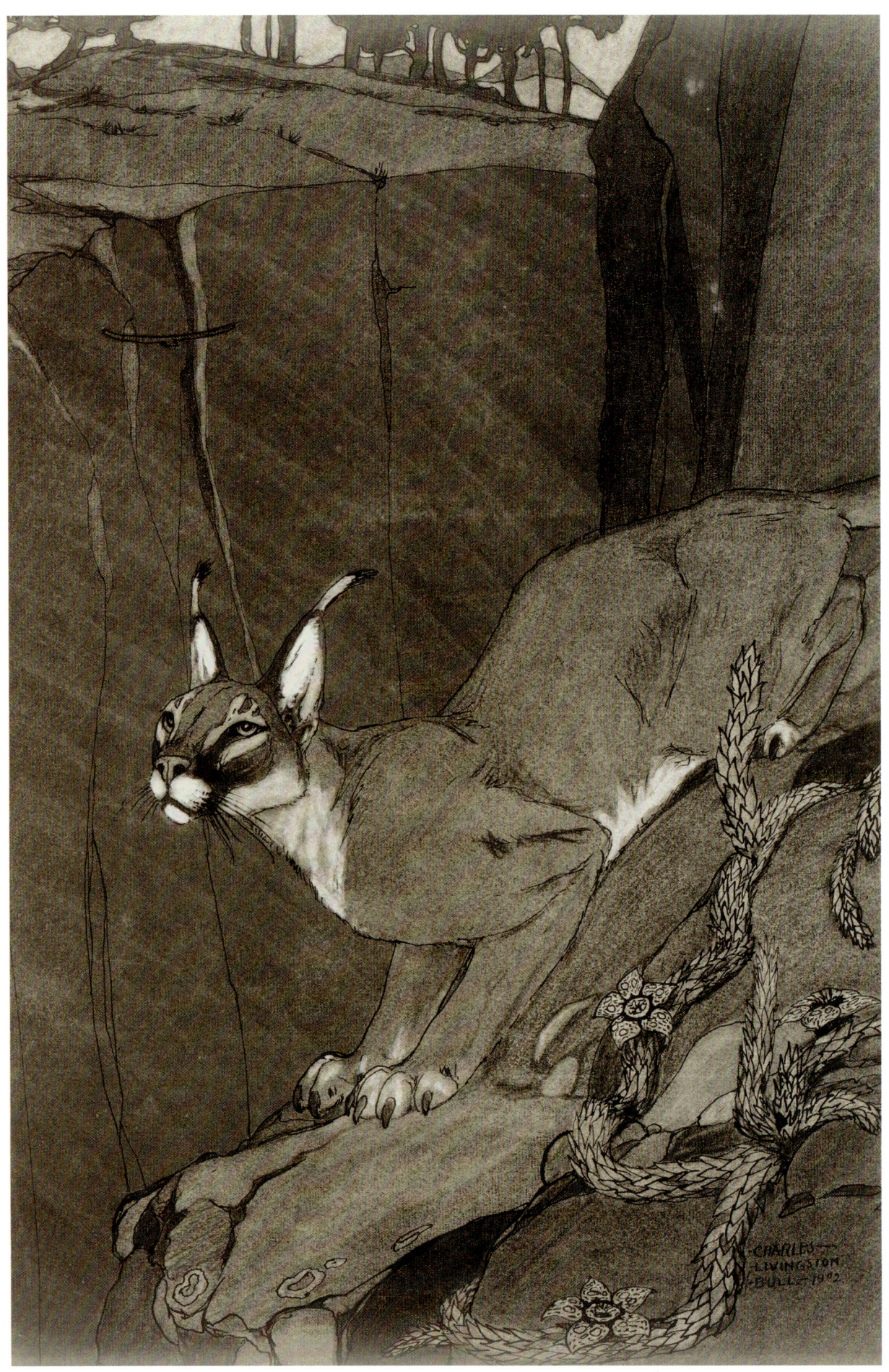

and is said to have been disheartened at the lack of respect her husband's work received. Bull's life is a prime example of the artist who never broke free from the demands of illustration to forge a fine art career. His work, however, had a tremendous impact on the next generation of artists. Robert Kuhn recalled searching for illustrations by Bull every week as new magazines hit the shelves of the local drugstore.

FIGURE 5.19.
CHARLES LIVINGSTON BULL
Caracal, 1902.
Ink, charcoal wash, and white gouache on
paper; 21¼ × 14½ inches.
JKM Collection.
JL2001.100.

LOUIS AGASSIZ FUERTES

United States, 1874–1927

The bold *Autumn in the Adirondacks* by well-known painter and illustrator of birds Louis Agassiz Fuertes presents a study of autumnal color and avian plumage, as well as a typical Adirondack mountain scene, with dense foliage and the hazy outline of a mountain in the distance (figure 5.20). Fuertes began experimenting with oils shortly before his tragic accidental death at the age of fifty-three. More typical of his oeuvre is *Arctic Gyr Falcon* (figure 5.21), with its crisp, clean lines, showing a bird in its natural habitat—evoking the best in field guide illustration and harkening back to giants in the field such as John James Audubon. Well-known naturalist Roger Tory Peterson wrote, "Although his passion for drawing birds was sparked by Audubon, Fuertes took a new direction, bringing the art of bird portraiture to its highest degree of excellence. Even today, two generations later, most bird painters are still influenced directly or indirectly by Fuertes."[36]

Fuertes was born on February 7, 1874, in Ithaca, New York, and was named after Harvard naturalist Louis Agassiz. At fourteen, Fuertes painted his first bird, a male red crossbill. His parents' disapproval of painting as a career led him to enroll in Cornell University's Engineering School in 1893. He graduated with an architecture degree but went on to study with renowned artist Abbot H. Thayer.[37] Beginning in 1894, Fuertes was mentored by Elliot Coues, an army surgeon and ornithologist who published *Key to North American Birds.* Fuertes illustrated a revised edition of the book for Coues in 1899. With encouragement from Coues and training from Thayer, Fuertes soon became an avian illustrator of the highest reputation.

Fuertes was a member of several scientific expeditions, including the Harriman Alaska expedition in 1899, which allowed him to study and draw birds from around the world. Fuertes's travels also led him to Europe, Africa, Mexico, South America, the Caribbean, and the Bahamas. He performed extensive field research, sketching birds in their natural habitats and collecting specimens for study in the studio. Robert Peck of the Academy of Natural Sciences of Philadelphia wrote, "At the height of his career, the demand for Fuertes' paintings came from most of the leading natural history writers of the period. . . . The editors of *National Geographic, St. Nicholas, Country Gentleman, Outing,* and other widely read national magazines also commissioned his illustrations." Peck

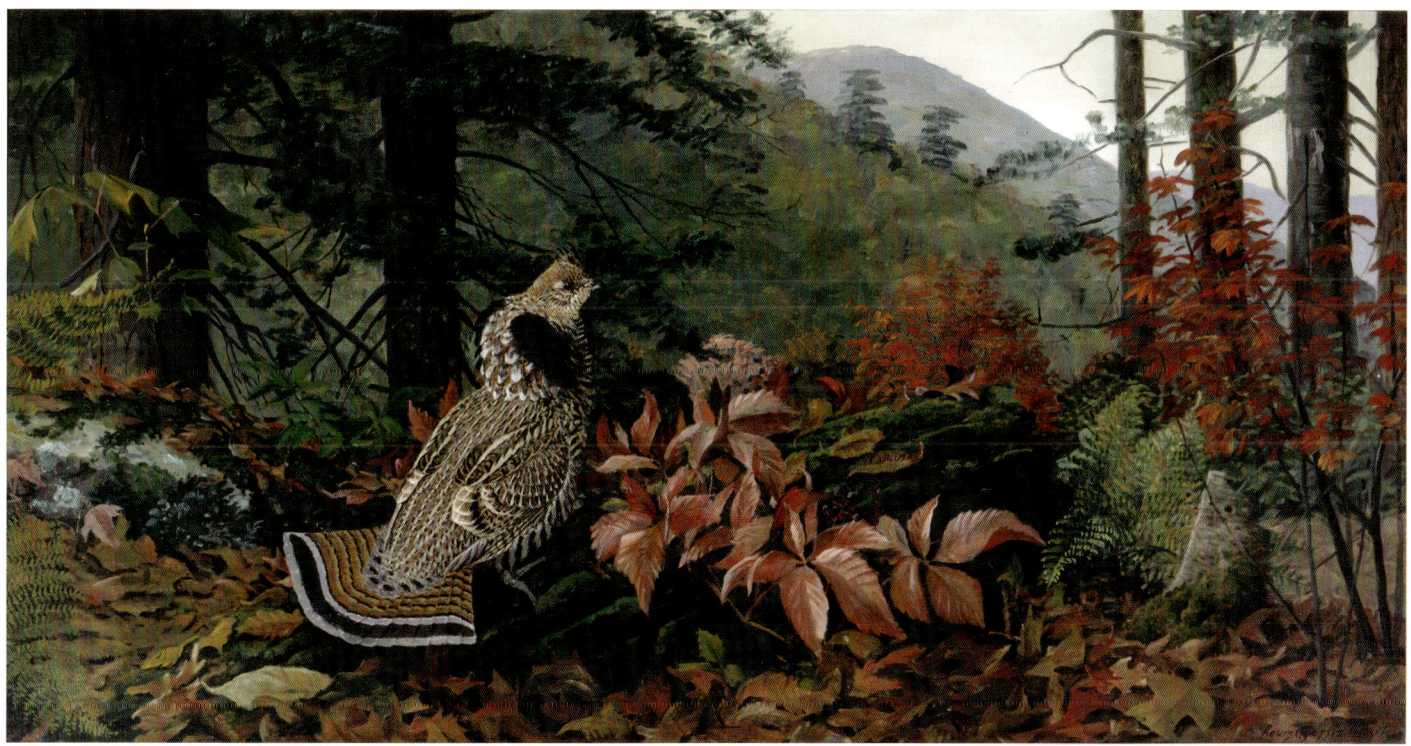

FIGURE 5.20.
LOUIS AGASSIZ FUERTES
Autumn in the Adirondacks, c. 1925.
Oil on canvas; 28 × 54 inches.
JKM Collection.
JL1996.045.

also noted that Fuertes illustrated more than thirty-five books and approximately fifty educational leaflets, handbooks, and bulletins.[38] In the 1920s, Fuertes created ninety watercolors that were reprinted as small cards and inserted into boxes of Arm & Hammer Baking Soda. These cards were widely distributed and avidly collected. In 1927, at the peak of his career and on the verge of painting more for himself and less for others, Fuertes was killed when a train struck his automobile. Peck summed up Fuertes's impact: "Through books, magazines and advertising promotions, Fuertes' accurate and appealing depictions of birds were given such wide distribution that, for many, his paintings became more memorable than the birds themselves."[39]

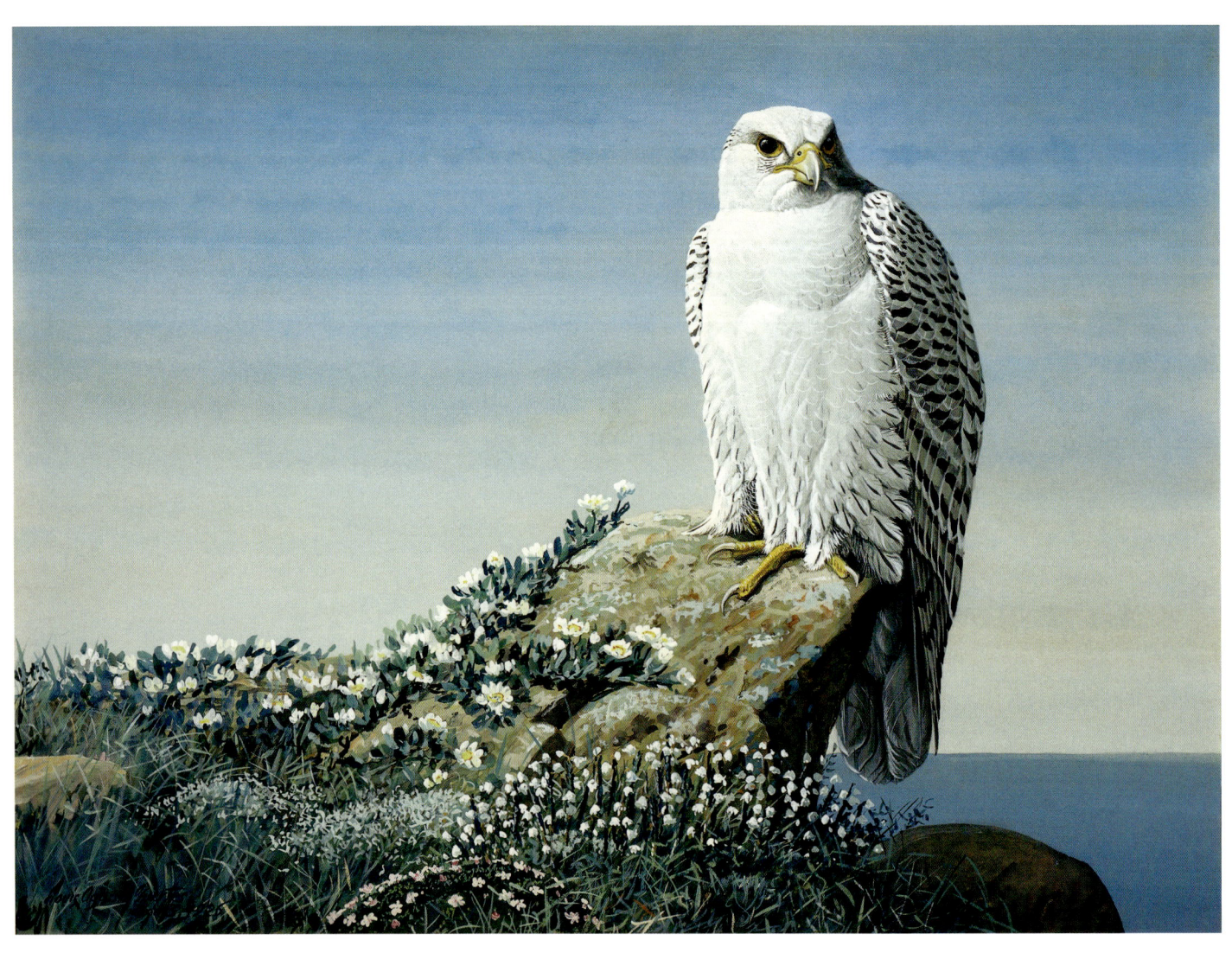

FIGURE 5.21.

LOUIS AGASSIZ FUERTES

Arctic Gyr Falcon, 1926.

Watercolor and gouache on board;

21½ × 29¼ inches.

JKM Collection.

JL2002.008.

ROLAND H. CLARK
United States, 1874–1957

Frank Benson, Richard Bishop, and Roland Clark were the foremost North American bird painters of their generation. While Fuertes is more closely associated with naturalism and field guide illustration, these three have greater ties to the world of sporting art. Their paintings and prints were appreciated across a broad spectrum of people who valued these pieces for their evocation of early morning forays into the wild, in search of migrating mallards, geese, and other game birds.

John Ordeman wrote of Clark's work, "Roland Clark had, like Frank Benson, observed birds all his life with the keen eyes of the hunter and the artist. He knew how birds employ the wind, the manner in which they flex their wings and the way they use their tails and hold their heads and necks when rising, dropping and landing. The subtle nuances of bird flight are there to be seen in Roland Clark's paintings and prints, and it is these subtleties that create the illusion of birds beating against the air, soaring in defiance of gravity."[40] A convincing depiction of flight is difficult to reproduce on canvas. Clark structured *Redheads at Sunrise* (figure 5.22) so that all of the action takes place above the horizon, emphasizing the birds' silhouettes by contrasting them against the blue sky and white clouds. To convey a sense of movement and individuality, he painted their wings in various states of extension as their bodies tilt into the wind. Clark also brought certain birds forward by painting them in clearer focus with bolder color, and he moved other birds back with muted tones. This lends a sense of depth to the flight as it descends into the marsh. Altogether, these elements make for a convincing picture of birds about to land.

Clark grew up hunting waterfowl in the marshes of the Long Island Sound and traveled extensively on hunting trips, shooting and sketching a wide variety of avian species. When he returned to the studio, he transformed his sketches into paintings. Clark studied at the Art Students League in New York and was preoccupied even then with sketching waterfowl. When he was twenty-six, he moved to Virginia to marry Ann Byrd. The couple lived in Virginia for twenty years before moving to New York City. In 1919, Clark began experimenting with drypoint and etching and was pleased with the results. He produced approximately two hundred drypoints during his lifetime. The multitalented Clark also published three books recounting his adventures in the field: *Stray Shots*

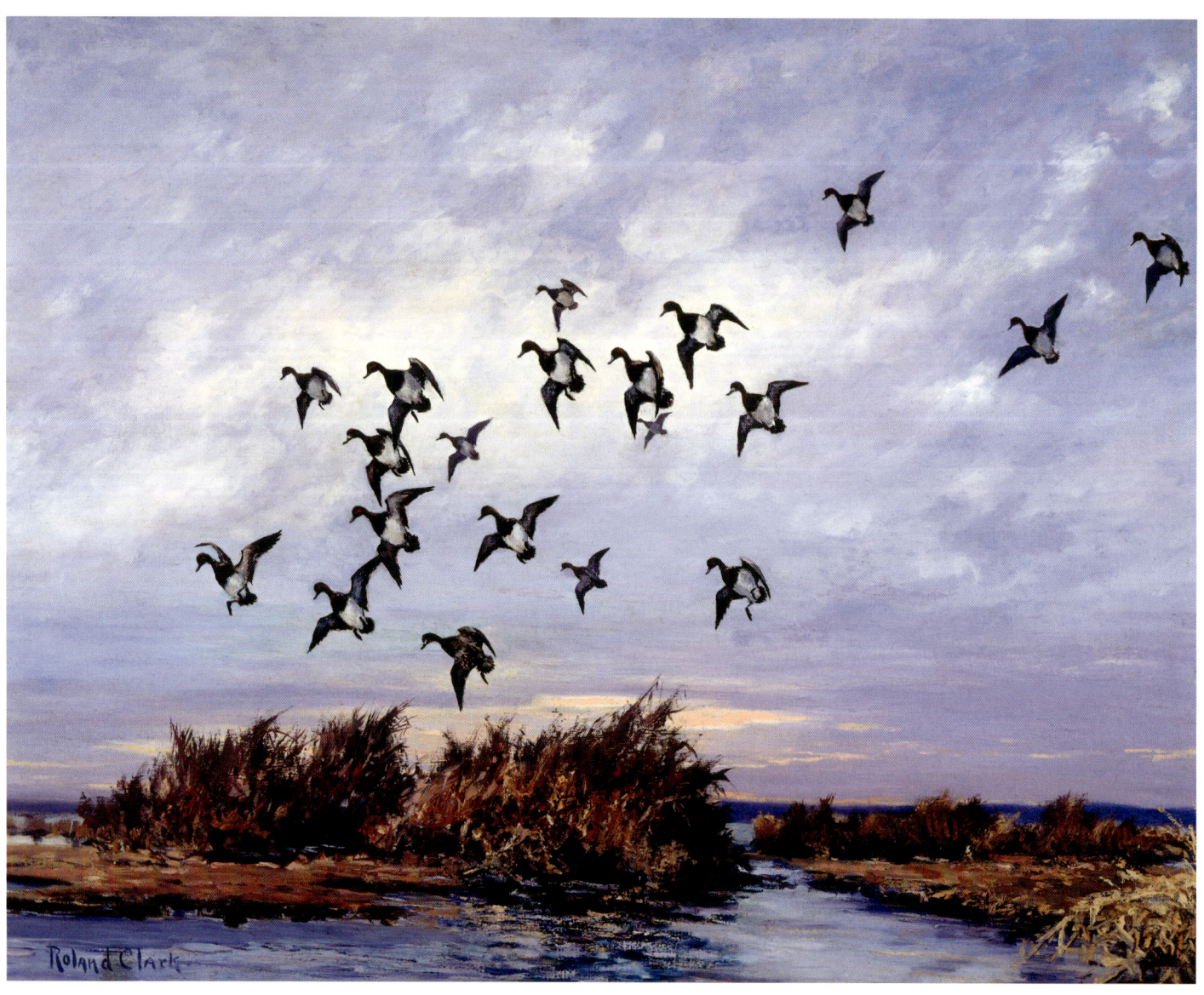

(1931), *Gunner's Dawn* (1937), and *Pot Luck* (1945). In 1938, Clark was the fifth artist featured in the nascent Federal Duck Stamp program, which began in 1934 as a means of generating funds to protect wildfowl and wetlands. Winning the annual contest has become a mark of the highest order for artists interested in portraying birds realistically. Also in 1938, Clark published a book featuring sixty-nine of his prints. He continued painting into his later years, living in Connecticut with his daughter.[41]

OLAF CARL SELTZER
DENMARK, 1877–1957

Becoming a more common sight in the West today, wolves have been both iconic and controversial for generations. In *Lone Wolf* (figure 5.23), Olaf Seltzer paints a solitary wolf on a cold winter night, capturing the chill in the air with just a wisp of breath emanating from the canine's nose. In *O. C. Seltzer: Painter of the Old West,* Mildred Ladner quoted a verse by Seltzer from 1919 that aptly sums up the sentiment of this work:

> This silent, weird and rugged west
> Where trails of men were dim and few
> Will soon be but a hazy past:—
> For step by step the struggling world
> Is slowly pushing into space.
> Each feature of the dying west:—
> From bloodshot Indian summer moon
> Down to the lonely night call of the loon.[42]

Lone Wolf is much more ominous than Frank Tenney Johnson's *Coyote Moonrise* (see figure 5.18), which portrays a similar subject. Seltzer's painting uses darker, colder tones to create this effect, echoing his sentiments that civilization was "slowly pushing into space[ ] / Each feature of the dying west." Seltzer portrayed a nearly featureless landscape in *Lone Wolf,* presenting a barren, flat expanse of snowy prairie, with one defoliated sagebrush hanging on in the middle ground. In contrast, Johnson's *Coyote Moonrise* features a mountain looming in the distance, touched by the last light of the setting sun. Metaphorically, the sun may be setting on the West in Johnson's work, but it is already long gone in Seltzer's.

Danish by birth, Seltzer and his mother immigrated to Great Falls, Montana, after he had begun attending art school. In Montana, Seltzer worked as a locomotive repairman for the Great Northern Railroad. In 1897, Seltzer met Charles Russell. Russell recognized Seltzer's artistic talent and invited him along on sketching expeditions. Seltzer learned his technique from Russell and, if harshly judged, can be accused of being an outright copyist. That reading discounts the talent of the younger painter but is not without merit. Although Seltzer clearly copied Russell's style (in some canvases, directly copying subjects and figures), in works such as *Lone Wolf* his ability is undeniable. In 1921, as a result of the postwar recession, Seltzer was laid off from the railroad and turned to painting full time. After Russell's death in 1926, Seltzer traveled to New York to work with collector Philip Cole. Seltzer stayed back east for two years, studying art and visiting museums and galleries. In 1930, Cole commissioned Seltzer to create a series of one hundred miniatures on the history of Montana (a task that severely taxed his eyesight). Seltzer completed more than twenty-five hundred paintings in his lifetime. A large collection of his work is housed at the Gilcrease Museum in Tulsa, Oklahoma.[43] Seltzer's work may never escape the shadow of his mentor, but success during his lifetime and the continued interest in his work from collectors and museums indicate the merit of his work. At his best, as in paintings such as *Lone Wolf,* Seltzer's artistic abilities shine through. The inclusion of animals in his oeuvre again shows how integral wildlife was to the western experience.

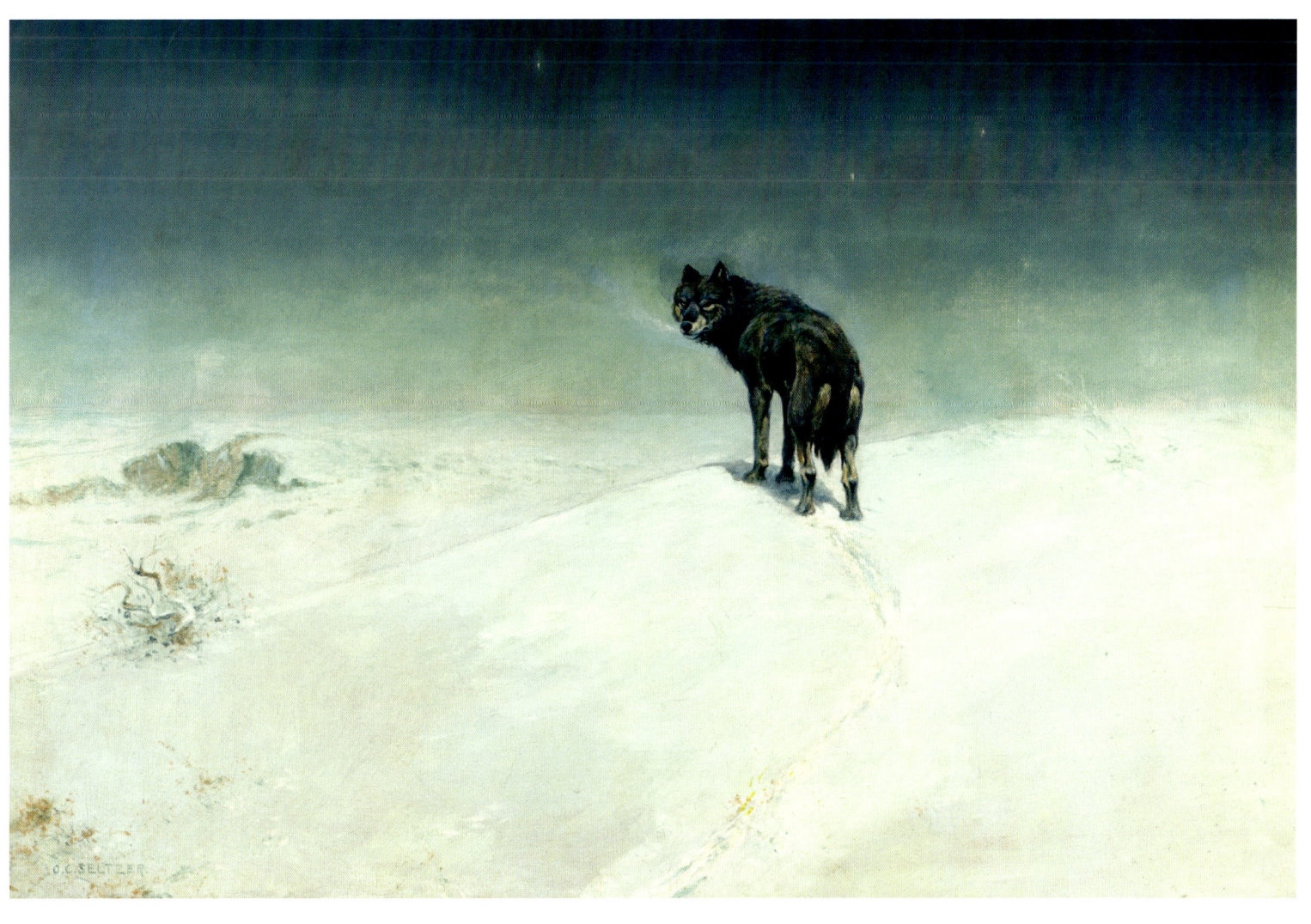

FIGURE 5.23.
OLAF CARL SELTZER
Lone Wolf, c. 1930.
Oil on canvas; 24 × 36 inches.
JKM Collection.
M1991.020.

BELMORE BROWNE
United States, 1880–1954

The nocturne *White River Moonlight* (figure 5.24) powerfully conveys the crisp air of a chilly night near the White River in the Canadian Rockies. This area was a favorite haunt of Belmore Browne, who had a studio in Banff, Alberta, for many years. Hard on the heels of Carl Rungius, Browne worked in and around Banff from 1921 until the late 1940s. Browne was an avid naturalist, outdoorsman, mountaineer, and artist. While he was a youth, his family spent five years living in Europe, summering in the Swiss Alps or the Italian lake country. When he was eight years old, his family moved to Tacoma, Washington, where his father founded a lumber company. Browne attended prep school back east but spent his summers in the rough and tumble town of Tacoma. In 1898, he began studying at the New York School of Art. In the city, he was inspired by the displays at the American Museum of Natural History. In 1902, he joined a museum expedition to the Yukon and Alaska to sketch and record wildlife and habitat.

According to John Ordeman and Michael Schreiber in *George and Belmore Browne: Artists of the North American Wilderness,* Browne spent nearly every summer from 1903 to 1913 "in the mountain ranges of the Yukon exploring, mapping, hunting and climbing."[44] He began to submit articles and illustrations to magazines such as *Collier's, Hearst's, Scribner's,* and *Harper's.* Browne also became interested in mountaineering. He was the first to ascend Mount Olympus in Washington state and made three attempts to climb Mount McKinley in Alaska (these attempts were recorded in his book *The Conquest of Mount McKinley* [1913]). Browne subsequently testified at congressional hearings that led to the establishment of Mount McKinley National Park (now Denali National Park).

The multitalented Browne wrote three boys' adventure stories: *The Quest of the Golden Valley* (1914), *The White Blanket* (1917), and *The Frozen Barrier* (1921). He married Agnes Evelyn Sibley in 1913. The couple had two children: Evelyn in 1916 and George in 1918. George would go on to become a renowned wildlife artist in his own right (see figure 5.33). The Brownes spent summers in Banff, where Belmore could sketch and paint. He succeeded in this field, as he had in his other endeavors, exhibiting regularly in New York, Philadelphia, Chicago, and Washington, D.C.

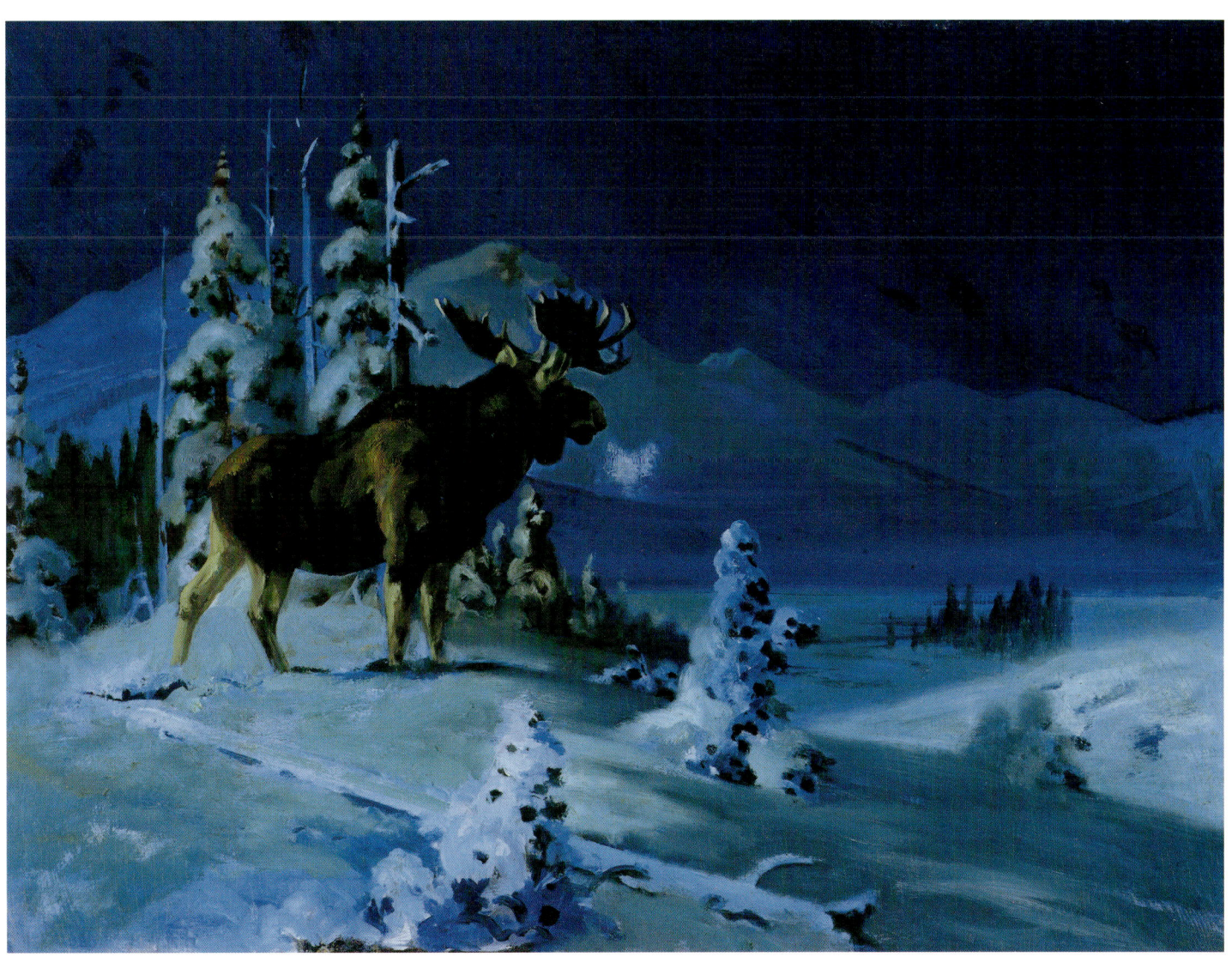

FIGURE 5.24.
BELMORE BROWNE
White River Moonlight, c. 1946.
Oil on plywood; 22 × 30 inches.
JKM Collection.
M1987.067.

NEWELL CONVERS WYETH

United States, 1882–1945

> As to the total numbers of these great animals, at the time of the first white
> occupation of the trans-Missouri, there is no such thing as computation.
> Certainly there were millions, but how many millions, one can only guess.
>
> Emerson Hough, "Wasteful West," 1

In 1905, Emerson Hough published the passage above in a mournful Saturday Evening Post report that described how commercial hunters and European settlers had decimated the vast herds of American bison, pushing the animals farther and farther across the continent as they cultivated the great middle West.[45] N. C. Wyeth's painting *How Many Millions, One Can Only Guess* (figure 5.25) appears in the middle of Hough's story, spanning the top of the page.[46] It depicts a vast herd of bison, stretching through the background to the horizon. The bison at the head of the herd make their way down a gully to a watering hole as ominous clouds roll in overhead. The painting is composed in somber colors, perfectly illustrating the dark tone of the story and ably capturing the situation of the nearly extinct American bison.

Wyeth began his training as a teenager, attending the Massachusetts Normal Art School. He soon transferred to the Eric Pape School of Art and then began studying with Charles H. Davis in Mystic, Connecticut, in 1902. Feeling his creativity blunted by the demands of the school, he submitted a portfolio to legendary illustrator Howard Pyle. To his surprise, Pyle accepted him; in October 1902, Wyeth began coursework at Pyle's studio in Wilmington, Delaware. Pyle encouraged his students to submit illustrations to magazines even as they were learning their trade, a practice that Wyeth took up with success. While still attending Pyle's classes, the young N. C. Wyeth began to make a name for himself in the world of illustration, particularly for his images of the West. His first *Saturday Evening Post* cover, which remains one of the magazine's most iconic, was of a lone rider on a bucking bronco, printed in 1903.[47]

Wyeth became known for his western subjects, though he had never ventured far beyond the East Coast. After graduating from Pyle's school in August of 1904, he made his first trip west, on a research expedition sponsored by the *Saturday Evening Post* and *Scribner's*. Wyeth's journey took him first to Denver and then to the Hashknife Ranch near Deer Trail, where he participated in a violent round-up, during which a variety of mishaps occurred, including the

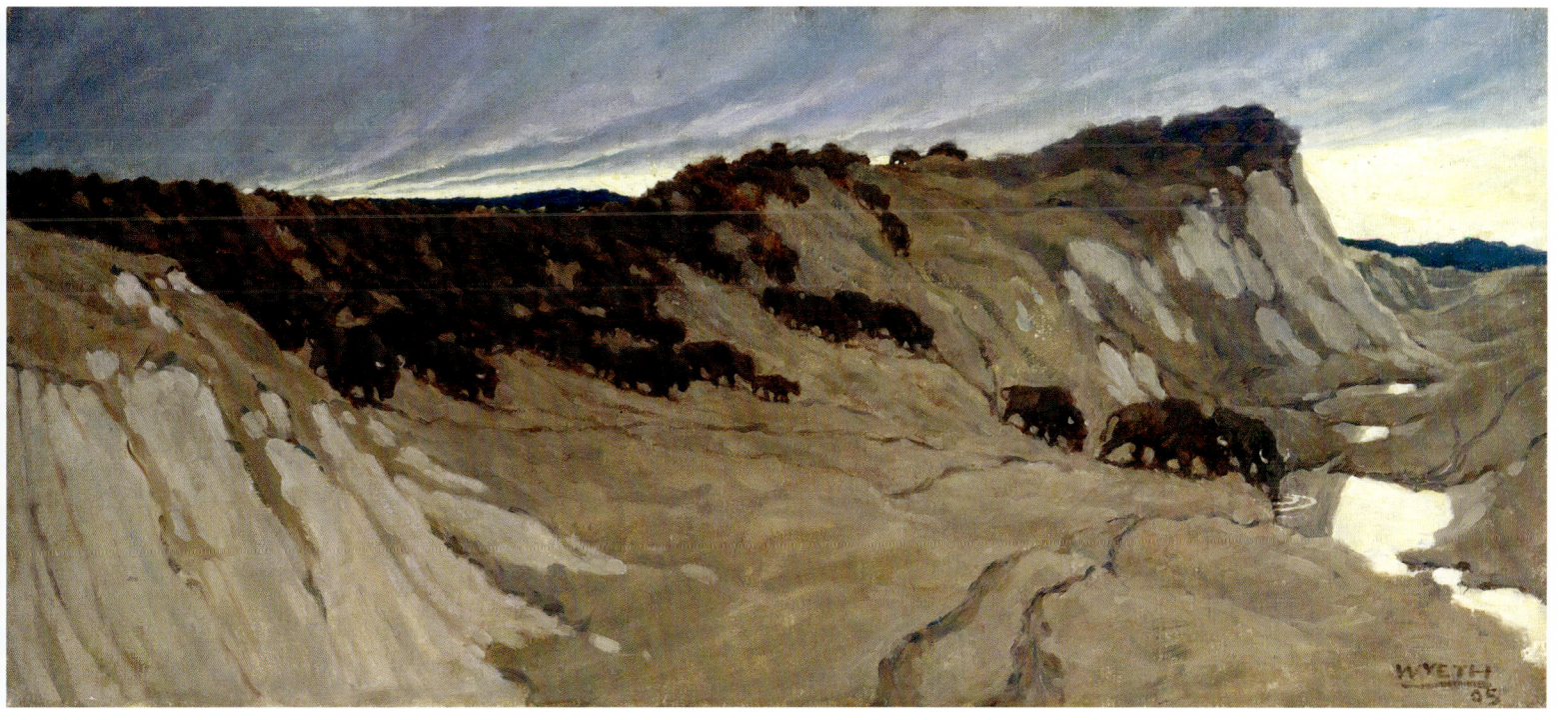

FIGURE 5.25.

NEWELL CONVERS WYETH

How Many Millions,
One Can Only Guess, 1905.

Oil on canvas; 16 × 36 inches.

JKM Collection.

J1995.029.

trampling death of one of the cowboys. Luckily, Wyeth suffered only a broken foot, which later healed, he professed, thanks to tight cowboy boots and tighter stirrup straps.[48] After spending about a month in Denver, painting and doing further study, Wyeth traveled to the Navajo Reservation in New Mexico. He returned home before Christmas, happy with the work he had done. Wyeth made only one more trip west, back to Colorado in 1906. Thereafter, his schedule became busier thanks to a steady stream of commissions for western-themed illustrations. By 1910, Wyeth had become burned out on the West. He wrote to a newspaper reporter, "My ardor for the West has slowly, but with increasing impetus, been dwindling, until my desires to go there to paint its people are already lukewarm. The West appealed to me as it would to a boy, a sort of external effervescence of spirit seemed to be all that substantiated my work."[49]

Wyeth eventually made a break with the West, but his success as an illustrator never faltered. Among his greatest accomplishments are illustrations for Robert Louis Stevenson's *Treasure Island* (1911), Paul Crewick's *Robin Hood* (1917), and Daniel Defoe's *Robinson Crusoe* (1920), to name a few. Wyeth's widely published work has had an inestimable impact on the way Americans envision some of the great heroes in literary history. In his early years, he helped cement an image of the West that remains relevant to this day.

PHILIP R. GOODWIN
United States, 1882–1935

> Lumberjacks, guides, packers and cowboys all populate [Goodwin's] work.
> But he was best known for his fishermen and hunters, thus broadening his
> appeal to a vast audience of deskbound urbanites who yearned to strip off
> their starched collars and business suits and don the clothing appropriate
> to what in their hearts was their true identity—hunting britches, laced
> boots, checked shirts or red flannels, and all the roughhewn garb of the
> out-of-doors.
>
> Brian Dippie, foreword to Peterson, *Philip R. Goodwin*, viii

The Surprise (figure 5.26) is classic Goodwin; clearly narrative, it immediately presents the elements of a story to viewers. This piece appeared posthumously on a calendar advertising the services of Pennsylvania taxidermist Fred P. Ayre in 1937, though it very likely also ran as an illustration to an adventure story during Goodwin's lifetime. The audience for this work, as for much of Goodwin's oeuvre, was obviously men interested in the outdoors. Known as *The Surprise* (or *Reel Adventure*), this painting features a young filmmaker, dressed in red flannel, approaching two cubs play-fighting while the mother bear looks on. The "surprise" was likely a sneak attack on the lower bear by the one that currently has the upper hand, but it could also be the young man's surprise at coming across this lively group. The secondary title, *Reel Adventure,* refers both to the reels on the film camera and to the reel on a fishing rod (note the fisherman in the far background, casting into a likely looking spot just below a shallow waterfall). For city dwellers and suburbanites alike, this picture would have provided a host of escapist imagery in which to become immersed as the workaday grind continued. Adding to the escapist nature of this piece, Goodwin provided enough realism to engage even a seasoned outdoorsman; one can easily imagine two men discussing recent outdoor adventures while standing before this work.

Though many people saw Goodwin's artwork reproduced on posters, in advertisements, and in calendars, neither his fame nor his fortune reached the heights of those of his contemporaries and friends Charles Russell and Carl Rungius.[50] Goodwin never broke away from illustration; consequently, his reputation suffered after his death in 1935. Not until recently have art historians, dealers, and collectors started to reexamine his work. At age eleven, Goodwin sold his first illustrated story to *Collier's.* He studied at the Rhode Island School of Design, the Art Students League in New York City, and the Drexel Institute in Philadelphia, as well as under famed illustrator Howard Pyle. At twenty-two, Goodwin contributed illustrations to Jack London's *Call of the Wild* (also illustrated by Charles L. Bull, 1903) and later to Theodore Roosevelt's *African Game Trails* (1910). At this time, he began illustrating the numerous posters, calendars, and other advertisements that would cement his place in sporting-art history. In 1904, he opened a studio in New York, where he drew pictures for *Collier's Weekly, Everybody's Magazine, Outdoor Life,* and *McClure's Magazine* and created cover illustrations for the *Saturday Evening Post.* He was an avid outdoorsman, befriending like-minded individuals such as Rungius, Russell, N. C. Wyeth, Theodore Roosevelt, Will Rogers, William H. Dunton, and Ernest Thompson Seton. Had Goodwin lived through the Great Depression and into his later years, he undoubtedly would have taken opportunities to break away from strictly assignment-driven artwork and found the freedom to create paintings on his own. However, as his career stands, people easily recognize his work, even if they have no idea who he was, because his massively reproduced renditions of hunters chasing moose or fishermen surprising bears have come to epitomize commercial sporting art of the early 1900s.[51]

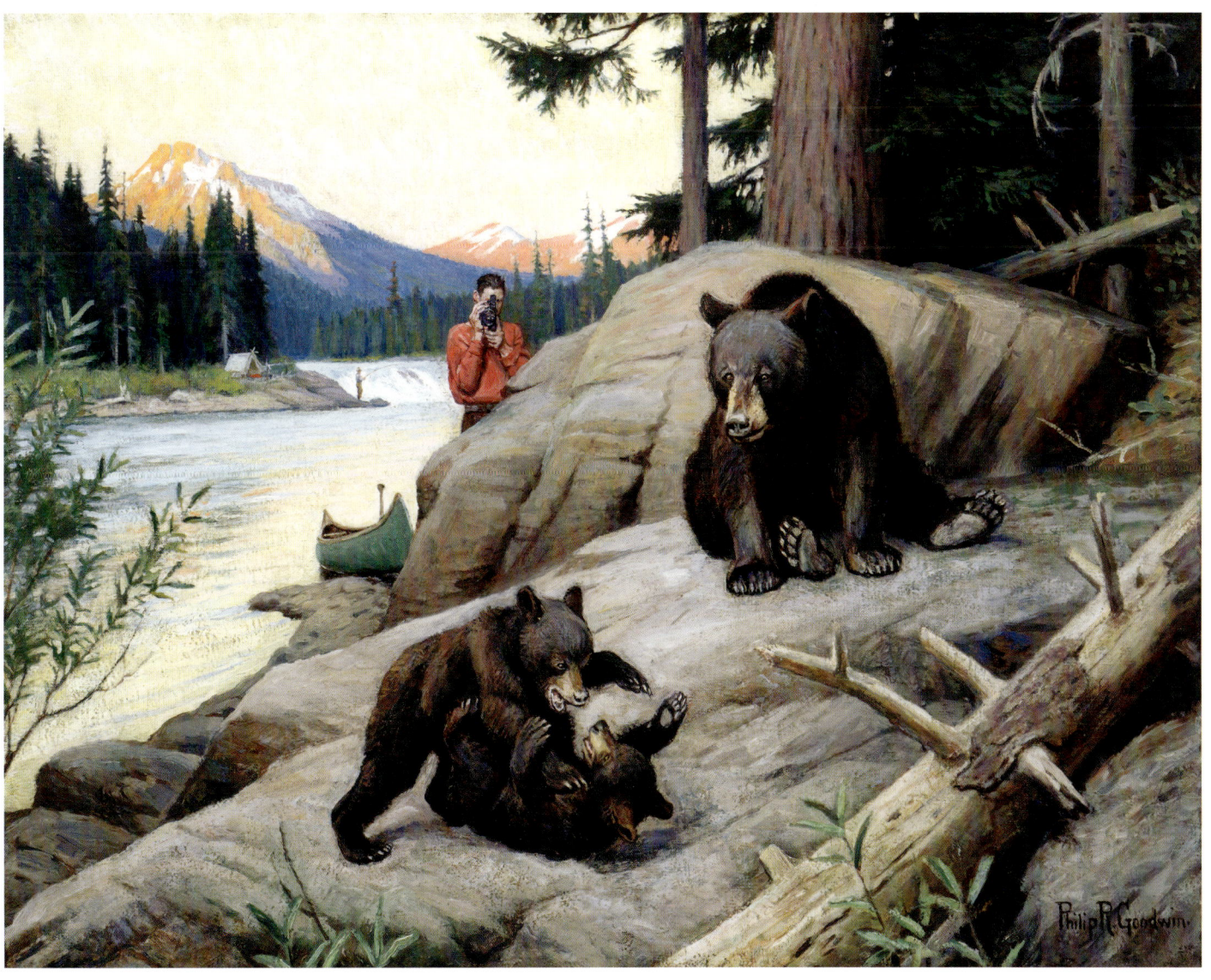

FIGURE 5.26.

PHILIP R. GOODWIN

The Surprise (aka *Reel Adventure*), c. 1925.

Oil on canvasboard; 30 × 39½ inches.

JKM Collection.

JL1997.027.

PAUL BRANSOM

United States, 1885–1976

> When I was a child (which was not the day before yesterday), there were in this country two great portrayers of wildlife. One was Charles Livingston Bull; the other was Paul Bransom. Their work decorated the pages of major magazines as well as those of many animal books. Bull was, undoubtedly, a superb designer, but my heart was stolen by the subtle, sensitive drawings and paintings of Paul Bransom.
>
> Robert Kuhn, foreword to Romero, *Paul Bransom*, 6

After examining a work such as *Leaping Cottontail* (figure 5.27), one can easily see why Paul Bransom was such a powerful influence on younger artists. Appearing on the cover of *Country Gentleman* magazine on April 5, 1924, this prime example of his work ably conveys action and anatomy within a well-designed overall composition. The piece focuses on the main protagonists while it leaves other elements to the imagination. The flat planes of color in the background and use of negative space give this work a slightly Asian feel, which ties directly to Bransom's appreciation for Japanese prints.

Bransom was a great proponent of studying live animals at the zoo; to create the artwork required for the wide variety of magazine assignments that came across his desk, he needed a clear sense of anatomy (and a hearty imagination). Bransom left school at thirteen to apprentice with Marion Fowler, creating mechanical drawings for patent applications. In 1903, Bransom moved to New York and helped illustrate the *Dodd-Mead Encyclopedia*. The *New York Evening Journal* hired him to continue Gus Dirk's comic strip, "The Latest News from Bugville." In New York, Bransom sketched animals at the New York Zoological Society (the Bronx Zoo) while searching for more assignments. The *Saturday Evening Post* purchased four paintings for the magazine's cover, jumpstarting his career as a wildlife illustrator. Bransom was also hired to illustrate stories and covers for *Ladies Home Journal, Country Gentleman, Century*, and *Good Housekeeping*. Beginning in 1947, Bransom spent sixteen summers in Jackson Hole, Wyoming. With artists Grant Hagen and Conrad Schwiering, he formed Teton Artists Associated, which successfully ran art classes in and around the Jackson Hole area for five or six years. Bransom led a long life, and his numerous illustrations in widely distributed magazines inspired a host of younger artists to take up their pencils and sketch the wildlife around them.[52]

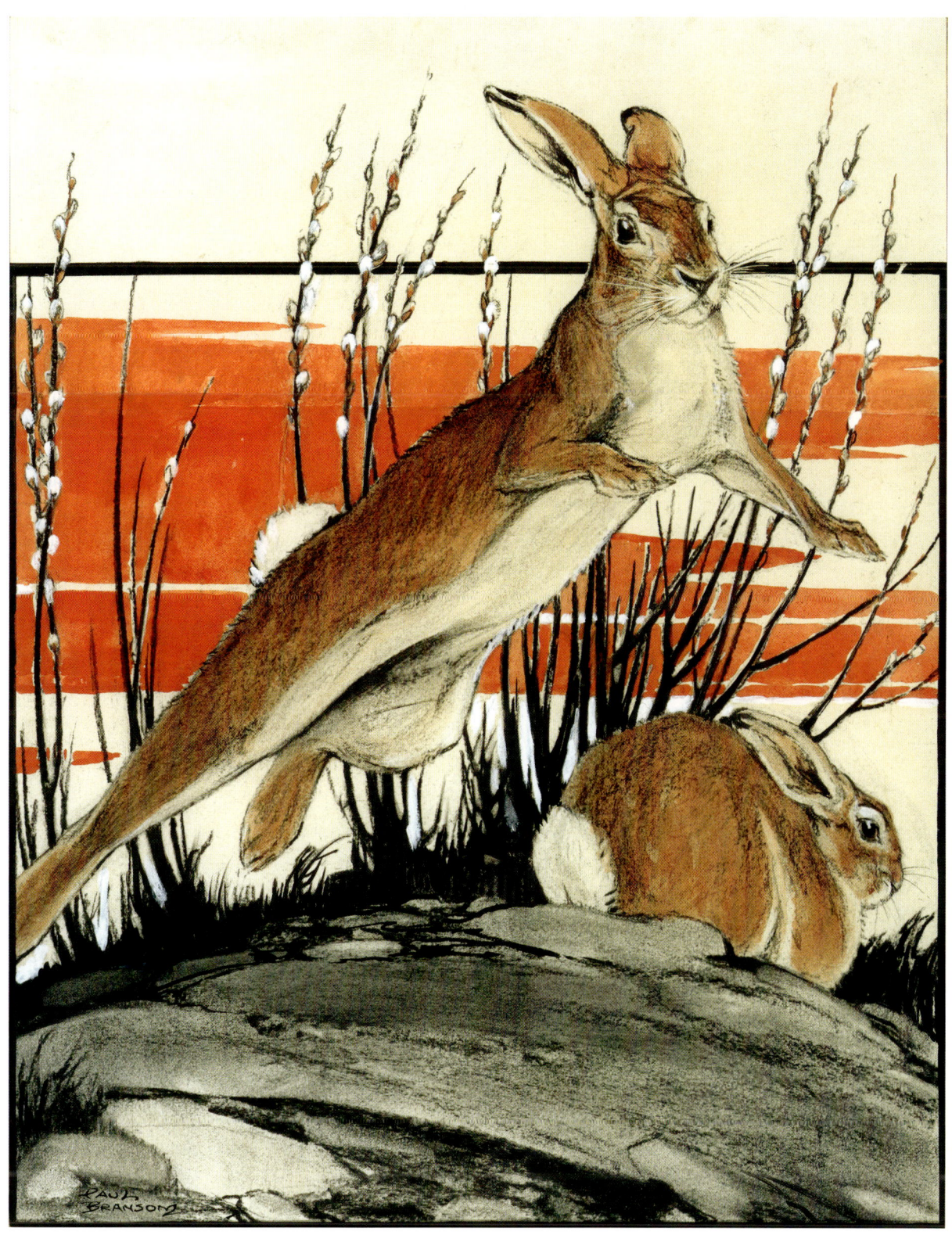

Carl Rungius and His Contemporaries

FRANCIS LEE JAQUES
UNITED STATES, 1887–1969

I n *Early Morning Whitetail* (figure 5.28), a deer stands on a slight slope before a small clearing. Crisp, clear morning light filters through the trees and creates a beautiful pattern of shadows on the snow blanketing the forest floor. Harmonious blues, greens, and browns work together throughout the painting to visually link all the elements, creating a cohesive whole. Jaques was a master at depicting scenes such as these, whether of native deer, Canadian musk ox, or migratory birds. In *The Shape of Things: The Art of Francis Lee Jaques*, Patricia Condon Johnson credited him with being "the first American bird artist to put his subjects *into* the landscape instead of merely against it."[53]

Growing up in Kansas, Jaques witnessed many migrations of ducks and geese. He developed an early interest in the beauty of nature and wildlife. Jaques accompanied his father on hunting trips and often sketched the birds they shot. These early drawings reveal close attention to the birds' colors and feathers and to their surroundings. As a teenager, he painted watercolors of birds in their natural environment and illustrated some of his father's *Field & Stream* articles. Without considering an art career, he worked as a taxidermist, lumberjack, electrician, and railroad fireman. The railroad job enabled him to travel throughout the country, introducing him to the splendid variety of North American wilderness and wildlife. In 1917, Jaques enlisted in the U.S. Army and was sent to San Francisco for artillery training. While in San Francisco, he visited the California Academy of Sciences and decided to pursue a career as a museum artist. In 1924, at the age of thirty-seven, Jaques sent two paintings as an application to the American Museum of Natural History; he was hired immediately. Johnson wrote, "During the next eighteen years, at the American Museum of Natural History in New York, he painted some fifty large diorama backgrounds, his best known work, each one a masterpiece. . . . Crediting him with bringing the diorama to its highest form of development, Roger Tory Peterson called him 'the dean of museum preparators.'"[54]

Jaques was in good company in the halls of the American Museum, with backgrounds by Carl Rungius, Belmore Browne, and William Leigh and taxidermy by James Clark, Louis Paul Jonas, and Robert Rockwell in close proximity. Jaques traveled with many museum expeditions to sketch, paint, and research landscapes for the dioramas. He also was one of the first Federal Duck Stamp winners, taking

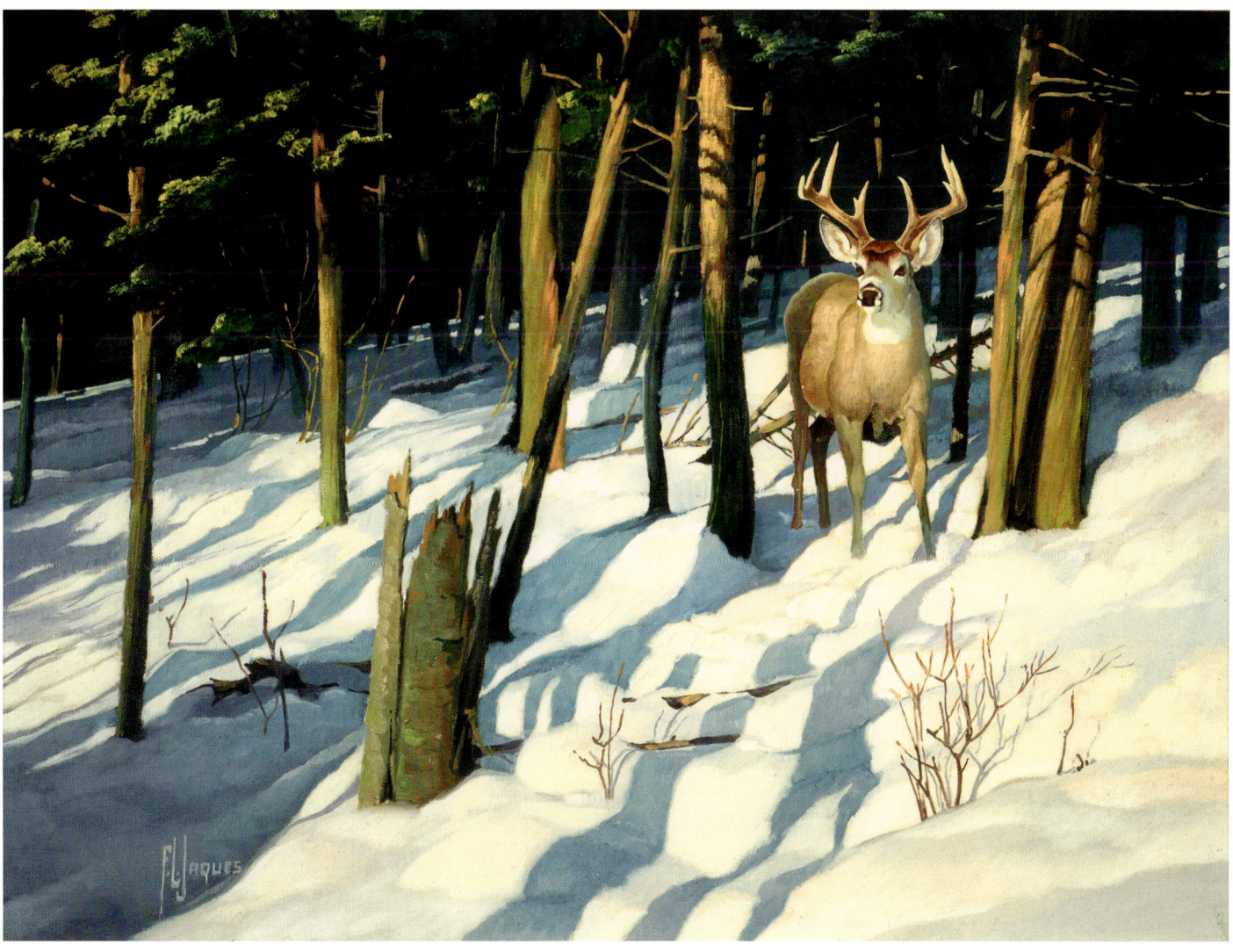

the prize in 1940. In addition to his museum work, Jaques created nature and wildlife illustrations for over forty books and countless magazine articles, including covers for *Outdoor Life* and the *Saturday Evening Post.* Jaques did not promote himself or his work and did not actively engage in the art market, selling his paintings for a few hundred dollars apiece. Consequently, he is better known today for his natural history work than for his wildlife art, but his reputation as a fine artist grows as more areas of wildlife art receive critical attention.

RICHARD E. BISHOP
United States, 1887–1975

The sporting aspect of wildlife art is evident in the work of Richard Bishop, who specialized in paintings and etchings of North American waterfowl and game birds. While the genesis of his art lies with hunting, its strength comes in the multifaceted way it can be interpreted. Today, artwork depicting moose or mallards in pristine natural settings can be used to support arguments for conservation, preservation, hunting, or not-hunting. At its core, Bishop's artwork displays a deep respect for unspoiled nature, wild places, and wild creatures, something to which the vast majority of people can relate.

Similar in design to *Wingmead,* Bishop's drypoint *Mississippi Mallards* depicts a flock of ducks descending into a marsh. In *Bishop's Wildfowl,* authors Earl Prestrud and Russ Williams wrote of the print, "Ole' Miss provides a paradise for the hunter who wants mallards. From below St. Paul, Minnesota, south through the picturesque valley of Prairie du Chien, on through the famous Illinois bottomlands and down into the fabulous shooting areas of the Grand Prairie around Stuttgart and DeWitt, Arkansas, there are countless acres of good mallard hunting grounds."[55] Close to Stuttgart and DeWitt, the area depicted in *Wingmead,* is a hunting retreat of the same name. The authors display a clear reverence for the ducks, the journey they make, and the landscape through which they fly. Part of the popularity of prints such as *Mississippi Mallards* and paintings such as *Wingmead* (figure 5.29) is their similarly reverential treatment of their subject, re-creating a sense of what it is like to be out in the middle of a marsh, interacting with nature.

Born in Syracuse, New York, Bishop grew up hunting and fishing with his father and developed a keen interest in waterfowl. He began etching while working as an electrical engineer in Philadelphia; ducks and geese were his primary subjects. Throughout his career, he created art using a variety of media, including etching, aquatint, drypoint, watercolor, and oil. He was a member of the Philadelphia print club and the Philadelphia Watercolor Society and was best known for capturing the beauty of birds in flight. In his introduction to *Bishop's Wildfowl,* Tom Davis wrote, "Richard Bishop was the last of a triumvirate of American artists, all early duck stamp honorees, whose portraits of wildfowl established the standard to which their successors still aspire."[56] The other artists of the triumvirate were, as previously noted, Frank Benson and Roland Clark.

FIGURE 5.29.
RICHARD E. BISHOP
Wingmead, 1943.
Oil on canvas; 27 × 20 inches.
JKM Collection.
JL1998.062.

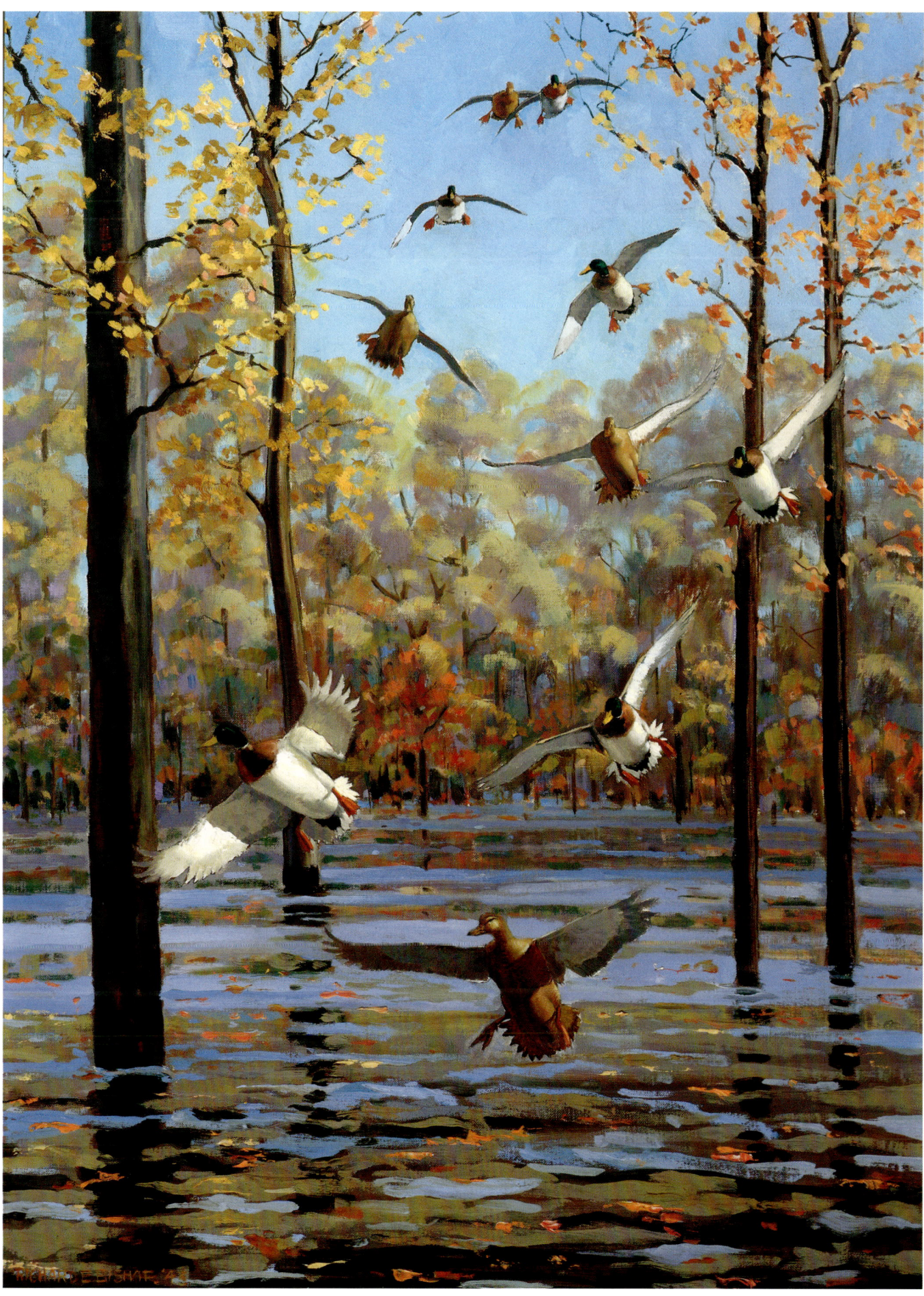

GERARD CURTIS DELANO

United States, 1890–1972

> The scene is at Surprise Lake in Summit County, Colorado. A bull elk takes
> a drink from that cold lake-water. This lake lies deep in the Arapaho Forest
> at an altitude of about 10,000 feet on the slope of Eaglenest Mountain, one
> of the snow covered peaks in the Gore Range. Here silence is supreme,
> evidence of Man is not apparent, and big game is plentiful.
>
> Gerard Curtis Delano, *Indians and Scenes of the Southwest,* 26

Known for his paintings of western life, especially of the Navajo people, Gerard Curtis Delano also painted wildlife on occasion. *Forest Primeval* (figure 5.30) is a departure from Delano's typically sunny, well-defined style. The combination of the dark undertones of the lake and quickly applied areas of paint laid-in for the foliage makes for a powerful painting that suggests a pristine wilderness, untouched by humankind (sentiments echoed in Delano's remarks about the work). This painting depicts the power and mystery of the wilderness rather than showing a literal depiction of it; the rich, dark tones imbue the canvas with a substantial feeling.

In 1908, in his late teens, Delano submitted a drawing to *St. Nicholas Magazine,* a popular children's publication of the era. His piece won an honorable mention, which encouraged him to continue submitting artwork. Later that year, *Life* magazine purchased one of his drawings, and his career as a professional artist began. Delano enrolled at the Swaine Free School of Design in New Bedford, Massachusetts, in 1909, before moving to New York City in 1910 to attend the Art Students League, where he studied under George Bridgeman, Frank Dumond, and Edward Dufer. Delano continued to take classes in the early phase of his career, attending the Grand Central School of Art in the 1920s and studying under prominent illustrators Harvey Dunn, Dean Cornwell, and N. C. Wyeth.

With some success in the field, Delano began to visit Colorado in 1919. In the early 1920s, he filed for a homestead and built a cabin and studio high in the Rocky Mountains, west of Denver. Returning to New York in the winters, he received illustration assignments from *Cosmopolitan, Collier's,* and *Western Stories.* After losing all of his money during the depression, Delano moved to Colorado permanently in 1933. Delano noted in his autobiography, "There followed two years of primitive living."[57] During those two years, Delano managed to sell a few illustrations to keep himself afloat. In 1936, he pitched an idea to *Western Story*

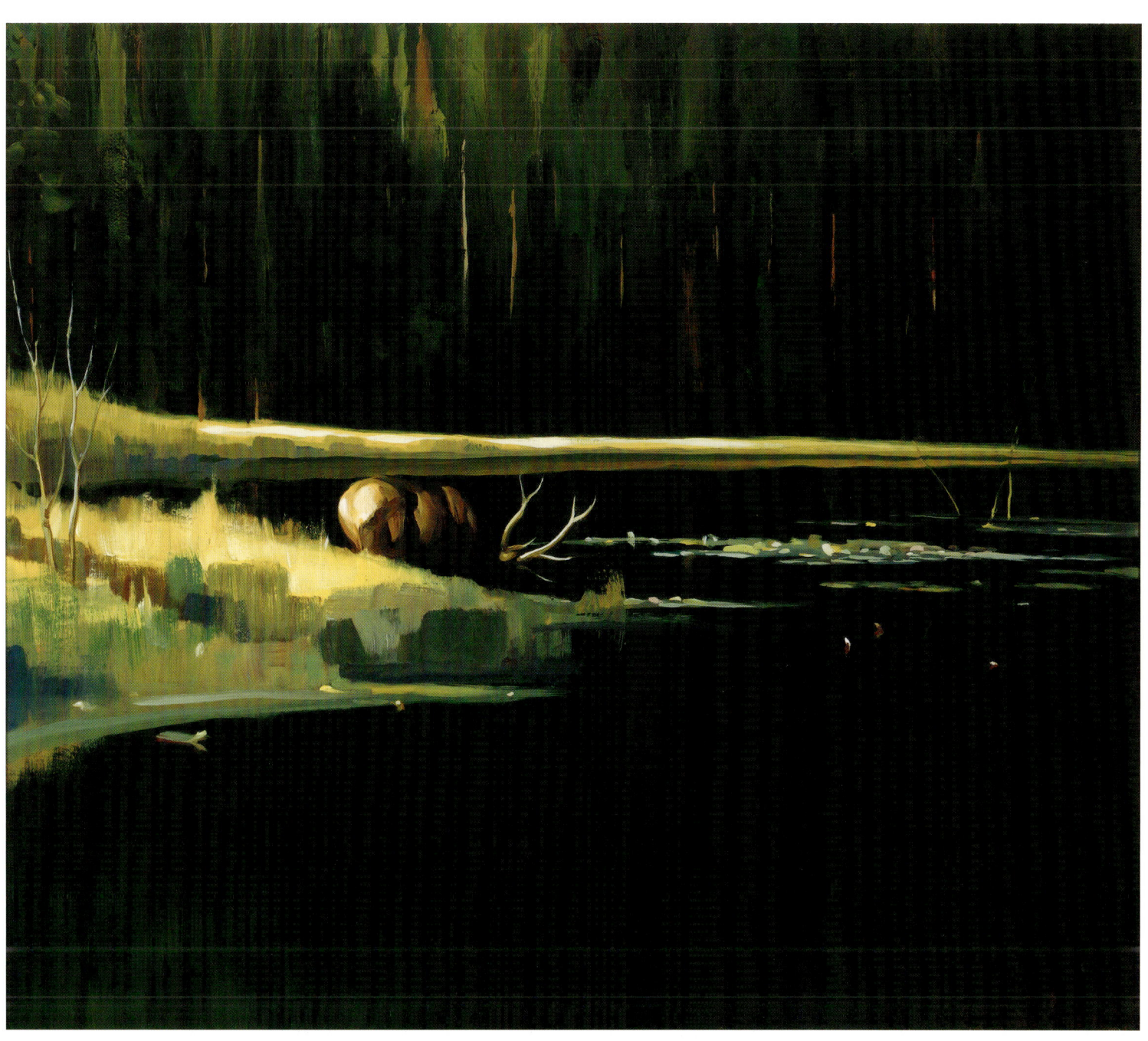

for a series called "The Story of the West." This series kept him employed until 1940. By that time, he had rented a studio in downtown Denver. Delano wrote, "I had collected quite a few preliminary color sketches and had, in the meantime, painted several very creditable pictures."[58] He took his artwork to a local gallery, which agreed to sell them. Though modest in price, the work sold, and this prompted Delano to put more time into his canvases (even though he continued to sell illustrations to pulp magazines, such as *Western Story, True West,* and *Star* magazine).[59] Interested in American Indian culture, Delano traveled through New Mexico and Arizona during the 1940s. He became intrigued with the Navajo people and spent much of the rest of his career depicting them. Like William Leigh and Frank Johnson, Delano branched out from a career in illustration; he continued painting popular subjects but imbued his later canvases with his own distinctive style and point of view.

JOHN CLYMER
United States, 1907–1989

Mountain goats inhabit the precipitous heights ably captured by John Clymer in *The Lookout* (figure 5.31). Though best known for his scenes of frontier life, Clymer often painted wildlife. In addition to mountain goats, he was drawn to grizzly bears and bison, preferring to paint the bigger animals of the West. His western paintings of trappers, explorers, and American Indians have been lauded for their historical accuracy. His wildlife work is no less precise; Clymer took great pride in the careful rendering of whatever subject he chose to paint. His wife, Doris, also deserves ample credit; she often researched the subjects John painted. Todd Wilkinson wrote in his article "The Clymers' Muse," "In retrospect, we need only ask John Clymer to sum up his wife's contributions to his career. He shared these words a few months before his death. 'I am the painter,' Clymer said. 'Doris is the inspiration.'"[60]

John Clymer was born in Ellensburg, Washington, in 1907. He sold two unsolicited drawings to the Colt Firearms Company when he was just sixteen years old. Prior to that, he had enrolled in an art correspondence school. His submissions received encouraging comment, prompting him to continue training. After high school, Clymer moved to British Columbia and took night classes at the Vancouver School of Art while working during the day at a studio that supplied drawings for mail-order catalogues. He soon began to provide illustrations for Canadian magazines. Working a full-time job and attending classes at night wore on Clymer, so he took a sabbatical in 1928 on a paddle wheeler that traveled up the Yukon River. Walt Reed wrote, "He got to visit with the Indians and trappers along the river and to become acquainted with their way of life. . . . [T]he experiences provided him with a wealth of artistic inspiration that he drew upon for the rest of his life."[61] Returning from the Yukon refreshed, Clymer began to paint again, eventually moving to Toronto to be closer to the major Canadian publishing houses. Contacts in New York led him to more assignments for magazines in the United States. Clymer wanted further training, so he traveled to Wilmington, Delaware, to study at the Wilmington Academy of Art, learning from students of Howard Pyle, such as Frank Schoonover and Harvey Dunn. N. C. Wyeth became a mentor, counseling him to take a day off from commercial work every week to paint something of his own choosing. According to Reed, Clymer followed this advice for much of his career.[62]

In 1932, Clymer married his high school sweetheart, Doris. The couple moved to Westport, Connecticut, a thriving artist colony, in 1937. There the Clymers met other illustrators, such as Robert Lougheed and Tom Lovell. Clymer migrated toward magazines such as *True* and *Field & Stream,* which played to his interest in the outdoors, but his work also appeared in *Cosmopolitan, Good Housekeeping,* and *American Magazine.* During his career as an illustrator, he created over eighty covers for the *Saturday Evening Post* and was known for his sweet, nostalgic renderings of American life. At the same time he was carving out a successful illustration career, Clymer had been selling paintings at Grand Central Art Galleries in New York City.

In 1964, at the age of fifty-seven, Clymer decided to give up illustration and dedicate himself to painting topics of his own choosing, including a newfound interest in history painting, for which his gallery had found a market. Clymer said of this change:

> For several years previously I had exhibited with Grand Central Art Galleries in New York. In the early years I had almost always painted wildlife subjects for them because I so much enjoy watching and painting animals out of doors in their natural surroundings. . . . [W]e made several camping trips to the Canadian Rockies for settings and material. Banff and Jasper National Parks are regions of mountain splendor where animals are protected and where there is every kind of wildlife to be seen. Now that the Galleries were asking for history paintings, however, our western trips came more and more to be history treks. Instead of looking for *Post* cover ideas or animal subjects, I was now looking for history subjects.[63]

In 1970, shortly after Clymer began transitioning from wildlife to historical scenes, he and Doris moved to Teton Village, Wyoming. The couple spent winters in the studio and summers traveling to research and sketch historical sites. After Clymer passed away in 1989, his family donated the contents of his studio to the National Museum of Wildlife Art, which re-created Clymer's studio space for visitors to enjoy.

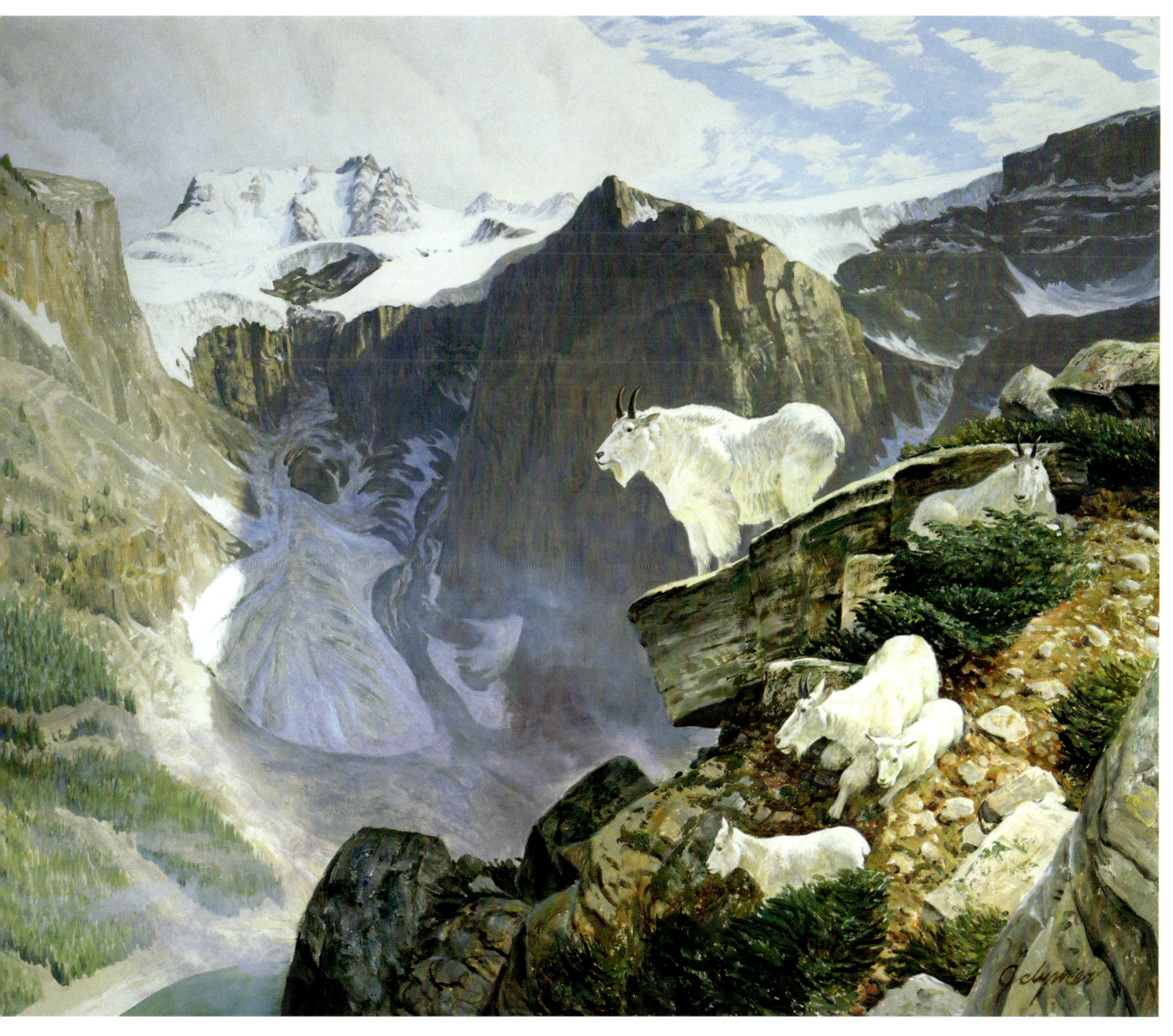

FIGURE 5.31.

JOHN CLYMER

The Lookout, 1963.

Oil on board; 30 × 36 inches.

Gift of Sybil and Tom Wiancko.

National Museum of Wildlife Art Collection.

W1995.025.

ROBERT LOUGHEED
CANADA, 1910–1982

In the Late March Sun (figure 5.32) depicts a bull elk and two cows in a sun-dappled snowfield, melting away as winter gives way to spring. Robert Lougheed was known for working outdoors, *en plein air,* his quick brushstrokes recording the changing colors of the day. Sunlight is as much the subject of this painting as are the elk, the snow, or the forest. Lougheed's mentor, Frank Dumond, was a great proponent of studying outside and offered his students the opportunity to travel to Nova Scotia each summer with him to paint the rugged Canadian terrain.[64]

Lougheed began his artistic career as an illustrator for the *Toronto Star.* In Toronto he met John Clymer, who would become a lifelong friend. Clymer was working for various Canadian publications when he decided to move to New York to train with Harvey Dunn; he urged Lougheed to move to New York as well. Lougheed agreed and, in 1935, made the journey south. He began taking classes with French-academy-trained Frank Dumond at the Art Students League in New York. Dumond was a major influence on Lougheed; under his tutelage, Lougheed's work improved dramatically. After moving to the artist enclave of Westport, Connecticut, where Clymer also lived, Lougheed illustrated articles for *Reader's Digest, Sports Afield, True,* and *Collier's.* According to Byron Price, Lougheed's most fruitful relationship was with *Reader's Digest,* for whom he created ninety-five covers and countless illustrations.[65] In addition to his commercial work, Lougheed spent six months of the year on his own paintings, a feat not many other illustrators could manage. He traveled widely, often with Clymer. Alaska, Canada, and New Mexico were some of his favorite places to study, sketch, and paint. In 1970, he and his wife, Cordy, moved to Santa Fe, where he continued to practice his trade.

Despite coming of age and making his career in the era of abstract painting, he made a plea for realism, saying, "I am a realist in painting. I know that a serious composition must include those emotional and spiritual qualities extolled by the professional art theorist; like every other artist, I also know that accurate reporting of detail does not, of itself, constitute art; but unlike other theorists, I cannot feel that realistic treatment need detract from any reasonable or sensible idea."[66] The interest from various museums in Lougheed's career and the careers of his contemporaries shows that others echo his sentiments. There is room under the broad umbrella of American art history to explore the ongoing development

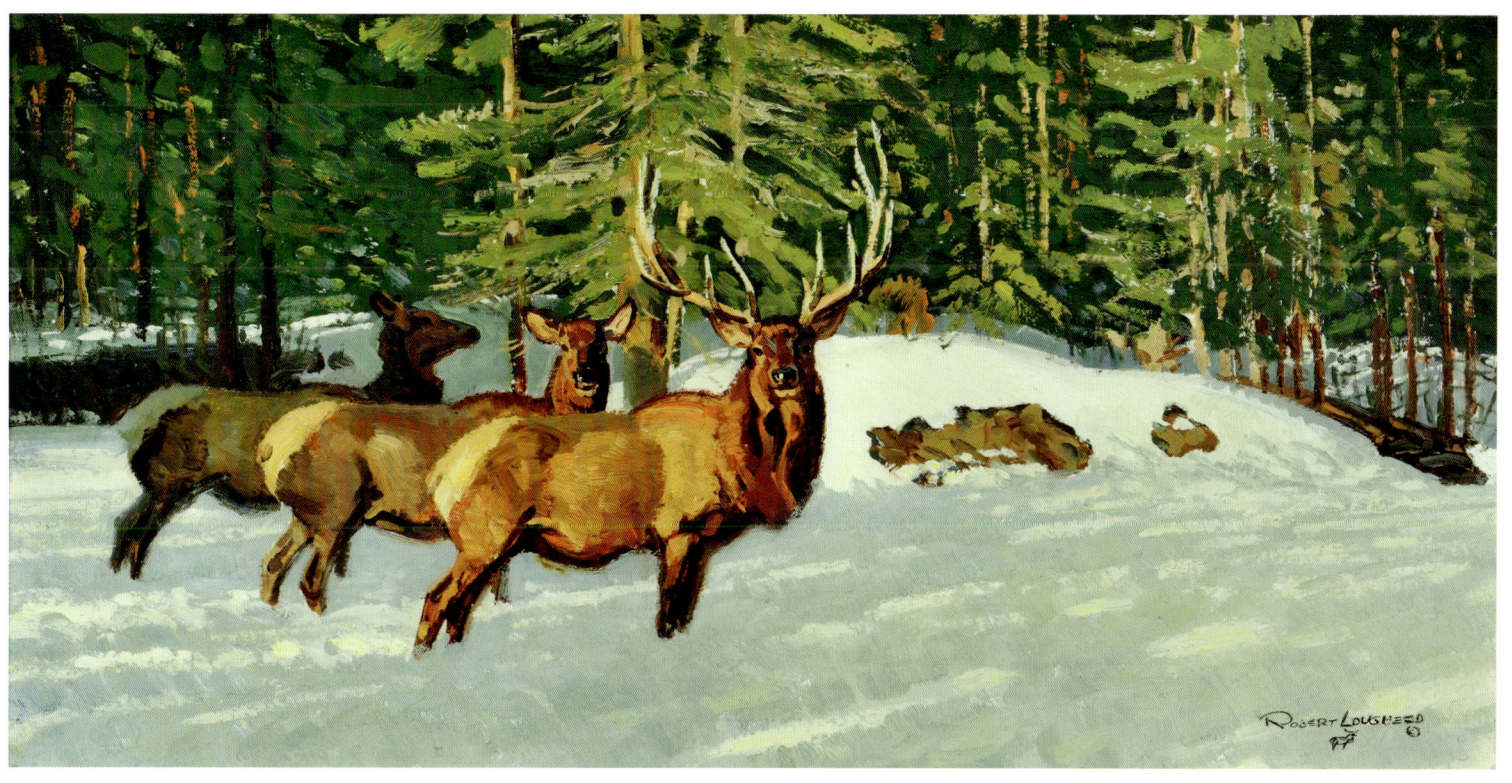

FIGURE 5.32.
ROBERT LOUGHEED
In the Late March Sun, c. 1975.
Oil on Masonite; 12 × 24 inches.
JKM Collection.
M1987.019.

of realism and naturalism in the twentieth and twenty-first centuries. These areas of painting did not end with the onset of abstract art but continued as artists, collectors, and museums sought out diverse art that represented different ideas, points of view, and perspectives across American culture.

GEORGE BROWNE
United States, 1918–1958

A recent book on Belmore Browne and his son, George, lauds the accomplishments of the younger: "George Browne was recognized throughout the United States in the mid-1950s as a sporting artist of the first rank, the ascending star among American wildlife painters of his generation. His oils of waterfowl and upland game birds in flight were compared favorably to the works of Frank Benson and Roland Clark, and his paintings of big game animals, to those of Carl Rungius. Every painting he completed sold quickly, and his dealers were continually pleading for more of his pictures to satisfy the demands of their customers."[67]

George Browne's childhood was spent in Banff, Alberta, the same territory that Carl Rungius was exploring and painting. For lovers of nature, the outdoors, and wildlife, there was no better place in North America. Banff was then a small town in the heart of some of the Rocky Mountain's most spectacular and rugged terrain, yet it was relatively accessible. The young Browne was clearly influenced by these surroundings; his paintings show a deep appreciation for the wilderness and wildlife (figure 5.33). In 1930, his family moved to Santa Barbara, California, where George's father served as the director of the Santa Barbara School of Fine Arts. With his parents' consent, Browne left school at age thirteen and devoted all his time to drawing and painting. He apprenticed under his father for two years, then enrolled at the California School of Fine Arts in San Francisco.

Two wildlife masters of a previous generation, Carl Rungius and Wilhelm Kuhnert, became inspirations for the young Browne. While serving in World War II, he continued painting, shipping works home for his father's critique. After the war, he moved to Norfolk, Connecticut, to be closer to the New York art world. He quickly rose to prominence, having a one-man show of his work at the Grand Central Art Galleries in 1950. Determined to support his family with his art, Browne produced more than two hundred oil paintings between 1948 and 1958, selling most of the works during his lifetime. Tragically, he was killed in a shooting accident in 1958, ending what was becoming a substantial career in wildlife art. Painter Francis Lee Jaques stated, "I fear I was a little jealous of George Browne's work, as I don't believe I was of any other artist. His work was a breakthrough. It was different—and better."[68]

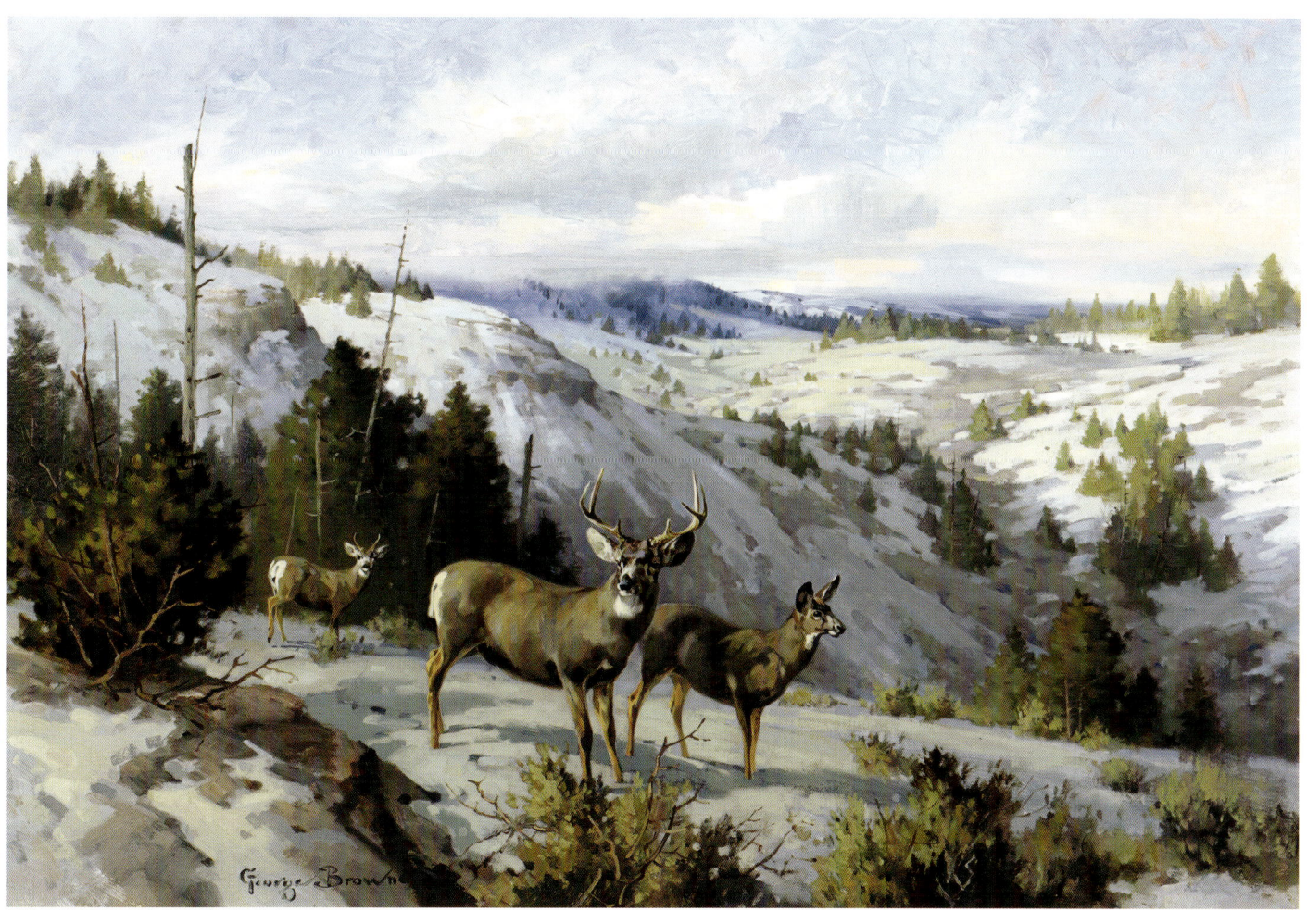

FIGURE 5.33.

GEORGE BROWNE

Quiet Canyon, c. 1955.

Oil on canvas; 20 × 30 inches.

Gift of Mr. and Mrs. Martin F. Wood.

National Museum of Wildlife Art Collection.

W1987.233.

LANFORD MONROE
United States, 1950–2000

Lanford Monroe's career illustrates the ongoing import of representational art in America. Instead of fading as artists such as Jackson Pollack and Franz Kline experimented with abstract-expressionism and dominated critical attention, some artists continued to build upon the work of their forebears and continued to hone their skills by venturing out into the field and sketching what they saw. Collectors also continued to support representational work of merit that evoked a mood or expressed a sentiment to which they could relate. Developing directly out of the artistic community that supported John Clymer, Robert Lougheed, and Robert Kuhn came Lanford Monroe, the daughter of illustrator C. E. Monroe and portrait artist Betty Monroe.

Monroe's parents encouraged her artistic endeavors from a young age. She completed her first commission by the age of six, designing an invitation for a new line of dolls produced by the Ginny Doll Company.[69] Monroe later received the Hallmark Scholarship in Fine Art and attended the Ringling School of Art in Sarasota, Florida. She traveled extensively throughout North America, settling in many places for short periods of time. Monroe began her fine art career as a watercolorist but eventually shifted to oils. Her atmospheric landscapes recall the work of greats such as Albert Bierstadt, but on a more intimate scale. Monroe's paintings do not promote the glories of the wilderness with elongated peaks but celebrate the quieter moments in nature with subtle, soft, gentle renderings that encourage contemplation. In *Leyburn Run*, she paints a misty field near Leyburn, in Yorkshire, England; the idyllic scene captures foxes running through lush, green grass (figure 5.34). The foxes are but one element within the greater composition; these are animals in a broader landscape, partially hidden, integrated into the scene. That careful integration of animal and setting is a Monroe hallmark, a principal quality that draws people to her work.

Monroe was just reaching the peak of her artistic powers when she passed away in 2000. In 2001, the National Museum of Wildlife Art initiated the Lanford Monroe Memorial Artist in Residence program. The goal of the program is to engage museum visitors in the art-making process, to encourage greater understanding of how the paintings and sculptures in the museum were created. Much like that of artists Louis Fuertes and George Browne, Monroe's life ended before she reached her full artistic potential. The success she enjoyed is evidence

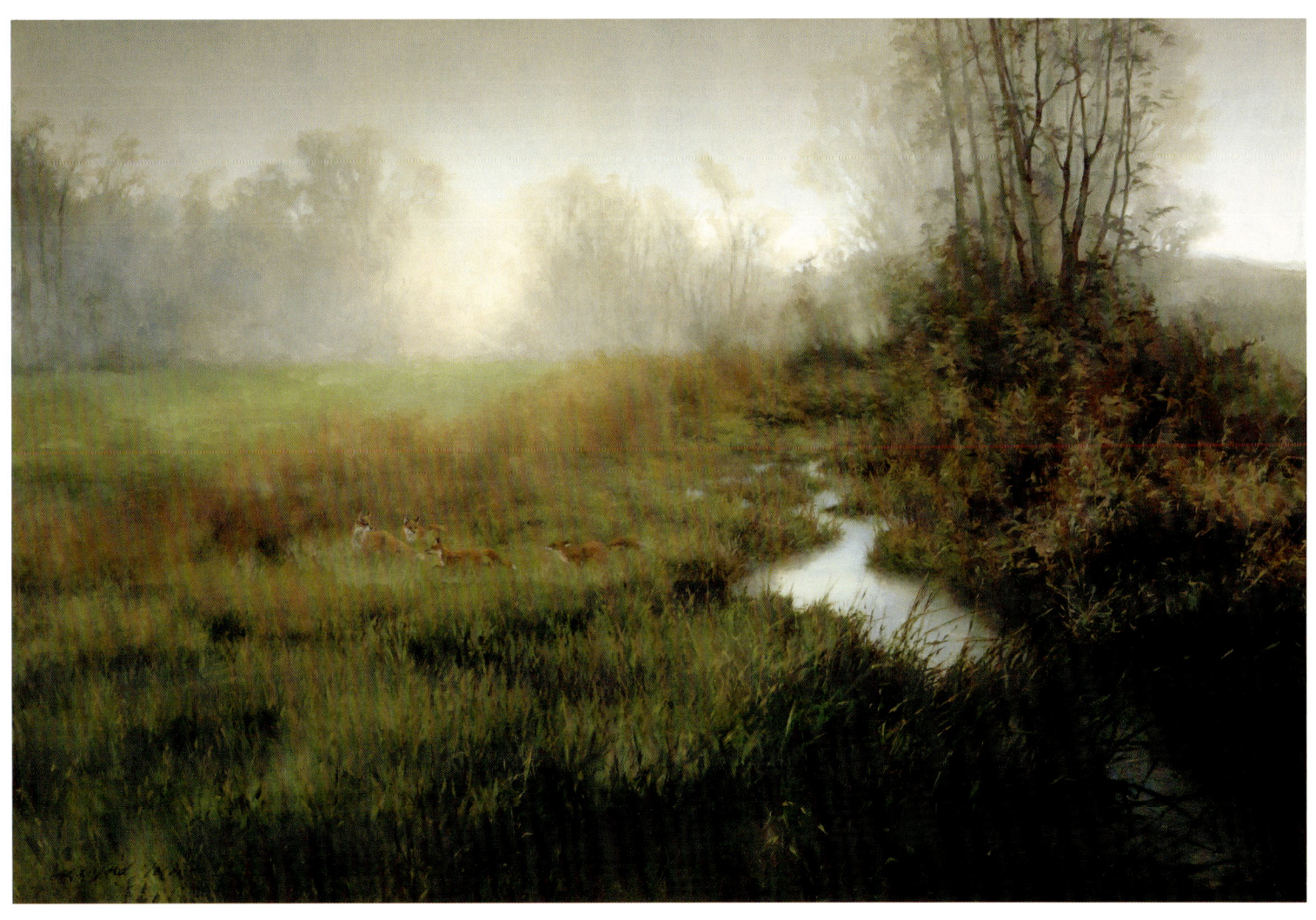

of her obvious ability but also serves as a prime indicator of contemporary interest in wildlife subject matter, an interest that stretches back to Audubon, Catlin, and Bodmer even as it extends forward to the many artists who continue exploring the rich field today.

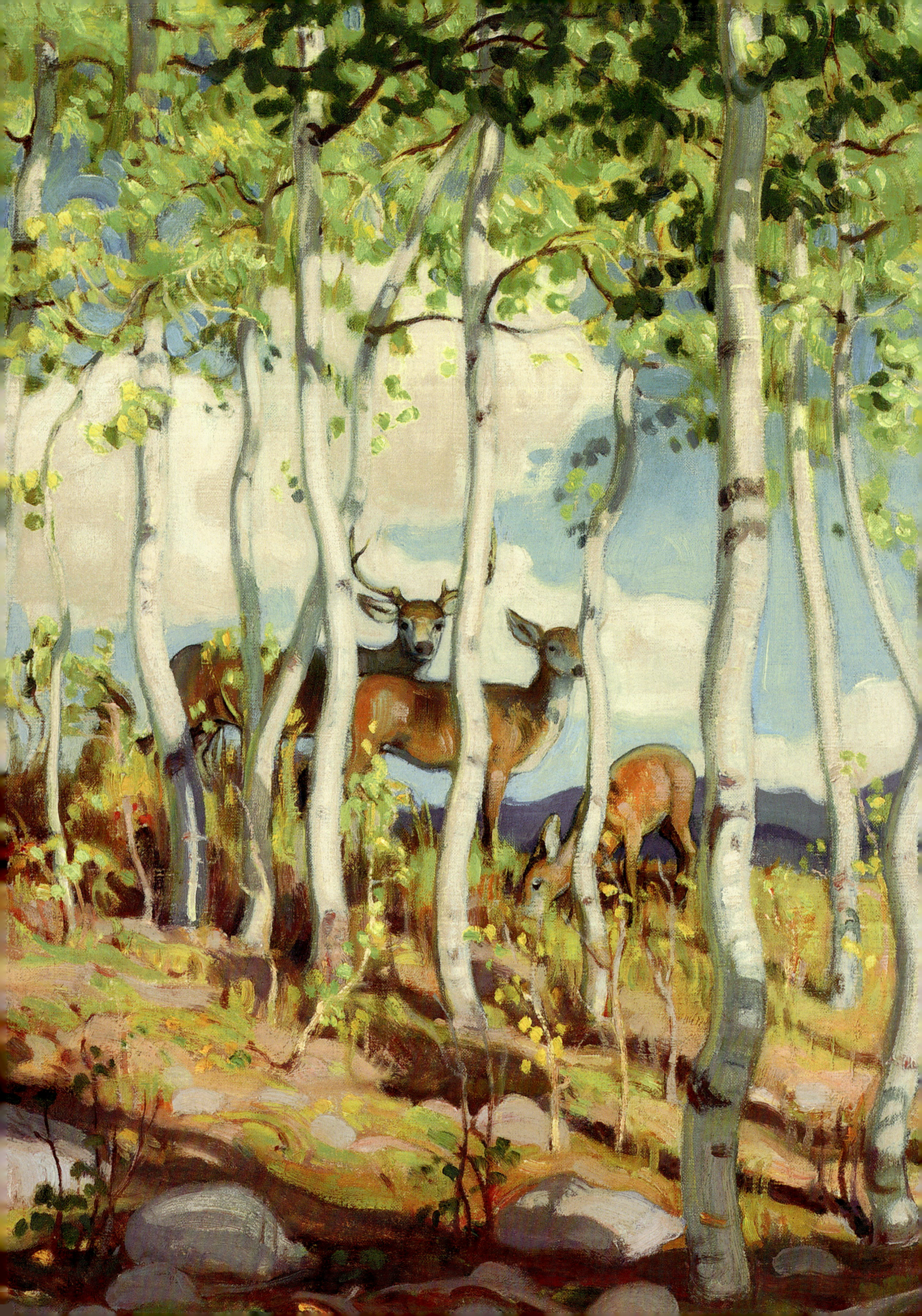

Chapter 6

Modern Movements: *New Styles, Familiar Subjects*

I t is noteworthy that one of the first images in this book, *Peaceable Kingdom* by Edward Hicks (see figure I.3), is considered a work of folk art, as is *Brown Rabbit* (figure 6.1) by Bill Traylor (1854–1947). Both Hicks and Traylor were "discovered" thanks to an interest in American folk art that arose during the first half of the twentieth century. *Peaceable Kingdom* (c. 1822–25) illustrates the depth of the folk art tradition in America, while *Brown Rabbit* (c. 1940) displays its continuance in modern times. Together, they exemplify a movement in collecting focused on art created by outsiders, by artists who had no formal link to art academies, galleries, or museums but were driven to create anyway, often despite hardship and disenfranchisement.

The simple outline of Traylor's rabbit, the flatness of the image, and its isolation in the picture are all modernistic elements. There is no attempt to depict the rabbit's habitat, fur, or musculature in detail, yet this is a charismatic, characteristic portrait of a rabbit just the same. Modern artists found kindred spirits in folk artists, whose often-naïve, immediate imagery came from inside themselves, without reliance on academic training. Folk art was seen as pure expression, uncurbed by the stifling effects of laborious classes on proper perspective or precise anatomical drawing. Carolyn Weekley noted in *The Kingdoms of Edward Hicks* that landmark exhibitions on American folk art held in the early 1930s at the Newark Museum in New Jersey and at the Museum of Modern Art in New York City set the stage for modern appreciation of the genre.[1] Abby Aldrich Rockefeller began collecting the work of Edward Hicks in the 1930s and amassed the largest single collection of his work (now housed in the Abby Aldrich Rockefeller Folk Art Museum at Colonial Williamsburg). These early exhibits and the emergence of a folk art market were the first steps in the launching of the genre. Interest in folk art steadily grew in strength as the twentieth century progressed; today, paintings by artists such as Hicks demand increasingly higher prices as museums and collectors outbid each other at auction.

The rabbit in Traylor's image may have been one he saw in a yard in Montgomery, Alabama, or a remembrance of one from the George Hartwell

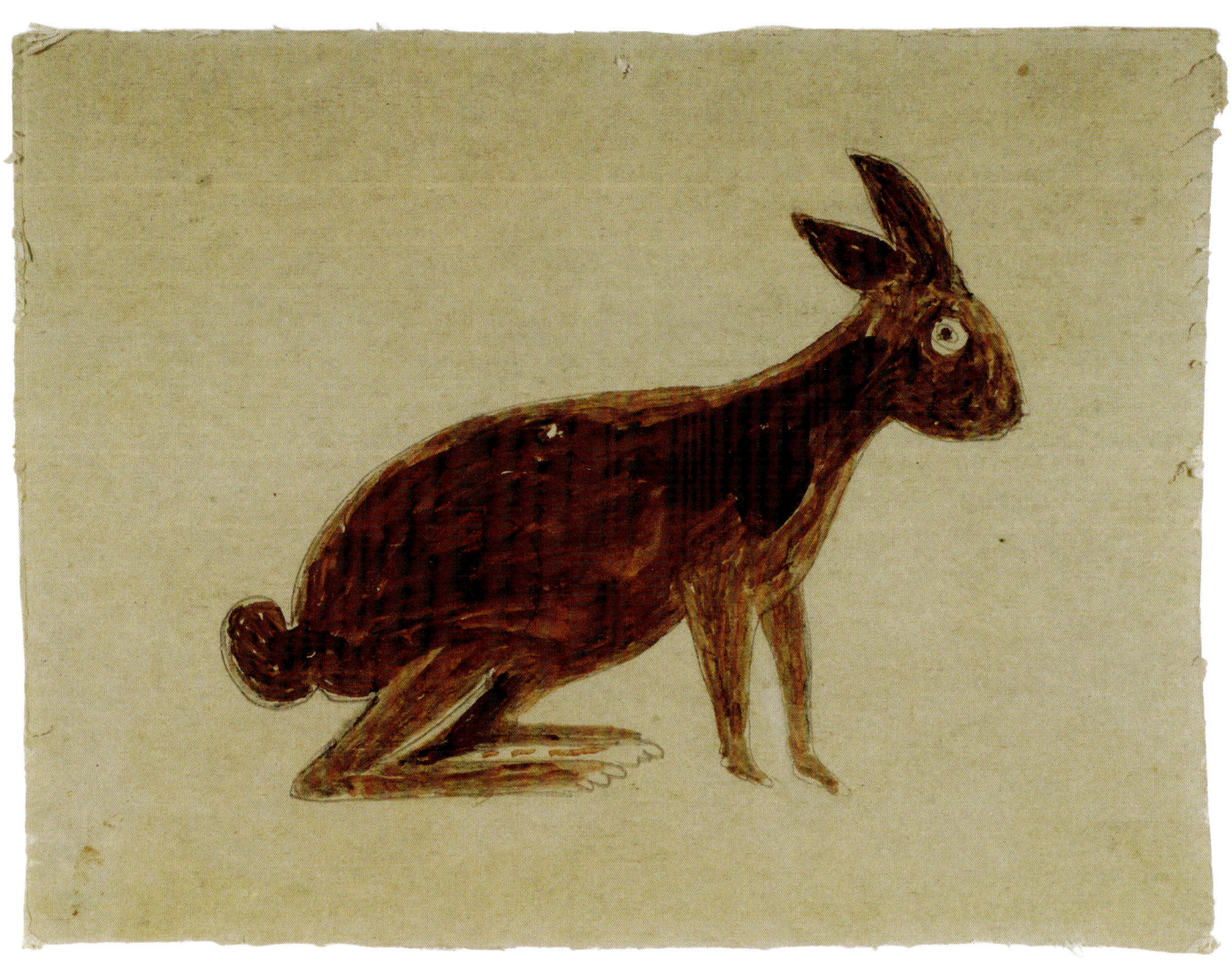

FIGURE 6.1.
BILL TRAYLOR
Brown Rabbit, c. 1940.
Pencil and gouache on cardboard;
7 ½ × 10 inches.
JKM Collection.
JL1997.092.

Traylor plantation near Montgomery, where he was born into slavery in 1854. After the Civil War, Traylor continued working on the plantation until 1938, when, at age eighty-four, he moved to Montgomery. He briefly worked in a shoe factory until rheumatism forced him to quit. He had a small state pension but little other income. Around 1939, he began to create pencil drawings on cardboard or scraps of paper. He sketched animals and people, along with scenes of lively Monroe Street. A young painter named Charles Shannon met Traylor in 1939 and quickly became his friend and supporter. Shannon provided Traylor with pencils, paints, and brushes and arranged gallery shows for him, the first at the New South Art Center. Traylor created over 1,500 drawings in the scant three years he lived in Montgomery. In 1942, he traveled north to Detroit and Washington, D.C., to live with his children. He returned to Montgomery in 1946 and died in 1947. Significant recognition came for Traylor in the 1980s, when his work was included in the landmark exhibition Black Folk Art in America at the Corcoran Gallery of Art in Washington, D.C.; his image of a coiled snake was featured on the cover of the catalogue.[2]

The fact that both Hicks and Traylor depicted wildlife sums up one of the underlying concepts of this book: that wildlife as subject matter is universal, spanning time, place, and art movements. Moreover, the tradition of depicting wildlife is particularly important in the formation of an American identity. Artists in the twentieth century melded modern art ideas with their own desires to paint the animals of North America. Applying principles of postimpressionist, expressionist, and abstract art to a subject that had previously been depicted by artists trained in traditional realism (or not trained at all) created a body of work that interprets American wildlife in a new light, opening the door for patrons who might not be drawn to a naturalistic painting of a deer in the woods but will eagerly seek out the same subject painted in a modernist idiom.

Instead of portraits of particular animals, landscape paintings such as Maynard Dixon's *Eagle's Roost* and William Dunton's *Tapestry of Autumn* incorporate wildlife as an integral part of the overall scene (see figures 6.2 and 6.3, respectively). These works look at nature more holistically, melding the animal into the environment. Georgia O'Keeffe's *Antelope* takes this concept a step further, more explicitly depicting how all living things return to the earth, as her pronghorn skull dissolves into the desert floor (see figure 6.7). Andy Warhol's *Endangered Species* portfolio takes the opposite direction, creating "celebritized" animal portraits with no hint of habitat, meant to draw attention to these harbingers of the animal kingdom in dire need of human assistance (see figure 6.10). The lovingly chiseled curves of William Zorach's *Pumas* (see figure 6.12) contrast markedly with the streamlined panels of Allan Houser's *Fabricated Bison* (see figure 6.13), but both show the influence of modernist ideas on wildlife subject matter. From evidence of the beneficence of a supreme being to enduring icons of American identity, images of wildlife have continued to intrigue artists and audiences alike. In the twenty-first century, these iconic images grow more powerful and more relevant as commercial interests continue to besiege wilderness areas and threaten wildlife habitat. A new generation of artists has risen to the challenge of creating art that is not only beautiful in and of itself but also reflects contemporary cultural concerns about the health of the planet on which we live.

MAYNARD DIXON
United States, 1875–1946

In *Escape to Reality: The Western World of Maynard Dixon*, art historian Linda Jones Gibbs noted, "In the dramatic scenery and profound silences of what he called 'my western world,' Dixon found what he referred to on numerous occasions as 'the Real Thing.' 'My object,' he explained, 'has always been to get as close to the Real Thing as possible—people, animals and country.'"[3] Dixon sought the authentic and the unspoiled, grand vistas that had not yet been crisscrossed by power lines, railroad tracks, or pavement; he found that and more in lonely corners of the Southwest. His "Real Thing" was the American West as it existed before modernization. He gravitated toward landscapes, American Indians, cowboys, and, on occasion, wildlife. Even the vertical *Eagle's Roost* (figure 6.2) shows Dixon's penchant for long horizons, stretching into the distance, reflecting the vast expanses of open land that still existed in the West. His strong horizons were often complemented by elements such as clouds in the sky or rocks on the ground. Dixon's clouds were not wispy, ephemeral things but seemingly solid objects, celestial counterparts to his earthbound boulders. Similar to paintings by Taos Society members William H. Dunton (see figure 6.3) and Ernest M. Hennings (see figure 6.6), *Eagle's Roost* presents the animal as an integral part of the landscape; Dixon provides a portrait not of an eagle but of a huge rock on which an eagle just happens to be landing.

Encouragement from none other than Frederic Remington helped Dixon decide to pursue a career in art. A natural sketcher, Dixon sent two notebooks to Remington when he was just sixteen years old (the venerable Remington was then about thirty). Dixon attended the California School of Design, studying under Arthur Matthews; he did not stay long, however, deciding after three months to travel throughout the West on his own, sketching as he went. In the 1890s, his illustrations began to appear in California magazines and newspapers. After the 1906 San Francisco earthquake destroyed his studio, he moved to New York City, where he published art in magazines such as *Harper's, Scribner's,* and *McClure's* and illustrated Clarence Mulford's Hopalong Cassidy stories.

The pressure and deadlines of illustration took their toll on Dixon. He returned to San Francisco in 1912 to focus on his art. In 1915, he attended the Panama-Pacific International Exposition and witnessed galleries full of modern art. Impressionism and postimpressionism provided a new visual language to work

FIGURE 6.2.
MAYNARD DIXON
Eagle's Roost, 1927–46.
Oil on canvasboard; 30 × 25 inches.
JKM Collection.
JL1996.081.

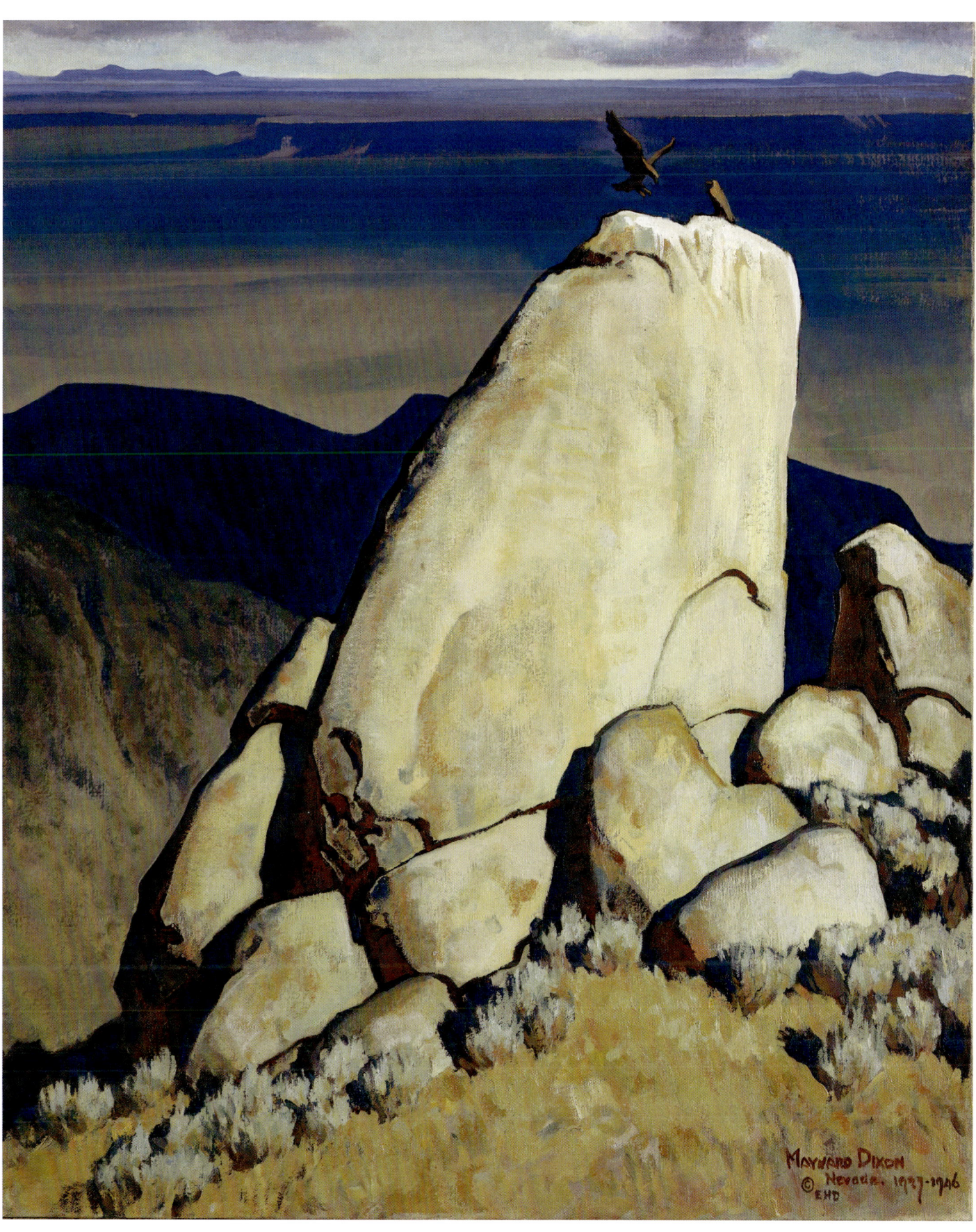

with, pushing him toward his signature style, which incorporated flat, broad planes of color and abstracted natural forms. For much of the 1920s, Dixon traveled throughout the West with his second wife, noted photographer Dorothea Lange. Together, they documented their experience, both focusing on the effects of the Great Depression on the American public. After their divorce, Dixon married muralist Edith Hamlin, and the couple set up a studio in Mount Carmel, Utah. There, he was able to concentrate on the landscapes he loved; he created some of his most spectacular work, investigating the shape and structure of rolling clouds, craggy mesas, and desert floors. In 1946, the same year he put the finishing touches on *Eagle's Roost,* Dixon died of emphysema.[4]

WILLIAM HERBERT DUNTON
United States, 1878–1936

William H. Dunton's wildlife paintings are prized for their beautiful sense of light, color, and overall decorative design. In *Tapestry of Autumn* (figure 6.3), the focus is not the deer but the beautiful light shining on the golden leaves of the majestic trees. In a manner typical of Dunton's mature style, the background is tilted up, so there is no visible horizon, just an undulating pattern of foliage, which serves as the backdrop for the scene in the foreground. This work displays the richly textured and intricately interwoven elements of fall in a southwestern forest in a tapestry-like fashion.

"Buck" Dunton was born in Augusta, Maine, in 1878. He grew up drawing and spending time outdoors with his grandfather. In 1894, at sixteen, he quit school to work in a men's clothing shop to save enough money to travel west and pursue his dream of becoming a cowboy. In 1896, Dunton began the first in a long series of western trips that would last until 1911. Also in 1896, he began to sell illustrations to newspapers, many with western and wildlife themes. Dunton traveled to different places each summer, ranging from Montana to Mexico, and returned east each winter. After trying his hand at being a cowboy, Dunton decided that the life of an artist was more to his liking, but he never outgrew his love for all things western.[5]

Back east, Dunton attended the Cowles Art School in Boston in 1897, and he married in 1900. Around 1903, he moved his winter base to New York City and began taking classes at the Art Students League with Frank DuMond. Dunton's early years in the city were filled with success; he sold illustrations to a wide variety of magazines, including *Collier's, Harper's Weekly,* the *Saturday Evening Post, Cosmopolitan, McClure's,* and *Scribner's.* He also illustrated a series of Zane Grey's westerns, including *Riders of the Purple Sage.* In 1911, he met Ernest Blumenschein and took Blumenschein's class at the Art Students League. Blumenschein invited him to visit Taos, New Mexico, to paint—and even encouraged him to relocate there.[6] Entranced by the light and landscape, Dunton established a studio in Taos in 1912 and became one of the founding members of the Taos Society of Artists. The Taos Society was formed to market the artwork of its members by organizing traveling exhibits to different parts of the country (at that time, there were no art galleries in Santa Fe or Taos).

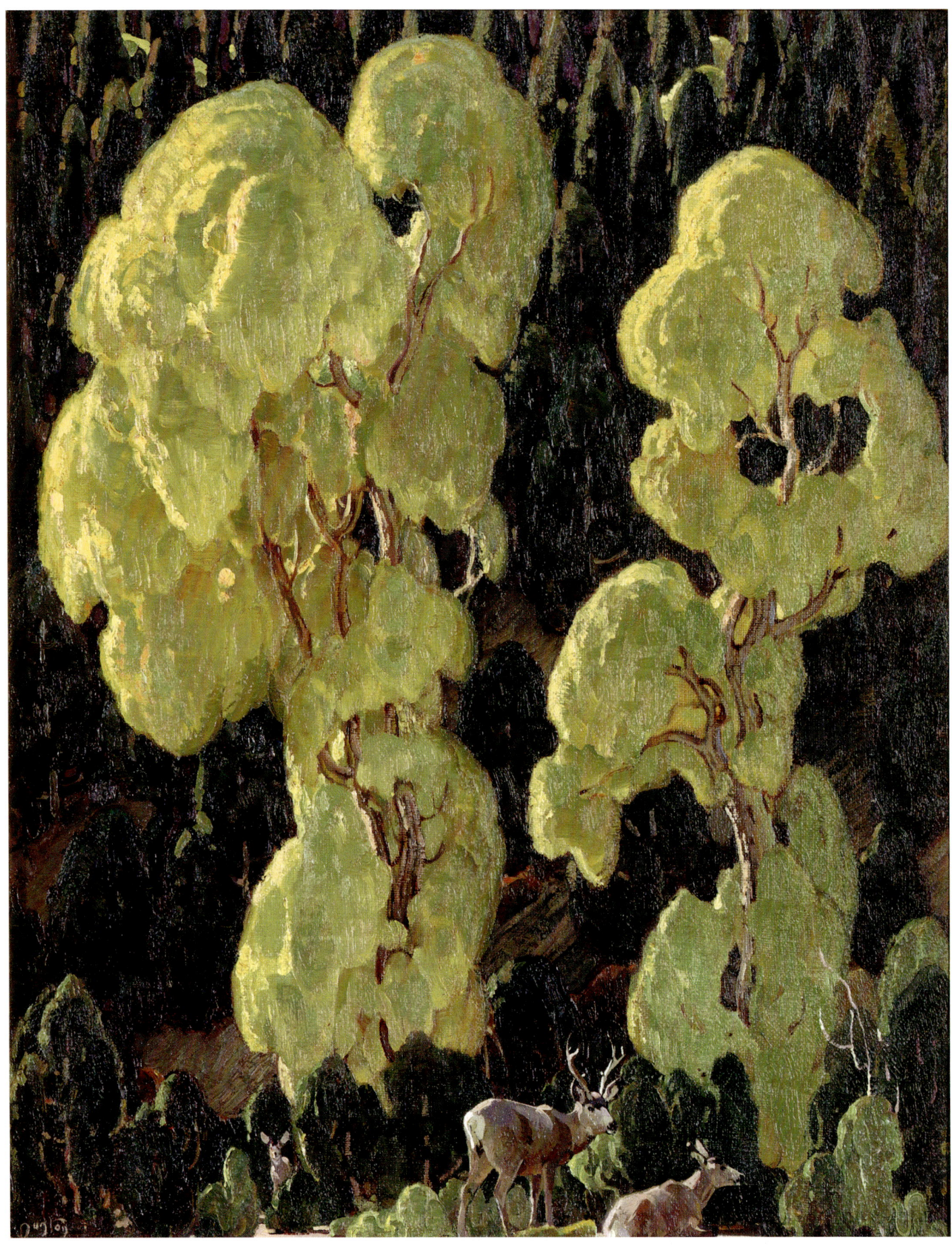

In contrast to the other Taos Society artists, Dunton did not focus on American Indian subject matter but preferred to paint the West he had dreamed of as a child. His oeuvre includes cowboys, cowgirls, goat herders, and other western characters. He also, always, had an interest in wildlife—bear, elk, and deer in particular. Early in life, he was an avid hunter and took great care studying the animals he shot, making careful sketches of an animal alive, dead, and then skinned, to reveal its musculature. The work Dunton is best known for is not tightly rendered anatomical realism, however. As he spent more time in Taos with other Taos Society artists, he developed a modernist style all his own, with abstracted forms, bold patterns, and simplified details, though his animals remained realistic. Dunton was not interested in depicting an elk in a clearing just as he had seen it; he was more concerned with how an animal fit into an overall pattern of trunks, branches, leaves, and light. He was clearly influenced by postimpressionist movements, the then-established schools of painting in which many of his cohort were working. Although Dunton's style was not revolutionary in terms of creating a new genre, he was among the first to apply modern tenets to depicting wildlife.

FIGURE 6.3.
WILLIAM HERBERT DUNTON
Tapestry of Autumn, 1927.
Oil on canvas; 20 × 16 inches.
JKM Collection.
M1997.048.

ROCKWELL KENT

United States, 1882–1971

The National Museum of Wildlife Art's *Mount Equinox, Vermont* (figure 6.4) displays the brilliant colors of fall foliage, with warm, low light on the landscape echoing the golden hues of soon-to-fall leaves. Rockwell Kent painted Mount Equinox at least twice. A companion piece, called *Mt. Equinox, Winter,* hangs in the Art Institute of Chicago. The Chicago painting also features two deer, one in the foreground and one in the background; the deer in front leaps to the left of the canvas in a variation on the same theme. The vantage point of the two paintings is similar, featuring the characteristic peak of Mt. Equinox. In *Rockwell Kent: The Mythic and the Modern,* Jake Milgram Wien reported that Kent could see Mount Equinox from his studio window (likely the view he depicted in these paintings).[7]

Kent's art training began during the summers of 1900–1903, when he took classes at the William Merritt Chase Summer School of Art. In the fall of 1900, Kent also began to study architecture at Columbia University and attended evening classes with Arthur Wesley Dow at the Art Students League. As he continued his studies, he took instruction from Robert Henri and became Abbot Thayer's studio assistant. Kent's teachers provided him with a solid combination of good draftsmanship and modernist thinking; Dow, for example, taught his students that artists should express their inner feelings on the canvas through line, color, and design, breaking away from traditional realism to be more expressionistic. The simplified shapes and heightened colors in *Mount Equinox, Vermont* are examples of how this teaching affected Kent's work. In his painting and illustration, he developed a bold style that can be seen particularly well in his graphic work, which is characterized by stark areas of black-and-white contrast and concise, clearly outlined forms.

Before settling in Vermont in 1919, Kent traveled to Newfoundland and Alaska and lived in various eastern locales such as Maine and New York City. Travel became a focus of Kent's life; during his nearly eighty years, he visited Tierra del Fuego, Ireland, Greenland, Denmark, Sweden, and Russia. Kent was an outspoken socialist, which caused him difficulty in the United States. In 1950, the U.S. State Department revoked his right to travel abroad and did not reinstate it until 1958. In 1960, he gave a large collection of his artwork to the people of the Soviet Union and, in 1967, received the International Lenin Peace Prize. Kent's numerous

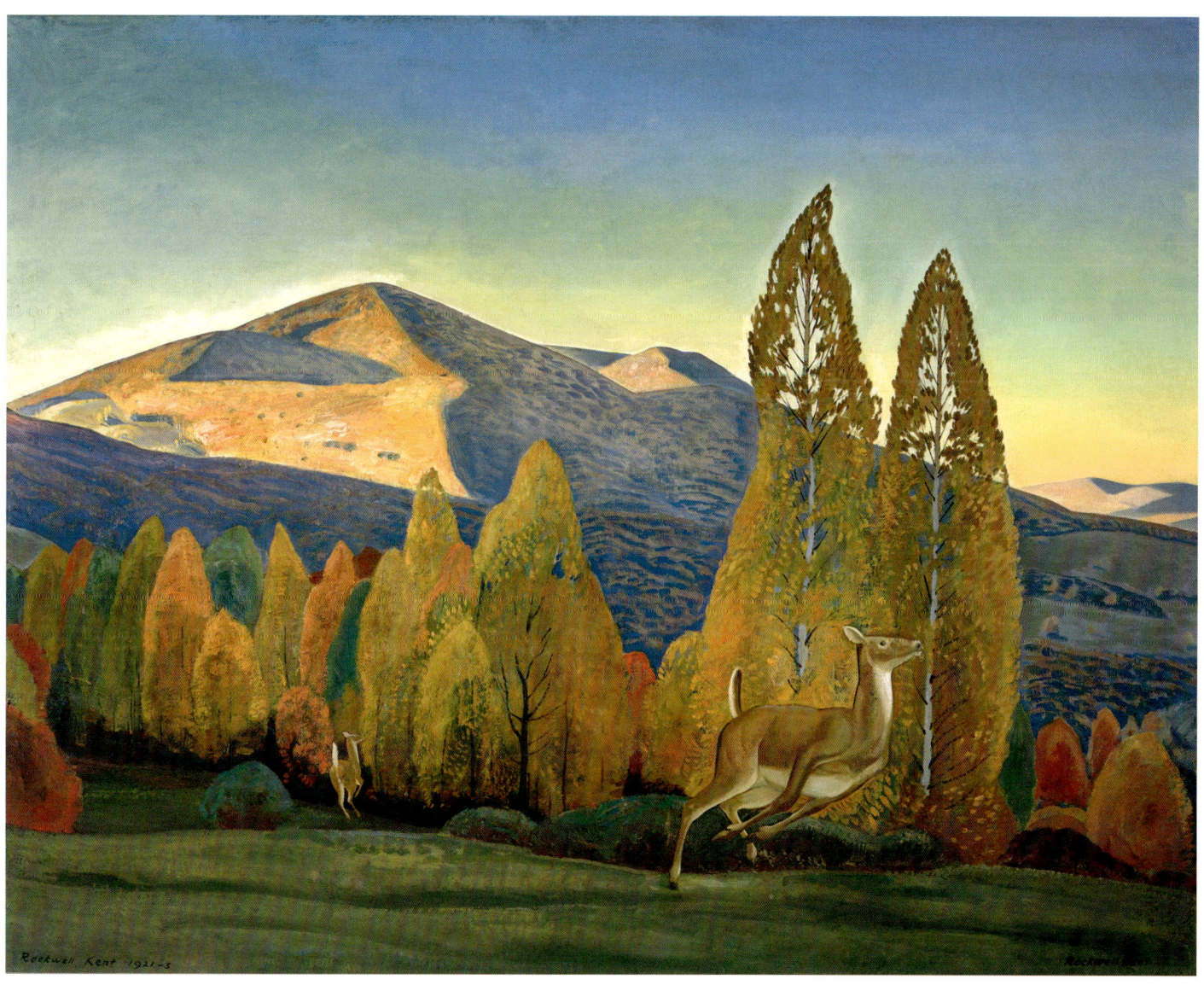

FIGURE 6.4.
ROCKWELL KENT
Mt. Equinox, Vermont, 1921–23.
Oil on canvas; 33 × 44 inches.
JKM Collection.
J1993.013.

illustration commissions include *Moby Dick* (1930), *Canterbury Tales* (1930), and *Paul Bunyan* (1941). A good record of his travels can be found in his considerable autobiographical work: *Wilderness: A Journal of Quiet Adventure in Alaska* (1920), *Voyaging: Southward from the Strait of Magellan* (1924), and *Greenland Journal* (1962). As a testament to his importance and outspokenness, Kent's obituary was printed on the front page of the *New York Times* when he died in 1971.[8]

JESSIE ARMS BOTKE

United States, 1883–1971

Commenting on her working skills after leaving the Art Institute of Chicago, Botke said, "I had no training in anything but art, and so far I had no style of my own, I was completely dominated by the teachers whose work I admired so much. . . . I kept working, and gradually my real talent began to come out, a strong feeling for decoration, two dimensional, flat pattern."[9] Botke's talent is clearly evident in *Black Peacocks with Japanese Persimmons* (figure 6.5), which showcases the flat, decorative nature of her mature style. In *Birds, Boughs, and Blossoms,* Patricia Trenton and Deborah Epstein Solon wrote, "By the late 1930s [Botke] had already begun to tilt the picture plane forward and to organize the composition on a diagonal. . . . Forms are large and placed directly against the picture plane. The effect of rippled water is achieved by several methods that she used for working with metal leaf, both gold and silver."[10]

This painting is made up of a series of different planes of color, from dark oils to brilliant gold leaf, and aptly communicates depth; the golden river recedes into the background, and the fanned-out tail of the peacock encircles his body, suggesting the shape of a seashell as the tail curves up and around behind him. The main goal of this type of work is to combine a variety of elements, which may be flat planes of color or different areas of pattern (such as the river or the tail), into a single, harmonious whole, in which everything comes together into a balanced and seamless composition.

At age fourteen, Botke displayed an early interest in art and took classes at the Art Institute of Chicago. In the summer, she participated in painting workshops in Michigan and Maine. Leaving the Art Institute two credits shy of graduating, Botke took jobs painting decorative friezes and illustrating books. Inspired by an exhibition of work from Herter Looms of New York, Botke moved to New York City in 1911. Initially, she worked in commercial illustration but was soon employed at Herter's, where she designed tapestries and painted friezes. The four years she spent working at the looms greatly influenced her later style. In 1914, she met artist Cornelius Botke; the couple married in 1915. The Botkes subsequently worked as artists in Chicago before moving to Carmel, California, and eventually to a ranch outside of Los Angeles. Botke studied birds all over the country, and the couple built their own aviary, where they kept peacocks and pheasants, among other exotics.[11] As Botke refined her style, she gained more prominent commissions

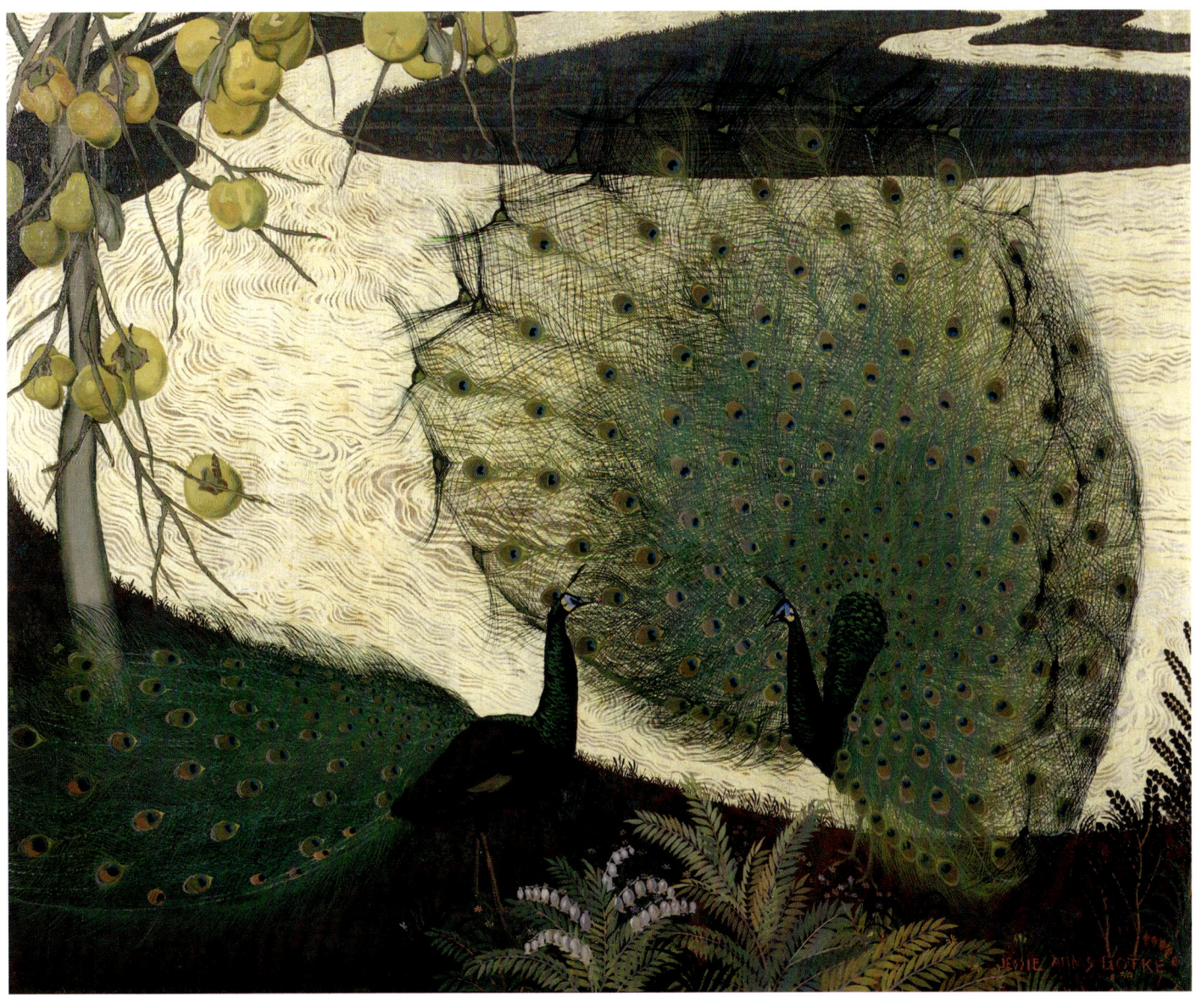

FIGURE 6.5.

JESSIE ARMS BOTKE

Black Peacocks with
Japanese Persimmons, c. 1940.

Oil and gold leaf on panel; 32 × 40 inches.

JKM Collection.

JL1998.015.

and was accepted by major galleries, such as Grand Central Art Galleries in New York and Stendahl Art Galleries in Los Angeles. Cornelius and Jessie Botke had a joint exhibition in 1942 at the Ebell Club in Los Angeles. Cornelius died in 1954. Jessie continued painting and traveling until 1967, when she suffered a stroke. She died in 1971 at the age of eighty-eight. Her abstracted scenes of birds celebrate the glorious colors and patterns to be found in nature, using modernist tenets to communicate these essential themes to twentieth-century viewers.[12]

ERNEST MARTIN HENNINGS
United States, 1886–1956

Landscape plays so important a part of my work, and subjects of sage,
mountain and sky. Nothing thrills me more, when, in the fall, the aspen and
cottonwoods are in color and with the sunlight playing across them—all the
poetry and drama, all the moods and changes of nature are there to inspire
one to greater accomplishment from year to year.

Ernest Martin Hennings, quoted in Broder, *Taos*, 253

The change of seasons and the cycles of life had a great influence on Hennings
and were the wellspring from which he drew inspiration. In *Deer Among the
Aspens* (figure 6.6), Hennings portrays a family of deer—stag, doe, and fawn—
safely grazing amidst a stand of aspens. The trunks of the trees create a beautiful
linear pattern across the canvas; the sunlight playing across the light bark and
on the still-green leaves is broken in a few places by shadows that stretch back
through the canvas, uniting the fore and middle grounds. Patricia Broder wrote
of Hennings's work, "The intricate linear designs, sinuous outlines, and expressive
contours of Hennings's paintings recall the rhythmic patterns and emphasis on the
forces of growth that are characteristic of Art Nouveau."[13]

Deer Among the Aspens also owes much to the decorative compositions
of William Dunton and the other artists painting in Taos. Inspired by the light,
landscape, and culture that had attracted the original six founding members of
the Taos Society of Artists (Joseph H. Sharp, Oscar E. Berninghaus, Ernest L.
Blumenschein, Bert G. Phillips, E. Irving Couse, and Dunton), Hennings set up
a studio in Taos in 1921. He was invited to join the society in 1924 and remained
a member until the group disbanded in 1927. Dunton and Hennings were the
only members of the group who regularly painted wildlife. While Dunton chose
to depict ranch life in his other work, Hennings more closely followed the Taos
Society habit of painting scenes of American Indians. These canvases show the
same interest in overall design as *Deer Among the Aspens*, focusing on people
placed within undulating patterns of foliage characteristic of New Mexico.

Hennings first visited Taos in 1917 at the behest of former Chicago
mayor Carter H. Harrison, Jr., and meat-packer Oscar Mayer, who supported his
travel and promised to buy Taos paintings from him upon his return. Harrison
instigated similar deals with painters William Ufer and Victor Higgins. Raised in
Chicago, Hennings showed an early aptitude for art. He graduated from the Art

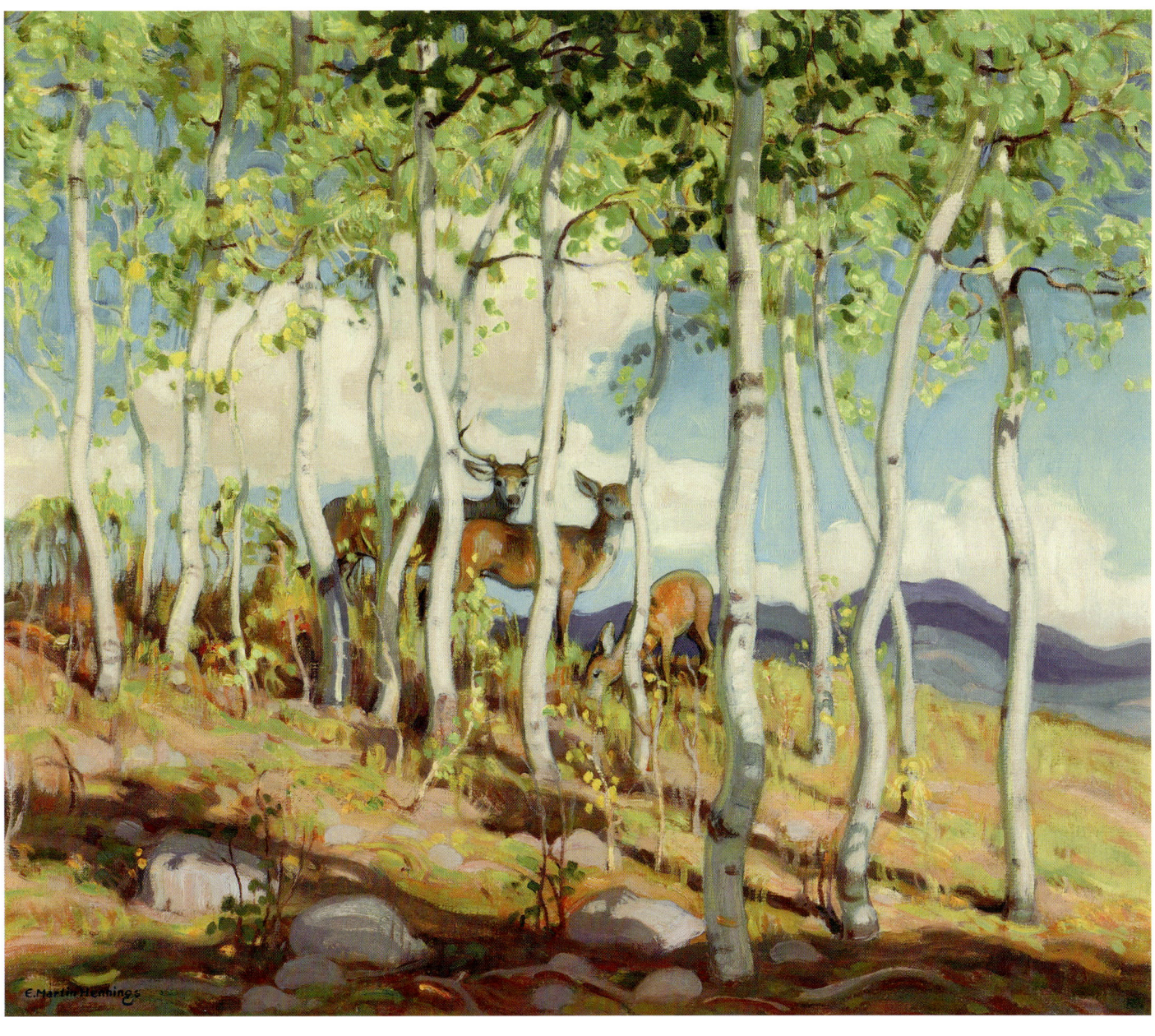

FIGURE 6.6.
ERNEST MARTIN HENNINGS
Deer Among the Aspens, 1939.
Oil on canvas; 20 × 24¼ inches.
JKM Collection.
M1987.136.

Institute in 1904 and then worked as a commercial illustrator. Disillusioned with illustration, Hennings traveled to Munich in 1912 to study with Franz von Stuck, a major proponent of *Jugenstihl,* Germany's version of art nouveau. When war broke out in Europe, Hennings made his way back to Chicago in 1915 and took a few commercial assignments, but he continued to concentrate on his own art. Two years later, he traveled to Taos, where he forged a successful painting career.[14]

GEORGIA O'KEEFFE
United States, 1887–1986

In 1939, Alfred Stieglitz held an exhibition at his American Place Gallery for Georgia O'Keeffe. In an exhibit statement, she wrote, "I have wanted to paint the desert and I haven't known how. So I brought home the bleached bones as my symbols of the desert. To me they are as beautiful as anything I know. To me they are strangely more living than animals walking around. The bones seem to cut sharply to the center of something that is keenly alive on the desert even tho' it is vast and empty and untouchable—and knows no kindness with all its beauty."[15] By the time O'Keeffe wrote that statement, she had been painting skulls and bones for nearly a decade. She continued painting them well into the 1950s, using different osseous materials as she found them on the desert or as they were given to her. Two known antelope (or, more properly, pronghorn) paintings come from this later period: *Antelope Head with Pedernal* (1953; now owned by the Gilcrease Museum), and the more simply titled *Antelope* (1954; at the National Museum of Wildlife Art). In a letter to Edith Halpert about an upcoming show at the Downtown Gallery in New York City, O'Keeffe wrote of *Antelope*, "[I]t is so different than the other things and I think one of the best."[16]

Antelope (figure 6.7) does take a different tack than her other skull paintings. It presents the skull on the horizon, emphasizing the organic relationship between bone and earth; we know that someday the skull will deteriorate back into the desert floor, providing nourishment for plant life that will, in turn, nourish another pronghorn or other animal. Earlier skull paintings showed the bones floating, disembodied, in the sky or juxtaposed them against other objects such as a brightly colored flower. The earthy *Antelope* is more temporal, emphasizing the limitless expanse of desert that meets the sky far, far in the distance of the painting. *Antelope* speaks directly to the relationship between all living things and the planet on which we live.

Born on November 15, 1887, O'Keeffe grew up on a farm in Sun Prairie, Wisconsin. Interested in art in her youth, she attended the Art Institute of Chicago from 1905 to 1906. She then went on to the Art Students League in New York in 1907, studying with William Merritt Chase. Not confident in her ability to make a mark on the art world, she quit painting until being reinspired by Alon Bement, who was teaching a course in 1912 on the principles of Arthur Wesley Dow (Rockwell Kent's instructor). Dow's philosophy was that art should be a reflection

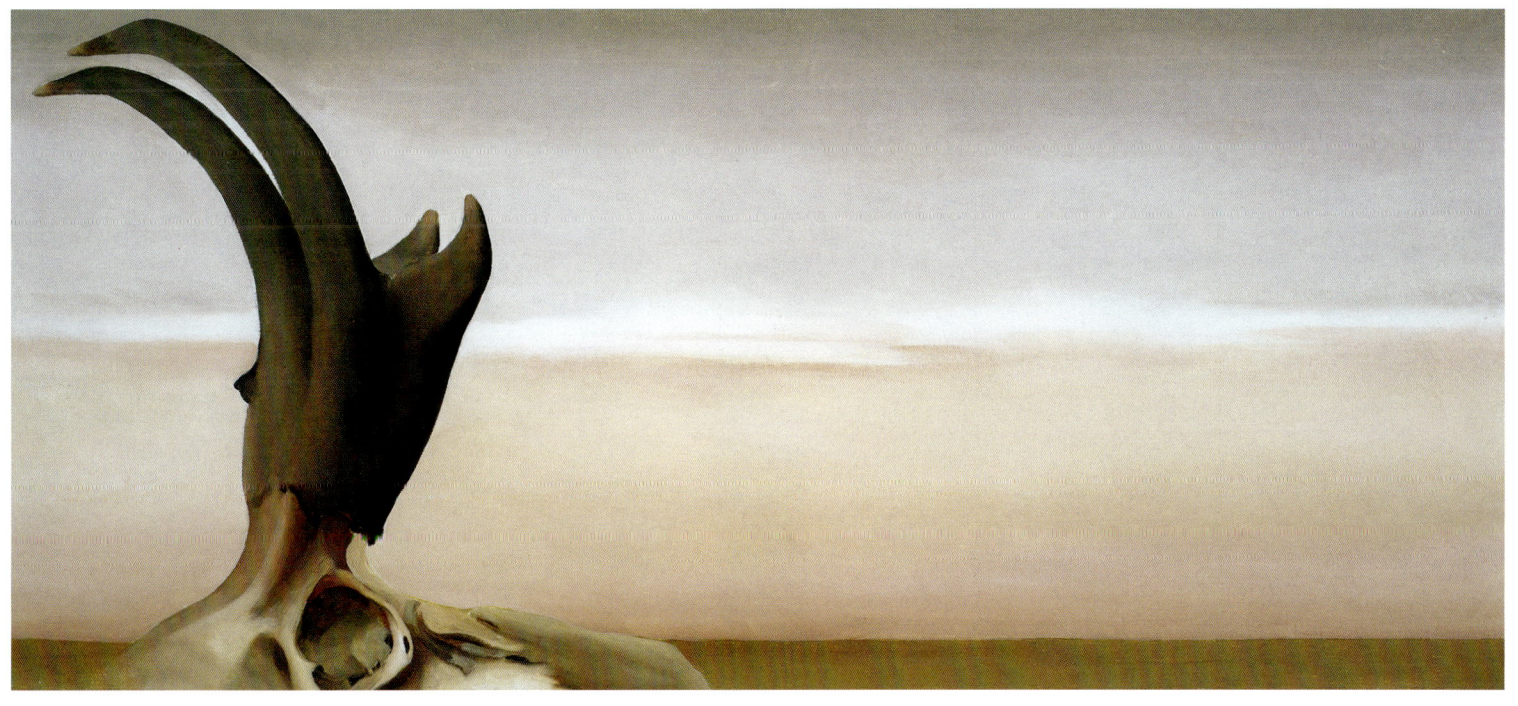

FIGURE 6.7.

GEORGIA O'KEEFFE

Antelope, 1954.

Oil on canvas, with painted
metal frame; 14½ × 32 inches.
This purchase made possible by previous
donations from Sandy Scott and the Widener
Charitable Limited Partnership, with addi-
tional assistance from Adrienne and John
Mars, Anne and John Marion, Ann and
Richard O'Leary, Charles D. Miller, Peggy
and Lowry Mays, and the Robert S. and
Grayce B. Kerr Foundation.
National Museum of Wildlife Art Collection.
M2007.033.

© 2009 Georgia O'Keefe Museum /
Artists Rights Society (ARS), New York

of the artist's inner feelings, expressed through color, line, and design. O'Keeffe taught art in Amarillo, Texas, and in the summers worked as Bement's assistant.

Growing more confident in her abilities, O'Keeffe sent some drawings to a friend, who showed them to Alfred Stieglitz. Steiglitz's 291 Gallery was renowned for exhibiting avant-garde art; he reacted favorably to her images and displayed ten of them in 1916. Stieglitz and O'Keeffe met, fell in love, and were married in 1924. O'Keeffe began traveling to the Southwest in 1929 and spent time there every year until 1946, when Stieglitz passed away. After a sojourn of three years, she moved to New Mexico and spent the rest of her life there, painting the desert, her Ghost Ranch home, and other local scenes. She died at the age of ninety-eight, in 1986, leaving a lasting legacy as a pioneer of American modernism.[17]

ALEXANDER CALDER

United States, 1898–1976

> When an animal is in rapid motion, or moves so that you do not expect it to return to its original position, leave what you have drawn and start a new sketch. . . . Do not trouble to have your drawings right side up or sequential. Keep rapidly transmitting your impressions of the animal's movements, and enjoy what you are drawing.
>
> Alexander Calder, *Animal Sketching*, 11

One of the twentieth century's most prominent modern artists, Alexander Calder is best known as the inventor of the mobile. His graceful, well-balanced, and impeccably designed kinetic sculptures hang in many of the world's finest museums. Calder is also known for his large, abstract sculptures, called stabiles, which occupy public spaces in cities from Chicago to Paris. Before these accomplishments, Calder created a series of animal sketches; some of these were included in his book *Animal Sketching*. Others remained relatively unknown until acquired by the National Museum of Wildlife Art in 2001.

In 1924, Calder began his artistic career at the Art Students League in New York City. During the winter of 1925, when he was twenty-seven years old, Calder ventured to the Bronx and Central Park zoos to sketch lions, leopards, and other animals. He was interested in the action and character of the animals, from the shapes, movements, and lines of their bodies to the personalities revealed in their faces. In 1926, Calder published a selection of these sketches in *Animal Sketching*. Additional drawings presumably prepared for the book were subsequently misplaced in his studio, only to be rediscovered in 1972. In 1974, the Archives of American Art published *Calder at the Zoo*, a small, loose-leaf set with twenty-five of the sketches reproduced on eight separate pages. The other sketches remained unpublished in a private collection until acquired by the National Museum of Wildlife Art (figures 6.8 and 6.9). This portfolio may consist of additional pages laid out for inclusion in *Animal Sketching* or were perhaps meant as a separate publication. The forty sheets in the NMWA portfolio of Calder sketches are numbered, but, according to the Calder Foundation, numbered by someone other than Calder. The numbers range from 1 to 49, with several sheets missing. The portfolio, published by the Archives of American Art as *Calder at the Zoo*, contains sheets with fewer sketches and with different animals combined on individual pages. The missing pages of the NMWA

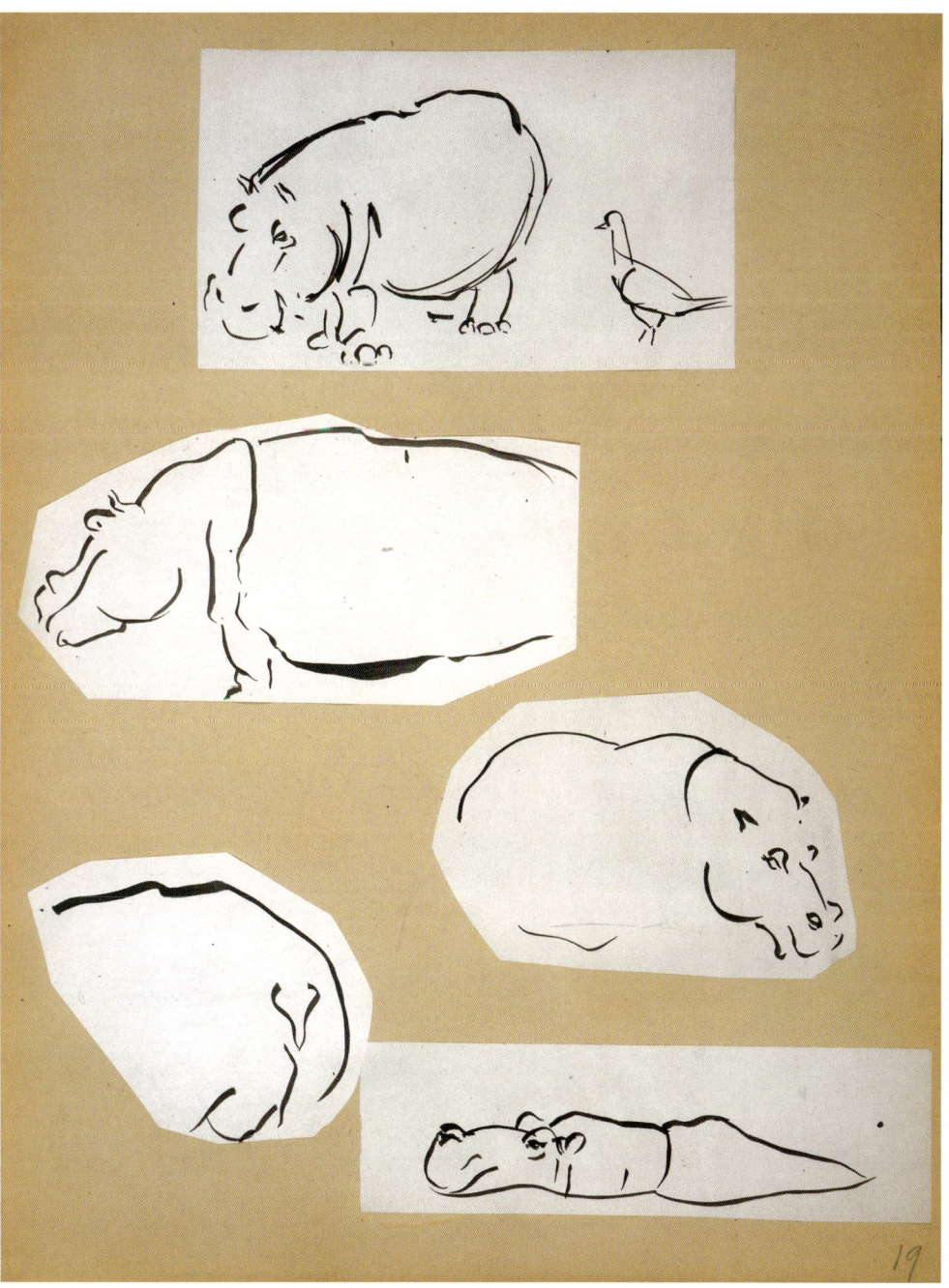

portfolio might be those reproduced in *Calder at the Zoo,* but it seems unlikely, as the layout is so different. One hypothesis is that after the zoo drawings were rediscovered, Calder and another person sat down and numbered them, then removed certain sheets that contained individual sketches that would then be reproduced in the Archives of American Art portfolio, and the selected sheets never made it back into the portfolio.

Calder's zoo sketches mark an important step in his development and predict the work he did as a mature artist, combining strong lines, biomorphic forms, and a sophisticated use of negative space into compositions that display great balance and a fluid sense of movement. Calder not only drew the sketches

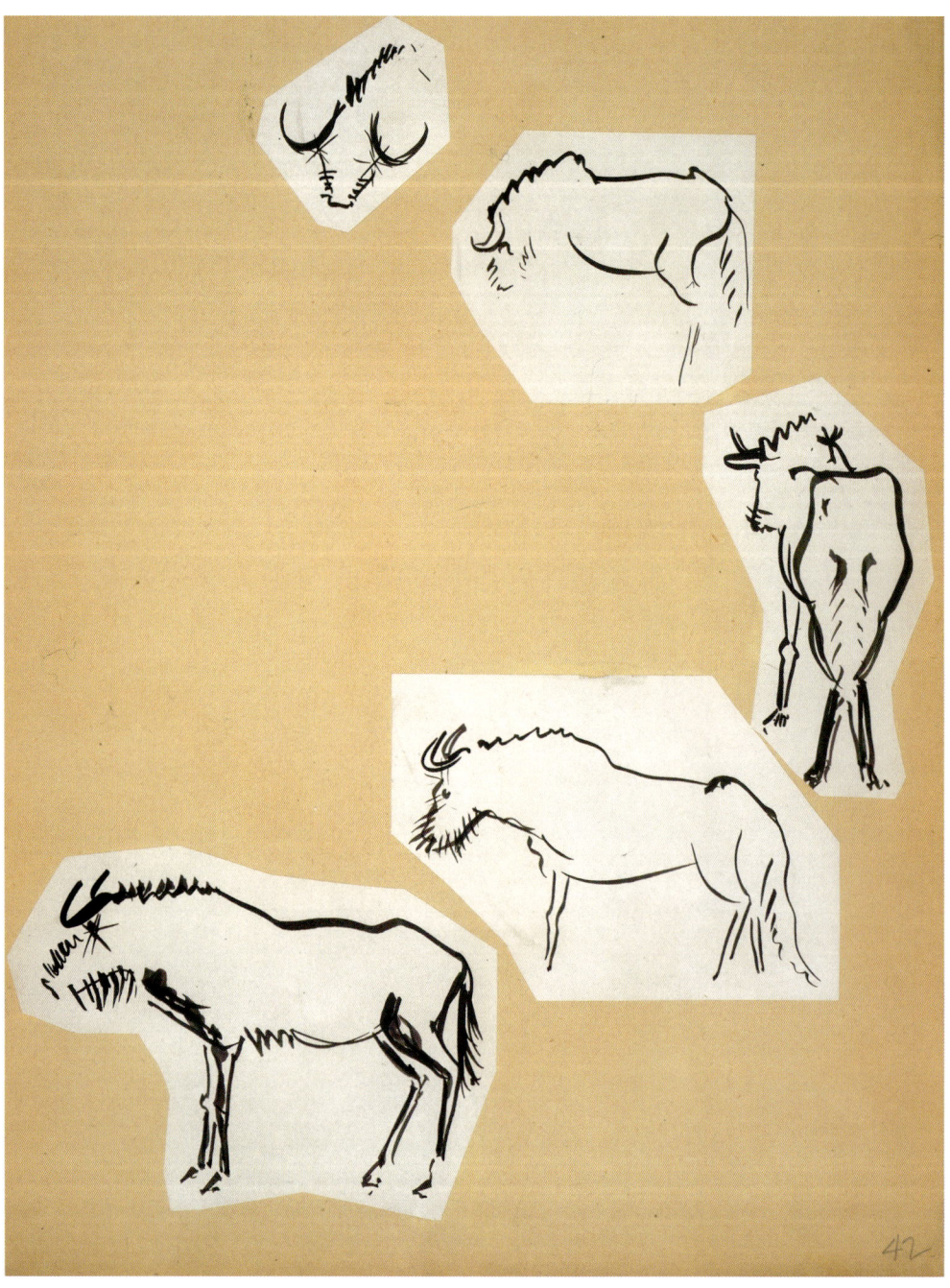

FIGURE 6.9.
ALEXANDER CALDER
Wildebeests, 1925.
India ink on white paper, mounted on
brown paper; 20 × 15 inches.
JKM Collection.
JL2001.185.035.
© 2009 Calder Foundation, New York /
Artists Rights Society (ARS), New York

but also cut them out and arranged them, creating geometrical shapes and
relationships between the animals on the page. The layout of the wildebeest
sketches (figure 6.9) bears a close resemblance to the undulating, well-balanced
forms found in his later mobiles. The simple progression up the page from large
sketch to small, the turning views of the wildebeest, and the shapes of the cut-outs
themselves tie this early animal work directly to his later sculptural efforts.

From his early sketches to his monumental sculptures, Calder communicated a sense of whimsy and humor in his art, which has made it both popular and
approachable. Throughout his lifetime, Calder continued to draw animals, adding
Calder creatures to four books, including *A Bestiary,* compiled by Richard Wilbur,

as well as an edition of *Aesop's Fables*. After Calder completed the sketches reproduced here, he journeyed to Paris, where he met art world luminaries such as Fernand Leger, Piet Mondrian, and Joan Miró; he continued to develop into one of the world's most renowned modern artists. These sketches show him at an early stage, when the mobile and the stabile were still years away. Looking closely at the shape, line, pattern, and rhythm of the drawings, one can see the same sense of composition and interest in movement that would emerge so engagingly in his mature work.[18]

ANDY WARHOL
United States, 1928–1987

Andy Warhol began his artistic career as an advertising and magazine illustrator. In the 1960s, he began to paint iconic American products such as Campbell's Soup cans and Coca-Cola bottles. Warhol was at the forefront of a movement known as pop art, which was a reaction to the dominant art of the era, abstract expressionism. Abstract expressionist artists painted completely abstract canvases, that is, they did not feature any recognizable figures, such as humans, skyscrapers, or wildlife. The often vast expanses of abstract patterning were lauded as records of the artist's inner self, usually a self in turmoil. The leading proponents of this style were Jackson Pollack, Franz Kline, and Mark Rothko. Going in the opposite direction, Warhol's work presented already well-known images, completely external to the artist. He even began having other people silk-screen his work for him—mass-producing his images of mass-produced objects, further removing himself from the process. Pop art made a strong and easily recognizable statement that had a major impact on the art world. The pop art movement included Roy Lichtenstein, Claes Oldenburg, and James Rosenquist in addition to Andy Warhol.

By playing with notions of production and by glamorizing everyday objects (or people with his celebrity portraits), Warhol made viewers see things they were intimately familiar with in a new light. In the 1980s, after critical and financial success, Warhol turned his attention to endangered species. In an essay on the *Endangered Species* portfolio, Matt Wrbican of the Andy Warhol Museum gave insight into Warhol's impression of the work: "Warhol commented that these unnatural, brightly colored works were 'animals in make-up,' thereby linking them to his society portraits on which he frequently performed a bit of visual surgery, making the lips fuller, the hair thicker, the nose straighter and thinner."[19] By giving eagles, elephants, and butterflies the Warhol treatment, he was both shedding new light on a popular topic and adding an air of celebrity to these creatures who had no voice of their own (figure 6.10).

Art dealers Ronald and Frayda Feldman commissioned the *Endangered Species* portfolio in 1983. The work arose from conversations with Warhol about ecological issues.[20] Warhol donated one hundred *Endangered Species* prints to a variety of conservation organizations, to be used in fund-raising auctions. Before Warhol died in 1987, he also created wildlife images for a book, *Vanishing*

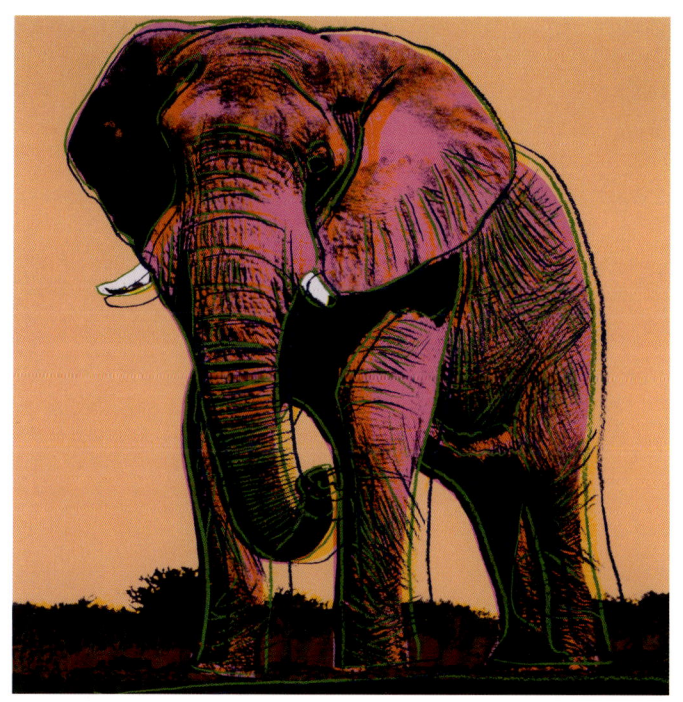

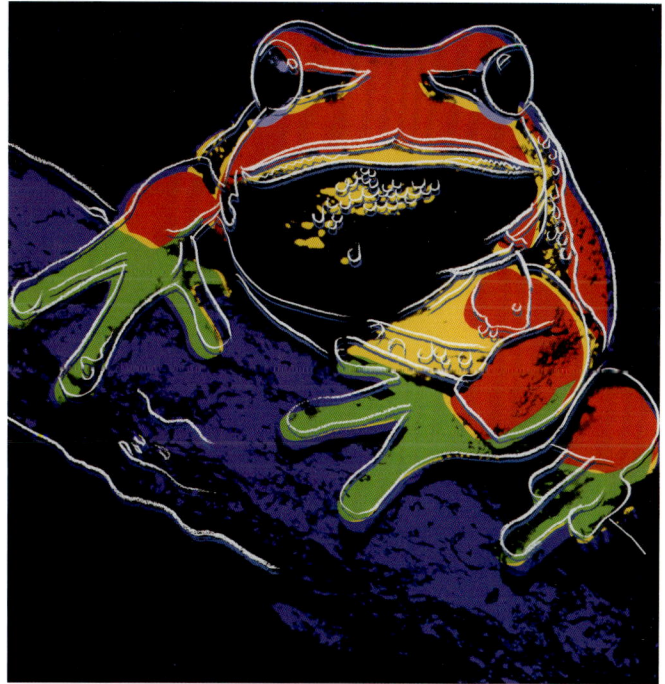

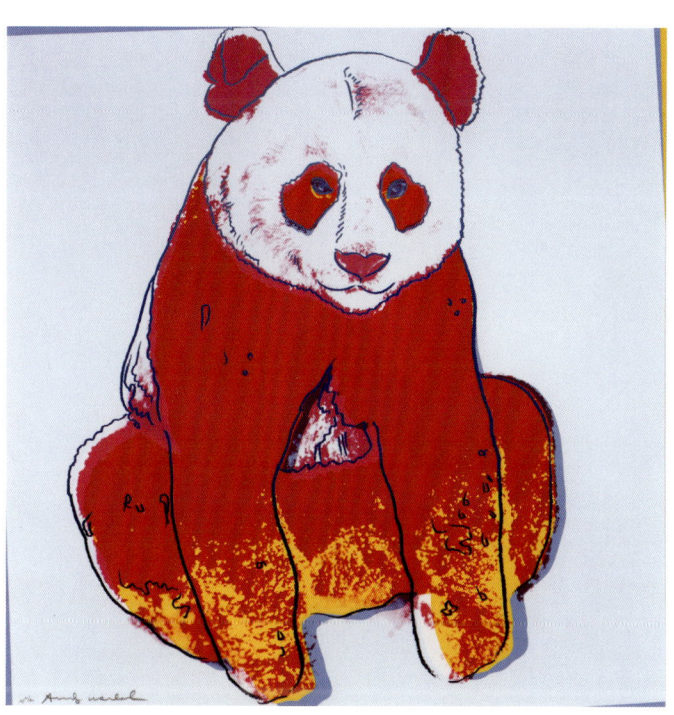

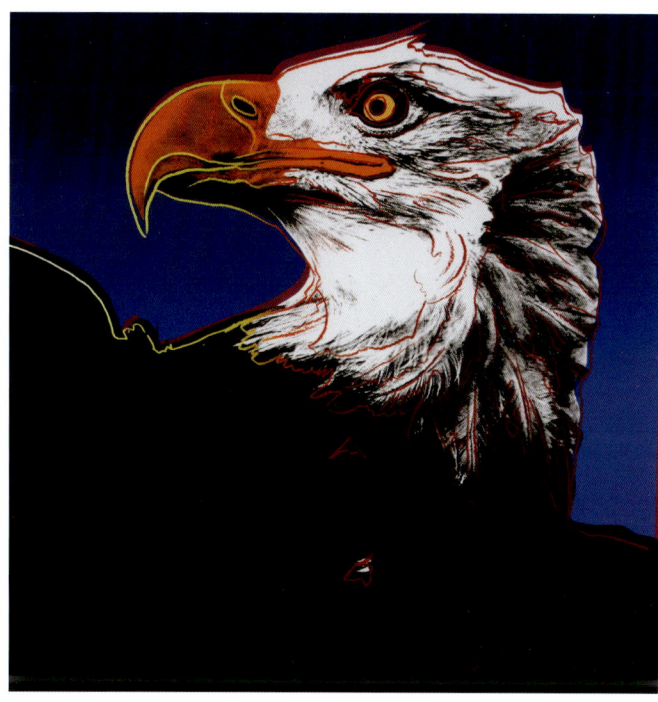

FIGURE 6.10.

ANDY WARHOL

Endangered Species Portfolio, 1983.
Each work, screenprint on
Lennox Museum Board; 38 × 38 inches.
Gift of the 2006 Collectors Circle, with
additional assistance provided by Lynn and
Foster Friess, the Robert S. and Grayce B.
Kerr Foundation, and the National Museum
of Wildlife Art Acquisitions Fund.
National Museum of Wildlife Art Collection.

© 2009 Andy Warhol Foundation for the
Visual Arts / Artists Rights Society (ARS), New
York. Courtesy Ronald Feldman Fine Arts,
New York

African Elephant
M2006.033.006

Giant Panda
M2006.033.010

Pine Barrens Tree Frog
M2006.033.009

Bald Eagle
M2006.033.007

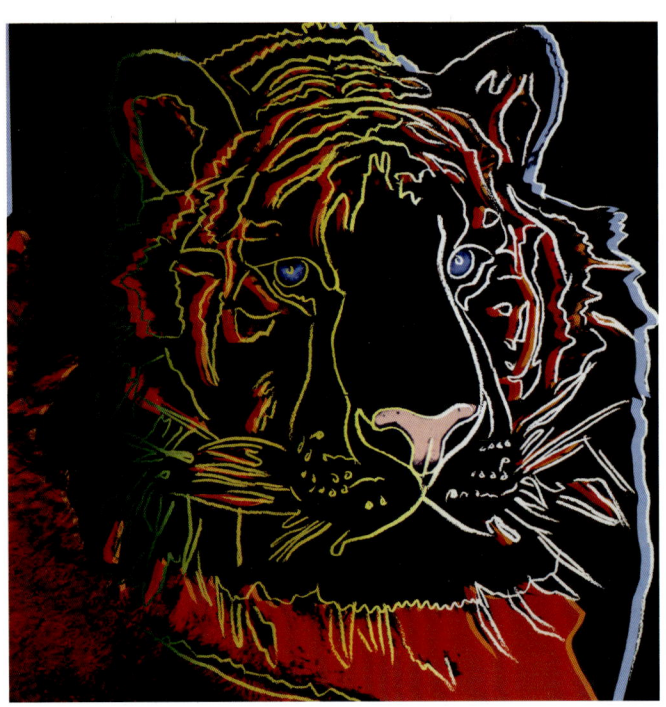

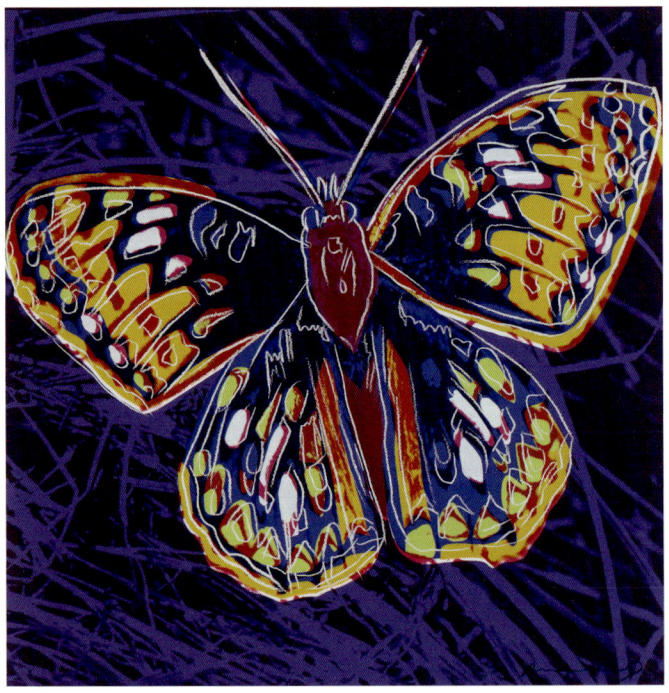

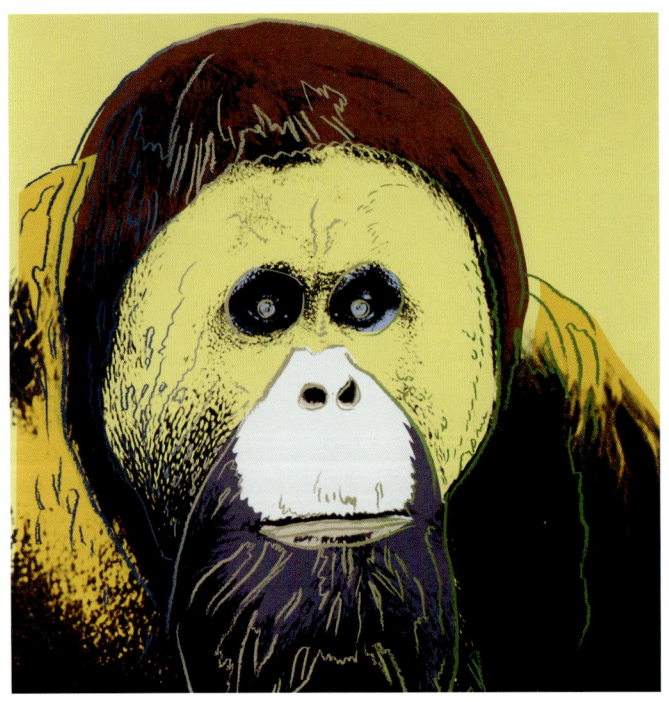

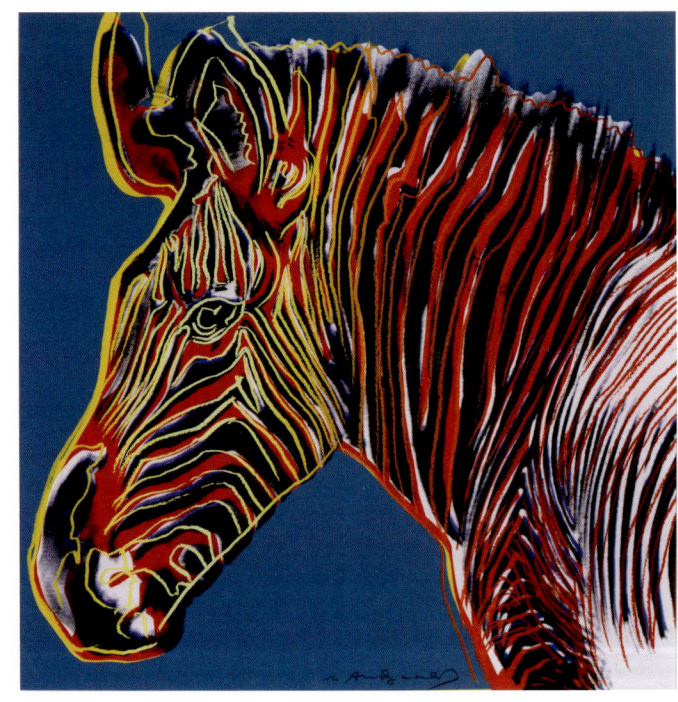

Siberian Tiger
M2006.033.008

San Francisco Silverspot Butterfly
M2006.033.005

Orangutan
M2006.033.004

Grevy's Zebra
M2006.033.003

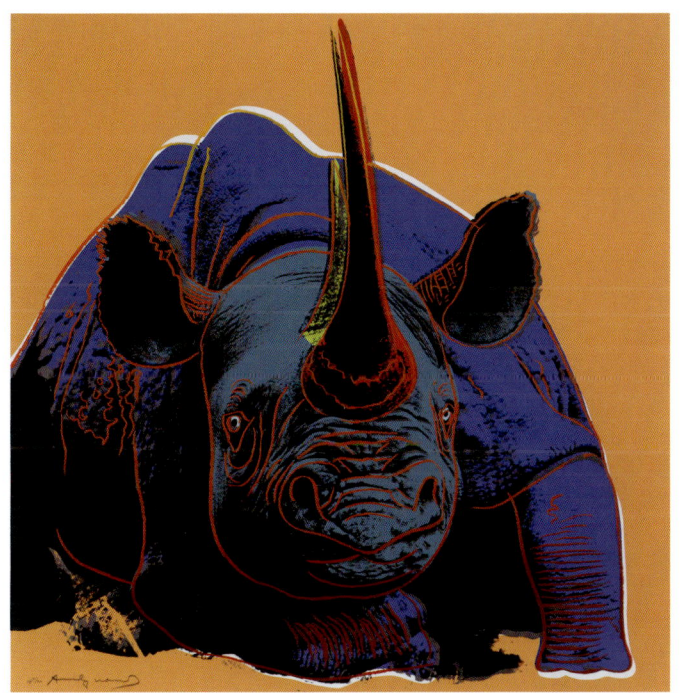
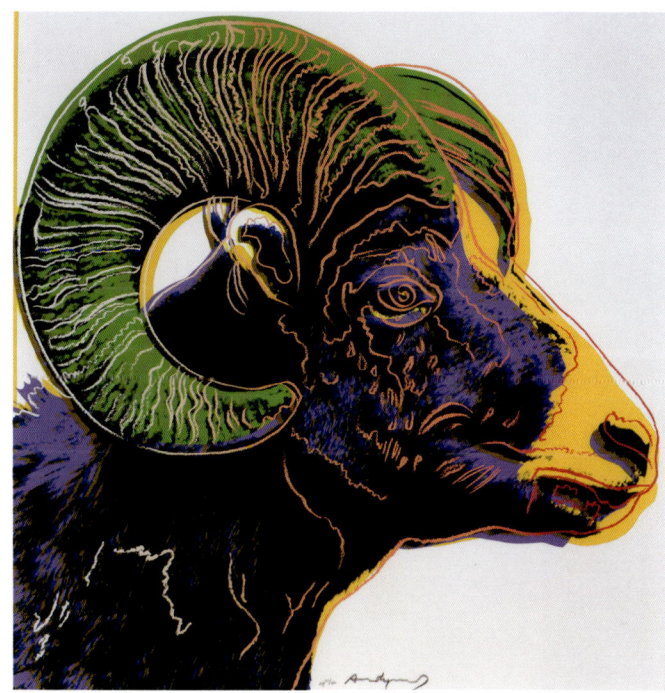

Black Rhinoceros
M2006.033.002

Bighorn Ram
M2006.033.001

Animals (1986), and for a print based on the film *Turtle Diary* (1985). Warhol cannot be described as an ardent environmentalist, but his work in this arena shows that he was aware of the plight of the world's wildlife and was willing to assist. These prints help the National Museum of Wildlife Art keep the ongoing peril of endangered species in the spotlight while they also provide a prime example of how animals have been used in art across time and place, in a variety of art movements.

PAUL MANSHIP
United States, 1885–1966

Paul Manship's *Indian and Pronghorn* (figure 6.11) captures a distinctly North American subject in a classically influenced manner. After studying at the Saint Paul School of Art during his high school years, Manship traveled to New York to study at the Art Students League. He apprenticed under famed sculptor Solon Borglum in 1905 before studying at the Pennsylvania Academy of Fine Arts in Philadelphia in 1907. Manship won a three-year scholarship to attend the American Academy in Rome in 1909. While in Italy pursuing his studies, Manship traveled widely, ranging from Greece to Holland, soaking up the diverse influences of art across Europe. These student years and his exposure to classical sculpture and mythology had a profound effect on his career. A glance at the titles of his major works amplifies this point: *Infant Hercules Fountain*, *Salomé*, *Diana*, and *Time and the Fates Sundial.* After returning to the United States in 1912, Manship met with almost instant success: he exhibited in New York and Philadelphia and won a gold medal at the Panama-Pacific International Exposition in San Francisco in 1915. For the remainder of his career, he traveled often to Europe, while keeping a studio in New York. Among his most well-known works is the *Prometheus Fountain* at Rockefeller Center, which oversees the often filmed and photographed ice skating rink.[21]

Commenting on Manship's style, art historian Harry Rand wrote, "In the 1920s, the general public was caught up in a new interest in the archaic. The startling finds from 'King Tut's' tomb in the Valley of the Kings, as well as the Berlin Museum's acquisition of the head of Nefertiti and the great sixth century Greek kouros, alerted the general public to a new aesthetic. This archaistic revival was part of the cluster of values subsumed under Art Deco, but Manship was ahead of his time."[22] On the leading edge of the art deco movement, Manship merged the classic with the modern to create his body of work. With its stylized surfaces and clear outline of forms, his sculpture looks back to historical references as it looks forward to a new machine-age sensibility, full of powerful lines and smooth surfaces.

In addition to the classics, Manship tackled American subject matter in works such as *Indian and Pronghorn.* Manship imbued this sculpture with classical allusions. The first is the lion skin draped over the American Indian's knee. The lion skin, emblematic of Hercules, represents his success at his first "Herculean task"— strangling the Nemean lion. *Indian and Pronghorn* also alludes to Hercules's

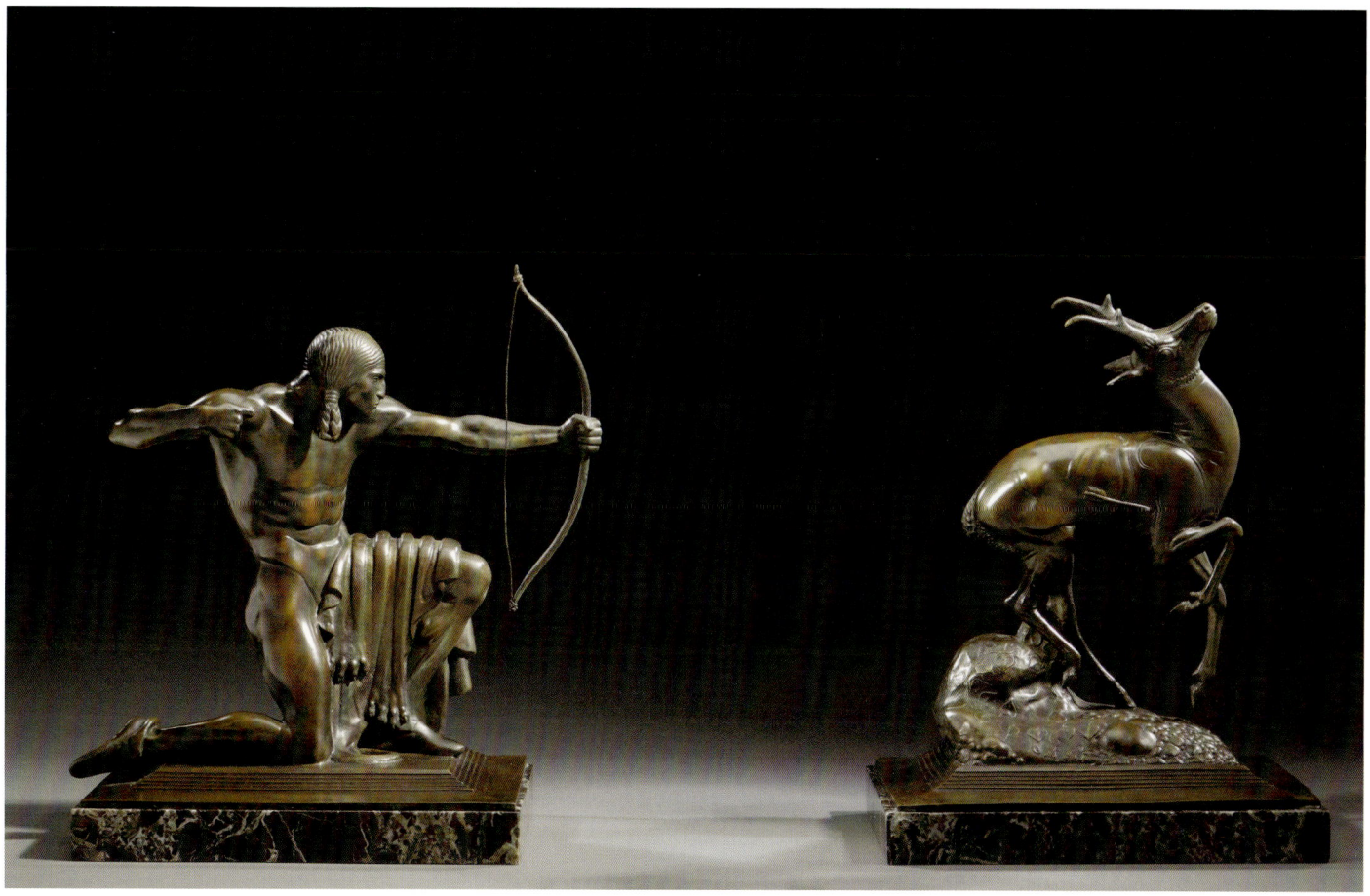

FIGURE 6.11.
PAUL MANSHIP
Indian and Pronghorn, 1914.
Bronze; 13½ × 10 × 8¼ inches (with base),
12½ × 10¼ × 8¼ inches (with base).
JKM Collection.
JL1998.035;
JL1998.036.

third labor, capturing the hind of Ceryneia. By associating the American Indian with the Greek hero, Manship paid homage to the then-disempowered hunters who had once ruled the North American forests and plains. As with nostalgic representations of the bison popular at this time, homages to American Indians became popular after the threat they posed to European settlers had been negated. While classical mythology and sculpture were clearly a major influence, Manship melded these ideas with a modernistic sensibility, refreshing the classics for a twentieth-century public and showing the ongoing potency of western and wildlife imagery.

WILLIAM ZORACH
LITHUANIA, 1887–1966

William Zorach was born Zorach Samovich in Lithuania. In 1893, his family immigrated to Cleveland, Ohio, where a teacher dubbed him William. Zorach studied at the Cleveland School of Art in 1903 and worked for the W. J. Morgan Lithograph Company. From 1907 to 1909, he took classes every winter in New York at the National Academy of Design (and briefly at the Art Students League) and spent the summers in Cleveland working at the Otis Lithograph Company. In 1910, Zorach scraped together enough money to travel to France, where he studied with Jacques Emil Blanche and John Duncan Fergusson, experimenting with cubism and fauvism.[23] While studying at the Académie de la Palette, Zorach met his future wife, Marguerite Thompson, who was also a painter. Returning to the United States, the couple married, pooled their resources, and took up residence in New York City. They spent the rest of their lives working and exhibiting together. Zorach did not begin sculpting until 1917; five years later, he began to sculpt exclusively. He taught at the Art Students League from 1929 until almost the end of his life. Major institutions such as the Whitney Museum of American Art collected and exhibited his sculpture during his lifetime. One of his best-known public pieces, *Spirit of the Dance* (1932) is installed at Radio City Music Hall in New York City.[24]

Zorach said of his influences, "I owe most to the great periods of primitive carving in the past—not to the moderns or to the classical Greeks, but to the Africans, the Persians, the Mesopotamians, the archaic Greeks and of course to the Egyptians."[25] One of the major influences on modern art, in general, was sculpture from non-Western cultures. A careful look at Pablo Picasso's seminal *Demoiselles d'Avignon* reveals that the face of the woman in the upper right-hand corner closely resembles a tribal mask, most likely one from Africa. The abstract nature of "primitive" carving (whether rounded or angular) was a rediscovered visual language of great appeal to modern artists after the turn of the nineteenth century. This interest in art from other cultures coincided with a rise in interest in folk or outsider art. Both primitive and folk art were thought to reveal a purer form of expression than art from academically trained artists.

Zorach, a great proponent of direct carving, created a version of *Pumas* in stone that reached forty inches high. Curator John Baur wrote, "Like Brancusi, Zorach allied himself naturally with the growing number of modern sculptors who

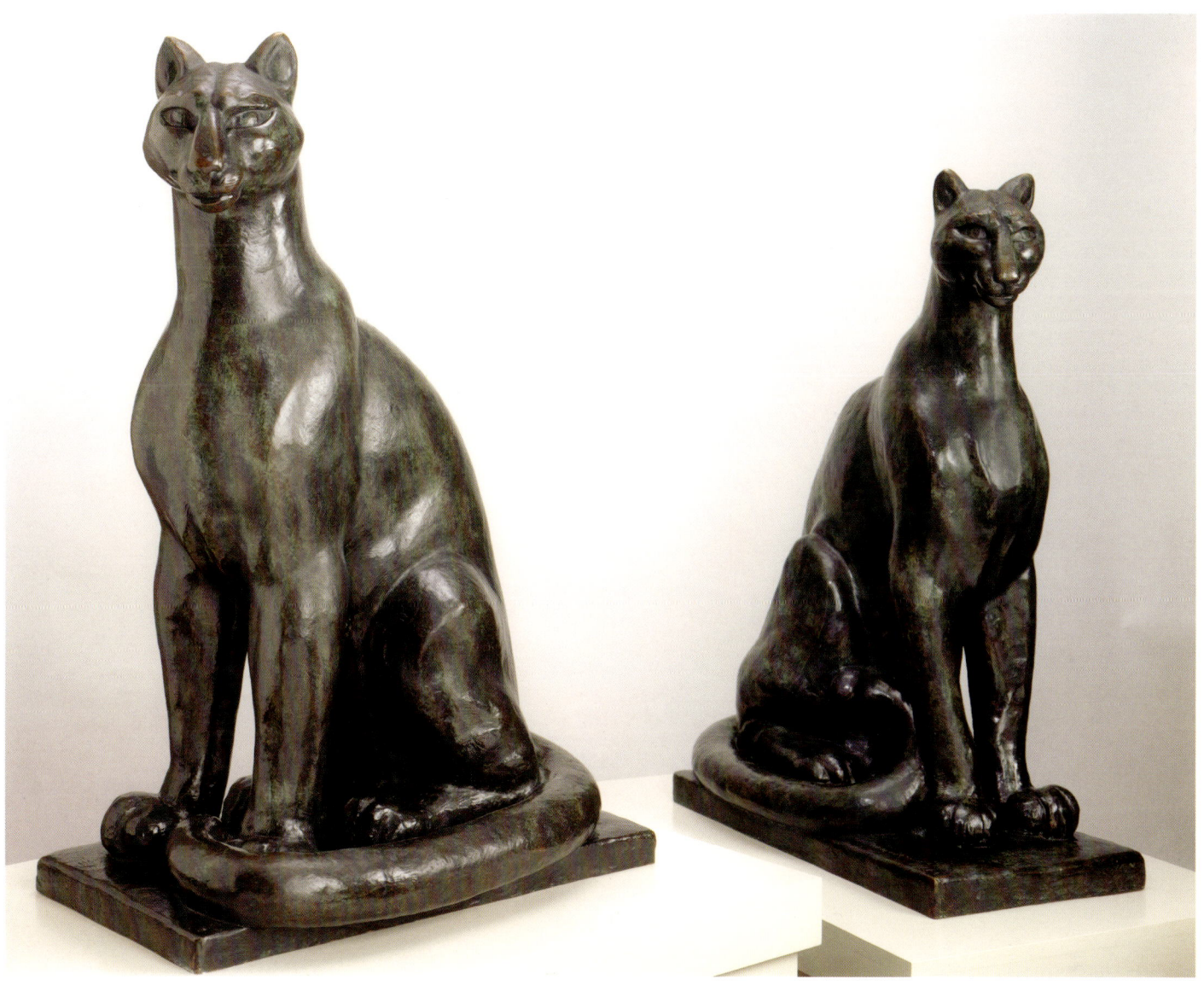

believed in the esthetic necessity of carving their own designs directly in the block of stone or wood rather than modeling them in clay to be copied by professional cutters in the harder material."[26] In Zorach's work, one can easily see the hand of the artist; his intent was not to create a classically refined surface that belied the impact of his chisel. The two bronze pumas in the museum collection look like hand-hewn stone in their shape and surface treatment (figure 6.12). The massive rounded forms closely resemble Zorach's characteristic sculpting in original, obdurate material.

The subject of two benignly cheerful pumas ties in closely with Zorach's oeuvre. From his earliest painting to his mature sculpture, Zorach had a soft, sensitive take on the world. One of his modernist paintings, *Interior and Exterior* (1918), shows a loving mother cradling her child as the family dog looks up and a father figure stands in the background. This semicubist experiment shows Zorach's proclivity toward the gently sentimental. He had a difficult time melding this sensibility with modernist tenets, which favored a harder, more analytic look at the world. His change from modernist painting to sculpting in a primitivistic style was a welcome one; the medium and style came to match the subject matter, for Zorach was sculpting basic, elemental themes of love and family. The two cats in *Pumas* (figure 6.21) are neither studies of form and motion, like Anna Hyatt Huntington's *Reaching Jaguar* and *Jaguar* (see figure 3.14), nor animals in combat, like Barye's *Lion Crushing a Serpent* (see figure 3.1). They are a loving pair, meant to be shown and appreciated together.

ALLAN HOUSER

United States, 1914–1994

In the 2004 catalogue commemorating the Smithsonian Museum of the American Indian's inaugural exhibit featuring Allan Houser and George Morrison, poet and artist Gail Tremblay wrote, "Clearly, as one examines the use of shape, line, texture, and mass in Houser's startlingly diverse body of work, one can see the way in which modernist aesthetics shape many of the most exciting examples of his art. . . . Houser creates works that dance on the edge between figuration and abstraction in ways that are richly magical. At the same time, one can see the absolute pride and appreciation for the culture he has inherited."[27] In *Fabricated Bison* (figure 6.13), Houser's distinctive modernism is readily apparent. The smooth bronze panels, carefully fitted together, combine to create a streamlined bison that looks toward the twenty-first century, while recalling the mythic status of the bison created during the late nineteenth. The bison is a complex symbol that continues to resonate with audiences; it represents all the promise of the American West, that is, the vast tracks of untrammeled land, endless opportunity, and plentiful resources. The bison also represents great loss and squander, in terms of both animal population and habitat. In addition, *Fabricated Bison* evokes the close association between bison and American Indians, who relied on them for food, shelter, and clothing.

Houser grew up in Oklahoma and began his artistic training with Dorothy Dunn at the Painting Studio of the Santa Fe Indian School in New Mexico from 1934 to 1938. While still in school, he had a solo exhibit at the Museum of Fine Arts in Santa Fe. In 1939, he exhibited paintings at the New York World's Fair, the National Gallery of Art in Washington, D.C., and the Art Institute of Chicago. Houser also trained with Norwegian muralist Olle Nordmark at the Fort Sill Indian School in Oklahoma. Seeing his obvious modeling ability, Nordmark encouraged Houser to practice his sculpture, and he soon began receiving commissions and awards. In 1948, he was asked to sculpt *Comrade in Mourning*, to honor American Indians who had died in World War II. He then received the Guggenheim Fellowship in 1949. He taught and later became the head of the sculpture department at the Institute of American Indian Arts in Santa Fe. Until 1968, when his first bronze was cast, he concentrated on direct carving in wood and stone. He retired from teaching to focus solely on sculpting in 1975. Houser passed away at his home in Santa Fe in 1994.[28] He left behind a body of work that

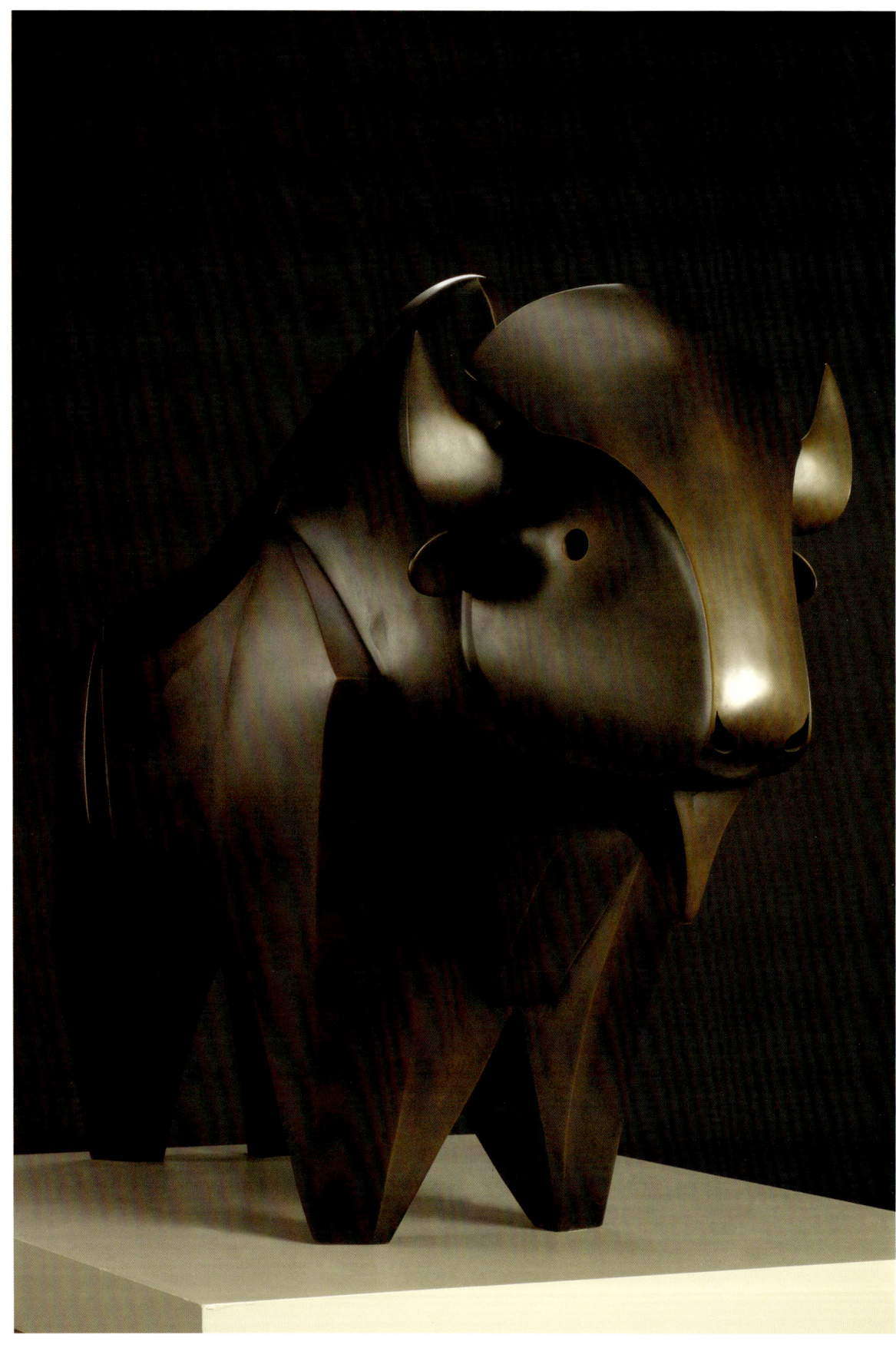

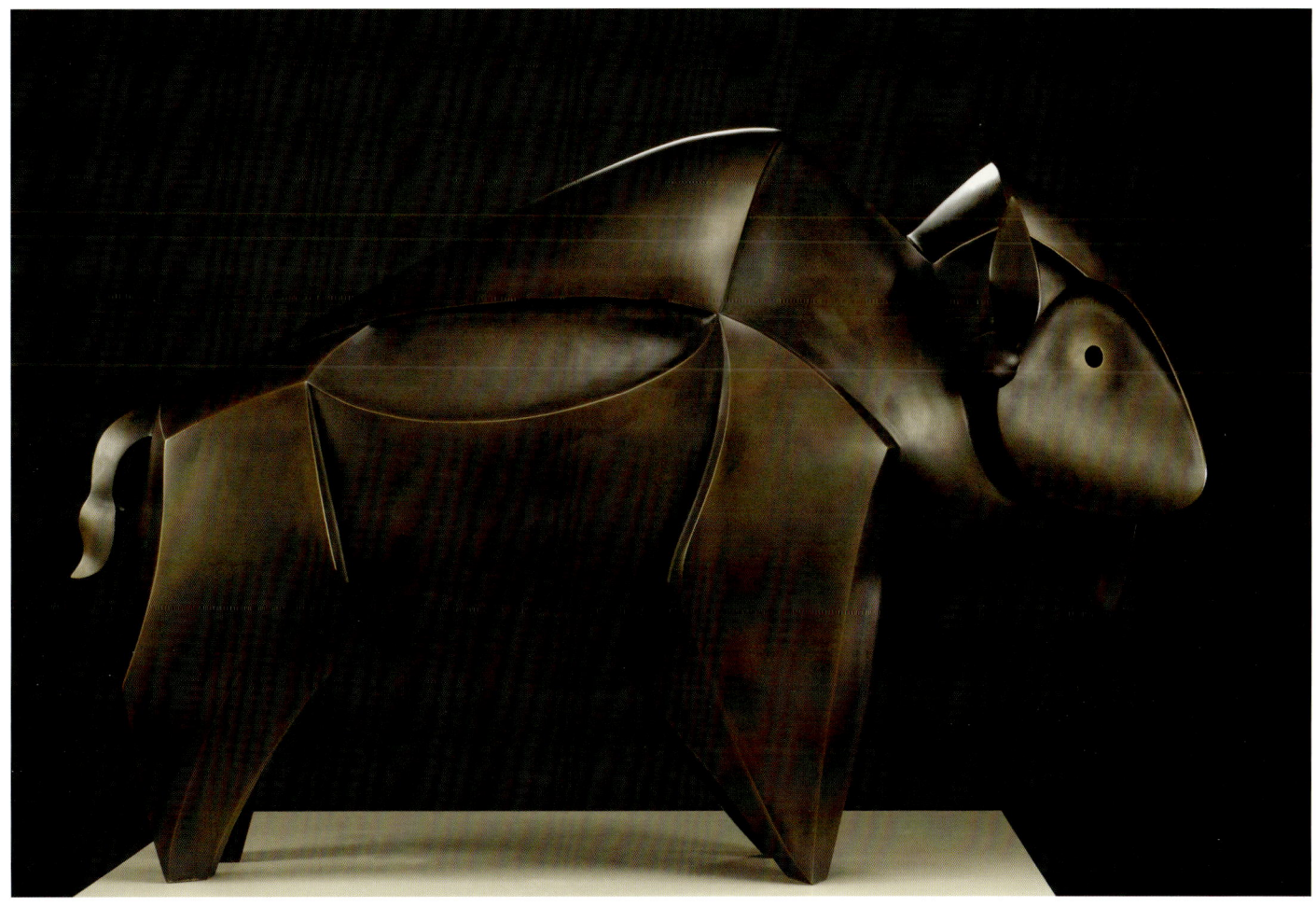

displays the ongoing importance of traditional American Indian ways of life; his career and imagery signal the potential for the rebirth of a downtrodden people. *Fabricated Bison* is a magnificent piece on its own, but taking into account the biography of the sculptor imbues it with added layers of meaning that have deep implications stretching back to some of the earliest images of animals produced on this continent.

LEONARD BASKIN
United States, 1922–2000

Owls, crows, and other avian subjects are prevalent in the sculpture of Leonard Baskin. He sometimes combined elements of these birds with human figures, creating mythic beasts that were half man and half animal. He also carved large wooden sculptures, such as *Roosting Predator* (figure 6.14), which were simply birds, presented in their own right. In 1960, he created an owl similar in shape and concept to *Roosting Predator*—a rounded mass of wood, deeply contoured to reveal the form of an animal within. Although this sculpture is not strictly representational, in no way was Baskin an abstract artist. He believed in the power of representational art and denounced abstract art, arguing for the necessity of the subject.[29]

Roosting Predator is menacing, with its skull-like head and deep red tone; this sense of menace emanates from Baskin's feeling about human predators; he uses the raptor family to embody this aggression. He wrote, "Birds of prey flutter ominously through my *oeuvre*. These predacious creatures symbolize their human counterparts. They exist as allegory, metaphor, and symbol, acting mimetic roles in the broadest sense. [Their] essential meaning in my work is as raptors, carrion devourer, and as startling bolts of death."[30] Baskin used predators to symbolize the negative aggression he saw in the culture around him. With their clearly organic nature, *Roosting Predator* and Baskin's other large wooden bird carvings can be interpreted in a broader sense as speaking to the intertwined relationship between bird and tree, animal and earth, life and nature. While there is aggression in the animal and human kingdom, that is part of the cycle of life, the cycle of seasons— those elemental, basic rhythms of the ecosystem in which we are all deeply rooted. *Roosting Predator* lends itself to this kind of interpretation because it is so clearly an element taken from nature that does nothing to belie that genesis.

Transfixed by a plasticene demonstration at Macy's in 1936, Baskin invested in some clay and immediately began modeling. In 1937, sculptor Maurice Glickman became his mentor, and Baskin enrolled at the New York University School of Architecture and Allied Art. In 1941, he accepted a two-year scholarship to Yale University of Fine Arts. While at Yale, he started his own printing press, Gehenna Press, which published more than one hundred books featuring his illustrations of obscure texts as well as examples of his own writing. After World War II, Baskin obtained his bachelor of art degree from the New School for

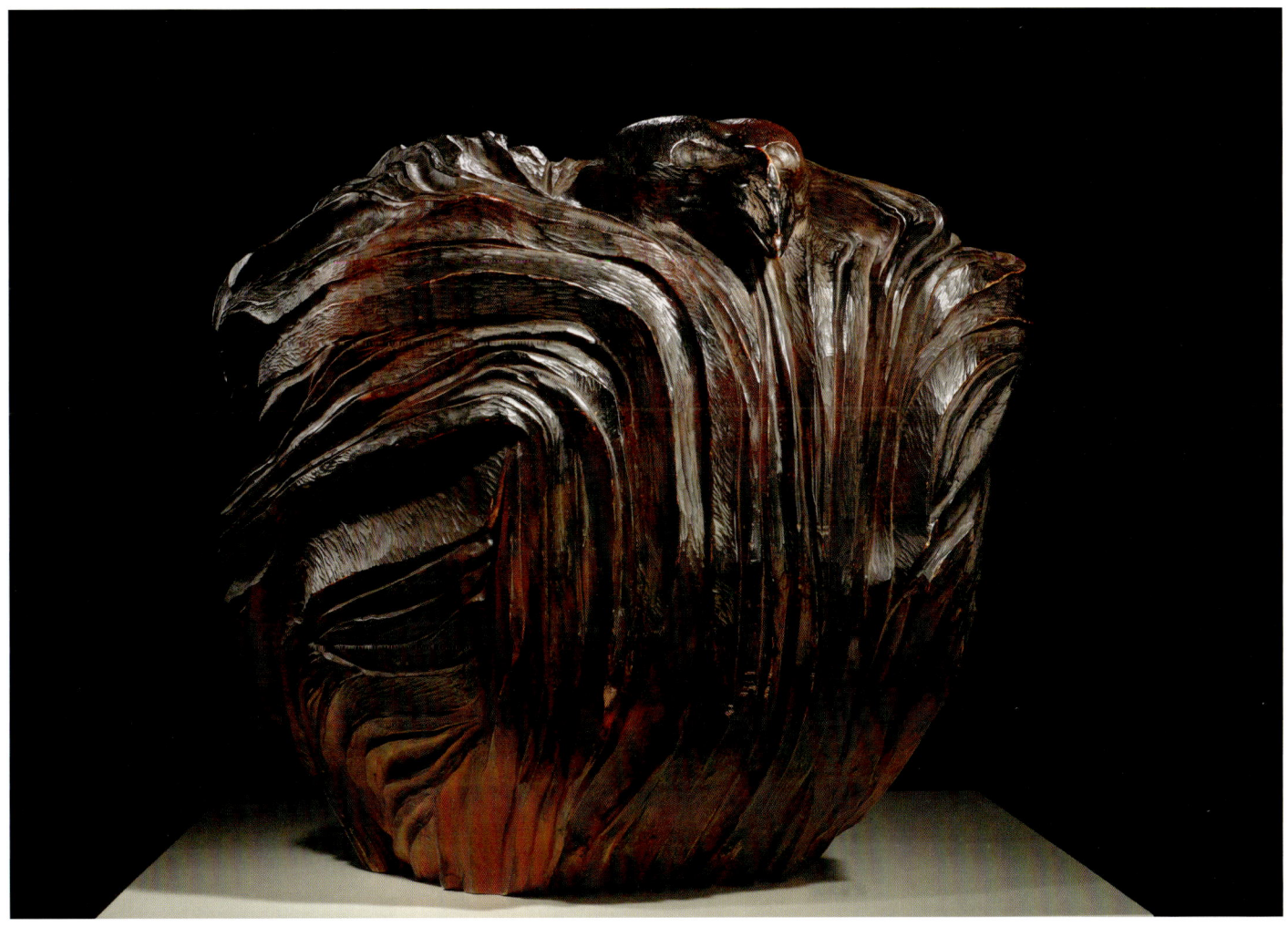

FIGURE 6.14.
LEONARD BASKIN
Roosting Predator, 1984.
Wood; 24 × 31 × 24 inches.
JKM Collection.
JL1999.077.

Social Research in New York; in 1950, he studied at the Académie de la Grande Chaumière in Paris, France. He returned to Europe in 1953 on a Guggenheim Fellowship. Baskin accepted many commissions, including the funeral cortege for the Franklin Delano Roosevelt Memorial in Washington, D.C., and a seven-foot-tall cast-bronze figure for the Ann Arbor Holocaust Memorial in Michigan. He created large wood-block prints, watercolors, and sculptures in limestone, bronze, and wood. His work is recognized in many private collections and museums, from the Vatican Museum to the Whitney Museum of American Art. Baskin's work often deals with the dark, troubled side of life; he used animal imagery to illustrate his sentiments about humanity, providing a modern take on the long tradition of using animals allegorically.[31]

WOLFGANG POGZEBA

GERMANY, 1936–1982

> My subject is nature and what I see to be the essence of its contents.
> A discerning eye can derive endless inspiration from the environment of
> nature. From the physical and mental response is produced a work of art,
> and through a search to create my own exciting visual world, I gain enlight-
> enment and spiritual advancement. The artistic process is inherently one of
> exploring new visions, new concepts, and new sensations of awareness.
>
> Wolfgang Pogzeba, *New Vision*, 1–2

The topic of wildlife in art is, in its very name, a subject-driven field. This topic is limited generally to figurative art—art that depicts recognizable figures. Is it possible to have a completely abstract painting and call it wildlife art? If Jackson Pollack had painted one of his huge drip canvases and named it *Spirit of the Elk*, then the answer would be yes. However, the National Museum of Wildlife Art has not yet come across anything of that nature, so one hundred percent of the art in the collection is figurative. In *Confronted Elks* (figure 6.15), Wolfgang Pogzeba has abstracted the forms of two elk battling, but the work still depicts two recognizable animals. By taking the specifics of each creature out of the equation and depicting the raw forms of the animals in jagged metal, Pogzeba rendered a popular subject in a different and dynamic fashion. Interpreters often use abstract art to discuss ideas or as a window into the soul of the artist. Because there are no identifiable figures or actions to examine in abstract art, interpretation moves onto another level, typically analyzing emotions or feelings. Similar discussions can be had about representational artwork, but one must at least acknowledge the figures and then discuss the mood of the work. By abstracting the forms in *Confronted Elks*, Pogzeba makes it easier to move past the literal and onto the idea or emotion presented. In this work, Pogzeba presents the force behind two elks butting heads; the raw edges of metal add to the feeling of raw, primal power. *Confronted Elks* is similar to Gerard Curtis Delano's *Forest Primeval* (see figure 5.30), which, through its title and its abstracted imagery, takes interpretation into a more mystical realm.

Patricia Broder in *Bronzes of the American West* wrote of Pogzeba, "Since he is interested primarily in the creation of a work of art, his goals are aesthetic rather than narrative or documentary. . . . He casts his own sculptures, after which he reworks the surface and applies several patinas to a single bronze. Smooth surfaces of gleaming bronze contrast with dark, rough, and unpolished areas."[32]

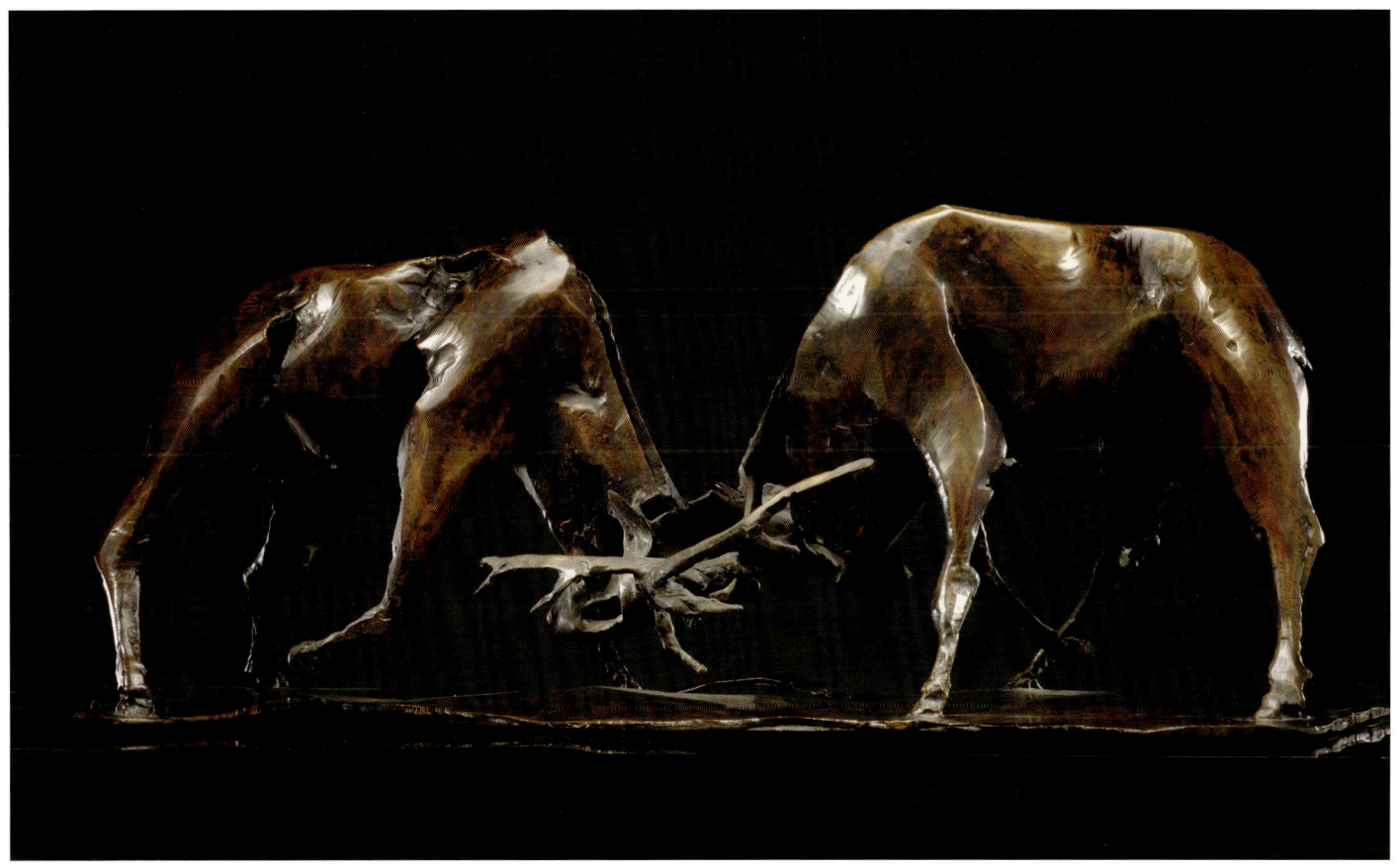

Broder laments the fact that Pogzeba stopped producing bronzes as his attention was drawn in other artistic directions. During his brief life, Pogzeba worked in sculpture, painting, and photography. His abstract vision spanned across these media, and he tackled each with equal enthusiasm. Pogzeba immigrated with his family to the United States from Germany in 1948; in 1950, he settled in Denver, where he studied at the Colorado School of Mines and then at the University of Colorado School of Architecture. He subsequently studied at the University of Mexico in Mexico City, at the Kunstakademie in Munich, and at the École des Beaux-Arts in Paris. Pogzeba had his first one-man show at the Historical Society Museum in Helena, Montana, in 1960 and then, while in the Air Force, had two exhibits: one in Montgomery and one in New York. His rapid rise to prominence allowed him to support himself as a full-time artist relatively early in his career. Unfortunately, this promising artist's career was cut short when he and his family died in an airplane accident in 1982, en route from Montana to Taos, New Mexico.[33]

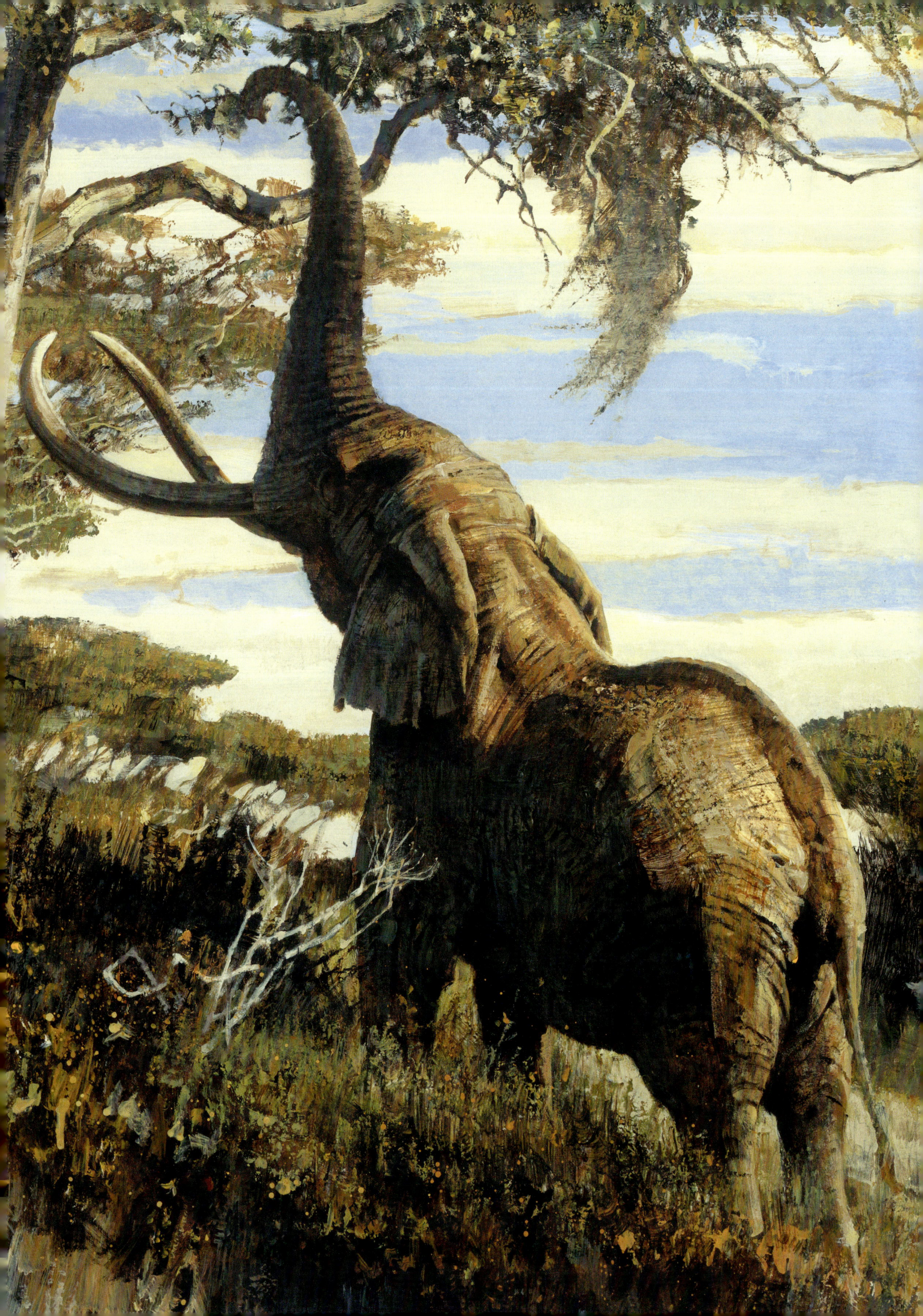

Conclusion

Robert Kuhn and Contemporary Wildlife Art

Absent from this catalogue is an analysis of living wildlife artists. As this book focuses on the history of wildlife in American art, contemporary practitioners have been excluded. However, two contemporary painters who passed away in the first decade of the twenty-first century make fitting subjects for an examination of wildlife art today. The last entry in chapter 5, on Lanford Monroe, aptly speaks for the careers of the many artists who continue working in the realist tradition, one that stems from a background in representational art and looks to the beauty of the natural world for inspiration. Monroe's career is a shining example of the enduring power of traditional painting in the history of American art. This conclusion addresses another stand-out in the field of contemporary art, Robert Kuhn (United States, 1920–2007). Kuhn epitomized the best in wildlife art of the twentieth century, freely drawing inspiration from sources that ranged from commercial illustration to abstract expressionism. Kuhn, like Monroe, played a significant role in a chapter of art history that all too often goes untold. His work, however, along with that of his contemporaries, is receiving greater critical attention as scholars examine more areas of art history and as museums and private collectors grow increasingly interested in the great diversity of art produced in North America.

Kuhn was one of the last in a long line of great illustrator-turned-artists of the twentieth century, a line that includes Frederic Remington, William Leigh, N. C. Wyeth, Maynard Dixon, William Dunton, Ernest Hennings, Gerard Delano, John Clymer, and Robert Lougheed. The unique historical moment that was the golden age of illustration gave birth to two generations of well-trained artists whose impact on the visual arts is just beginning to be understood. Kuhn, who passed away during the fall of 2007, based his career on years of experience gleaned from illustrating magazine articles about African, North American, and Asian animals. He supplemented that knowledge with constant practice, sketching animals he saw in the wild, in zoos, in magazines, or on video (figures C.1 and C.2). His deep-seated sense of curiosity, plus a keen sense of good design, gave him the drive and the ability to see his visions through to finished paintings. During his forty-plus-year

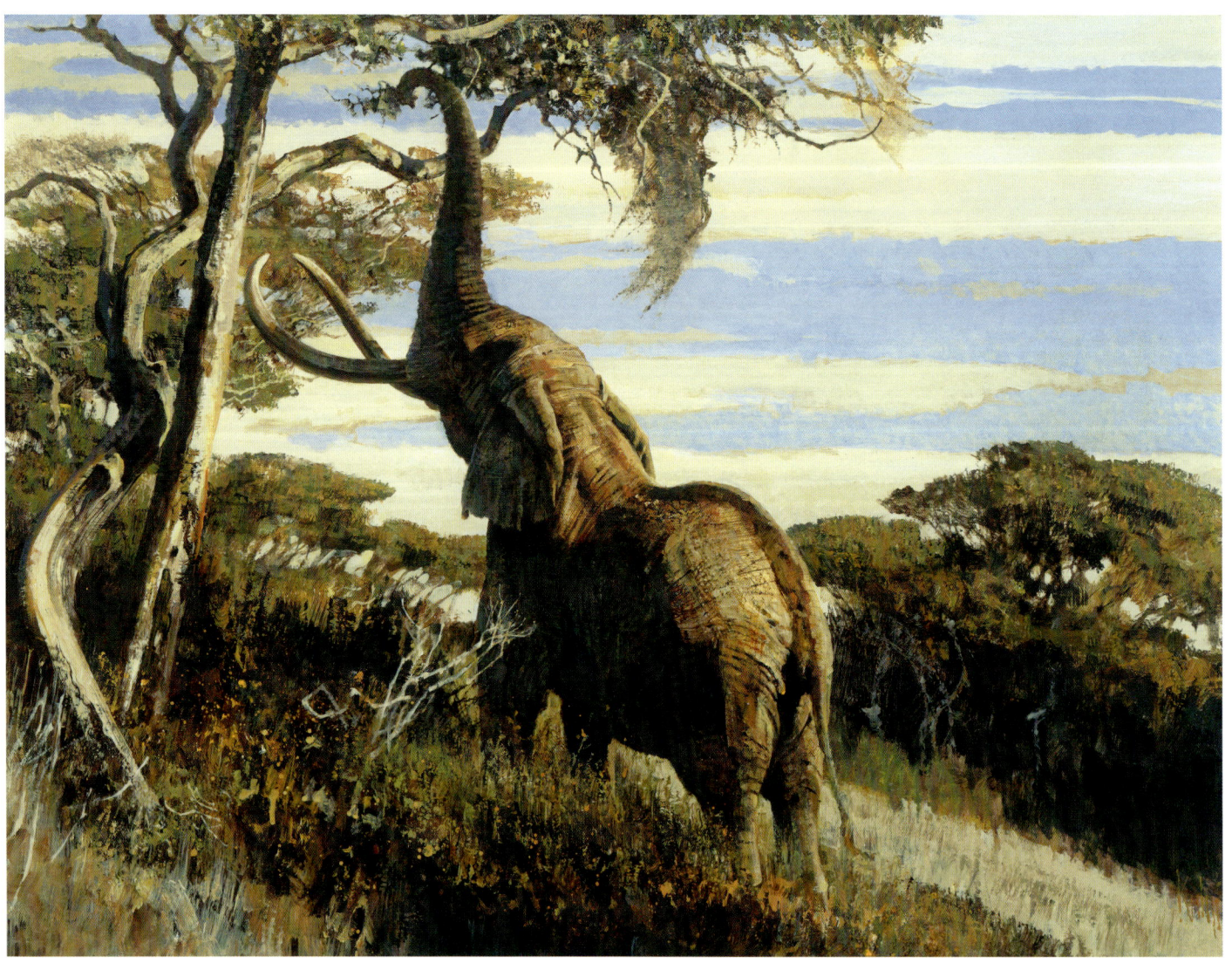

painting career, he created work of immediate significance, work that has set the standard for other wildlife artists working in the late twentieth and early twenty-first centuries.

Kuhn was born on January 20, 1920, in Buffalo, New York. By age five, he was copying illustrations from his favorite magazines; the work of animal artists Paul Bransom and Charles Livingston Bull was particularly influential. In later years, Kuhn began to frequent the Buffalo Zoo, sketch pad and pencil in hand. While in high school, he sent a letter and a selection of sketches to Bransom, asking for advice from the professional. Bransom replied with encouraging words and a solid critique. In 1936, after his senior year, Kuhn drove to the Adirondacks, paying a visit to Bransom's studio along the way. Bransom received him warmly and so began a mentorship and lifelong friendship. Of the many pieces of advice Bransom gave, one nugget in particular stuck with Kuhn through his life. Bransom advised Kuhn to "keep going to the zoo and keep drawing. When you look at an animal, look at it as though you may never see it again."[1] Thereafter, Kuhn

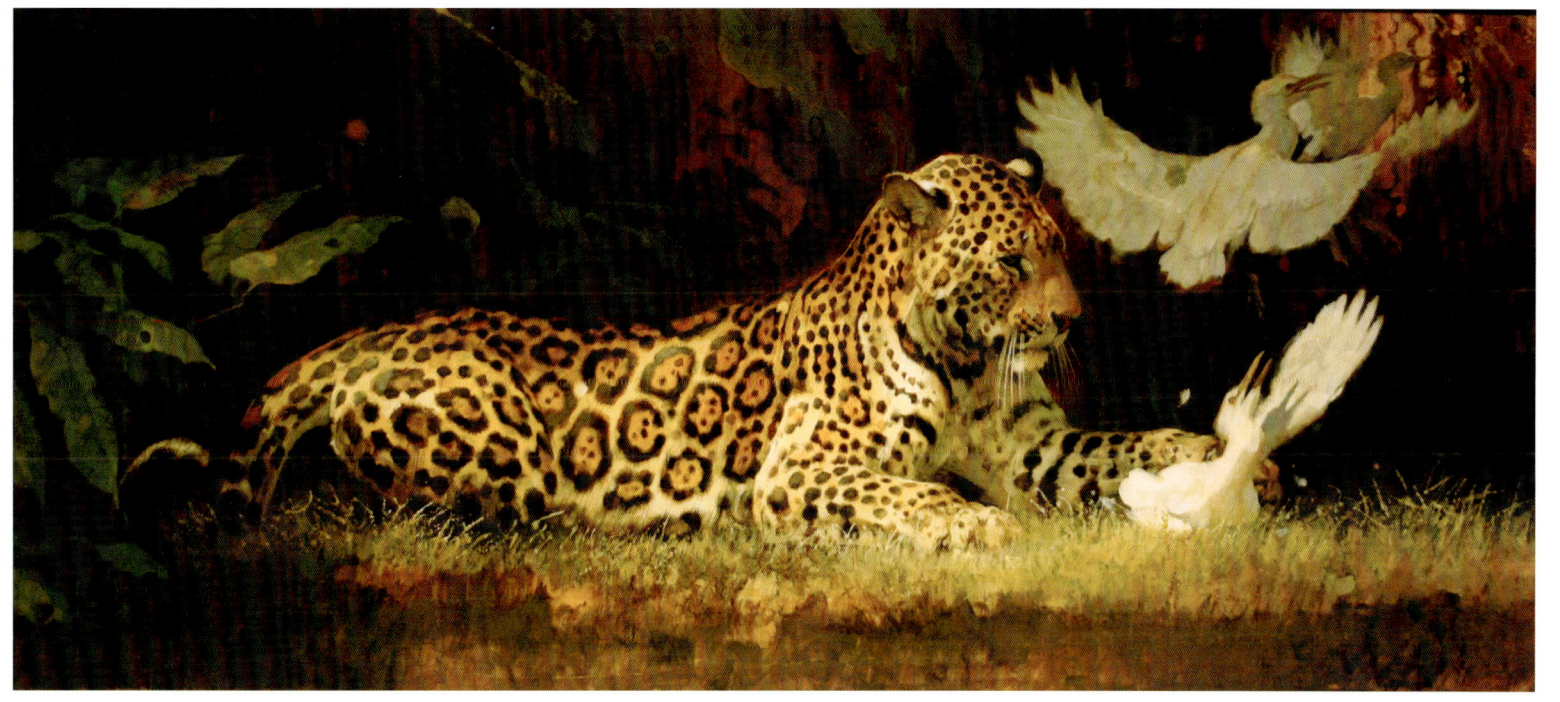

became an inveterate sketcher, sketching at breakfast, while watching television, or whenever else he got a chance. He drew on artist's paper, check stubs, or any available scrap. Kuhn later passed on Bransom's advice to the many younger artists who sought his council.

In September 1937, Kuhn enrolled at the Pratt Institute in Brooklyn. After graduating in 1940, he began working as a freelance illustrator and the following year married fellow Pratt student Elizabeth Casey. The two lived in New York City, where he illustrated children's books such as Felix Salten's *Forest World* and *Good Comrades* (both 1942) and contributed to magazines such as *Outdoor Life* and *Field & Stream.* With World War II raging in Europe, Kuhn joined the merchant marines, shipping out from New York in 1944. In 1945, Kuhn returned to his family and moved to Roxbury, Connecticut. For the next twenty-five years, Kuhn was an active commercial illustrator, but in addition, he began painting larger pieces and selling them, with some success. In 1965, the gallery at Abercrombie and Fitch in New York City held Kuhn's first solo exhibition. In 1970, he quit commercial illustration completely to focus on easel painting.

Kuhn observed, "Picasso spoke of the tyranny of the thing seen. In painting you've got to be the boss and not let the subject matter rule. Use only what you want and toss the rest. Control is the name of the game."[2] Yet when one looks at a Kuhn painting, control is not likely to be the first word to enter the viewer's mind. His work evokes a sense of freedom and vibrancy, with flowing movements and loose brushwork. When one thinks of control, more-detailed "fur and feather" paintings come to mind. Kuhn's sense of control, however, is not about concisely painting minute details but about controlling what goes into the composition.

Whereas other artists strive to paint every blade of grass in the foreground, Kuhn made conscious choices to limit the amount of information supplied in each painting, suggesting details with broad strokes and not belaboring every element in the field of view.[3]

Kuhn's style derives from several diverse sources. On a bulletin board in his studio were a variety of clippings and small pictures, including reproductions of mountain sheep by Carl Rungius, the Tetons by Conrad Schwiering, horse racing by Alfred Munnings, and ducks by Bruno Liljefors. Going beyond animal-related material, the board also held pictures of a Winslow Homer watercolor, an Edgar Degas dancer, and an abstract painting by Stuart Davis. When asked about the influence of abstraction and modern art, Kuhn remarked that artists such as Richard Diebenkorn and Mark Rothko, among others, were truly inspirational. Kuhn found the looser abstractions with the boldest use of color to be the most interesting. Remarking on a completely abstract work by Diebenkorn, he said, "I don't even know what he's trying to do there, but . . . I love that sort of thing, the totally abstract. If it tries to be something, I don't like it. . . . The figure stuff does nothing for me at all, but these random abstractions I really love."[4]

More than being simply appealing objects, abstract paintings often provided the spark of inspiration for the color scheme of a Kuhn painting. A close look at the transitions between sky, cloud, and landscape in many Kuhn works reveals an understanding of color that comes straight out of the work of artists such as Rothko. Kuhn said, "What I like is how [Rothko] juxtaposes rich colors so similar in value that you really have to look to see where one begins and the other ends. The colors are so close in tone that they vibrate. . . . People say, 'How can you like that non-objective stuff, nothing is happening.' I respond, 'What's happening is terrific color; what else has to happen?'"[5]

That terrific color, filtered through Kuhn's considerable artistic sensibility, can be seen in his work from the late 1970s onward. His interest in modernism is hardly surprising, given the era in which he grew up and the era in which he began easel painting. His ability to absorb the artistic atmosphere (as he had to do with color and style in his illustration career) allowed him to look at the field of modern art and borrow positive and useful elements, such as abstract passages and lively color combinations.

Kuhn's style did not emerge fully formed in 1970, when he began easel painting in earnest, of course. In early works such as *Ahmed* (1973; see figure C.1), Kuhn provided ample detail in the depiction of both animal and setting and used a restrained, more naturalistic palette. Throughout the 1970s and 1980s, he experimented with bolder colors and greater abstraction. By 1985, he was painting works such as *Come to Mama* (figure C.3), which features clear, horizontal bands of blue and gray that echo the combinations and transitions of a Rothko color-field painting.

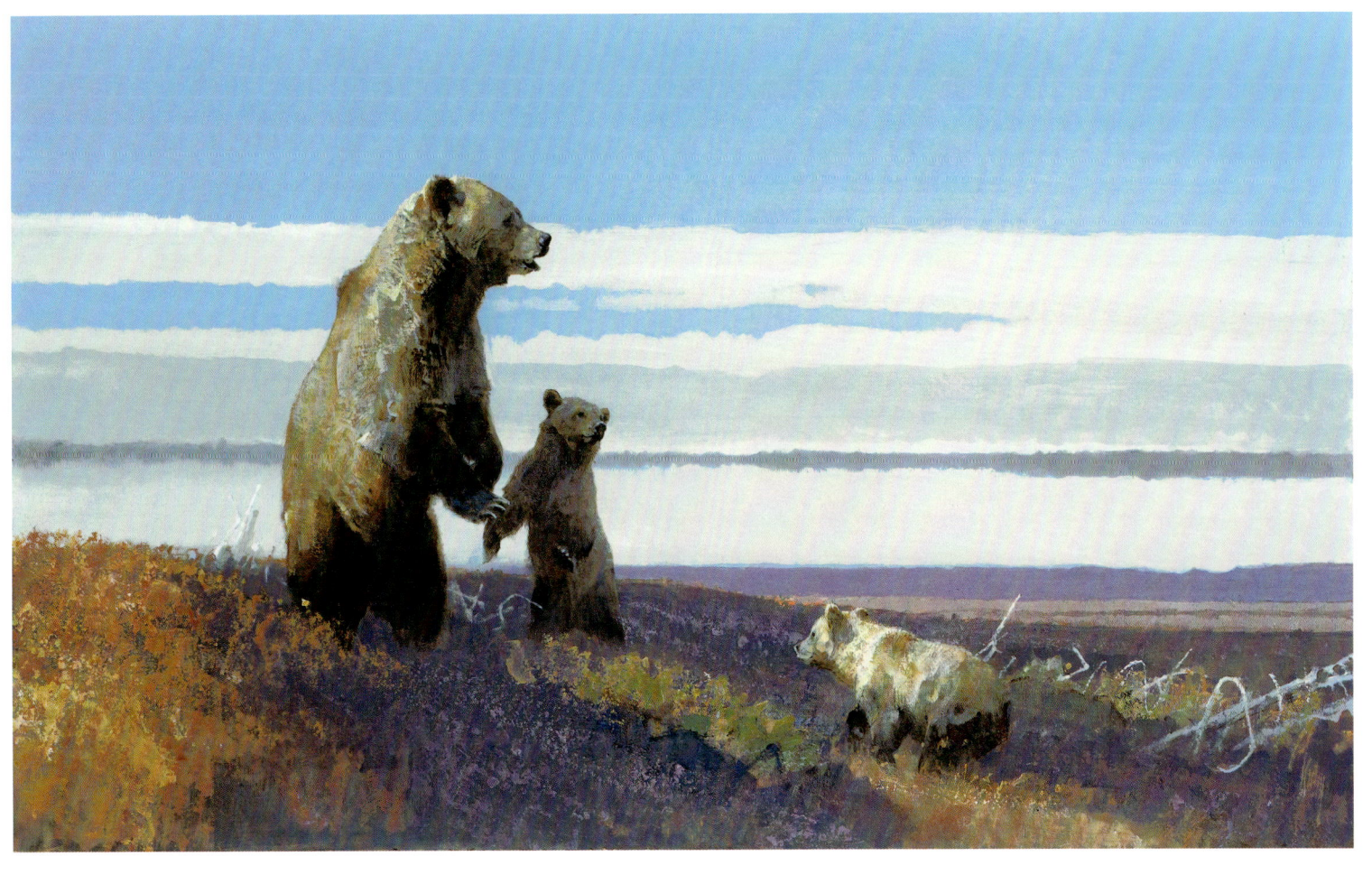

FIGURE C.3.
ROBERT KUHN
Come to Mama, c. 1985.
Acrylic on board; 24½×40 inches.
JKM Collection.
M1987.012.
© Estate of Robert Kuhn

In addition to his innovative use of color, Kuhn also brought action into many of his canvases. One of his favorite topics to paint was the predator/prey relationship, aptly represented in *Pas de Deux* (figure C.4). Here, Kuhn depicts a deadly dance between fox and hare on a snowy North American plain. All of the trademark elements of his style come together in this seminal work—color, abstraction, action, and anatomy. The red-orange fox dominates the bottom half of the picture, making a quick turn to nip at the hare, forming an "S" curve with head up and back, tail swinging around and forward. The curve leads the viewer into the painting and gives it its initial sense of depth. The eye goes up from the fox's nose to the airborne legs of the leaping snowshoe hare. The hare is stretched out, flying through the air, inches away from the fox's jaws. As with the dimensionality of the fox, the hare's hind legs extend slightly out, toward the viewer. Rapid brushwork and judicious use of white splatter representing snow kicked up by both fox and hare reinforce the motion. The composition is a sinuous series of lines and shapes that pulls the eye into and around the painting, providing depth to the image and aptly capturing the event. There is a delicate tension in *Pas de Deux* between the hare and the fox, both in terms of space and in terms of narrative. Does the fox capture the rabbit, or does the rabbit get away? The question is posed, but unanswered, leaving viewers to decide for themselves.

Kuhn was drawn to scenes of predators and prey, but he strived not to repeat himself and became known for the breadth of his oeuvre. He painted African elephants, Alaskan moose (figure C.5), and American cats. He painted majestic males, families interacting, and predators after prey in pictures that were sometimes humorous, sometimes poignant, but always moving in one way or another. Although Kuhn painted a broad range of animals and behaviors, he generally set his animals in habitats without signs of human incursion. In this sense, his work aligns with the Romantic notion of the wilderness as a pristine place—a vision of the wilderness he shared with greats such as Carl Rungius. Like Rungius, Kuhn painted vigorous, healthy wildlife: ideal specimens of the species. It was no revelation to Kuhn that he was painting idealized views. He said, "I could be accused of being a romantic, of romanticizing the scenes by making the animals bolder, stronger. I make a lion look like what you *think* a lion is supposed to look like."[6] Kuhn's paintings make the leap from depicting an animal in its environment to epitomizing a specific, celebratory definition of wildlife and the wilderness, a definition shared by generations of North Americans who grew up with Yellowstone, Yosemite, Nairobi, and Masai Mara as the prime examples of what it meant to be wild (and he was fully conscious of what he was doing—as he said, he made his animals look the way people thought they should look). There is certainly room in the field of wildlife art to take a different approach, to paint animals as they appear to the typical viewer through fence lines and across roads or to depict the breadth of creatures in the animal kingdom—prime, ordinary, even

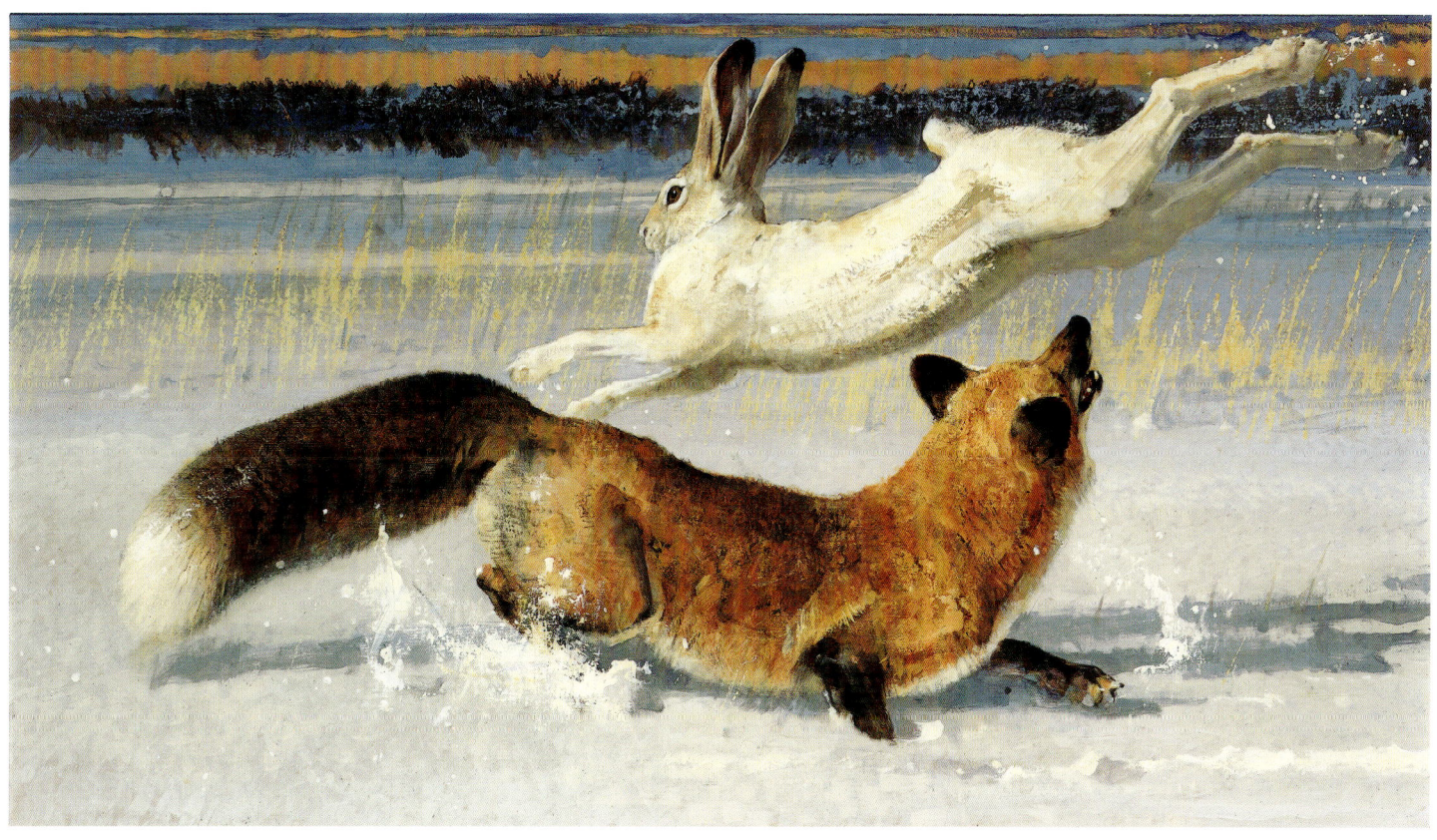

sickly subjects alike. That, however, will have to be the subject of someone else's oeuvre. Kuhn's work represents a contemporary apex in a long, undulating line of artistic endeavor that values the wilderness and wildlife as subjects to be venerated, protected, and cherished; and that line of endeavor continues to spur the American imagination and inform a sense of national identity.

Kuhn's vision shows the ongoing power of a specific wilderness ideal that has captivated audiences since the earliest artists began recording the animals of North America. Explorer-artists such as Titian Ramsay Peale, George Catlin, and Karl Bodmer documented the fauna of a wild continent for eastern and European audiences eager for imagery of what lay beyond the frontier. Each in their own way, later artists such as Albert Bierstadt, Arthur Tait, and Worthington Whittredge celebrated the glories of the continent and its wildlife. In sculpture, Edward Kemeys, Alexander Proctor, and Henry Shrady modeled the distinct characteristics of wild cats, bears, and bison: iconic animals of the West that represented a national sense of identity based on nature and natural resources. Carl Rungius's paintings of the proud denizens of the wilderness coronated a vision of wildlife that reigns to this day, setting the benchmark for all who followed. Georgia O'Keeffe, Alexander Calder, and Andy Warhol embraced animals as fitting subjects to express their ideas about modernity's interconnected relationship with nature. In the twenty-first century, artists continue to depict wildlife as the United States wrestles with its place in the world and its sense of self. In an era when national parks are

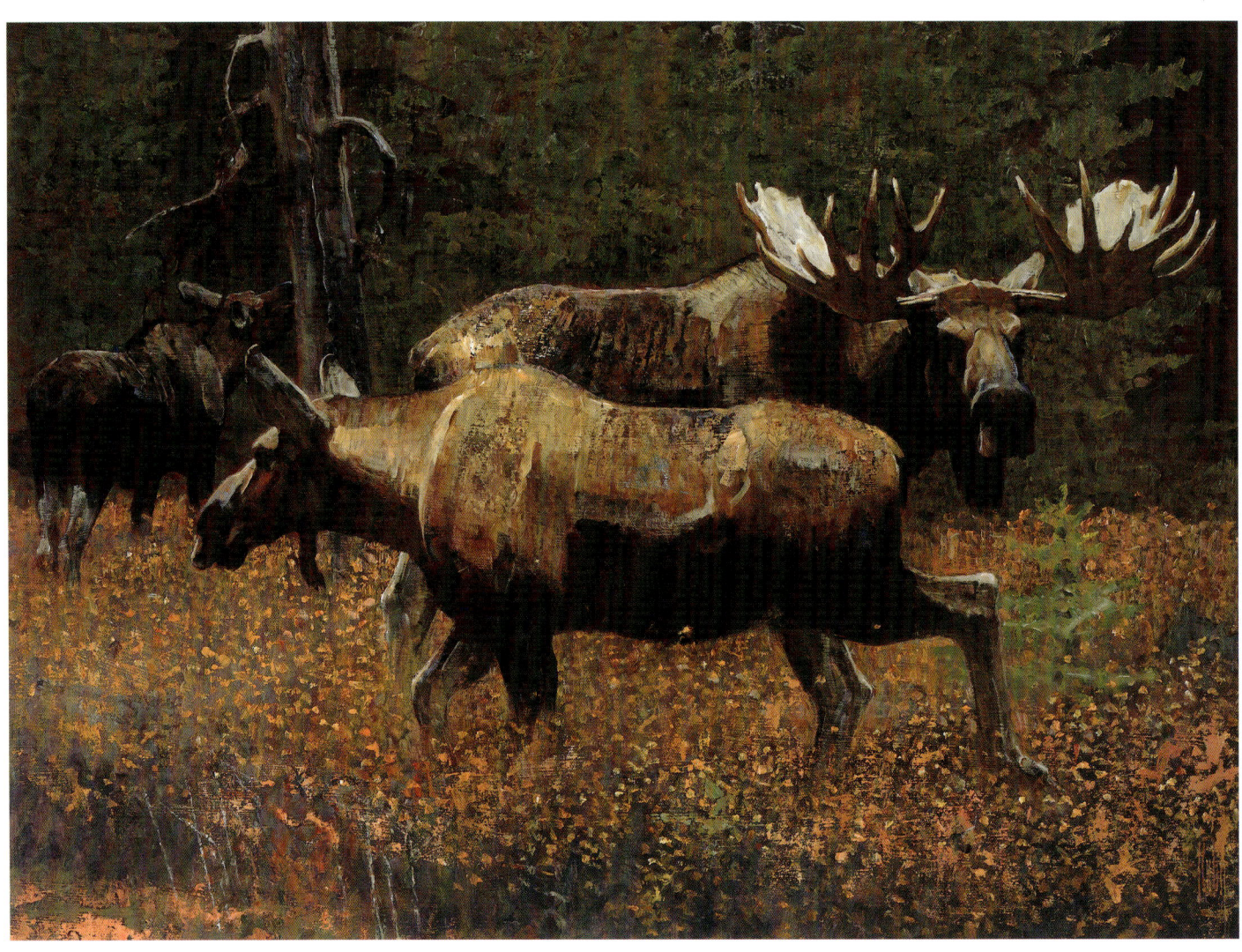

being loved to death while other wilderness areas are being mined for natural resources, wilderness and wildlife remain among the most pertinent subjects of national debate. Contemporary depictions of wildlife reflect these cultural concerns as they contribute to the long line of artistic attempts, stretching back thousands of years, to understand, record, and portray the enigmatic nature of our relationship with the wild.

Notes

INTRODUCTION

1. Asian animals, to a slightly lesser extent, have inspired artists as well. The tiger and Asian elephant appear most regularly in art inspired by Asia in the museum's permanent collection.
2. Anonymous, "How Carl Rungius Combines Art with the Adventures of a Sportsman," *New York Times*, February 2, 1913 (available online at query.nytimes.com).
3. A 1947–48 catalogue from New York's Crossroads of Sport Gallery offers sporting and wildlife art side by side; Carl Rungius's *Alert Old Prospector—Grizzly,* for example, is mere pages away from Ogden Pleissner's *New England Stone Wall—Grouse Shooting.* The catalogue also includes a host of decorative items associated with hunting, including miniature trophy heads, duck decoys, and gun racks.
4. When Rungius did return to including humans in his paintings, they were either cowboys on round-up or guides leading pack strings in the wilderness.
5. Whyte and Hart, *Carl Rungius,* 38.
6. Weekley, *Kingdoms of Edward Hicks,* 90. Hicks's inspiration for the subject was an illustration (also called *The Peaceable Kingdom*) by Richard Westall that appeared in many American Bibles. The illustration depicted a young boy, also holding grapes, leading similar animals down a forested path. Hicks did not slavishly copy the engraving but used it as a point of departure.
7. Ibid., 81. Hicks appropriated this image from a popular print of his day, which depicted Benjamin West's painting *Penn's Treaty with the Indians* (1771), in the Pennsylvania Academy of Fine Arts, Philadelphia.
8. Ibid., 36–38.
9. Nash, *Wilderness,* 69. Emphasis in original.
10. The highly regarded Buffon, author of a thirty-six-volume series on the natural history of the world published between 1749 and 1788, wrote, "In America, therefore, animated Nature is weaker, less active, and more circumscribed in the variety of her productions; for we perceive, from the enumeration of the American animals, that the numbers of species is not only fewer, but that, in general, all the animals are much smaller than those of the Old Continent. No American animal can be compared with the elephant, the rhinoceros, the hippopotamus, the dromedary, the camelopard, the buffalo, the lion, the tiger, &c." Buffon, *Histoire naturelle,* vol. 5.
11. Nash, *Wilderness,* 68.
12. Jefferson to Meriwether Lewis, June 20, 1803.
13. For a fuller discussion of the development of concepts of the wilderness, see Dean, "Natural History."
14. Ibid., 75.
15. Miller, "Fate of Wilderness," 95.
16. Catlin, *Letters and Notes,* 1:261. Emphasis in original.
17. Miller, "Fate of Wilderness," 106.
18. For a full discussion, see Brian Dippie, "Now or Never Is the Time," in Dippie, *Vanishing American;* see also John F. Reiger, "Conservation Begins with Wildlife" in Reiger, *American Sportsmen.*
19. According to Anthony Janson, Whittredge visited Mexico in 1893 with Frederic Church. The pair may have stopped in Yellowstone en route, but that remains undocumented. Whether Whittredge visited the park or not does not change the fact that the image he presented of Yellowstone in *Deer in Yellowstone National Park* represents a distinct vision of the park in line with the arguments presented above. See Janson, *Worthington Whittredge,* 197. Intended as a Promised Gift to the Museum from Lynn and Foster Friess, this painting was being stored at a gallery in Montana. Sadly, just prior to publication, the work was destroyed in a gas explosion that burned down the gallery and several other businesses.
20. Reiger, *American Sportsmen,* 62–63.
21. Grinnell quoted in Reiger, *American Sportsmen,* 126.
22. Miller, "Fate of Wilderness," 93.

CHAPTER 1. EXPLORING NEW GROUND

1. For this and other early bison prints, see Barsness, *Heads, Hides and Horns,* 10–11.
2. For a complete discussion, see Wagner, *American Wildlife Art,* 5–16.
3. Even Catesby relied on the work of others, but at least he had the experience of seeing the animals himself to back up his borrowing; see the discussion of Catesby with figure 1.2.
4. Wagner, *American Wildlife Art,* 30.
5. For a complete discussion on Audubon, see ibid., 61–97.
6. Peale's *American Indian and Bison* print was produced in 1832. Catlin's *Letters and Notes on the Manners, Customs, and Condition of the North American Indians* was published in 1841. Bodmer's illustrations for Maximilian's *Travels in the Interior of North America* were published in America in 1844. The University of Oklahoma Press has recently published the first volume of *The North American Journals of Prince Maximilian of Wied,* edited by Stephen S. Witte and Marsha V. Gallagher.
7. For a complete description of early artists on the Missouri River, see Hassrick, *Treasures of the Old West;* Ladner, *William de la Montagne Cary,* 11–15.
8. Catlin, *Letters and Notes,* 1:260. Emphasis in original.
9. For further discussion of Fraser's coin, see Dippie, *Vanishing American,* 225. See also all of chapters 13 and 14 (esp. pp. 223–28) in *The Vanishing American* for a cogent discussion of related issues.
10. This is true during the early to middle 1800s, when American Indians were relegated to

reservations run by Christian missionaries, and later, in the post–Civil War era, when the missionaries argued for assimilation and the end of the reservation system.

11. For a concise biography of Catesby, see Wagner, *American Wildlife Art*, 17–31.

12. McBurney, *Mark Catesby's Natural History*, 120.

13. For a brief description of Audubon's life, see Pohl, *Framing America*, 182. For more depth, see Rhodes, *John James Audubon*; Souder, *Under a Wild Sky*.

14. Peck, "Audubon and Bachman," 80.

15. Audubon met Stewart in 1843 in Saint Louis as Audubon was preparing to journey up the Missouri. Stewart, who was heading out for one more trip to the Wind River Mountains, invited Audubon to accompany him (Rhodes, *John James Audubon*, 421).

16. Peck, "Audubon and Bachman," 86.

17. Poesch, *Titian Ramsay Peale*, 35.

18. *Dusky Wolf* is illustrated in Miller, *Peale Family*, 192.

19. For a discussion of related images, see Haltman, *Looking Close*, 133–72.

20. In 1837, the French sculptor Antoine Louis Barye sculpted *Virginia Deer Reclining*, also of a whitetail deer. Barye only studied animals at menageries, so the whitetail's presence at the Jardin des Plantes or at another private zoo is fairly certain.

21. Truettner, *Natural Man Observed*, 12.

22. Dippie, "Green Fields," 30.

23. Tyler, *Prints of the West*, 51–52.

24. Ibid., 54–55.

25. Ibid., 55.

26. For a concise biography of Catlin, see Goetzmann and Goetzmann, *West of the Imagination*, 15–35.

27. Goetzmann, "Introduction," 4–8.

28. Trenton and Hassrick, *Rocky Mountains*, 31.

29. Goetzmann, "Introduction," 21–22.

30. Ibid., 5.

31. See Rudd, *Karl Bodmer's North American Prints*, Appendix E, for reference to this work, published in Bodmer's *Eaux-fortes: Animaux et paysages* (Paris: Jules Géruzet, 1863), n.p.

32. See Rudd, *Karl Bodmer's North American Prints*, Appendix D, for a description of the distribution of Bodmer's imagery in the 1840s.

33. See Ross, *West of Alfred Jacob Miller*, xi–xix; Goetzmann and Goetzmann, *West of the Imagination*, 58–68.

34. Strong, *Sentimental Journey*, 23.

35. Goetzmann and Goetzmann, *West of the Imagination*, 67.

36. Ross, *West of Alfred Jacob Miller*, note to plate 113.

37. For a concise biography of Miller, see Strong, *Sentimental Journey*, 13–25.

38. Peck, "Audubon and Bachman," 101, 115. The museum's *Mountain Brook Minks* is reproduced on 116–17.

39. Ibid., 101.

40. Goetzmann and Goetzmann, *West of the Imagination*, 39. The epigraph is from Paul Kane, "Wanderings of an Artist among the Indians of North America," in Harper, *Paul Kane's Frontier*, 80.

41. The National Gallery of Canada's version of Kane's painting is known as *Buffalo Reposing near Sturgeon Creek, Sixteen Miles West of Fort Edmonton*.

42. Ewers, *Artists of the Old West*, 137.

43. Ibid., 137–38.

44. Ibid., 149.

45. Kurz, *Journal*, 274. See also Kelly, *On the Upper Missouri*.

46. Penny, "Illustrating America," 153–54.

47. Hodges, *Carl Wimar*, 11.

48. Ibid., 29.

49. Museums holding Wimar's work include the Fine Arts Museums of San Francisco, the Rockwell Museum (in Corning, New York), the Autry National Center, the Amon Carter Museum, the Gilcrease Museum, the St. Louis Art Museum, and the National Cowboy and Western Heritage Museum.

50. The classically trained Wimar may have done these small, finished pastels as studies for larger compositions or as pictures in their own right, diversifying his output. Their scarcity may also indicate that he was trying a new medium, in which, for whatever reason, he did not continue working.

51. Ketner, "Indian Painter in Düsseldorf," 39.

52. Thanks to dampness and unstable media, Wimar's murals quickly began to deteriorate. In 1888, his half-brother, the painter August Becker, restored them. Miller, "A Muralist of Civic Ambitions," 218.

53. Ranchers felt that prairie dogs competed for food with grazing cattle. The expanse of holes dug by the colony also was thought to wreak havoc on the lower legs of horses and cattle.

54. McNally, *Art of William Jacob Hays*, 4–8.

55. A similar prairie dog painting by Hays is in the collection of the Tweed Museum of Art, located on the campus of the University of Minnesota, Duluth.

56. According to Brian Dippie, the figure in the painting could be a Métis buffalo hunter. The Métis people are defined as Canadian aboriginals, descended from French-Canadian and Native peoples. They were known for being expert fur traders, guides, and middlemen who acted as agents between European settlers and Native peoples (Brian Dippie, e-mail message to author, February 4, 2008).

57. Quoted in Ladner, *William de la Montagne Cary*, 118.

58. Samuels and Samuels, *Encyclopedia of Artists*, 490.

59. Arthur Wardle employs a similar technique in *Silent Watchers* (figure I.2).

60. Murray, *Last Buffalo*, 30–31.

61. Ibid., 104.

CHAPTER 2. FROM BIERSTADT TO CHASE

1. Hughes, *American Visions*, 194.

2. The stuffed mountain goat appears in a picture of Bierstadt's Broadway studio, into which he moved in 1874; for a reproduction of this picture, see Anderson and Ferber, *Albert Bierstadt*, 228.

3. Lubin, *Picturing a Nation*, 274.

4. Pohl, *Framing America*, 282.

5. Minks, *Hudson River School*, 9.

6. Ibid., 18.

7. Herman, *Hunting*, 188.

8. Goetzmann and Goetzmann, *West of the Imagination*, 148.

9. Nash, *Wilderness*, 67–69.

10. Anderson and Ferber, *Albert Bierstadt*, 140.

11. Bierstadt had not formally enrolled at the famed Düsseldorf Academy, though "he learned a great deal from fellow artists" (ibid., 23).

12. Built in 1857 by architect Richard Morris Hunt to house artists, the Tenth Street Studio Building housed such occupants as William Merritt Chase, Albert Bierstadt, and Winslow Homer at various times.

13. Anderson and Ferber, *Albert Bierstadt*, 246, 249.

14. For biographical material, see Johnson, "Shepard Alonzo Mount." See also Benjamin Genocchio, "Brothers Who Painted a 'New America,'" *New York Times*, July 9, 2002 (available online at query.nytimes.com).

15. Dorst, *Framing the Wild*, 6–7.

16. Edgell, Karolik, and Baur, *M. and M. Karolik Collection*, 354.

17. Samuels and Samuels, *Encyclopedia of Artists*, 227.

18. Cadbury and Marsh, *Arthur Fitzwilliam Tait*, 327–28.

19. Ibid., 41.

20. Janson, *Worthington Whittredge*, 145.

21. For a brief biography and

discussion of a related painting, *Woods of Ashokan,* see Hagood and Harrison, *American Art,* 89.

22. Gerdts, *William Holbrook Beard,* 10. For biographical details, see ibid., 5–23; see also Driesbach, *Direct from Nature,* 11–98.

23. Driesbach, *Direct from Nature,* 21.

24. Lewis, *American Paintings,* 28.

25. Biographical information in ibid. and in Lewis, "Herman Herzog."

26. Article from *Boston Herald* (October 5, 1902), quoted in Frankenstein, *After the Hunt,* 140.

27. Lubin, *Picturing a Nation,* 273.

28. Phillips, "William Merritt Chase," 49.

29. Hagood and Harrison, *American Art,* 129.

30. Chase quoted in ibid., 129.

31. Gallati, *William Merritt Chase,* 40.

CHAPTER 3. AMERICAN ANIMALIERS

1. Broder, *Bronzes,* 48–49.

2. Adler, Hirschler, and Wienberg, *Americans in Paris,* 11.

3. Barye made his debut at the annual Salon in 1827, with plaster busts, but not until 1831 were his animal sculptures accepted. Pieces such as *Tiger Devouring a Gavial* opened the door to a much wider acceptance of animal sculpture. See Johnston and Kelly, *Untamed,* 6.

4. Ibid., 54–55.

5. "Nature, red in tooth and claw" comes from Alfred Lord Tennyson's poem *In Memoriam A.H.H.,* section 56, line 15, written 1833–50 and published 1850. Reprinted in M. H. Abrams, ed., *The Norton Anthology of English Literature,* 1251.

6. Benge, "Tiger Devouring a Gavial," 127.

7. Ibid., 128.

8. The complete inscription reads, "25 Juillet 1899, Le Personnel de la Maison, Rheims Auscher et C—, Souhaite de Bonheur." The museum's *Lion* was cast by F. Barbedienne Fondeur, a well-known foundry that created reasonably priced reductions of monumental sculptures around Paris.

9. Lockman, "Interview with Frederick Roth."

10. Eisenman, *Nineteenth Century Art,* 305.

11. Johnston and Kelly, *Untamed,* xi.

12. Butler, "Auguste Rodin," 327.

13. The loose style of Rodin's bronzes has now become commonplace among sculptors and is generally referred to as being impressionistic. If the surface is very rough, the term "expressionistic" is often used.

14. The lion and the device "Garde Bien" written on a banner lying at the lion's feet formed the Turquet's family coat of arms. Information on the Rodin lion comes from an e-mail written by Helene Marraud at the Musée Rodin in Paris, November 14, 2007.

15. Butler, "Auguste Rodin," 327.

16. Harris, *Cultural Excursions,* 112.

17. Hassrick, *Wildlife and Western Heroes,* 38.

18. Taft, *History of American Sculpture,* 114.

19. If Brown was not the very first, he was definitely among the first artists to cast bronze on this continent. Beginning in the late 1840s, he was producing sculptures on a regular basis from a foundry in his Brooklyn studio. Brown cast *The Choosing of the Arrow* for the American Art Union in 1849 and a statue of De Witt Clinton for Greenwood Cemetery in 1852. Brown also sculpted portrait busts and equestrian statues, so he was not solely focused on American Indians or animals.

20. For biographical details and analysis on Brown, see Broder, *Bronzes,* 30–33; Craven, *Sculpture in America,* 144–58.

21. For further discussion of *Panther and Cubs,* see Tolles, "Henry Kirke Brown" and "Panther and Cubs" in Tolles, ed., *American Sculpture,* 1:41, 46–47.

22. Precedent for the protective mother can be found in many places but is noticeably present in Horatio Greenough's *Rescue Group* (1837–52), installed on the right blocking of the east front entry of the U.S. Capitol. This sculpture features a mother sheltering her child as the father battles an American Indian. A snarling dog is also included in the composition.

23. Quoted in Richman, *Edward Kemeys, 1843–1907,* 3.

24. David Wagner postulates that the installation of Auguste Cain's *Tigress and Cubs* and John Quincy Adams Ward's *Indian Hunter* in Central Park during Kemeys's early years in New York also likely served as inspiration (Wagner, *American Wildlife Art,* 157–59).

25. The youthful Alexander P. Proctor also completed twelve life-sized sculptures for the fair.

26. For additional information on Kemeys and a picture of the *Still Hunt* bas-relief, see Tolles, "Edward Kemeys," in Tolles, ed., *American Sculpture,* 1:191, 196–97.

27. The differences between the two felines may not be as readily apparent as the Winslow Brothers promotional piece would have its readers believe; however, close examination reveals that the jaguar in *At Bay* does have a more compact body and comparatively larger head when compared to the mountain lion, or cougar, in *At Play.* For Kemeys aficionados, these two rare bas-reliefs are an extraordinary find. The reason for the paucity of located casts of these sculptures may be that if they were installed as elements of decorative friezes in private homes, they are either still in situ or have been destroyed as subsequent generations have remodeled their living rooms. Text from sales brochure, Winslow Brothers, *The Kemeys Collection,* n.p.

28. Taft, *History of American Sculpture,* 472.

29. Richman, *Edward Kemeys, 1843–1907,* 10.

30. Craven, *Sculpture in America,* 521.

31. Proctor, *Alexander Phimister Proctor,* 82.

32. Hassrick, *Wildlife and Western Heroes,* 31.

33. Ibid., 31, 102, 106.

34. Taft, *History of American Sculpture,* 477.

35. Harvey, *Autobiography of Eli Harvey,* 40.

36. Ibid., 34. For biographical details, see also Tolles, "Eli Harvey," in Tolles, ed., *American Sculpture,* 1:374.

37. Hassrick, *Wildlife and Western Heroes,* 118.

38. Another casting of *Mutual Surprise* is in the Metropolitan Museum of Art. For biographical details, see Tolles, "Edwin Willard Deming," in Tolles, ed., *American Sculpture,* 1:371, 373.

39. Taft, *History of American Sculpture,* 374.

40. Craven, *Sculpture in America,* 429.

41. Hassler, "Paul Wayland Bartlett," in Tolles, ed., *American Sculpture,* 2:454.

42. Bartlett's statue of Lafayette was a reciprocal gift to France from the United States for Frédéric-Auguste Bartholdi's Statue of Liberty. *Apotheosis of Democracy* (1908–16), Bartlett's sculpture for the pediment of the House of the U.S. Capitol, represents the apex of his storied career. For more biographical details, see ibid.

43. See Broder, *Bronzes,* 241; Hassler, "Henry Murwin Shrady" and "George Washington at Valley Forge," in Tolles, ed., *American Sculpture,* 2:544 and 547.

44. Quoted in Garrett, "New American Sculptor," 546.

45. Broder, *Bronzes,* 241.

46. Craven, *Sculpture in America,* 541. Roth won the Ellen P. Speyer Award from the

academy twice; this award was given exclusively to a sculpture of an animal or a sculpture portraying an act of kindness toward an animal. In 1915, Roth won a gold medal from the academy for his work with Alexander Stirling Calder and Leo Lentelli on *The Alaskan,* which was displayed at the Panama-Pacific International Exposition in San Francisco.

47. Hassler, *"Polar Bear,"* in Tolles, ed., *American Sculpture,* 2:554.

48. Craven, *Sculpture in America,* 540.

49. Biographical details from Hassler, "Frederick George Richard Roth," in Tolles, ed., *American Sculpture,* 2:551.

50. Quoted in Heyneman, *Arthur Putnam, Sculptor,* 41.

51. Ibid., 113.

52. Hassler, "Arthur Putnam," in Tolles, ed., *American Sculpture,* 2:570.

53. For more information on Señor Lopez and the Bronx Zoo, see Bridges, *Gathering of Animals,* 132–39.

54. For a concise biography and analysis of Huntington, see Conner and Rosenkranz, *Rediscoveries in American Sculpture,* 71–78; Marter, "Anna Hyatt Huntington," *"Reaching Jaguar,"* and *"Jaguar,"* in Tolles, ed., *American Sculpture,* 2:600–601, 603–606.

55. For a concise biography and analysis of Laessle (including the life-casting controversy), see Conner and Rosenkranz, *Rediscoveries in American Sculpture,* 105–12; Marter, "Albert Laessle," in Tolles, ed., *American Sculpture,* 2:615.

56. This bronze was cast in 1911 (copyrighted in 1912) at the Gorham Foundry; it is listed as 1911:8 in the catalogue raisonné (Conner, Lehmbeck, and Tolles, *Captured Motion,* 223).

57. Quoted by Tolles in ibid., 20. Frishmuth's small eagle is titled *Small Spread Eagle* (1910).

58. Quoted in ibid., 15.

59. For biographical details, see Marter, "Harriet Whitney Frishmuth," in Tolles, ed., *American Sculpture,* 2:640.

60. During the years she worked in the converted stable, she often employed the dancer Desha Delteil, who was known for her ability to hold difficult poses. Delteil served as the model for many of Frishmuth's best-known whimsical nude sculptures.

61. Marter, "Harriet Whitney Frishmuth," in Tolles, ed., *American Sculpture,* 2:640.

62. Ambler, *Katherine Lane Weems,* 4.

63. The bronze medal was for a pigmy African elephant sculpture.

64. Ambler, *Katherine Lane Weems,* 103.

CHAPTER 4. CARL AKELEY AND A NEW BREED OF ARTIST-NATURALIST

1. Unrecorded conversation with Peter Hassrick, Rick Stewart, and Adam Harris, National Museum of Wildlife Art galleries, April 12, 2008.

2. Clark, *Trails of the Hunted,* 15.

3. Ibid., 14–15.

4. The American West was and still is a huge source of inspiration for people in many realms of artistic endeavor; however, the fresh sense of the unexplored has vanished.

5. Akeley, *In Brightest Africa,* 178.

6. Akeley cast several other models during his life, including a bust of a gorilla, a battle between a lion and a cape buffalo, and another elephant, titled *Stung* (figure 4.2), which depicts a single elephant confronting a cobra. Castings of *Stung* and *Lion and Cape Buffalo* are also in the National Museum of Wildlife Art collection.

7. Czerkas and Glut, *Dinosaurs, Mammoths, and Cavemen,* 19.

8. For biographical material on Knight, see ibid., 1–39.

9. Broder, *Bronzes,* 249.

10. Clark, *Trails of the Hunted,* 12.

11. Ibid., 14.

12. Quinn, *Windows on Nature,* 42.

13. See "Robert Henry Rockwell," in Proske, *Brookgreen Gardens Sculpture,* 192–94.

14. See "Louis Paul Jonas," in ibid., 195–97.

15. Ibid., 196.

16. Quotation written by John A. McGuire appears on the base of the Jonas sculpture located outside Denver's Museum of Natural History.

CHAPTER 5. CARL RUNGIUS AND HIS CONTEMPORARIES

1. Craven, *Sculpture in America,* 536.

2. Hough, "Wasteful West," 18.

3. Nash, *Wilderness,* 67.

4. Both paintings are set not far from where they hang today at the National Museum of Wildlife Art and not far from a thriving bison herd that occupies a portion of the National Elk Refuge across from the museum.

5. Lubin, *Picturing a Nation,* 274.

6. Ibid., 275.

7. In Schaldach, *Carl Rungius,* 104–105.

8. Sarah Milroy wrote, on wildlife artist Robert Bateman, "While an abstract exhibition in Unionville delivers admirably on the museum's mandate to educate, the McMichael's Robert Bateman show is a betrayal of public trust" (Milroy, "A Tale of Two Shows," *Globe and Mail,* October 4, 2007; available online at www.theglobeandmail.com). Milroy's biggest complaints arose from the fact that the exhibit was packed with people and therefore suspiciously popular and that the artist has made a success by selling prints of his work. Milroy wrote a slightly less condemnatory review of a Carl Rungius retrospective several years earlier, under the tagline "Wild Things." "By turns gruesome, sentimental and weird, the paintings of Carl Rungius may not be great art. But," writes Sarah Milroy, "the history

behind them is fascinating." In this article, she wrote, "[H]ere comes the unspeakable part—I enjoyed the show," before likening wildlife art, its artists, and collectors to a cult (Milroy, "Wild Things," *Globe and Mail,* July 10, 2002; available online at www.theglobeandmail.com).

9. Anonymous, "How Carl Rungius Combines Art with the Adventures of a Sportsman," *New York Times,* February 2, 1913 (available online query. nytimes.com).

10. Milroy, "Tale of Two Shows."

11. See Lippincott and Blühm, *Fierce Friends;* Morton, *Oudry's Painted Menagerie.*

12. Meyerheim was not a great advocate of studying animals in the field. Instead, he advised students to fabricate suitable backgrounds from their imagination or to place some chunks of coal into a box of sand and shake it, creating a rocky desert landscape they could copy for a background.

13. In the case of some contemporary wildlife artists, this movement has led to an overreliance on field photography and an under-reliance on the imagination and creativity. That lack of perceived freedom to create often results in boring, repetitive imagery that fails to go beyond the mundane. Good wildlife art, like any good representational art, combines a thorough knowledge of the subject with the creative spark that only the artist can bring.

14. For a similar argument, see Wagner, *American Wildlife Art,* 257–67.

15. Schaldach, *Carl Rungius,* 68.

16. Ibid., 34.

17. Ibid., 81–82.

18. Ibid., 49.

19. Hornaday quoted in Whyte and Hart, *Carl Rungius,* 110.

20. The Great Northern Railroad purchased a total of 347 paintings (Peterson, *Call of the Mountains,* 42).

21. Previously, artists such as

Thomas Moran and Newbold Hough Trotter had painted the range from the western slope in the late 1870s and early 1880s. Their depictions of the range, although magnificent, do not capture the mountains from the most dramatic vantage point.

22. For biographical details, see Peterson, *Call of the Mountains;* Hedgpeth, *Mountain Majesty.*

23. Partial inscription in Williams, *Woolaroc,* 127. Full inscription thanks to Linda Stone, Woolaroc curator of art, e-mailed March 20, 2007.

24. Troccoli, "Sketchbooks of Emil Lenders," 31.

25. Quoted in Sarchet, "He Lives as a Cowboy to Paint the Wild West," *Kansas City Star Magazine,* June 13, 1926.

26. For a comprehensive look at Russell's sculpture, see Stewart, *Charles M. Russell.*

27. For an overview of Russell's career, see Price, *Charles M. Russell;* Hassrick, *Charles M. Russell.*

28. Congreve, *Mourning Bride,* act 1, scene 1 (1697).

29. For biographical details on the life of Hudson, see Boynton, *Painter Lady.*

30. Dubois, *W. R. Leigh,* 51. See this work for biographical details.

31. Maxwell, "Painters of the West," 8.

32. Quoted in Webster, *Frank Tenney Johnson,* 7.

33. Dates and events in ibid., 27. See also McCracken, *Frank Tenney Johnson Book.*

34. Cooper, "Charles Livingston Bull," n.p.

35. Biographical information from Choppa, *Charles Livingston Bull,* 5–16.

36. Roger Tory Peterson, introduction to Peck, *Celebration of Birds,* xii.

37. Fuertes's *Autumn in the Adirondacks* clearly reflects the influence of Thayer's series of camouflage paintings, showing how natural coloration

helped animals blend into their surroundings.

38. Peck, "Louis Agassiz Fuertes," 144–45.

39. Ibid., 145–46.

40. Ordeman, *To Keep a Tryst,* 20.

41. Biographical details in ibid., 15–17.

42. Ladner, *O. C. Seltzer,* 45.

43. For biographical details, see ibid.

44. Ordeman and Schreiber, *George and Belmore Browne,* 14. See this work for biographical details.

45. By 1905, very few bison remained on the plains, numbering as few as one thousand, down from an estimated 50 million at their peak in the early 1800s. William Temple Hornaday at the New York Zoological Society in the Bronx had saved a few bison and began breeding them in 1899. By 1907, the society had shipped fifteen bison to the Wichita Mountain Reserve in Oklahoma. Soon thereafter, other small groups were sent to preserves in Nebraska, Montana, and South Dakota. With great care, these tiny herds began to grow; many of the bison roaming the West today are descendants of the Bronx Zoo bison.

46. The Wyeth illustration is in Hough, "Wasteful West," 2.

47. Allen and Allen, *N. C. Wyeth,* 23–24, 27. See this work for biographical details.

48. Harris, *N. C. Wyeth's Wild West,* 46, 49.

49. Allen and Allen, *N. C. Wyeth,* 53.

50. See Peterson, *Philip R. Goodwin,* 168.

51. For a complete biography of Goodwin, see ibid.

52. For biographic material, see Romero, *Paul Bransom;* see also Bransom and Hays, *All Unplanned.*

53. Johnson, *Shape of Things,* 26.

54. Ibid. See this work for biographical details.

55. Prestrud and Williams, *Bishop's*

Wildfowl, 115. See this work for biographical details.

56. Tom Davis in ibid., viii.

57. For Delano's autobiography, see Bowman, *Walking with Beauty,* 110.

58. Delano in ibid., 110.

59. Highlights of Delano's career published in "Chronology," in Hagerty, *Heart of the Desert,* 84–86.

60. Wilkinson, "Clymers' Muse," 74.

61. Reed, *West of John Clymer,* 9.

62. Reed, *John Clymer,* 9–10.

63. Ibid., 27.

64. Price, *Lougheed, A Painter's Painter,* 12.

65. Ibid., 22.

66. Mayberry Fine Art, *Robert Lougheed,* 5.

67. Ordeman and Schreiber, *George and Belmore Browne,* 9.

68. Quoted in ibid., 10. See this work for biographical details.

69. Thompson, *Homefields,* 23. See this work for biographical details.

CHAPTER 6. MODERN MOVEMENTS

1. Weekley, *Kingdoms of Edward Hicks,* 2.

2. See chronology and list of exhibitions in Maresca and Ricco, *Bill Traylor,* 179–83.

3. Gibbs, *Escape to Reality,* 8.

4. Biographical details from ibid. and from Hagerty, *Desert Dreams.*

5. Schimmel, *Art and Life,* 22–24. See also Porter, Ebie, and Campbell, *Taos Artists.*

6. Broder, *Taos,* 170–71.

7. Wien, *Rockwell Kent,* 61.

8. See chronology in ibid., 162–68.

9. Botke quoted in Trenton and Solon, *Birds, Boughs, and Blossoms,* 11.

10. Ibid., 51.

11. Ibid., 50.

12. Complete biographical details in ibid.

13. Broder, *Taos,* 256.

14. Ibid., 257–58. See this work for biographical details.

15. Goodrich, *Georgia O'Keeffe,* 23.

16. Georgia O'Keeffe to Edith Halpert, February 26, 1955,

Archives of American Art, Washington, D.C.

17. Biographical details from Lisle, *Portrait of an Artist* and from Bry and Callaway, *Georgia O'Keeffe.*

18. Complete portfolio and biography published in Harris, *Wild Work.*

19. Wrbican, "Wildlife."

20. Ibid.

21. Biographical details from Rand, *Paul Manship.*

22. Ibid., 32.

23. Cubist painting breaks down a subject into component parts, while fauvism, which means "wild beasts" in French, uses bright, bold colors as a means of expression.

24. Chronology in Baur, *William Zorach,* 109–10.

25. Ibid., 18.

26. Ibid., 20.

27. Tremblay, "Different Tracks," 87–88.

28. Houser chronology in Lowe, *Native Modernism,* 106–107.

29. Jaffe, *Sculpture of Leonard Baskin,* 112–13. Jaffe cites a speech given by Baskin at the Yale School of Art, entitled "The Necessity for the Image."

30. Baskin quoted in ibid., 122.

31. Biographical material from ibid. and from Cate McQuaid, "Dark Passage: Artist Leonard Baskin at the Art Institute of Boston," *Boston Phoenix,* November 6, 1992, sec. 3, p. 6.

32. Broder, *Bronzes,* 296–97.

33. Biographical material from Cunningham and Schriever, *Masterpieces,* n.p.

CONCLUSION

1. Quoted in Davis, *Bob Kuhn,* 72.

2. Quoted in Bailey, "Bob Kuhn," 22.

3. An earlier, longer version of this chapter appears in Harris, *Bob Kuhn.*

4. Robert Kuhn, interview with the author, July 15, 2001, Tucson, Arizona.

5. Quoted in McGarry, "Bob Kuhn," 89.

6. Ibid., 93.

Bibliography

Adler, Kathleen, Erica E. Hirschler, and H. Barbara Wienberg. *Americans in Paris, 1860–1900.* London: National Gallery Company, 2006.

Akeley, Carl. *In Brightest Africa.* Garden City, N.Y.: Doubleday, Page and Company, 1924.

Allen, Douglas, and Douglas Allen, Jr. *N. C. Wyeth: The Collected Paintings, Illustrations, and Murals.* New York: Crown, 1972.

Ambler, Louise Todd. *Katherine Lane Weems: Sculpture and Drawings.* Boston: Boston Athenaeum, 1987.

Anderson, Nancy, and Linda Ferber. *Albert Bierstadt: Art and Enterprise.* New York: Hudson Hills, 1990.

Bailey, Patricia Black. "Bob Kuhn: The Wildlife Artist's Wildlife Artist." *Art Today* (Spring 1986): 22.

Barsness, Larry. *Heads, Hides and Horns: The Compleat Buffalo Book.* Fort Worth: Texas Christian University Press, 1985.

Baur, John I. H. *William Zorach.* New York: Frederick A. Praeger, 1959.

Beard, William Holbrook. *Humor in Animals: A Series of Studies in Pen and Pencil.* New York: G. P. Putnam's Sons, 1885.

Benge, Glenn. "Tiger Devouring a Gavail of the Ganges." In *The Romantics to Rodin: French Nineteenth-Century Sculpture from North American Collections,* edited by Peter Fusco and Horst W. Janson, 127–28. Los Angeles: Los Angeles County Museum of Art, in association with George Brazillier, 1980.

Boehme, Sarah E., Annette Blaugrund, Robert McCracken Peck, and Ron Tyler. *John James Audubon in the West: The Last Expedition, Mammals of North America.* New York: Harry N. Abrams, in association with the Buffalo Bill Historical Center, 2000.

Bowman, Richard G. *Walking with Beauty: The Art and Life of Gerard Curtis Delano.* Denver: Richard G. Bowman, 1990.

Boynton, Searles R. *The Painter Lady: Grace Carpenter Hudson.* Ukiah, Calif.: Sun House Guild, 1978.

Bransom, Paul, and Helen Ireland Hays. *All Unplanned: Memoirs of the Golden Age of Illustration.* Johnston, N.Y.: Baronet Litho, 1983.

Bridges, William. *Gathering of Animals: An Unconventional History of the New York Zoological Society.* New York: Harper and Row, 1974.

Broder, Patricia Janis. *Bronzes of the American West.* New York: Harry N. Abrams, 1974.

———. *Taos: A Painter's Dream.* Boston: New York Graphic Society, 1980.

Bry, Doris, and Nicholas Callaway, eds. *Georgia O'Keeffe in the West.* New York: Knopf, 1989.

Buffon, comte de [George-Louis Leclerc]. *Histoire naturelle, generale et particuliere,* vol. 5. Translated by William Smellie, 1781. http://faculty.njcu.edu/fmoran/vol5new.htm.

Butler, Ruth. "Auguste Rodin." In *The Romantics to Rodin: French Nineteenth-Century Sculpture from North American Collections,* edited by Peter Fusco and Horst W. Janson, 326–28. Los Angeles: Los Angeles County Museum of Art, in association with George Brazillier, 1980.

Cadbury, Warder H., and Henry F. Marsh. *Arthur Fitzwilliam Tait: Artist in the Adirondacks.* Newark, N.J.: University of Delaware Press, 1986.

Calder, Alexander. *Animal Sketching.* 3rd ed. New York: Dover, 1973.

Catlin, George. *Letters and Notes on the Manners, Customs, and Condition of the North American Indians.* 2 vols. New York, 1841. Reprint, New York: Dover, 1973.

Choppa, Karen A. *Charles Livingston Bull, 1874–1932: A Retrospective.* Oradell, N.J.: Hiram Blauvelt Museum, 1994.

Clark, James Lippitt. *Trails of the Hunted.* Boston: Little, Brown, and Company, 1928.

Congreve, William. *The Mourning Bride: A Tragedy.* London: J. Bell, 1797.

Conner, Janis, Leah Rosenblatt Lehmbeck, and Thayer Tolles. *Captured Motion: The Sculpture of Harriet Whitney Frishmuth.* New York: Hohmann Holdings, 2006.

Conner, Janis, and Joel Rosenkranz. *Rediscoveries in American Sculpture: Studio Works, 1893–1939.* Austin: University of Texas Press, 1989.

Cooper, Anice Page. "Charles Livingston Bull: Portrait Painter of Wild Animals." In Cooper, *About Artists.* Garden City, N.Y.: Doubleday, Page and Company, 1926.

Craven, Wayne. *Sculpture in America.* New York: Thomas Y. Crowell, 1968.

Crossroads of Sport. *1947–1948 Annual Catalogue.* New York: Crossroads of Sport Gallery, 1947.

Cunningham, Elizabeth, and George Schriever. *Masterpieces of the American West: Selections from the Anschutz Collection.* Denver: A. B. Hirschfield Press, 1983.

Bibliography

Czerkas, Sylvia Massey, and Donald Glut. *Dinosaurs, Mammoths, and Cavemen: The Art of Charles R. Knight.* New York: E. P. Dutton, 1982.

Davis, Tom. *Bob Kuhn.* Camden, S.C.: Briar Patch Press, 1989.

Dean, Bradley P. "Natural History, Romanticism, and Thoreau." In *American Wilderness: A New History,* edited by Michael Lewis, 73–90. New York: Oxford University Press, 2007.

Delano, Gerard Curtis. *Indians and Scenes of the Southwest by Gerard Curtis Delano.* Tustin, Calif.: Foster Art Service, n.d.

Dippie, Brian. Foreword to *Philip R. Goodwin: America's Sporting and Wildlife Artist,* by Larry Len Peterson. Hayden, Idaho: Coeur d'Alene Art Auction; Tucson, Ariz.: Settlers West Galleries, 2001.

————. "Green Fields and Red Men." In *George Catlin and His Indian Gallery,* edited by Therese Thau Heyman and George Gurney, 27–61. New York: W. W. Norton, in association with the Smithsonian American Art Museum, 2002.

————. *The Vanishing American: White Attitudes and U.S. Indian Policy.* Lawrence: University Press of Kansas, 1982.

Dorst, John. *Framing the Wild: Animals on Display.* Laramie: University of Wyoming Art Museum, in association with the National Museum of Wildlife Art, 2002.

Driesbach, Janice. *Direct from Nature: The Oil Sketches of Thomas Hill.* Sacramento, Calif.: Crocker Art Museum, 1997.

Dubois, June. *W. R. Leigh: The Definitive Illustrated Biography.* Kansas City, Mo.: Lowell Press, 1977.

Edgell, G. H., Maxim Karolik, and John I. H. Baur. *M. and M. Karolik Collection of American Paintings, 1815 to 1865.* Boston: Museum of Fine Arts, 1949.

Eisenman, Stephen F. *Nineteenth Century Art: A Critical History.* New York: Thames and Hudson, 1996.

Ewers, John C. *Artists of the Old West.* Garden City, N.Y.: Doubleday, 1965.

Frankenstein, Alfred. *After the Hunt: William Harnett and Other American Still Life Painters, 1870–1900.* Berkeley: University of California Press, 1953.

Frink, Maurice. *Edwin Deming: "That Man, He Paint!"* Tulsa, Okla.: Thomas Gilcrease Institute of American History and Art, 1971.

Fusco, Peter, and Horst W. Janson. *The Romantics to Rodin: French Nineteenth-Century Sculpture from North American Collections.* Los Angeles: Los Angeles County Museum of Art, in association with George Brazillier, 1980.

Gallati, Barbara. *William Merritt Chase.* New York: Harry N. Abrams, 1995.

Garrett, Charles Hall. "The New American Sculptor." *Munsey's Magazine* (July 1903): 545–52.

Gerdts, William. *William Holbrook Beard: Animals in Fantasy.* New York: Alexander Gallery, 1981.

Gibbs, Linda Jones. *Escape to Reality: The Western World of Maynard Dixon.* Provo, Utah: Brigham Young University, 2000.

Goetzmann, William H. "Introduction: The Man Who Stopped to Paint America." In *Karl Bodmer's America,* edited by David C. Hunt, Marsha V. Gallagher, and William J. Orr, 1–23. Lincoln: University of Nebraska Press, in association with the Joslyn Art Museum, 1984.

Goetzmann, William H., and William N. Goetzmann. *The West of the Imagination.* New York: W. W. Norton, 1986.

Goodrich, Lloyd. *Georgia O'Keeffe.* New York: Whitney Museum of American Art, 1970.

Hagerty, Donald G. *Desert Dreams: The Art and Life of Maynard Dixon.* Rev. ed. Salt Lake City, Utah: Gibbs Smith, 1998.

———. *Heart of the Desert: The West of Gerard Curtis Delano.* Santa Fe, N.Mex.: Gerald Peters Gallery, 2001.

Hagood, Martha N., and Jefferson C. Harrison. *American Art at the Chrysler Museum: Selected Paintings, Sculpture, and Drawings.* Norfolk, Va.: Chrysler Museum of Art, 2005.

Haltman, Kenneth. *Looking Close and Seeing Far: Samuel Seymour, Titian Ramsay Peale, and the Art of the Long Expedition, 1818–1823.* University Park: Pennsylvania State University Press, 2008.

Harper, J. Russell, ed. *Paul Kane's Frontier.* Austin: University of Texas Press, 1971.

Harris, Adam Duncan. *Bob Kuhn: Painting the Wild.* Jackson, Wyo.: National Museum of Wildlife Art, 2002.

———. *Wild Work: Animal Drawings by Alexander Calder.* Jackson, Wyo.: National Museum of Wildlife Art, 2004.

Harris, Géné E. *N. C. Wyeth's Wild West.* Chadds Ford, Penn.: Brandywine River Museum, 1990.

Harris, Neil. *Cultural Excursions: Marketing Appetites and Cultural Tastes in Modern America.* Chicago: University of Chicago Press, 1990.

Harvey, Eli. *The Autobiography of Eli Harvey: Quaker Sculptor from Ohio.* Wilmington, Ohio: Clinton County Historical Society, 1966.

Hassrick, Peter H. *Charles M. Russell.* New York: Harry N. Abrams, 1989.

———. *Treasures of the Old West: Paintings and Sculptures from the Thomas Gilcrease Institute of American History and Art.* New York: Harry N. Abrams, 1984.

———. *Wildlife and Western Heroes: Alexander Phimister Proctor, Sculptor.* Fort Worth, Tex.: Amon Carter Museum, 2003.

Hedgpeth, Don. *Mountain Majesty: The Art of John Fery.* Jackson, Wyo.: William P. Healey and John B. Fery, 1997.

Herman, Daniel Justin. *Hunting and the American Imagination.* Washington, D.C.: Smithsonian Institution Press, 2001.

Heyman, Therese Thau, and George Gurney, eds. *George Catlin and His Indian Gallery.* New York: W. W. Norton, in association with the Smithsonian American Art Museum, 2002.

Heyneman, Julie Helen. *Arthur Putnam, Sculptor.* San Francisco: Johnck and Seeger, 1932.

Hodges, William Romaine. *Carl Wimar: A Biography.* Galveston, Tex.: Charles Reymershoffer, 1908.

Hough, Emerson. "The Wasteful West: How America's Most Wasteful Blunder Cost the West a Great Opportunity and the Country a Food-Supply." *Saturday Evening Post* (October 14, 1905): 1–3, 18.

Hughes, Robert. *American Visions: The Epic History of Art in America.* New York: Alfred A. Knopf, 1997.

Hunt, David C., Marsha V. Gallagher, and William J. Orr. *Karl Bodmer's America.* Lincoln: University of Nebraska Press, in association with Joslyn Art Museum, 1984.

Irving, Washington. "A Tour on the Prairies." In *Washington Irving: Three Western Narratives.* New York: Library Classics of the United States, 2004.

Jaffe, Irma B. *The Sculpture of Leonard Baskin.* New York: Viking Press, 1980.

Janson, Anthony F. *Worthington Whittredge.* New York: Cambridge University Press, 1989.

Jefferson, Thomas. Thomas Jefferson to Meriwether Lewis, June 20, 1803. www.library.csi.cuny.edu/dept/history/lavender/jefflett.html.

Johnson, Deborah J. "Shepard Alonzo Mount, His Life and Art." *American Art Review* (May–June 1998): 116–21.

Johnson, Patricia Condon. *The Shape of Things: The Art of Francis Lee Jaques.* Camden, S.C.: Live Oak Press, 1994.

Johnston, William R., and Simon Kelly. *Untamed: The Art of Antoine-Louis Barye.* Baltimore, Md.: Walters Art Museum, 2006.

Kane, Paul. "Wanderings of an Artist among the Indians of North America." In *Paul Kane's Frontier,* edited by J. Russell Harper, 47–157. Austin: University of Texas Press, 1971.

Kelly, Carla. *On the Upper Missouri: The Journal of Rudolph Friederich Kurz, 1851–1852.* Introduction by Scott Eckberg. Norman: University of Oklahoma Press, 2005.

Ketner, Joseph D., II. "The Indian Painter in Dusseldorf." In *Carl Wimar: Chronicler of the Missouri River Frontier,* by Rick Stewart, Joseph Ketner II, and Angela Miller, 30–75. New York: Harry N. Abrams, 1991.

Kort, Pamela, and Max Hollein, eds. *I Like America.* Munich, Germany: Prestel, in association with Schirn Kunsthalle, Frankfurt, 2006.

Kuhn, Robert. Introduction to *Paul Bransom, 1885–1979: Dean of American Animal Artists,* by Mario Cesar Romero. Nyack, N.Y.: Edward Hopper Landmark Preservation Foundation, 1987.

Kurz, Rudolf Friederich. *Journal of Rudolf Friederich Kurz: An Account of His Experiences among Fur Traders and American Indians on the Mississippi and the Upper Missouri Rivers during the Years 1846 to 1852.* Translated by Myrtis Jarrell. Reprint, Lincoln: University of Nebraska Press, 1970.

Ladner, Mildred D. *O. C. Seltzer: Painter of the Old West.* Norman: University of Oklahoma Press, 1979.

———. *William de la Montagne Cary: Artist on the Missouri River.* Norman: University of Oklahoma Press, 1984.

Leigh, William R. *Frontiers of Enchantment: An Artist's Adventures in Africa.* New York: Simon and Schuster, 1938.

Lewis, Donald S., Jr. *American Paintings of Herman Herzog.* Chadds Ford, Penn.: Brandywine River Museum, 1992.

———. "Herman Herzog (1831–1932), German Landscapist in America." *American Art Review* (July–August 1976): 52–66.

Lewis, Michael, ed. *American Wilderness: A New History.* New York: Oxford University Press, 2007.

Lippincott, Louise, and Andreas Blühm. *Fierce Friends: Artists and Animals, 1750–1900.* New York: Merrell Publishers, in association with Van Gogh Museum and Carnegie Museum of Art, 2005.

Lisle, Laurie. *Portrait of an Artist: A Biography of Georgia O'Keeffe.* Rev. ed. New York: Washington Square Press, 1997.

Lockman, DeWitt McClellan. "Interview with Frederick Roth. Sherwood Studios. 1927." National Museum of Wildlife Art Library and Archives Artist Biography Files from Transcript, Manuscripts Department, New York Historical Society. Microfilmed for DeWitt McClellan Lockman Papers, Archives of American Art, Smithsonian Institution, Washington, D.C., 1927.

Lowe, Truman T., ed. *Native Modernism: The Art of George Morrison and Allan Houser.* Washington, D.C.: National Museum of the American Indian, Smithsonian Institution, 2004.

Lubin, David. *Picturing a Nation: Art and Social Change in Nineteenth-Century America.* New Haven, Conn.: Yale University Press, 1994.

Maresca, Frank, and Roger Ricco. *Bill Traylor: His Art—His Life.* New York: Alfred A. Knopf, 1991.

Maxwell, Everett Carroll. "Painters of the West—F. Tenney Johnson, A.N.A." *Progressive Arizona* (March 1931): 8.

Mayberry Fine Art. *Robert Lougheed (1910–1982): A Painter's Legacy.* Winnipeg: Mayberry Fine Art, 2003.

McBurney, Henrietta. *Mark Catesby's Natural History of America: The Watercolors from the Royal Library, Windsor Castle.* London: Merrell Holberton, 1997.

McCracken, Harold. *The Frank Tenney Johnson Book.* Garden City, N.J.: Doubleday and Company, 1974.

McGarry, Susan Hallsten. "Bob Kuhn: Colorful Critters." *Southwest Art* (May 1994): 86–93.

McNally, Kathleen. *The Art of William Jacob Hays.* Art Exhibition Series 5. Calgary, Alberta: Glenbow Museum, 1986.

Miller, Angela. "A Muralist of Civic Ambitions." In *Carl Wimar: Chronicler of the Missouri River Frontier,* by Rick Stewart, Joseph Ketner II, and Angela Miller, 188–226. New York: Harry N. Abrams, 1991.

———. "The Fate of Wilderness in American Landscape Art." In *American Wilderness: A New History,* edited by Michael Lewis, 91–112. New York: Oxford University Press, 2007.

Miller, Lillian B., ed. *The Peale Family: Creation of a Legacy, 1770–1870.* New York: Abbeville Press, 1996.

Minks, Louise. *Hudson River School.* Avenal, N.J.: Crescent Books, 1989.

Morton, Mary, ed. *Oudry's Painted Menagerie: Portraits of Exotic Animals in Eighteenth-Century Europe.* Los Angeles: Getty Trust Publications, J. Paul Getty Museum, 2007.

Murray, Joan. *The Last Buffalo: The Story of Frederick Arthur Verner, Painter of the Canadian West.* Toronto: Pagurian Press, 1984.

Nash, Roderick. *Wilderness and the American Mind.* 3rd ed. New Haven, Conn.: Yale University Press, 1982.

O'Keeffe, Georgia. Georgia O'Keeffe to Edith Halpert, February 26, 1955. Archives of American Art, Washington, D.C.

Ordeman, John T. *To Keep a Tryst with the Dawn: An Appreciation of Roland Clark.* Henderson, N.C.: John T. Ordeman, 1989.

Ordeman, John T., and Michael M. Schreiber. *George and Belmore Browne: Artists of the North American Wilderness.* Toronto: Warwick, 2004.

Peck, Robert McCracken. "Audubon and Bachman: A Collaboration in Science." In *John James Audubon in the West: The Last Expedition, Mammals of North America,* by Sarah E. Boehme, Annette Blaugrund, Robert McCracken Peck, and Ron Tyler, 71–115. New York: Harry N. Abrams, in association with the Buffalo Bill Historical Center, 2000.

———. *A Celebration of Birds: The Life and Art of Louis Agassiz Fuertes.* New York: Walker and Company, for the Academy of Natural Sciences of Philadelphia, 1982.

———. "Louis Agassiz Fuertes (1874–1927)." *Southwest Art* (November 1983): 144–45.

Penny, H. Glenn. "Illustrating America: Images of the North American Wild West in German Periodicals, 1825–1890." In *I Like America,* edited by Pamela Kort and Max Hollein, 140–57. Munich, Germany: Prestel, in association with Schirn Kunsthalle, Frankfurt, 2006.

Peterson, Larry Len. *The Call of the Mountains: The Artists of Glacier National Park.* Tucson, Ariz.: Settlers West Galleries, 2002.

———. *Philip R. Goodwin: America's Sporting and Wildlife Artist.* Hayden, Idaho: Coeur d'Alene Art Auction; Tucson, Ariz.: Settlers West Galleries, 2001.

Peterson, Roger Tory. Introduction to *A Celebration of Birds: The Life and Art of Louis Agassiz Fuertes,* by Robert McCracken Peck, xi–xiii. New York: Walker and Company, for the Academy of Natural Sciences of Philadelphia, 1982.

Phillips, Duncan. "William Merritt Chase." *American Magazine of Art* (December 1916): 49.

Poesch, Jessie. *Titian Ramsay Peale, 1799–1885, and His Journals of the Wilkes Expedition.* Philadelphia: American Philosophical Society, 1961.

Pogzeba, Wolfgang. *New Vision: Photographs of the American West.* Flagstaff, Ariz.: Northland Press, 1977.

Pohl, Francis. *Framing America: A Social History of American Art.* New York: Thames and Hudson, 2002.

Porter, Dean, Teresa Hayes Ebie, and Suzan Campbell. *Taos Artists and Their Patrons, 1898–1950.* Notre Dame: Snite Museum of Art, University of Notre Dame, 1999.

Prestrud, Earl, and Russ Williams. *Bishop's Wildfowl: A Collection of Etching and Oil Painting Reproductions by Richard E. Bishop.* Camden, S.C.: Live Oak Press, 1994.

Price, Byron, ed. *Charles M. Russell: A Catalogue Raisonné.* Norman: University of Oklahoma Press, 2007.

———. *Lougheed, A Painter's Painter: The Life and Art of Robert Lougheed.* Bozeman, Mont.: Nygard and Elliot, 1991.

Proctor, Alexander Phimister. *Alexander Phimister Proctor, A Sculptor in Buckskin: An Autobiography.* Norman: University of Oklahoma Press, 1971.

Proske, Beatrice Gilman. *Brookgreen Gardens Sculpture.* Rev. ed. Brookgreen Gardens, S.C.: Brookgreen Gardens, 1968.

Quinn, Stephen Christopher. *Windows on Nature: The Great Habitat Dioramas of the American Museum of Natural History.* New York: Harry N. Abrams, 2006.

Rand, Harry. *Paul Manship.* Washington, D.C.: National Museum of American Art, Smithsonian Institution, 1989.

Reed, Walt. *John Clymer: An Artist's Rendezvous with the Frontier West.* Flagstaff, Ariz.: Northland Press, 1976.

———. *The West of John Clymer.* Oklahoma City: National Cowboy Hall of Fame and Western Heritage Center, 1991.

Reiger, John F. *American Sportsmen and the Origins of Conservation.* 3rd ed. Corvallis: Oregon State University Press, 2001.

Rhodes, Richard. *John James Audubon: The Making of an American.* New York: Random House, 2006.

Richman, Michael. "Edward Kemeys (1843–1907), American Animal Sculptor." Master's thesis, George Washington University, 1970.

———. *Edward Kemeys, 1843–1907: America's First Animal Sculptor.* Middleburg, Va.: Kemeys Foundation, 1972.

Romero, Mario Cesar. *Paul Bransom, 1885–1979: Dean of American Animal Artists.* Nyack, N.Y.: Edward Hopper Landmark Preservation Foundation, 1987.

Ross, Marvin C. *The West of Alfred Jacob Miller.* Norman: University of Oklahoma Press, 1951.

Rudd, Brandon K., ed. *Karl Bodmer's North American Prints.* Lincoln: University of Nebraska Press, in association with Joslyn Art Museum, 2004.

Samuels, Peggy, and Harold Samuels. *Samuels' Encyclopedia of Artists of the American West.* Edison, N.J.: Book Sales, 1985.

Schaldach, William J. *Carl Rungius: Big Game Painter, Fifty Years with Brush and Rifle.* Camden, S.C.: Live Oak Press, 1993.

Schimmel, Julie. *The Art and Life of W. Herbert Dunton, 1878–1936.* Austin: University of Texas Press, 1984.

Souder, William. *Under a Wild Sky: John James Audubon and the Making of the Birds of America.* Berkeley, Calif.: North Point Press, 2005.

Stewart, Rick. *Charles M. Russell, Sculptor.* Fort Worth, Tex.: Amon Carter Museum, 1994.

Stewart, Rick, Joseph Ketner II, and Angela Miller. *Carl Wimar: Chronicler of the Missouri River Frontier.* New York: Harry N. Abrams, 1991.

Strong, Lisa Maria. *Sentimental Journey: The Art of Alfred Jacob Miller.* Fort Worth, Tex.: Amon Carter Museum, 2008.

Taft, Lorado. *The History of American Sculpture.* New York: MacMillan, 1903.

Tennyson, Alfred Lord. *In Memoriam.* In *The Norton Anthology of English Literature,* vol. 2, edited by M. H. Abrams, 1251. 7th ed. New York: W. W. Norton, 2000.

Thompson, Chipper. *Homefields: The Art of Lanford Monroe.* Columbia, S.C.: Sporting Classics, Islet Bay Press, 2007.

Tolles, Thayer, ed. *American Sculpture in the Metropolitan Museum of Art,* vol. 1, *A Catalogue of Works by Artists Born before 1865.* Catalogue by Lauretta

Dimmick, Donna J. Hassler, and Thayer Tolles. New York: Metropolitan Museum of Art, 1999.

———, ed. *American Sculpture in the Metropolitan Museum of Art,* vol. 2, *A Catalogue of Works by Artists Born between 1865 and 1885.* Catalogue by Donna J. Hassler, Joan M. Marter, and Thayer Tolles. New York: Metropolitan Museum of Art, 2001.

Tremblay, Gail. "Different Tracks, Paths Worth Following." In *Native Modernism: The Art of George Morrison and Allan Houser,* edited by Truman T. Lowe, 78–102. Washington, D.C.: National Museum of the American Indian, Smithsonian Institution, 2004.

Trenton, Patricia, and Peter H. Hassrick. *The Rocky Mountains: A Vision for Artists in the Nineteenth Century.* Norman: University of Oklahoma Press, 1983.

Trenton, Patricia, and Deborah Epstein Solon. *Birds, Boughs, and Blossoms: Jessie Arms Botke (1883–1971).* Carmel, Calif.: William A. Karges Fine Art, 1995.

Troccoli, Joan Carpenter. "The Sketchbooks of Emil Lenders: Down to the Souls of the Moccasins." *Gilcrease Journal* (Spring 1993): 31–46.

Truettner, William H. *The Natural Man Observed: A Study of Catlin's Indian Gallery.* Washington, D.C.: Smithsonian Institution Press, 1979.

Tyler, Ron. *Prints of the West.* Golden, Colo.: Fulcrum Publishing, 1994.

Wagner, David J. *American Wildlife Art.* Seattle: Marquand Books, 2008.

Webster, Melissa J. *Frank Tenney Johnson: The Rimrock Years.* Cody, Wyo.: Buffalo Bill Historical Center, 1986.

Weekley, Carolyn J. *The Kingdoms of Edward Hicks.* Williamsburg, Va.: Colonial Williamsburg Foundation, in association with Harry N. Abrams, 1999.

Whyte, Jon, and E. J. Hart. *Carl Rungius: Painter of the Western Wilderness.* Calgary, Alberta: Glenbow-Alberta Institute, 1985.

Wien, Jake Milgram. *Rockwell Kent: The Mythic and the Modern.* New York: Hudson Hills Press, 2005.

Wilbur, Richard. Alexander Calder, illus. *A Bestiary.* London: Fourth Estate, 1993.

Wilkinson, Todd. "The Clymers' Muse." In Walt Reed, *The West of John Clymer,* 70–74. Oklahoma City: National Cowboy Hall of Fame and Western Heritage Center, 1991.

Williams, Joe. *Woolaroc.* Bartlesville, Okla.: Frank Philips Foundation, 1991.

Winslow Brothers. *The Kemeys Collection.* Chicago, Ill.: Winslow Brothers, 1894. Art Institute of Chicago Pamphlet files, P-13870.

Witte, Stephen S., and Marsha V. Gallagher, eds. *The North American Journals of Prince Maximilian of Wied,* vol. 1, *May 1832–April 1833.* Norman: University of Oklahoma Press, 2008.

Wrbican, Matt. "Wildlife: Nature as Culture in Andy Warhol's Art." In *Silent Spring: Andy Warhol's Endangered Species and Vanishing Animals.* Exhibit brochure. Jackson, Wyo.: National Museum of Wildlife Art, 2006. Exhibit originated at the Andy Warhol Museum, Pittsburgh, Pennsylvania.

Index

Page numbers in italic type refer to illustrations.

Staff and Board of Trustees

Frontispiece: John Fery, *Red Eagle Lake, Glacier National Park,* 1915 (figure 5.10, p. 163).

Page v: Francis Lee Jaques, *Early Morning Whitetail,* 1945 (detail; figure 5.28, p. 201).

Page vi: Worthington Whittredge, *Deer Watering,* c. 1875 (detail; figure 2.7, p. 69).

Page viii: Gerald Curtis Delano, *Forest Primeval,* c. 1940 (figure 5.30, p. 204).

Page x: Albert Bierstadt, *Elk Grazing in the Wind River Country,* 1861 (figure 2.3, p. 61).

Page xv: Frank Tenney Johnson, *Coyote Moonrise,* c. 1920 (figure 5.18, p. 178).

Pages xvi–1: Robert Kuhn, *Come to Mama,* c. 1985 (figure C.3, p. 259).

Page 16: William de la Montagne Cary, *Lost Buffalo Calf,* c. 1875 (detail; figure 1.17, p. 49).

Page 54: Thomas Hill, *Two Stags Battling,* 1883 (detail; figure 2.9, p. 72).

Page 81: Henry Merwin Shrady, *Elk Buffalo,* 1900 (detail; figure 3.11, p. 107).

Page 126: James Lippitt Clark, *Ovis Poli,* 1930 (detail; figure 4.5, p. 138).

Page 145: Olaf Carl Seltzer, *Lone Wolf,* c. 1930 (detail; figure 5.23, p. 189).

Page 216: Earnest Martin Hennings, *Deer Among the Aspens,* 1939 (detail; figure 6.6, p. 231).

Page 254: Robert Kuhn, *Ahmed,* 1973 (detail; figure C.1, p. 256).

Copyedited by Sally P. Bennett

Photography credit: Garth Dowling

Text design and composition by David Alcorn, Alcorn Publication Design

      Set in New Caledonia, with display heads set in New Caledonia Semibold

Jacket design by Tony Roberts

Image prepress by University of Oklahoma Printing Services

Printed in Singapore by CS Graphics Pte. Ltd. on 157 gsm Gold East Matt